TURKEY

TURKEY

CONTENTS

DISCOVER 6

EXPERIENCE ISTANBUL 56

EXPERIENCE TURKEY 174

NEED TO KNOW 362

Left: İznik tiles inside Istanbul's Blue Mosque
Previous page: Alanya's iconic Red Tower
Front cover: Hot-air balloons over Cappadocia

DISCOVER

Houses in a Cappadocia rock-cut town

WELCOME TO TURKEY

Pristine beaches and jagged mountains. Ancient ruins and bustling modern cities. Traditional festivals and some of the world's most delicious cuisine. Turkey has all this to offer and more. Whatever your dream trip to this captivating country includes, this DK travel guide is the perfect companion.

1 Intricate tiling in Istanbul's Topkapi Palace.

2 Ancient remains in the city of Side.

3 A spread of traditional Turkish meze dishes.

4 City views in Şanlıurfa, Eastern Anatolia.

Straddling the border between Europe and Asia, Turkey has long been home to a dazzling diversity of influences. It has roots in both Western and Eastern traditions, with countless sites left behind by the many empires that ruled here over the centuries. These iconic structures – from the impressive ancient ruins of Ephesus to Istanbul's Ottoman Topkapı Palace – stand as lasting testaments to Turkey's varied past. Within the country's cities and towns, artisanal crafts, literary legacies and vibrant food scenes have been shaped by the same rich cultural heritage. This is especially visible in Istanbul, which is historically divided into European and Asian sides by the Bosphorus Strait.

Turkey's transcontinental position means the country is home to a variety of landscapes, with tall mountains looming above impressive canyons in the central Anatolian Plateau; waves lapping the golden Mediterranean beaches in the south; and dense forests leading up to the Black Sea in the north. Among it all, natural wonders like the towering fairy chimneys of Cappadocia and the extraordinary travertine terraces of Pamukkale are not to be missed.

With so much to pack in, any visit to Turkey requires thoughtful planning. We've broken the country down into easily navigable chapters, with detailed itineraries, expert local knowledge and comprehensive maps to help you plan the perfect trip. However long you plan to stay, this DK travel guide will ensure that you see the very best of the country. Enjoy the book, and enjoy Turkey.

REASONS TO LOVE TURKEY

Impressive ruins from the ancient world, relaxing beaches, historical cities and some of the world's best cuisine. There are endless reasons to love Turkey, but here are some of our favourites.

1 OTTOMAN ARCHITECTURE

Safranbolu's townhouses *(p304)*, Topkapı Palace *(p72)*, Süleymaniye Mosque *(p108)* and countless others like it: Turkey's Ottoman buildings are an architectural delight.

ANCIENT CITIES 2

The architects of the classical world left behind many ancient cities here. Explore famous Bergama *(p200)* and Ephesus *(p206)*, as well as less-visited ruins like Termessos *(p258)*.

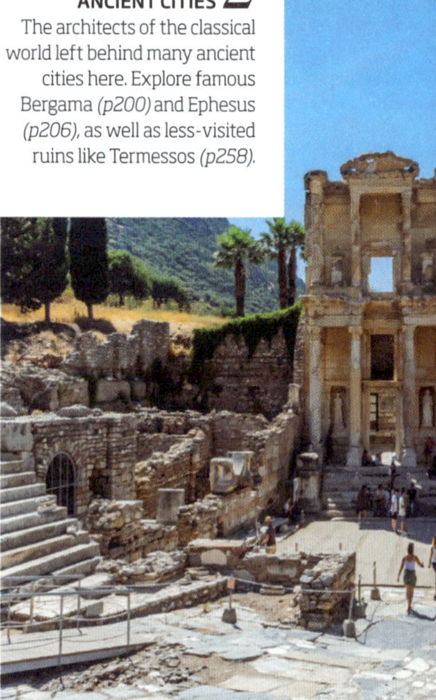

3 SHOPPING AT LOCAL MARKETS

From weekly bazaars in Istanbul's suburbs to farmers' markets in rural Anatolia, you can take your pick of the best seasonal produce at one of Turkey's local markets *(p35)*.

CAPPADOCIA 4

The unique fairy chimneys of Cappadocia *(p324)* are world famous for a reason. For the best views of this iconic landscape, take a hot-air balloon flight over the rock formations.

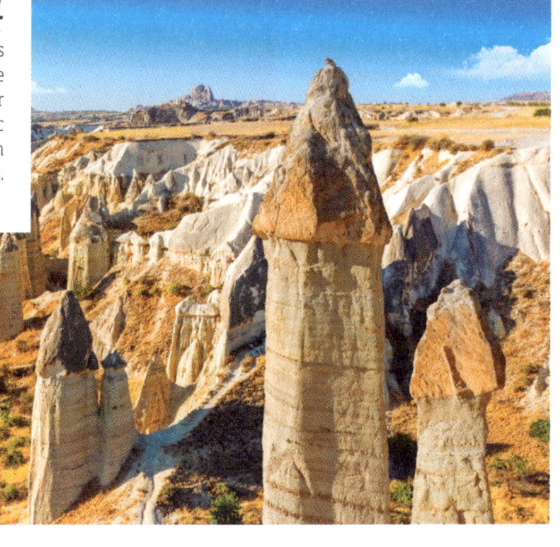

SAILING THE MED 5

Turkey's southern coast is best enjoyed from the water. Hop aboard a gulet boat *(p41)* to explore the ancient sites, hidden beaches and villages along the Mediterranean.

REGIONAL CUISINE 6

Turkey is vast, so it's no surprise that it has a variety of regional cuisines. From familiar meze and kebabs to local "Turkish pizza" *(pide)* and hearty *güveç* stews, there's plenty to enjoy.

BAZAAR QUARTERS 7

See the best of local life by exploring one of Turkey's bazaar quarters, made up of narrow covered streets. Those in Gaziantep, Mardin and Istanbul are especially vibrant.

HIKING TRAILS 8

Get close to nature along one of Turkey's many trails. Some of the best include the Lycian Way *(p252)*, Western Anatolia's St Paul Trail *(p294)* and the route up the Kaçkar Mountains *(p316)*.

9 SOAKING IN A TURKISH BATH

The hammam is a Turkish institution, and few places are as relaxing. You can find many all over Turkey, but Istanbul's Baths of Roxelana *(p96)* is one of the most luxurious.

10 BLISSFUL BEACHES

Turkey's beaches are varied and plentiful. Kick back on popular city beaches like Marmaris' İçmeler *(p218)*, or seek out quieter shores such as those near Çıralı *(p257)*.

ARTS AND CRAFTS 11

There is a long tradition of craftsmanship in Turkey. Head to Istanbul's Museum of Turkish and Islamic Arts *(p97)* to see historic İznik pottery and finely woven carpets.

MUSIC AND DANCE 12

Music and dance cultures in Turkey are deep rooted. See traditional whirling dervish dances *(p288)* or enjoy music by modern Anatolian rock groups such as Altin Gün.

EXPLORE TURKEY

This guide divides Turkey into eight colour-coded sightseeing areas, as shown on this map. Find out more about each area on the following pages.

UKRAINE
Rozdol'ne
Dzhankoy
Simferopol
Foros
Yalta
Black Sea
BULGARIA
Edirne
Kırklareli
Babaeski
Tekirdağ

ISTANBUL
p56

THRACE AND THE SEA OF MARMARA
p176

THE BLACK SEA
p300

Karabük
Kastamonu
Adapazarı
Düzce
İzmit
Yalova
Bandırma
Bolu
Çanakkale
Karacabey
Bursa
Çankırı
İskilip
Çorum
Edremit
Balıkesir
Eskişehir
Ankara
Yozgat
Kırıkkale
Polatlı
Kütahya

THE AEGEAN
p196

ANKARA AND WESTERN ANATOLIA
p272

Akhisar
Simav
Manisa
Kulu
Uşak
Afyonkarahisar
İzmir
Salihli
Nevşehir
Akşehir
Aksaray
Aydın
Denizli
Burdur
İsparta
Konya
Niğde
Milas
Tavas
Muğla
Bodrum
Ereğli
Antalya
Dalaman
Side

THE EASTERN MEDITERRANEAN
p260

THE WESTERN MEDITERRANEAN
p238

Alanya
Mut
Silifke
Mediterranean Sea
CYPRUS

0 kilometres 150
0 miles 150
N

LOCATOR MAP
DENMARK
POLAND
BELARUS
RUSSIA
GERMANY
CZECH REP.
UKRAINE
SLOVAKIA
FRANCE
AUSTRIA
HUNGARY
SWITZ.
CROATIA
ROMANIA
SERBIA
ITALY
BULGARIA
GEORGIA
ALBANIA
TURKEY
GREECE
SYRIA
TUNISIA
Mediterranean
CYPRUS
IRAQ
ALGERIA
JORDAN
LIBYA
EGYPT
Korenovsk
Krasnodar
Feodosiya
Anapa
RUSSIA
Gelendzhik
Tuapse
GEORGIA
Bafra
Samsun
Terme
Ünye
Hopa
Artvın
Ardahan
Rize
Ordu
Giresun
Kars
ARMENIA
Niksar
Gümüşhane
Turhal
Tokat
Şebinkarahisar
Bayburt
Suşehri
Iğdir
Yıldızeli
Zara
Erzurum
Ağrı
Sivas
Erzincan
CAPPADOCIA AND CENTRAL ANATOLIA
p318
Divriği
EASTERN ANATOLIA
p342
Patnos
IRAN
Tunceli
Bingöl
Elazığ
Muş
Van
Tatvan
Malatya
Elbistan
Ergani
Silvan
Siirt
Gölbaşı
Adıyaman
Diyarbakır
Hakkâri
Kahramanmaraş
Siverek
Şırnak
Midyat
Kızıltepe
Gaziantep
Adana
Nizip
Şanlıurfa
Payas
Sêmêl
Arbīl/Hewlêr
Antakya
Aleppo
Al Mawşil (Mosul)
Ar Raqqah
Ash Shadādah
SYRIA
Dayr az Zawr
Dāqūq
Salamiyah
Al Mayādīn
IRAQ
Homs
Tikrīt
Abū Kamāl
Sāmarrā'
Tudmur (Palmyra)
LEBANON
Baalbek
Haditha
Al Khāliş
Beyrouth (Beirut)

GETTING TO KNOW TURKEY

Stretching from the edge of Europe to the Middle East, Turkey is huge and varied. The west is home to its most cosmopolitan cities, including Istanbul; the coasts offer outstanding beaches; the interior and the east boast sublime scenery; and all over, there are reminders of the country's dramatic history.

PAGE 56

ISTANBUL

One of the world's largest and most spectacular cities, Istanbul may not be Turkey's capital, but it is unquestionably the country's beating heart. Home to several of Turkey's most famous sights, including the Hagia Sophia, Topkapı Palace and the Grand Bazaar, it's also where you'll find the country's best restaurants and most vibrant nightlife, from Michelin-starred establishments to trendy rooftop bars. Istanbul's buzzing central districts of Seraglio Point, Sultanahmet and Beyoğlu draw the most visitors, but the wider city is also well worth exploring.

Best for
Iconic sights, contemporary culture, nightlife

Home to
Numerous historic sights, including Topkapı Palace, Hagia Sophia and the Grand Bazaar

Experience
Cruising along the Bosphorus, past waterfront villas

THRACE AND THE SEA OF MARMARA

PAGE 176

At the eastern edge of Europe, Thrace is where the city of Edirne can be found, an ancient settlement famous these days for the Selimiye Mosque, considered the masterwork of the renowned Ottoman architect Sinan. Thrace is cut off from the rest of Turkey by the Sea of Marmara, on the eastern shore of which is Bursa, dotted with some of Turkey's most impressive Ottoman-era architecture. A little further inland lies the town of İznik, known for its outstanding pottery industry.

Best for
Historic towns, rural landscapes, thermal spas

Home to
Edirne, İznik, Bursa

Experience
Exploring the former Ottoman capitals of Edirne and Bursa

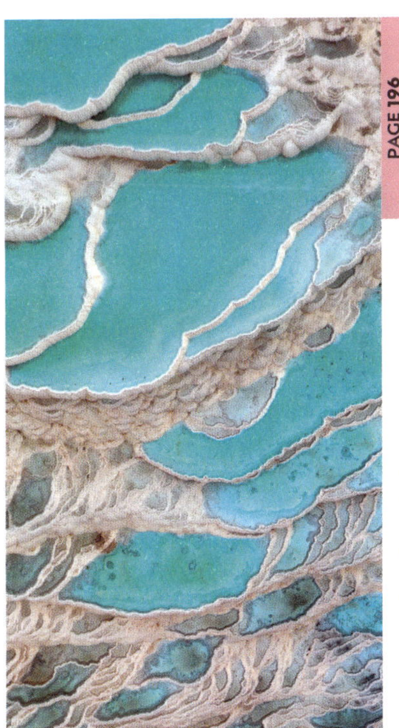

THE AEGEAN

PAGE 196

The western coast of Turkey borders the Aegean Sea, so it's perhaps no surprise that the region is where many of Turkey's ruins linked to the ancient world can be found. Troy and Bergama are just two of the most impressive, but the region's highlight is the simply stunning Ephesus and its famous library. Towns such as Bodrum and Marmaris have countless splendid beaches to be enjoyed, while inland is another of Turkey's most iconic sights: the unique "cotton-candy" limestone formations and geothermal pools of Pamukkale.

Best for
Ancient sites, village life, culinary delights

Home to
Bergama, İzmir, Ephesus, Hierapolis, Aphrodisias, Bodrum, Marmaris, Gallipoli Peninsula

Experience
Walking the ancient Roman roads of Ephesus

PAGE 238

THE WESTERN MEDITERRANEAN

This stretch of Turkey's southern coast is dotted with many of its most popular beach resorts, and no wonder – the coastline here is stunning. Antalya, Turkey's fifth-largest city, has an attractive old town, while the coast in either direction of the city is where a number of outstanding ancient ruins can be found, such as Aspendos and Myra. The Western Mediterranean is also an excellent region for outdoor activity: rafting in the Köprülü Canyon and hiking the Lycian Way are two popular choices.

Best for
Golden beaches, coastal hikes, ancient ruins

Home to
Antalya, Side

Experience
Hiking the Lycian Way

PAGE 260

THE EASTERN MEDITERRANEAN

The eastern Mediterranean coast sees fewer visitors than the west, but is no less fascinating. The seaside resort town of Alanya makes a great base for exploring the region, while along the coast are beautiful ancient ruins such as Anemurium and the gorgeous Mamure Castle, overlooking a splendid sandy beach. The large city of Adana – famous for its spicy kebabs – offers a taste of big-city life, and just a short drive east is the mysterious hilltop Hittite settlement of Karatepe.

Best for
Beach resorts, idyllic ruins, coastal views

Home to
Adana

Experience
Taking a "Blue Voyage" on a traditional gulet (wooden yacht)

PAGE 272

ANKARA AND WESTERN ANATOLIA

As Turkey's capital and second-largest city, Ankara is home to many of the country's finest museums and cultural experiences. The Museum of Anatolian Civilizations – a rich collection spanning Turkey's earliest beginnings to the classical period – is a must-see, but the city also offers a fascinating insight into modern Turkey at the Atatürk Mausoleum. Further south, Konya is one of the country's most devout cities, and is famous for its whirling dervishes.

Best for
Museums, wooden mosques

Home to
Ankara, Konya, Kütahya

Experience
Stepping back in time at Ankara's Museum of Anatolian Civilizations

→

PAGE 300

THE BLACK SEA

The Black Sea coast is a unique part of Turkey, a semitropical zone of lush greenery occupying a strip between the sea to the north and mountain ranges to the south. Most visitors head for the town of Safranbolu to wander the pretty streets of traditional Ottoman houses, while at the eastern end of the coast, the ancient city of Trabzon is well worth a stop for its splendid Byzantine-era Hagia Sophia church. A little way inland, and high up in the mountains, lies the 4th-century CE Sumela Monastery, clinging to a sheer rock face – a fabulously romantic sight.

Best for

Rugged coastline, unique cultures, Ottoman villages

Home to

Safranbolu, Trabzon, Sumela Monastery

Experience

Hiking in the yayla (highland pastures) of the Kaçkar range

PAGE 318

CAPPADOCIA AND CENTRAL ANATOLIA

Cappadocia needs little introduction: its remarkable rock formations are among the most frequently seen images of Turkey. This unique landscape is now an adventure playground for outdoorsy types, who come here to hike, and ride hot-air balloons over the otherworldly landscapes. This is also a rewarding area for history-lovers. Early Christians carved out rock churches here, and many incredible, colourful frescoes have been perfectly preserved inside.

Best for
Magical landscapes, Hittite history, Seljuk architecture

Home to
Göreme Open-Air Museum, Kayseri, Hattuşaş, Amasya

Experience
Floating over "fairy chimneys" in a hot-air balloon

PAGE 342

EASTERN ANATOLIA

The fascinating but often-overlooked eastern regions of Turkey offer fine rewards for those who venture into the mountains and plains at this end of the country. Here, you'll find stunning Armenian ruins, mountaintop monuments, and, at Göbeklitepe, some of the oldest archaeological remains in the world. Turkey's highest mountain, the imposing Mount Ararat, and its largest lake, Lake Van, are highlights of the region's gorgeous natural scenery. Meanwhile, urban centres such as Gaziantep and Mardin make perfect places to enjoy a spot of cosmopolitan city life.

Best for
Remote ruins, Kurdish and Arabic culture

Home to
Mount Nemrut, Göbeklitepe, Diyarbakır, Ani, Erzurum

Experience
Visiting the windswept ruins of Ani, on the Armenian border

1 The impressive Imperial Hall, Topkapı Palace.

2 A vibrant stall in the Spice Bazaar.

3 The imposing Galata Tower.

4 An antique red tram.

3 DAYS

in Istanbul

Day 1

Morning Start at the Topkapı Palace *(p72)*, seat of imperial Ottoman power for 400 years. Wander through its elegant courtyards, grand state rooms and intriguing museums before heading downhill to Gülhane tram stop. Ride the T1 tram to Eminönü, admiring the Moorish façade of Sirkeci Station *(p80)*, once the terminus of the *Orient Express*, and grab a quick bite at one of the quayside vendors – the fish sandwiches are very good.

Afternoon Board the ferry for the Short Bosphorus Cruise *(departs 14:40 daily; sehirhatlari.istanbul)* and enjoy a glass of Turkish *çay* (tea) from the onboard café as you take in the spectacular views. Back on terra firma, browse Eminönü's aromatic Spice Bazaar *(p112)*, a short walk from the quay. Spices secured, make your way to adjacent Hamdi *(hamdi.com.tr)*, a charming restaurant that serves some of the best *lahmacun* (spicy mincemeat flatbread) in the city. A comfy bed awaits in the nearby Ottoman Hotel Imperial *(p97)*, your base for the trip.

Day 2

Morning Begin your day with a stroll in Gülhane Park *(p79)*, spotting herons and taking in the lofty Goth's Column before stopping for *çay* at a local café. Refreshed, make the short walk to the splendid Archaeological Museums *(p68)*, where you can fully immerse yourself in Turkey's past.
Afternoon A short tram ride and uphill stroll brings you to the magnificent Süleymaniye Mosque complex *(p108)*, known for its majestic architecture. Admire the domes and minarets – the work of architect Sinan – before stopping for lunch at Süleymaniye Erzincanli Ali Baba *(7 Professor Sıddık Sami Onar Cad)*, which serves delicious *kuru fasulye* (creamy, chilli-topped beans in tomato sauce). Head across the iconic Galata Bridge and order a sunset beer at one of the cafés lining its bottom deck. Intimate Salon Galata *(p136)*, with its fine cocktails and sophisticated Turkish menu, ensures a delicious and relaxed end to a busy day.

Day 3

Morning Rise early and take the short tram ride to Karaköy, home to Istanbul Modern *(p130)*. Allow a couple of hours to explore the museum before walking along the Bosphorus waterfront to Galata Bridge. Here, the quaint, 19th-century Tünel funicular will whizz you up to İstiklal Caddesi *(p140)*, where you can order a Turkish coffee and a slice of cake from Mandabatmaz *(mandabatmaz.com.tr)*.
Afternoon Make the short walk past the historic Pera Palace Hotel *(p132)*, whose illustrious guests included crime writer Agatha Christie *(p42)*. Then stroll down bustling İstiklal Caddesi towards Galata Mevlevi Lodge Museum *(p134)*. Once home to whirling dervishes, it's now a museum set in tranquil gardens. After exploring, make your way to the Galata Tower *(p133)*, a former watchtower that now offers visitors stunning views. For dinner, head to Ali Ocakbaşı Karaköy *(p136)*, renowned for its charcoal-grilled meats and Golden Horn vistas – the perfect setting for your last meal in this vibrant city.

1

2

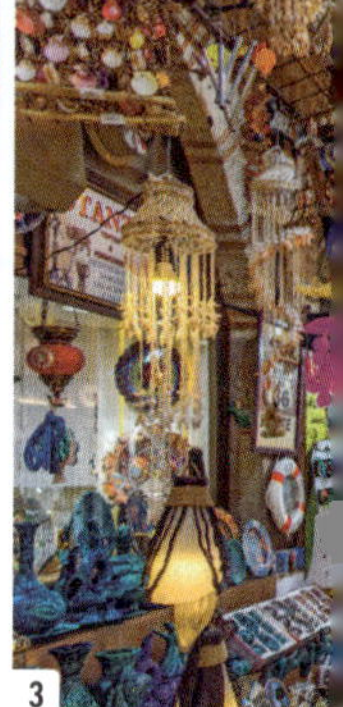

3

A WEEK
on the Aegean Coast

Day 1

Begin your Aegean journey on the Gallipoli Peninsula *(p220)*, where one of World War I's key campaigns was fought. For an immersive, walk-in-their-footsteps experience, take a guided battlefields tour with Crowded House Tours *(crowdedhousegallipoli.com)*. Afterwards, have a simple lunch at Tarihi Eceabat Köftecisi *(İsmetpaşa Mahallesi Zübeyde Hanım Meydanı 43)*, then head to Kilitbahir Castle *(p222)* for views across the Dardanelles. Take the ferry to Çanakkale *(p222)* and spend what remains of the afternoon exploring this lively town. End the day with a seafood feast at waterfront Yalova Restaurant *(yalovarestoran.com)*.

Day 2

Rise early to traverse the 30 km (18 miles) south to Troy *(p222)*. Visit the brilliant Troy Museum first, then tour the site itself, which incorporates ruins from several different eras of occupation. Leaving Troy behind, drive 64 km (40 miles) south to Behram Kale *(p223)*, where houses cluster above the ruins of Assos. Have lunch at Cleanthes Cafe *(cleanthescafe.com)*, then stroll the town's alleyways to the Temple of Athena, following the trail through the ruins down to the harbour. In the evening, grab dinner on the balcony of Assos Köyüm Restaurant *(Behram Köyü Yolu)* for sunset views.

Day 3

This morning, set off on the 102-km (64-mile) drive around the Bay of Edremit to Ayvalık *(p223)* and delve into its back alleys, brimming with preserved Ottoman-Greek architecture. Then hop on the ferry to Alibey Island, for a tasty meze lunch at Lal Girit Mutfağı *(Ayvalık Cad 20)* before exploring the island's nature trails or beaches. Back on the mainland, enjoy dinner and drinks at Komşu Meyhane *(komsumeyhane.com)* on Ayvalık's harbour.

Day 4

Don't leave Ayvalık without trying an Ayvalık *tost* (the town's famed toasted sandwich) for breakfast. Afterwards, it's

1 A memorial at Gallipoli. ↑

2 Boats lining the promenade in Ayvalık.

3 İzmir's Kemeraltı Bazaar is a shopper's paradise.

4 The Library of Celsus at ancient Ephesus.

68 km (42 miles) southeast to Bergama and the dramatic ruins of Pergamon *(p200)*, where you can devote the rest of the day to rambling around its colossal remnants. Bed down in one of Bergama old town's boutique hotels – but not before tucking into dinner in the atmospheric garden at Akropoli Restaurant *(İttihati Terraki Cad 78)*.

Day 5

Today starts with a 115-km (72-mile) drive to İzmir. Begin your exploration of this bustling city at the İzmir Culture and Arts Factory *(p202)*, then visit the Agora *(p205)* before pausing for lunch at Deniz Restaurant *(p203)*. In the afternoon, venture into the labyrinthine Kemeraltı Bazaar *(p202)*; you can book a tour of the bazaar's synagogues at izmirjcc.org. If you're a foodie, don't miss a trip 40 km (24 miles) west of town to Michelin-starred OD Urla *(p224)*.

Day 6

After five days on the road, it's time for a two-night stop, and there's no better place to do that than Selçuk *(p224)*, home to the ruins of Ephesus *(p206)*; it's an 80-km (50-mile) drive south from İzmir. In town, visit the excellent Ephesus Museum *(p225)* and the Basilica of St John *(p224)* before having lunch at Kybele Gastro Restaurant *(kybelegastro.com)*. Cap an afternoon of exploring the grand ruins at Ephesus itself with dinner at Ejder Restaurant *(Cengiz Topel Cad 9)*, under the arches of Selçuk's Byzantine aqueduct.

Day 7

On your last day, embark on Selçuk's most popular day trip: a loop around the Meander Valley's ancient cities. First, head 56 km (35 miles) south to Priene *(p227)*, with its Greco-Roman ruins. From here, it's 22 km (14 miles) to Miletus *(p228)*, while Didim and the ruins of Didyma *(p229)* lie a further 20 km (13 miles) south. Have lunch at Lavin Restaurant *(Atatürk Bulvarı)*, before exploring Didyma's Temple of Apollo next door. After, drive back to Selçuk for an evening amble along the cobblestone lanes, and dinner at Agora Restaurant *(agorarest.com)*.

1

A WEEK
in Mediterranean and Anatolian Turkey

Day 1

The buzzing city of Antalya *(p242)* is a great place to begin your journey. In the morning, strike out for the Psidian ruins of Termessos *(p258)*, 36 km (22 miles) west of Antalya. After exploring the site, enjoy lunch back in Antalya at Sauvignon Restaurant (*sauvignonrestaurant.com*). Devote the afternoon to the city: stroll the alleys of Keleiçi, then ride the antique tram to the Antalya Archaeological Museum (*Bahçelievler, Konyaaltı Cad 88*). In the evening, head to one of the restaurants perched above the Old Harbour *(p242)* for dinner and drinks.

Day 2

A full day of ancient-city sightseeing awaits. First, Perge *(p258)*, 16 km (10 miles) east of Antalya, where you can hike up to the Acropolis for a panoramic view across the entire site. Next, hop 33 km (20 miles) east to Aspendos *(p259)* and its Roman theatre, the best preserved in the world. Split the onward 35-km (22-mile) drive to Side with a relaxed lunch at aptly named Riverside Restaurant in Belkis (*Aspendos Yolu*). In Side *(p246)*, scramble around the 2nd-century-CE theatre and agora ruins, then wander to the harbour for dinner at Apollonik Café (*Apollon Sok 35*), overlooking the seafront's Temple of Apollo.

Day 3

Start today by veering north from the coast to Beyşehir *(p294)*, 140 km (87 miles) away, to see the Eşrefoğlu Mosque. When you've finished gazing at its stunning wooden interior, drive onto Konya *(p284)*, 90 km (56 miles) to the east. Lunch on local *tirit* kebabs at Tarihi Tiritci Mithat (*Yusufağa Sok 21/A*), then visit the Mevlâna Museum *(p284)*. Spend the rest of the day exploring the lanes of Konya's bazaar district before dining on richly spiced dishes at Sultan Somati (*sultansomati.com.tr*).

Day 4

Staying in Konya for another night means you can dig deeper into this fascinating city, once capital of the Sultanate of Rum.

1 Antalya's Old Town. ↑

2 The monumental Roman Theatre at Aspendos.

3 Sultanhanı Caravanserai, a 13th-century traders' inn.

4 Hot-air balloons floating above the otherworldly landscapes of Göreme.

First though, head further back in time by driving 50 km (31 miles) southeast to the Neolithic settlement of Çatalhöyük *(p294)*. Back in Konya, check out the city's many Seljuk monuments, including the Karatay Museum *(p285)* and the Alaeddin Mosque *(p284)*. For dinner, try Şıfa Restaurant (*sifarestaurant.com*), a Konya stalwart.

Day 5

Hit the road again, beginning with a 109-km (68-mile) drive northeast to Sultanhanı Caravanserai (*İstikamet, Ufuklar Sok*). This 13th-century traders inn is renowned for its Seljuk artistry. Afterwards, head 70 km (44 miles) east to the Ihlara Valley *(p339)*. Have lunch in one of the restaurants perched above the Melendiz River in Belisırma before hiking the valley trail between fresco-decorated Byzantine churches and hermit hideouts.

Day 6

Today is all about exploring the Cappadocian countryside on the way to Göreme, 89 km (55 miles) to the northeast. The first stop is Güzelyurt *(p338)* and the Monastery Valley, then continue onto Derinkuyu *(p334)* to explore the underground city's cavern system. Once in Göreme *(p322)*, have a late lunch with valley views at Nazar Börek Café (*Karamızrak Sok*) before hiking Pigeon Valley to Uçhisar, where you can wind your way up to the top of the rock. Back in Göreme, make a beeline to Topdeck Cave (*Hafız Abdullah Efendi Sok 15*) for dinner.

Day 7

Wake up before the birds for a hot-air balloon ride over Cappadocia's valleys of wind-eroded rocky spires. Then spend the rest of the day delving into central Cappadocia's key sights. Explore the frescoed churches of the unforgettable Göreme Open-Air Museum *(p322)* before driving to Avanos *(p335)* for a lazy lunch by the river. Finally, head into the neighbouring rock valleys of Zelve *(p334)* and Paşabağı, before finishing up with a sunset walk in Göreme's Rose Valley.

Rock Stars

Turkey's rich geological past has created some spectacular rock formations. Among the most famous examples are those in the Cappadocia region *(p318)*, where volcanic eruptions some 12 million years ago created "fairy chimneys" – spire-like, conical rocks. If you don't make it to Cappadocia, then head to Afyonkarahisar *(p295)* to see similar formations. Over in the east, the area around Lake Van *(p360)*, known as "Vanadocia", is home to similar fairy-chimney-style rocks.

Some of the impressive rock formations in Cappadocia

TURKEY FOR NATURAL WONDERS

Turkey is a land of rugged beauty. From stunning coastlines to towering mountain ranges, with iconic geological formations in between, there's a huge variety of exhilarating scenery to enjoy.

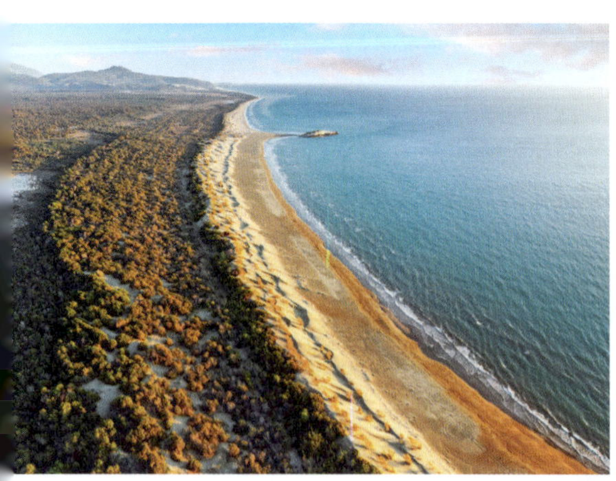

↑ Golden sand stretching along the shores of Patara on Turkey's Turquoise Coast

Captivating Coastlines

With blue waters lapping on sandy shores, Turkey's beaches are some of the world's most beautiful. The Turquoise Coast is dotted with hidden coves, while Anamur *(p267)* is an especially picturesque seaside spot.

Did You Know?

Turkey's diverse natural habitats are home to around 10,000 plant, 500 bird and 150 mammal species.

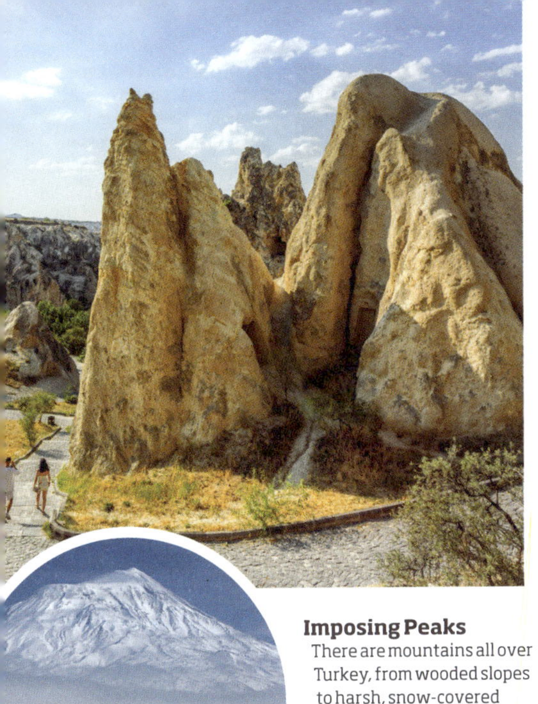

Imposing Peaks

There are mountains all over Turkey, from wooded slopes to harsh, snow-covered summits. The mountainous regions make for stunning trekking country: head to the Kaçkar Mountains *(p316)* in the east and the Taurus and Aladağlar mountains in the south *(p338)* to see some of the best vistas. Over in the far east, the tremendous bulk of Mount Ararat towers over the town of Doğubayazıt *(p359)*, near the Armenian border.

↑ The snow-covered slopes of striking Mount Ararat

TOP 5 **HIGHEST PEAKS IN TURKEY**

Mount Ararat
At 5,137 m (16,853 ft) high, this is Turkey's tallest mountain, found in Dogubayazit *(p359)*.

Mount Cilo
Looming over Hakkarı, at 4,134 m (13,562 ft) tall, Mount Cilo is summitable again after years of political unrest.

Mount Süphan
The tallest of the peaks around Lake Van *(p360)*, at 4,058 m (13,313 ft) high, Mount Süphan is an imposing sight.

Mount Kaçkar
The tallest mountain in the Kaçkar Range *(p316)*, this peak reaches 3,932 m (12,900 ft) above pretty alpine meadows.

Mount Erciyes
Cappadocia's Mount Erciyes *(p337)* towers at 3,917 m (12,851 ft) and is one of the country's top ski spots.

Limpid Lakes

Thanks to its mountainous landscape, Turkey is home to a huge number of lakes. Head to its largest, Lake Van *(p360)*, to see views of the surrounding snowy mountains and visit Armenian ruins on its southern shores and islands. Further west, Tuz Gölü (Salt Lake, *p339*) is entirely different: a very shallow, saline lake, where you can spot plenty of wildlife, including bright-pink flamingos.

↑ An Armenian church on the shores of one of Lake Van's islands

Mosques and Palaces

As its former imperial centre, Istanbul is home to some of Turkey's most impressive mosques and palaces. Head to the well-preserved Topkapı Palace *(p72)* to see one of the most significant, along with the Blue Mosque *(p92)*. Beyond Istanbul, the Selimiye Mosque in Edirne *(p184)* is thought to be the pinnacle of Ottoman architecture.

One of the ornately decorated rooms inside Istanbul's Topkapı Palace

TURKEY FOR AMAZING ARCHITECTURE

From opulent palaces to dome-topped basilicas and mosques, the scope of architecture in Turkey is unparalleled. But it's not all about the grand sites: many of its most interesting buildings lay beyond the old imperial cities.

TURKEY'S FIRST NATIONAL ARCHITECTURE MOVEMENT

The First National Architecture Movement style was prominent during the early 20th century, as the Ottoman era ended. Proponents of it sought to bring together Ottoman and Seljuk elements in modern architecture. Key examples of it include the Grand Post Office in Istanbul's Sirkeci area, and Ankara's Ethnography Museum *(p277)* and archetypal Painting and Sculpture Museum *(p276)*.

Ottoman Konaks

Many of Turkey's *konaks* (18th- and 19th-century Ottoman houses) have been transformed into hotels. For a stay full of creaky, quirky ambience, bed down in one of Safranbolu's timber-framed merchant mansions *(p305)*, or Amasya's *(p330)* clutch of stone-and-wood riverfront houses, with rooms projected over the water.

→

Konaks making up much of the Safranbolu skyline

Byzantine Structures

Istanbul was once the capital of the Byzantine Empire, and today the city is where many of its greatest relics stand. The Hagia Sophia *(p88)* may be the most famous of these, but sights like the Basilica Cistern *(p94)* and Theodosian Walls *(p150)* impress. In east Turkey, the Sumela Monastery *(p310)* is one of the most unique sights.

INSIDER TIP

The Theodosian Walls online

Istanbul's Byzantine fortifications, one of the ancient world's greatest defensive structures, can also be explored online *(istanbulsurlari.ku.edu.tr/en)*.

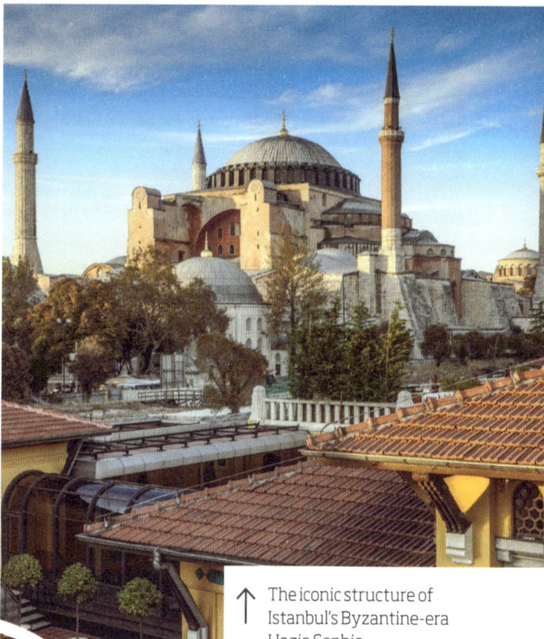

↑ The iconic structure of Istanbul's Byzantine-era Hagia Sophia

Seljuk Architecture

Before the Ottoman Empire came the Seljuk Empire, which left its mark on Turkey, particularly Anatolia. Explore early examples like Divriği's Great Mosque *(p357)*, the stone doorways of which are considered a masterpiece of Islamic architecture. Anatolian cities are home to countless other Seljuk monuments, including the impressive Alaeddin Mosque *(p284)* in the former Seljuk capital Konya.

← Intricately carved stonework decorating the mihrab of Divriği's Great Mosque

Medieval Mosques

The Wooden Hypostyle Mosques of Medieval Anatolia are unique structures dating back to the 13th and 14th centuries. Head to Eşrefoğlu Mosque in Beyşehir *(p294)* or Kasaba's Mahmut Bey Mosque to take in the woodwork artistry, full of *kundekari* (interlocking-wood) designs and carved wooden *muqarnas* (stalactite vaulting).

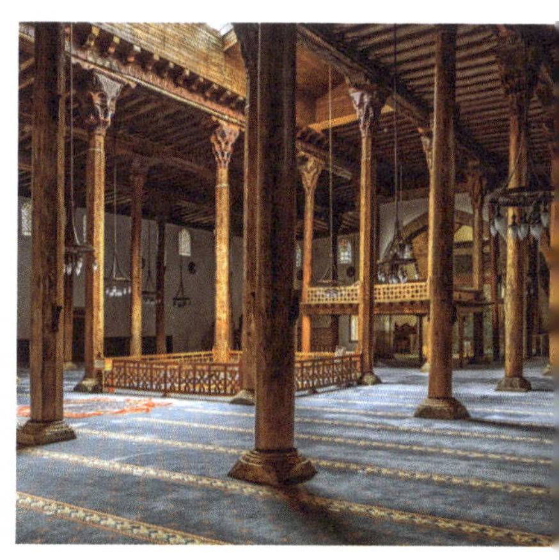

→ Detailed woodwork adorning Beyşehir's Eşrefoğlu Mosque

↑ The Ottoman-era Süleymaniye Mosque, in Istanbul's Fatih district

EXPLORING MOSQUES

Befitting Turkey's largest city, there are over 3,000 mosques in Istanbul, ranging in style from Ottoman and Byzantine to more contemporary buildings, and from small, local neighbourhood mosques to towering landmarks like the Hagia Sophia and the Blue Mosque. Over 99 per cent of Turkey's population is Muslim, with most belonging to the Sunni branch of Islam, although there are also a few Shiites.

A soaring sense of space characterizes the vast prayer halls found in many of Istanbul's great historic mosques. Islam forbids images of living things (human or animal) inside a mosque, so there are never any statues or figurative paintings; but the geometric and abstract architectural details of the interior can be exquisite. Men and women pray separately; women often use a screened-off area or a balcony.

Mosques also function as community hubs, with courtyards often busy with families, students and worshippers going about their day. While visitors are welcome at Istanbul's mosques, it's best to plan your visit outside the main periods of worship.

Key features

Müezzin Mahfili

▲ The *müezzin mahfili* is a platform found in large mosques. The muezzin (mosque official) stands on this when chanting responses to the prayers of the imam (head of the mosque).

Mihrab

▲ The mihrab, a niche in the wall, marks the direction of Mecca - generally south-southeast from Istanbul. The prayer hall is laid out so that most people within this often vast, central space can see the mihrab.

MOSQUE COMPLEXES

A mosque complex, or *külliye*, such as the Süleymaniye Mosque *(p108)* shown here, was built not only to be a place of worship but also as a charitable foundation. In addition to the central mosque, the complex would typically include a hospital *(darüşşifa)*; a school *(medrese)*; Islamic study halls; a *han* or caravanserai, which acted as lodgings for travellers; a public soup kitchen *(imaret)* that served the mosque officials, the *medreses'* students and the community's sick and poor; and a bathhouse (hammam). Today, most such buildings no longer fulfil their original functions.

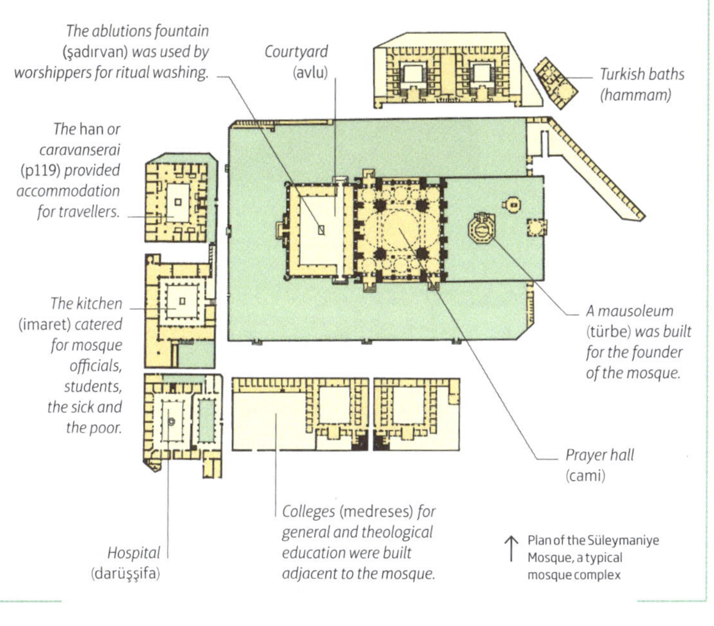

↑ Plan of the Süleymaniye Mosque, a typical mosque complex

Minbar

△ The *minbar* is a lofty pulpit to the right of the *mihrab*. This is used by the imam when he delivers the Friday sermon (known as the *khutba*).

Loge

△ The loge (*hünkar mahfili*) provided the sultan with a screened-off balcony where he could pray, safe from would-be assassins.

Kürsü

△ The *kürsü*, from the Arabic for "chair", is seen in some mosques and is a throne used by the imam while he reads extracts from the Koran.

Mezes and Meyhane Culture

The best way to sample Turkish cuisine and culture is with a meze at a *meyhane*. These traditional Turkish taverns aren't about big main courses. Instead, they offer up typical meze dishes such as *mercimek köfte* (spiced lentil balls), *paçanga böreği* (pastries stuffed with cheese and dried beef) and olive-oil-drenched artichokes, along with plenty of raki. In Istanbul, Beyoğlu *(p126)* is the area for traditional *meyhanes*, while modern fare can be found outside the capital at the likes of Lavinia Meyhane *(p280)* in Ankara and İskele Meyhanesi *(p309)* in Trabzon.

→ A table packed with traditional Turkish meze dishes

TURKEY FOR FOODIES

While Turkey may be famous for kebabs and meze, there's so much more to the country's culinary catalogue. You'll find a mosaic-like gastronomical tradition here that showcases Arabic, Persian and Mediterranean influences, not to mention a bounty of fresh produce and delectable desserts.

EAT

Turk Fatih Tutak

Turkey's only two-Michelin-starred restaurant is a real treat for serious foodies. Chef Fatih Tutak's delicious 14-course tasting menu takes diners on a culinary adventure across Turkey, with traditional regional dishes and innovative modern delights served up on the menu.

Yeniyol Sok 2, off Cumhuriyet Hacıahmet Silahşör Cad, Istanbul
turkft.com

Contemporary Fine-dining

A new wave of chefs are putting a fresh spin on high-end Turkish food, fusing Anatolia's plentiful produce with modern cooking methods. The best in sustainable excellence can be tried at OD Urla *(p224)*, helmed by Michelin-starred chef Osman Sezener. At Neolokal *(neolokal.com)* in Istanbul, chef Maksut Aşkar has mastered quirky takes on traditional dishes.

→ Chefs at work in the kitchen of OD Urla

TURKISH WINE

Alongside its bounty of produce, Turkey also has a burgeoning, yet oft-overlooked, wine industry, which stretches back to before 5,000 BCE. Viticulture thrived here until the Ottomans, who ruled that only non-Muslims were permitted to produce wine. But since the fall of the Ottomans in 1922, the industry has dramatically grown and today there are hundreds of producers cultivating native grapes, primarily in Cappadocia, Ankara and Tokat.

Desserts

Turkish people love a sweet treat, whether it's a traditional *künefe* (syrup-soaked *kadayıf* pastry and cheese), a *muhallebi* (milk pudding) or, of course, *lokum* (Turkish delight). Those with a sweet tooth should head to Istanbul to try *künefe* at Hafız Mustafa 1864 (*hafizmustafa.com*) and the famous *lokum* at the historic Hacı Bekir shop (*hacibekir.com*). If baklava is more your thing, visit Gaziantep (*p358*), which is ground zero for this flakey pastry: Tarihi Elmacıpazarı Güllüoğlu (*elmacipazarigulluoglu.com*) has been making baklava since 1843.

Different types of Turkish delight stacked high

Buying fresh produce at a local market near the city of Alanya

Market Days

Local markets, known as a *pazar*, are a weekly staple of towns and villages throughout Turkey, and a visit to one is not to be missed. All sorts of vendors come to town laden down with goods ranging from fruit and vegetables to nuts and olives, plus speciality items such as *pekmez* (fruit molasses) and *biber salçası* (red pepper paste). Among the best regular markets are those held in Avanos (*p335*) on Fridays, Tire (northeast of Selçuk) on Tuesdays, and Ayvalık (*p223*) on Thursdays.

Neolithic Relics

Remnants of Turkey's ancient past are scattered all over the country. In the southeast, at Şanlıurfa *(p358)*, the sites of Karahan Tepe *(muze.gov.tr)* and Göbeklitepe *(p348)* have transformed what we know of early humans. Over to the southwest are the mudbrick houses of Çatalhöyük *(p294)*, one of the largest Neolithic settlements ever unearthed.

Remains of the temple at Göbeklitepe, a UNESCO World Heritage Site

TURKEY FOR HISTORY BUFFS

As the bridge connecting West to East and Europe to Asia, Turkey has a long and fascinating history, influenced by many powerful civilizations. Neolithic sites, ruins from the Hittites, Greeks and Romans, and opulent Ottoman buildings all provide a window into Turkey's storied past.

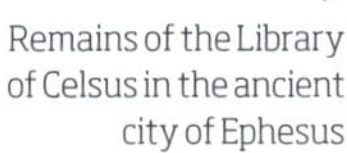

→

Remains of the Library of Celsus in the ancient city of Ephesus

THE LYCIAN STATE

In the Classical era, the area around the Teke Peninsula (between Fethiye and Antalya) was home to the Lycian state, a confederation of 23 cities. The Lycians had been granted autonomy by the Romans in 168 BCE and set about forming a union of the cities. Elections were held annually, and each city had voting rights. Though the state was dissolved in 42 CE, it is regarded as one of the earliest attempts at a proto-democratic union and even influenced the US constitution.

The Classical Era

In antiquity, Turkey was part of Asia Minor, a land fought over by the Greeks and Persians, conquered by Alexander the Great, then consumed by the Roman Empire. The Romans named Ephesus *(p206)* their capital, and today, the ruins of this city are among the most evocative ancient sites in the world. Remains of powerful cities can also be found at the summit-site of Bergama *(p200)* and on the Mediterranean coast at Xanthos *(p253)*, former capital of the fiercely independent Lycian state.

↑ İsak Paşa Palace, and *(inset)* decorated arches inside the palace

Ottoman Grandeur

Turkey brims with vestiges of the Ottoman era, hardly surprising given they ruled from c 1300 to 1922. Istanbul is the place to start, with sites including the Blue Mosque *(p92)* and Topkapı Palace *(p72)*, while the earlier capitals (Bursa and Edirne) brim with grand remains, headlined by Bursa's sprawling bazaar area *(p192)* and Edirne's Selimiye Mosque *(p184)*. There are also fascinating sites in far-flung corners, such as the imposing İsak Paşa Palace, close to the Iranian border.

INSIDER TIP

Take a Tour

Istanbul Walks *(istanbulwalks.com)* offers a great range of history-themed walking tours throughout the city, from day-long trips of the Asian shore to a half-day walk devoted to Istanbul's lesser-known Jewish heritage.

Hittite History

The Hittites were one of Turkey's first major civilizations, ruling the Anatolian region during the Bronze Age. Get an introduction to them at the Museum of Anatolian Civilizations *(p278)* in Ankara, home to the world's largest collection of Hittite artifacts. Then dive into their former heartland at Boğazkale for the walled capital Hattuşaş *(p328)* and the inscribed rock faces of the Hittite sanctuary, Yazılıkaya. Those who want to delve deeper can visit Çorum's Hittite-heavy museum *(p340)* and the site of Alacahöyük *(p340)*.

→ An inscribed Hittite rock face at Yazılıkaya

Floating in the Air

There is nothing quite like soaring in the sky over Cappadocia; it might be the most romantic experience in Turkey. Here, balloons rise above "fairy chimneys", giving passengers an unparalleled view over this moon-like landscape. Those with a head for heights can also float over the unique white travertines in Pamukkale *(p210)* or enjoy memorable sunrise trips over Lake Emre in the Phrygian Valley *(p298)*.

INSIDER TIP

Check your Operator

Rogue balloon companies have been known to scam tourists: check websites and reviews, and speak to other travellers to ensure you have a good flight.

TURKEY FOR OUTDOOR ADVENTURES

With well-marked hiking trails, slick ski resorts and natural hot springs, Turkey offers something for everyone, and its dramatic scenery provides the perfect backdrop to every outdoor pursuit.

Soaking in the Springs

When it comes to geothermal springs, Turkey is one of the best destinations in Europe. The white limestone travertine at Pamukkale *(p210)* has been favoured by bathers since at least the Roman era. But it isn't the only great spot: the spas at Afyonkarahisar *(p295)* are some of the best modern baths in Turkey, while those at Haymana *(p292)* are also excellent and within easy reach of Ankara.

Bathers taking a dip in the travertine pools and terraces at Pamukkale

Colourful hot-air balloons hovering over Cappadocia

TOP 3 SCENIC HIKES IN TURKEY

The Lycian Way
The longest and most famous hiking route in Turkey is the 520-km (320-mile) coastal Lycian Way *(p252)*. Give yourself around 30 days to complete it.

Love Valley
This Cappadocian highlight, known as Aşıklar Vadisi in Turkish, offers an easy walk amid stunning scenery.

St Paul Trail
Follow the footsteps of St Paul on this trail *(p294)*, which runs from the coast near Antalya to the Turkish Lakeland.

Turkish Trekking

The best way to see Turkey's stunning nature is in a pair of hiking boots. Serious hikers can tackle the long-distance paths in Western Anatolia, such as the Lycian Way *(p252)*, or the lesser-known, but equally spectacular, trails around the Kaçkar Mountains *(p316)*. Conversely, the valleys in Göreme *(p322)* offer easier walks in Turkey's most impressive landscapes.

Hiker admiring the views on the Lycian Way

Hit the Slopes

Turkey may not be the first place that springs to mind for skiing, but perhaps it should be. There are great slopes for all abilities at the likes of Palandöken *(p356)*, Lake Salda or Mount Erciyes *(p337)*, while those who prefer to do their shredding on a snowboard can enjoy the "crystal snow" at Sarıkamış.

Skiers enjoying the powder at the Salda Ski Centre

Epic Water Sports

There are a wealth of places along Turkey's vast coastline where you can take part in water sports. Take to the waves at Alaçatı, on the Çeşme peninsula *(p224)*, the country's capital of kitesurfing, or on the Datça *(p236)* and Bodrum *(p214)* peninsulas, where windsurfing rules. To explore the coast from beneath the sea, try scuba diving off Kaş *(p253)*; in the clear waters here, divers can see the flooded remains of ancient Lycian ruins.

A scuba diver exploring the plentiful waters off the coast of Kaş

TURKEY FOR THE COAST

With over 8,000 km (5,000 miles) of coastline, Turkey's abundant shores have plenty to offer. Whether you're looking to unwind on a tranquil beach, discover quiet coves off the beaten track or explore the rich marine life beneath the waters, Turkey delivers in spades.

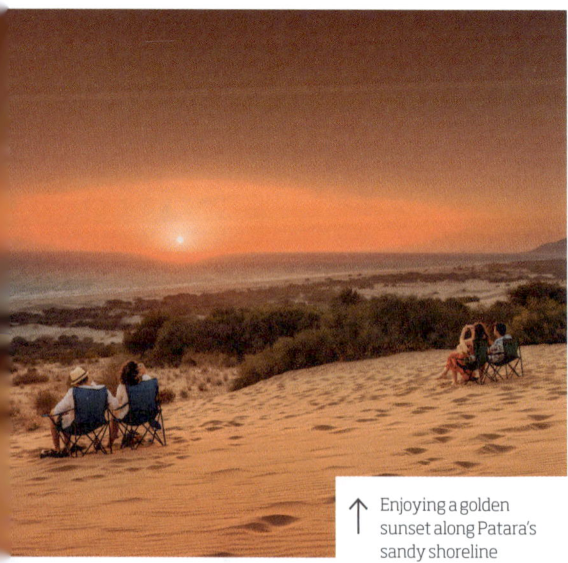

↑ Enjoying a golden sunset along Patara's sandy shoreline

Golden Sands

Head almost anywhere along the Aegean and southern coasts, and you'll find long stretches of golden sand, lapped by turquoise water. Patara's long beach *(p256)* is a Mediterranean highlight, while the sandy shores of Ölüdeniz, on the Aegean coast, wind along to the Blue Lagoon.

INSIDER TIP

Sand Sculpture Museum

In Antalya *(p242)*, head to the open-air museum of sand sculptures run by locals making use of the plentiful shores *(sandlandantalya.com/en/home)*.

KAŞ'S SUNKEN LYCIAN CITIES

A number of submerged ancient Lycian cities are under the waters off Kaş's coast *(p253)*. Located just east of Kaş lie the remains of the Kekova Sunken City, thought to have been flooded as a result of earthquakes. Nearby are the ruins of the ancient city of Aperlae *(p256)*, founded between the 4th and 3rd centuries BCE; today, these remains can be seen from the coast, emerging partially from the sea.

Turtle Beaches

Thanks to pioneering campaign work in the 1980s, there are a number of protected conservation areas where loggerhead sea turtles breed in Turkey. See the endangered species at the Göksu Delta *(p268)* or İztuzu Beach near Dalyan *(p248)*. The latter is also one of the most unspoiled beaches in Turkey: here, you can catch a glimpse of the turtles from a distance and enjoy the pristine sands outside of nesting season.

← A turtle hatchling making its way to the sea on a beach near Dalyan

Blue Cruises

Take in the best of the Turkish coast onboard a Blue Cruise, which tour the seas in traditional gulet boats. Hop on a Blue Cruise at places such as Bodrum *(p214)* or Antalya *(p242)* and get ready to explore the coast away from tourist crowds, stopping off at quiet beaches and coves accessible only by sea.

↑ A traditional Turkish gulet boat crossing Bodrum's harbour

Istanbul's Libraries

The libraries of Istanbul are not your average book havens. Many are heritage buildings that have been converted into public spaces. The Rami Library (*Rami Kışla Cad 98/1*) was originally an 18th-century military barracks, but it's now a library with exhibition halls and specialist reading rooms. Likewise, the old Imperial Ottoman Bank headquarters is now the SALT Galata *(p135)* cultural centre, home to a famous research library, while Beyazıt's old trolleybus power station has become the Trolleybus Library (*Prof Dr Cavit Orhan Tütengil Sok 4*).

→ Visitors using a reading room at the historic Rami Library

TURKEY FOR BOOKWORMS

With its stunning landscapes and historic cities, Turkey has provided rich inspiration for poets and authors throughout the centuries. While foreign writers, such as Agatha Christie, have made the country globally famous, there is also a strong home-grown literary tradition.

Turkey on the Page

Turkey has inspired countless writers. In the rolling hills around Adana *(p264)*, discover the landscape described in Yaşar Kemal's *Memed, My Hawk* (1955). See where Elif Shafak set her fictionalized account of the poet Rumi in *The Forty Rules of Love* (2009) on a stroll through Konya *(p284)*, or head to Istanbul to visit the Pera Palace Hotel *(p132)*, where Agatha Christie wrote *Murder on the Orient Express* (1934).

The opulent interior of the Pera Palace Hotel

Did You Know?

Agatha Christie's favourite room in the Pera Palace Hotel was Room 411, now named after her.

SHOP

Homer Kitabevi

This Beyoğlu spot has English-language books.

H3 Yeni Çarşı Cad 52-1, Istanbul homerbooks.com

Minoa

Choose from over 45,000 titles at this bookshop.

D3 Süleyman Seba Cad 52/A, Istanbul minoa.com

Rumi's Legacy

As a scholar, author of the *Mesnavi* poems and founder of the Mevlevi Sufi order, the influence of the poet Rumi (1207-73) is manifold. Devotees can see his tomb and the earliest edition of the *Mesnavi* in the Mevlâna Museum *(p284)*, and learn about his life at the Galata Mevlevi Lodge Museum *(p134)*.

The decorated sarcophagus of the poet Rumi

Museums for Modern Writers

Literature enthusiasts are spoiled for choice when it comes to exploring Turkish authors. Learn about the short-story writer Sait Faik Abasıyanık at his former Burgazadası home, or trace the life of novelist Ahmet Hamdi Tanpınar in his museum and library *(p79)* in Gülhane Park. Alternatively, take a deep dive into Orhan Pamuk's *The Museum of Innocence* at the museum *(p138)* of the same name.

↑ The Ahmet Hamdi Tanpınar Literature Museum & Library in Gülhane Park

Marvellous Museums

Turkey has a line-up of world-class museums, showcasing a mind-boggling array of cultural artifacts from across the country. Foremost among these is the award-winning Troy Museum in Troy *(p223)*, which demystifies the real site of one of the world's most mythical cities. Elsewhere, the Şanlıurfa Museum offers eye-opening insight into the art and culture of Turkey's Neolithic Age, while the Zeugma Mosaic Museum *(p358)*, in Gaziantep, contains arguably the single greatest collection of Roman mosaic art in the world.

→ Columns on display outside Gaziantep's impressive Zeugma Mosaic Museum

TURKEY FOR ART AND CULTURE

From the primitive artistry of early humans to cutting-edge modern exhibits, the vibrant cultural scene in Turkey is never less than awe-inspiring. And it isn't just confined to galleries - head out to provincial towns, and you're likely to see a few of the local folk dances Turkey is famous for.

TOP 4 TURKISH CULTURAL FIGURES

Şükriye Dikmen (1918-2000)
Cubism trailblazer in Turkish modern art.

Bariş Manço (1943-99)
Pioneer of the 1960s Anatolian Rock genre.

Sezen Aksu (1954-)
Arguably the country's most influential pop music figure.

Nuri Bilge Ceylan (1959-)
Award-winning film-maker of *Once Upon a Time in Anatolia* (2011).

The Modern Art Scene

Historically viewed as traditional and sedate, Turkish art has been transformed in the last century and is now the place for inventive new exhibitions. Nowhere is this more true than in Istanbul, where the likes of Arter *(p139)*, Istanbul Modern *(p130)* and SALT Beyoğlu *(p135)* display works by some of Turkey's key modern artists.

→ A contemporary artwork on dispay inside the Istanbul Modern

Traditional Handicrafts

Crafts have been woven into Turkish culture since ancient times. Where to go to enjoy these depends on what you're interested in: for carpets, the collection in Istanbul's Museum of Turkish and Islamic Arts *(p97)* is among the world's best; for *kilims* (flat weaves), there's the Vehbi Koç House in Istanbul; and for ceramics, the towns of İznik *(p187)* and Kütahya *(p290)* have long-standing traditions.

EBRU ART

The Turkish art of marbling *(ebru)* has long been associated with the country, despite originating elsewhere in Central Asia around the 11th century. Traditional pieces are created by applying paints first to oily water before the finished work is transferred onto paper or fabric. The artform has experienced a revival in the last decade, and workshops can be found in Cappadocia and Istanbul.

← Intricate decorations adorning bright tiles in İznik

Whirling dervishes performing at Hodjapasha Culture Centre ↑

Whirling Dervishes

The Mevlevi Sufi *sema* (whirling dervish ceremony, *p288*) may have begun as a form of medieval meditation, but it's now one of Turkey's most distinct contributions to global culture, and recognized by UNESCO. To witness the *Mevlevis* (performers) whirling away, visit Bursa *(p188)* where the congregation of the Tasavvuf Cultural Centre *(mevlana.org.tr)* opens the doors to visitors every evening. Alternatively, be entranced by a ceremony in the historic surroundings of Hodjapasha Culture Centre *(hodjapasha.com)* in Istanbul.

Outdoor Adventures

It's easy to keep the whole family busy on an adventure in Turkey's great outdoors. Teenagers and parents alike can take to the skies and try tandem paragliding in Ölüdeniz *(p250)* or hot-air ballooning in Cappadocia *(p322)*. Prefer to stay out of the air? Then hop aboard a boat trip with swim-stops from Antalya *(p242)*, Fethiye *(p250)* or Bodrum *(p214)*, which also have family-friendly beaches, or head to Kaş *(p253)* for a kayaking tour over one of Kekova's sunken ruins.

Paragliders enjoying stellar views of the Mediterranean Sea

TURKEY FOR FAMILIES

World-class beaches and warm weather to relish, fascinating ancient history and rich wildlife to discover, unforgettable vistas and endless outdoor adventures to enjoy: there are so many reasons why Turkey is one of the most popular destinations for families.

Historical Exploration

There are more ways to learn about Turkish history than by simply visiting sights. In Cappadocia, families with children can enjoy learning more about the area's history while scrambling around the tunnel mazes of Derinkuyu *(p334)* and Kaymaklı *(p336)* or peeping into the hidden churches of Ihlara Valley *(p339)*. In Hierapolis, history is underfoot: visitors must remove shoes (to protect the site) before exploring part of Pamukkale's surreal calcite terraces *(p210)*.

Exploring some of the impressive rock formations of Cappadocia

ISTANBUL EXPLORATIONS

Taste of Two Continents Tour
This popular tour offers a family-friendly, food-focused stroll *(yummyistanbul.com)*.

The Grand Bazaar
This treasure trove is packed with vendors offering delicious snacks and samples.

Turkish Arts
This family-run art shop holds mosaic, tile-painting and *ebru* workshops for all ages (*turkisharts.com*).

Impressive Views

Turkey has countless epic viewpoints, many of which can be easily accessed without a strenuous hike – making them ideal for families. In Dalyan, enjoy a riverboat tour to see dramatic cliff-side tombs *(p248)*. The short uphill stroll to Simena Castle *(p256)* leads to views of the bay, while the climb up Uçhisar's citadel (around 120 steps) in Cappadocia opens up to views of the valleys beyond.

→ A riverboat passing ancient riverside tombs near Dalyan

Spectacular Wildlife

Plenty of wildlife roams Turkey: elusive brown bears, wolves and the Anatolian leopard all reside here. But for guaranteed sightings, take a trip to Butterfly Valley near Fethiye *(p250)* to spot some of 100 butterfly species, including the endemic Jersey tiger. At the Sultansazlığı Bird Sanctuary *(p338)*, you can see aquatic birds, as well as amphibians and turtles.

A beautiful butterfly resting on a leaf

A YEAR IN TURKEY

JANUARY

Bocuk Night *(early Jan).* A Halloween-inspired event in the Edirne region, in which villagers dress up in scary costumes and parade the streets.

△ **Epiphany** *(6 Jan).* In Istanbul, the Orthodox devout dive into the Bosphorus to retrieve a wooden cross to celebrate the Baptism of Christ.

FEBRUARY

Erciyes Winter Festival *(early Feb).* A celebration of the snowy season at Mount Erciyes, near Kayseri.

△ **Datça Almond Blossom Festival** *(mid-Feb).* The Datça Peninsula's principal agricultural product is honoured with music and dance.

Ramadan *(Feb–Mar).* Muslims fast during the holy month of Ramadan, which ends with Eid al-Fitr.

MAY

△ **Hıdırellez** *(6 May).* Folk festival celebrating the meeting of the prophets Al-Khidr and Elijah and symbolizing the arrival of spring.

Istanbul Opera and Ballet Festival *(May–Jun).* Performances of opera and ballet from local and international artists at venues across Istanbul.

JUNE

Istanbul Music Festival *(mid-Jun).* Classical music festival with performances from Turkish and international ensembles and soloists.

△ **International İzmir Festival** *(Jun–Jul).* Festival featuring music and dance performances, taking place in venues across İzmir and beyond.

SEPTEMBER

Aspendos Opera and Ballet Festival *(mid-Sep).* The ancient theatre of Aspendos on Turkey's south coast hosts outstanding opera and ballet performances.

△ **Bosphorus Cup Istanbul Regatta** *(mid-Sep).* Nearly 100 boats take part in this annual sailing race along the Bosphorus through the city of Istanbul.

OCTOBER

Bodrum Cup Regatta *(early Oct).* A thrilling five-day sailing event where classic yachts and traditional gulets compete in a race along the Bodrum Peninsula.

△ **Republic Day** *(29 Oct).* This national holiday celebrates the 1923 establishment of the Turkish Republic with impressive firework displays and cultural performances.

MARCH

İzmir European Jazz Festival *(mid-Mar).* This annual music festival hosts performances all across İzmir and showcases the work of jazz musicians from Turkey and Europe.

△ **Newroz** *(mid-Mar).* Persian New Year festivities take place each year across Turkey, especially in the eastern city of Diyarbakır.

Mesir Macunu Festival *(21–24 Mar).* A festival in Manisa marking the recovery of Hafsa Sultan.

APRIL

△ **Istanbul Tulip Festival** *(1–30 Apr).* Colourful displays of tulips bloom across the city.

ANZAC Day *(25 Apr).* Memorial day for the fallen soldiers of the Australian and New Zealand Army Corps (ANZAC) in World War I's Gallipolli campaign.

Istanbul Film Festival *(Apr–Jun).* Screenings of both Turkish and international films are held in Istanbul.

JULY

Kırkpınar Oil-Wrestling Championships *(late Jun/early Jul).* The oil-wrestling competition in Edirne have been held annually since 1360.

△ **Ephesus Opera and Ballet Festival** *(early Jul).* Opera and ballet performances are held in the splendid setting of the ancient Ephesus theatre.

AUGUST

△ **Bosphorus Cross-Continental Swim** *(mid-Aug).* A 6.5-km (4-mile) swimming race from the eastern to the western shore of the Bosphorus.

Troy Festival *(mid-Aug).* Cultural performances, focusing on the legend of the Trojan War, are hosted in Çannakale.

NOVEMBER

Istanbul Marathon *(early Nov).* The world's only intercontinental marathon follows a route between the eastern and western shores of the Bosphorus.

△ **Anniversary of Atatürk's Death** *(10 Nov).* Turks commemorate the founding father of the Turkish Republic on the anniversary of his death with a two-minute silence.

DECEMBER

△ **Mevlana Festival** *(early Dec).* Sufi music and dance performances in Konya commemorate Rumi, the Mevlevi Order's founder.

Bursa Photography Festival *(Dec/Jan).* Themed photography exhibitions are displayed in numerous venues across the city of Bursa.

A BRIEF HISTORY

Turkey's history has been shaped by powerful empires - Greeks, Romans, Byzantines, Seljuks, Ottomans - through the millennia. Each has added a unique flavour to the country's make-up, resulting in a remarkable nation that has exerted considerable influence on the history of the entire world.

The First Settlements and Early City-States

The territory that is now Turkey was settled as far back as 12,000 years ago. We know little of these early hunter-gatherers, but the temples they built at places such as Göbeklitepe suggest a sophisticated culture. Influences from Mesopotamia and Syria brought agriculture and, as a consequence, settlements like Çatalhöyük. The Bronze Age was dominated by city-states and, later, empires. The most powerful was the Hittite civilization, which flourished in the 2nd millennium BCE, with its capital at Hattuşaş, although Troy is the more famous city today.

Did You Know?

The Trojan Horse, where Greek soldiers allegedly entered Troy in a wooden horse, is mentioned in Homer's *Iliad*.

Timeline of events

c 9500 BCE

Construction of Göbeklitepe, the world's oldest temple.

c 7000 BCE

Proto-cities like Çatalhöyük reveal the sophistication of Anatolia's early inhabitants.

c 1600 BCE

The Hittite Empire is at its peak.

c 1200 BCE

Greeks destroy the city of Troy during The Trojan War.

New Civilizations and the Hellenistic Age

After the fall of the Hittite Empire in c 1180 BCE, Anatolia suffered a sharp decline in the Late Bronze Age. From the ruins, new civilizations emerged: the Urartians established a kingdom around Lake Van, while western Anatolia saw the appearance of the Lydians, Lycians and Phrygians. Anatolia came under active Greek rule when Alexander the Great invaded in 334 BCE. After Alexander's death, his generals established Hellenistic kingdoms, appointing themselves as rulers.

The Roman Era

During the first century BCE, the Hellenistic kingdoms surrendered to the Roman Empire, after which Rome sought to expand its influence over the entirety of Anatolia. But the empire was becoming too unwieldy, so in 284 CE, Emperor Diocletian split it in two. The eastern capital later became Constantinople, the city conquered in 324 CE by Constantine the Great, the man responsible for the adoption of Christianity as the official Roman religion.

1 Ancient map of Turkey. ↑

2 Illustration of the temple at Göbeklitepe.

3 Troy, a powerful city-state during the Bronze Age.

4 Painting depicting Alexander the Great at the Battle of Issus.

c 850 BCE

The Kingdom of Urartu emerges as a powerful state.

c 700 BCE

The states of Lydia, Lycia and Phrygia dominate southwest Anatolia.

334 BCE

Alexander the Great's Anatolian campaigns.

c 270 BCE

The city of Pergamon reaches its greatest extent.

190 BCE

Roman influence in Anatolia begins.

324 CE

Constantinople renamed.

1

2

Byzantium

The Western Roman Empire collapsed in 476 CE, but the Eastern Roman Empire endured for nearly a thousand years more. At its height around 555 CE, the Byzantine Empire, as it was known, encompassed all of Anatolia, the Balkans, the Middle East and much of North Africa. Constantinople became fabulously wealthy and powerful, but its emperors often neglected their duties, becoming embroiled in deep theological questions – with the result that the empire was ill prepared to withstand assaults from new powers that encroached on its territory.

The Seljuks and the Crusades

The Seljuk Turks originated in Central Asia, and had migrated westward during the 10th century. In 1071, they inflicted a crushing defeat on the Byzantine Empire at the Battle of Manzikert, after which they captured much of Anatolia from the increasingly unsteady Byzantines. The Seljuks set up their capitals at Nicaea (now İznik) and Iconium (present-day Konya), and called their empire the Sultanate of Rum – Rum being derived from Rome. Hoping to redress the balance, Byzantine

↑ Preaching of the Crusade by Peter the Hermit and Pope Urban II in 1095.

Timeline of events

537

Emperor Justinian builds the Hagia Sophia in Constantinople.

634

Arabic attacks on southern Byzantine territory.

1054

Byzantium's religious schism with Rome.

1071

Defeat of Byzantines by Seljuk Turks at the Battle of Manzikert.

emperor Alexius Comnenus looked to Western Europe for help; in response, Pope Urban II called for a religious crusade. In 1096, in the first of four separate crusades that stretched over a century, Western armies rampaged through Byzantine territory, taking Jerusalem and establishing crusader states across the Middle East. Despite thwarting the Byzantines and, ultimately, the crusaders, the Seljuks were eventually destroyed by another invader from the east: the Mongols.

Collapse of Byzantium

Having defeated the Seljuks, the Mongols did not push further west, instead establishing relatively friendly relations with Byzantium. Even so, the Byzantine Empire had other problems: after (ironically) finding itself the target of a crusade in 1204, the empire became a shadow of its former self, and was no match for the rising power of the Ottomans. Named after the dynasty's founder, Osman, the Ottomans had by the early 1400s conquered the entirety of Anatolia, with Constantinople itself the only hold-out. The inevitable defeat came in 1453, when Sultan Mehmet II captured the city, earning himself the sobriquet "the Conqueror".

1 Fresco of Byzantine emperor Constantine IX, the last Christian ruler of Constantinople. ↑

2 Triumphant Seljuk Turks at the Battle of Manzikert.

3 Illustration depicting the Siege of Nicaea in 1097, during the First Crusade.

4 The fall of Constantinople in 1453.

1096

Emperor Alexius' call for aid leads to the First Crusade.

1243

Seljuks defeated by the Mongols.

1299

Osman I founds the Ottoman Empire.

1453

Ottoman capture of Constantinople.

The Rise of the Ottoman Empire

Constantinople was restored by the Ottomans, who added a number of sumptuous buildings. Their westward expansion continued, with Sultan Süleyman the Magnificent capturing Budapest and leading his armies to the gates of Vienna. Throughout the territory that is now Turkey, the Ottomans installed an efficient bureaucracy, allowing easy rule from the centre. They showed a degree of religious tolerance across their empire, rejecting the notion of forced conversions, although the tax burden on non-Muslim subjects was considerably higher.

The "Sick Man of Europe"

After Süleyman's death in 1566, the Ottomans produced a long line of increasingly ineffectual sultans, who could do nothing to halt the empire's eventual collapse. As rebellions challenged the centralized power of the state, newly confident powers such as Russia snapped up territory in the empire's east. Nascent Nationalism in the Balkans resulted in independence for Greece in 1820, followed by Bulgaria, Romania, Serbia and Montenegro. The Ottoman Empire had become "the sick man of Europe".

1 Süleyman I, better known as Süleyman the Magnificent, was the Ottoman Empire's longest-reigning sultan. ↑

2 Illustration depicting the Battle of Kars, a significant Russian victory during the Russo-Turkish War (1877-78).

3 Mustafa Kemal - Atatürk - founder of the Turkish Republic.

4 Crowds outside the Hagia Sophia in Istanbul.

Timeline of events

1529

Süleyman the Magnificent besieges Vienna.

1609–16

Sultan Ahmed I builds the Blue Mosque (Ayasofya).

1877

Kars and Ardahan ceded to Russia during a disastrous war.

1914

Outbreak of World War I.

3

4

The New Republic

The last straw for the Ottoman Empire was World War I, during which it fought the Russians in the east, the British in the west, and the Arabs in the south. Collapse swiftly followed, with the army's commander Mustafa Kemal – later known as Atatürk ("Father of the Turks") – abolishing the sultanate and becoming head of state of the new Turkish Republic in October 1923. Atatürk modernized the country, bringing in sweeping reforms and ultimately becoming Turkey's most-loved historical figure.

Turkey Today

Since 2003, Turkey has been under the rule of Recep Tayyip Erdoğan, who first took office as prime minister, and became president in 2014. Although Erdoğan was initially popular, domestic criticism of his rule has risen, particularly following the government's response to the devastating earthquake of 2023. The country's accession talks for EU membership – begun in 1987 – have been effectively stalled since 2016, but its tourism industry remains vibrant: in 2024, Turkey was the fourth most-visited destination in the world.

ISTANBUL'S RELIGIOUS MINORITIES

Events since the 1923 compulsory Greece-Turkey population exchange, which relocated Orthodox Christians and Muslims based on religion, have altered Istanbul's fabric. The launch of a tax on non-Muslims in 1942, Jewish migration after the creation of Israel in 1948, and 1955's Istanbul Riots led many to emigrate.

1923

Foundation of the Turkish Republic.

1938

Death of Atatürk.

2003

Recep Tayyip Erdoğan takes office as Prime Minister of Turkey.

2014

Erdoğan sworn in as Turkey's president.

2023

A 7.8-magnitude earthquake devastates southeast Turkey.

EXPERIENCE ISTANBUL

Shopping at Istanbul's Grand Bazaar

EXPLORE ISTANBUL

This map divides Istanbul into five sightseeing areas: Seraglio Point, Sultanahmet, The Bazaar Quarter, Beyoğlu and Further Afield, as shown on this map. Find out more about each area on the following pages.

KAPTANPAŞA
KULAKSIZ
KADI MEHMET EFENDI
BALAT
Golden Horn
DERVIŞ ALI
YAVUZ SULTAN SELIM
KARAGÜMRÜK
HIRKA-IŞERIF
CIBALI
HOCA GIYASETTIN
ALI KUŞÇU
ZEYREK
MOLLA HÜSREV
Süleymaniye Mosque
İSKENDERPAŞA
ŞEHREMINI
KALENDERHANE
THE BAZAAR QUARTER
p104
MOLLA GÜRANI
BALABANAĞA
Beyazıt Mosque
MESIHPAŞA
SARAÇ İSHAK
MUHSINE HATUN

TURKEY

BULGARIA
ISTANBUL
GEORGIA
ARMENIA
TURKEY
IRAN
SYRIA
IRAQ
CYPRUS

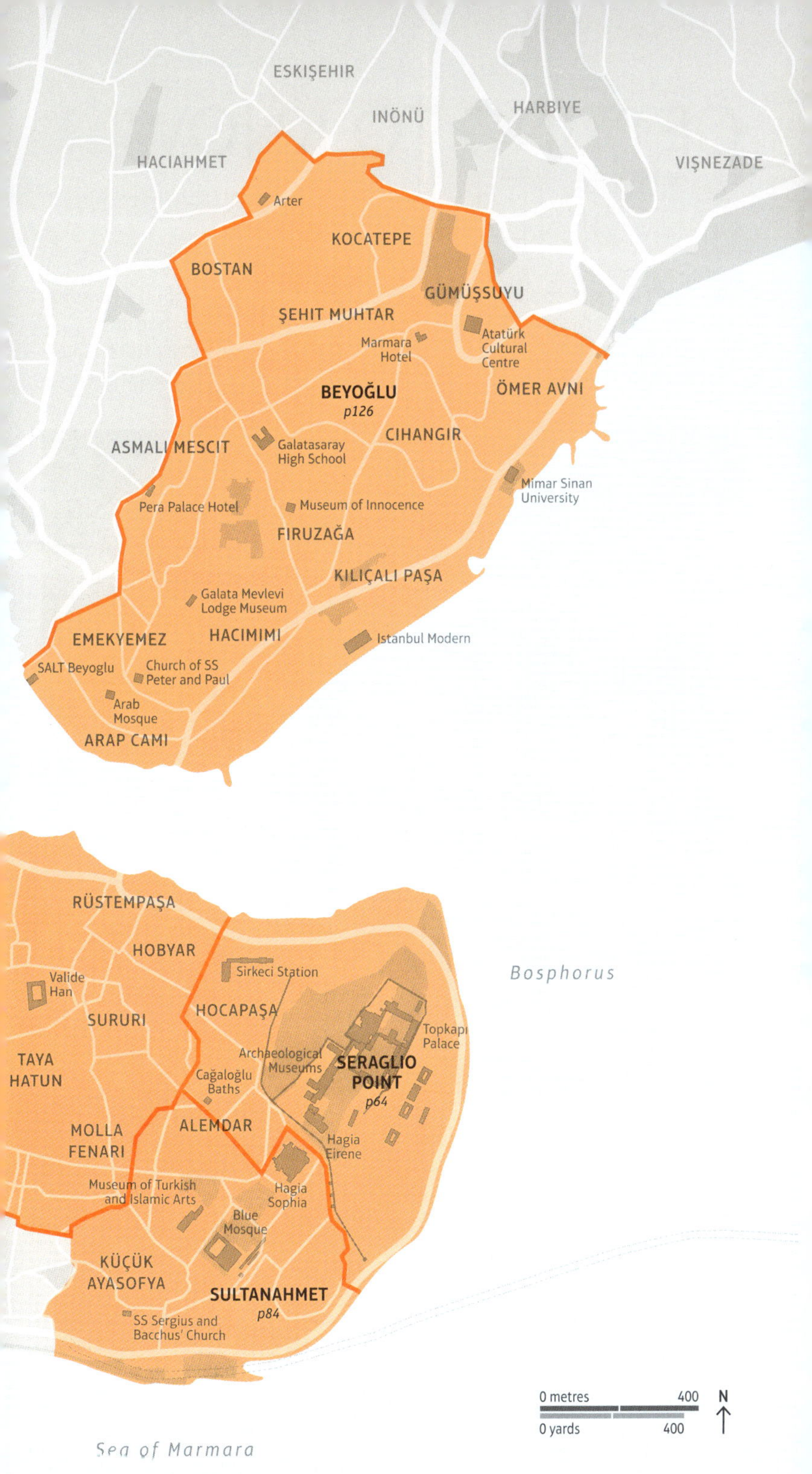

ESKIŞEHIR
INÖNÜ
HARBIYE
HACIAHMET
VIŞNEZADE
Arter
KOCATEPE
BOSTAN
GÜMÜŞSUYU
ŞEHIT MUHTAR
Marmara Hotel
Atatürk Cultural Centre
BEYOĞLU
p126
ÖMER AVNI
ASMALI MESCIT
Galatasaray High School
CIHANGIR
Mimar Sinan University
Pera Palace Hotel
Museum of Innocence
FIRUZAĞA
KILIÇALI PAŞA
Galata Mevlevi Lodge Museum
EMEKYEMEZ
HACIMIMI
Istanbul Modern
SALT Beyoglu
Church of SS Peter and Paul
Arab Mosque
ARAP CAMI
RÜSTEMPAŞA
HOBYAR
Sirkeci Station
Bosphorus
Valide Han
SURURI
HOCAPAŞA
Topkapı Palace
TAYA HATUN
Archaeological Museums
SERAGLIO POINT
p64
Cağaloğlu Baths
MOLLA FENARI
ALEMDAR
Hagia Eirene
Museum of Turkish and Islamic Arts
Hagia Sophia
Blue Mosque
KÜÇÜK AYASOFYA
SULTANAHMET
p84
SS Sergius and Bacchus' Church
0 metres 400
0 yards 400
N
Sea of Marmara

GETTING TO KNOW ISTANBUL

One-time capital of the Byzantine and Ottoman empires, Istanbul is Turkey's (and Europe's) largest city. Straddling the Bosphorus – the dividing line between Europe and Asia – the city's districts are further split by the smaller Golden Horn. Most sights are found on the western side of the Bosphorus.

PAGE 64

SERAGLIO POINT

Hilltop Seraglio Point, the promontory where Istanbul was founded, is dominated by one of the city's biggest attractions: the spectacular Topkapı Palace, Mehmet III's main abode, which is now stuffed with a sparkling array of treasures. Riches of a different kind can be found in the adjacent Archaeological Museums, which between them house arguably the finest collection of artifacts from across the Ottoman Empire, while nearby leafy Gülhane Park is a popular refuge for both locals and visitors alike seeking respite from the busy metropolis outside.

Best for
Ottoman art and architecture

Home to
Archaeological Museums, Topkapı Palace

Experience
Exploring the corridors and courtyards of Topkapı Palace

PAGE 84

SULTANAHMET

The heart of old, imperial Istanbul, Sultanahmet is a honeypot of architectural magnificence, most notably in the forms of the Hagia Sophia and Blue Mosque. Most visitors make a beeline for these two towering landmarks, but Istanbulites are drawn to the area, too, especially at weekends, to pray here or to simply enjoy their heritage – and an ice-cream. Named after Sultan Ahmed I, the 14th Ottoman sultan, the district is a pleasant, largely pedestrianizsed area, perfect for wandering, with plenty of benches on which to sit and admire the domes, minarets and sea views.

Best for
Elegant squares, museums

Home to
Hagia Sophia, Blue Mosque, Basilica Cistern

Experience
Gazing upward at the domes of the Hagia Sophia

PAGE 104

THE BAZAAR QUARTER

This intriguing area is a heady mix of piety, commerce, tourism and academia. Dominating the district, the Grand Bazaar hums with locals as well as tourists, as does the magnificent Süleymaniye Mosque complex, perched atop one of Istanbul's seven hills. Set in between them, Istanbul University brings a youthful energy, with cheap-and-cheerful cafés catering for students, while the nearby streets are a warren of hole-in-the-wall shops selling everything from wooden spoons to dried fruits.

Best for
Bartering in bazaars

Home to
Süleymaniye Mosque, Grand Bazaar

Experience
Shopping for ceramics, rugs and lokum (Turkish Delight) in the Grand Bazaar

→

PAGE 126

BEYOĞLU

Istanbul's entertainment quarter par excellence is split by pedestrianized Istiklal Caddesi, linking historic Galata and its iconic tower with Taksim Square. This buzzing thoroughfair, serviced by tinkling trams, is lined with mainstream clothing stores, cafés and cinemas, while the smaller alleys that run off it are home to hidden boutiques and vintage clothes shops. The area's vibe is youthful and hip, with contemporary galleries and museums like the stylish Istanbul Modern and the quirky Museum of Innocence regularly drawing in a younger crowd.

Best for
Gallery hopping, trendy restaurants

Home to
Istanbul Modern

Experience
Admiring the sunsets from the Galata Tower

PAGE 144

FURTHER AFIELD

The areas beyond the city's central districts provide visitors with a greater insight into everyday life in Istanbul. The traditional neighbourhoods of the Western Districts, beyond the Bazaar Quarter, contrast with lively Beşiktaş, east of Beyoğlu, while, on the Asian shore, vibrant Kadıköy rubs shoulders with conservative Üsküdar. Highlights include the Ottoman palaces of Dolmabahçe and Beylerbeyi, both with extravagant interiors, while few people pass up the chance to take a cruise on the Bosphorus, hopping between its scattered fishing villages.

Best for
Waterfront palaces, local life

Home to
Kariye Mosque, Theodosian Walls, Dolmabahçe Palace, Yıldız Park

Experience
Cruising along the Bosphorus, past waterfront villas

Imperial Hall, Topkapı Palace

SERAGLIO POINT

The hilly, wooded promontory that marks the meeting point of the Golden Horn, the Sea of Marmara and the Bosphorus, Seraglio Point occupies a natural strategic position. Greek king Byzas founded Byzantion here around 667 BCE, and in the Byzantine era, monasteries and public buildings stood on this site. Today, this nub of land is dominated by the grandiose complex that makes up the Topkapı Palace, the construction of which began in 1460 under Sultan Mehmet II and continued, in the form of alterations and expansions, into the 19th century. The residence of the Ottoman sultans and the women of the harem for 400 years, the palace is now open to the public as a rambling museum, with lavish apartments and glittering collections of jewels and other treasures. Originally, the Topkapı Palace covered almost the whole of Seraglio Point with its gardens and pavilions; indeed, "Seraglio" derives from the Persian word for palace. Part of the grounds have now been turned into a tranquil public park, while adjacent to the palace lie the Archaeological Museums, a renowned collection of finds from Turkey and the Near East that opened here in 1891.

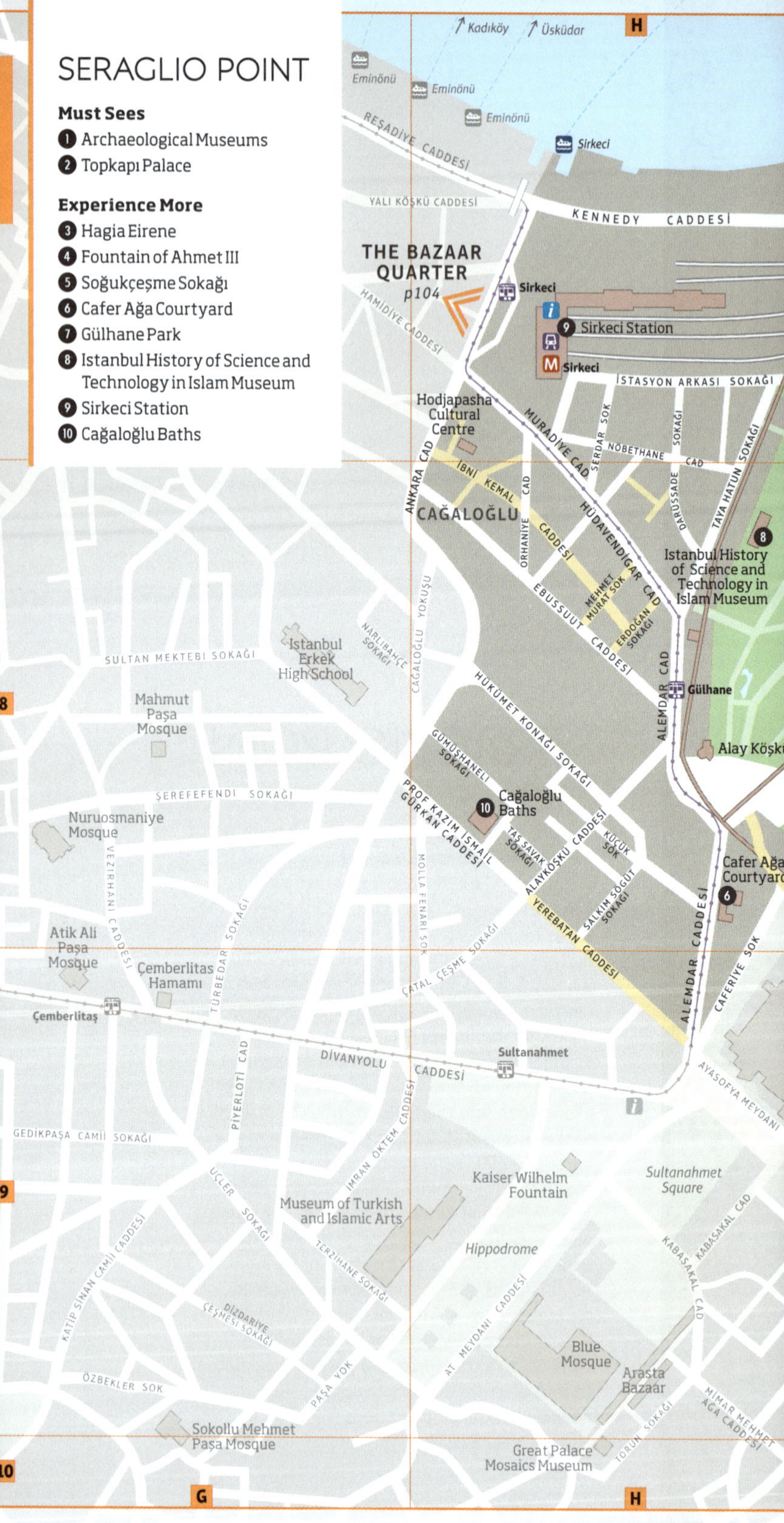

SERAGLIO POINT
Must Sees
1 Archaeological Museums
2 Topkapı Palace
Experience More
3 Hagia Eirene
4 Fountain of Ahmet III
5 Soğukçeşme Sokağı
6 Cafer Ağa Courtyard
7 Gülhane Park
8 Istanbul History of Science and Technology in Islam Museum
9 Sirkeci Station
10 Cağaloğlu Baths
Kadıköy
Üsküdar
H
Eminönü
Eminönü
Eminönü
Sirkeci
REŞADİYE CADDESİ
YALI KÖŞKÜ CADDESİ
KENNEDY CADDESİ
THE BAZAAR QUARTER
p104
HAMİDİYE CADDESİ
Sirkeci
Sirkeci Station
Sirkeci
İSTASYON ARKASI SOKAĞI
Hodjapasha Cultural Centre
MURADİYE CAD
SERDAR SOK
NÖBETHANE CAD
SOKAĞI
ANKARA CAD
İBNİ KEMAL CADDESİ
CAĞALOĞLU
ORHANİYE CAD
HÜDAVENDİGAR CAD
DARÜSSADE
TAYA HATUN SOKAĞI
Istanbul History of Science and Technology in Islam Museum
EBUSSUUT CADDESİ
MEHMET MURAT SOK
ERDOĞAN SOKAĞI
CAĞALOĞLU YOKUŞU
NARLIBAHÇE SOKAĞI
Istanbul Erkek High School
SULTAN MEKTEBİ SOKAĞI
Mahmut Paşa Mosque
8
ALEMDAR CAD
Gülhane
HÜKÜMET KONAĞI SOKAĞI
Alay Köşkü
GÜMÜŞHANELİ SOKAĞI
ŞEREFEFENDİ SOKAĞI
PROF KAZIM İSMAİL GÜRKAN CADDESİ
Cağaloğlu Baths
TAŞ SAVAK SOKAĞI
ALAYKÖŞKÜ CADDESİ
KÜÇÜK SOK
Nuruosmaniye Mosque
VEZİRHANI CADDESİ
MOLLA FENARİ SOK
SALKIM SÖĞÜT SOKAĞI
Cafer Ağa Courtyard
YEREBATAN CADDESİ
ALEMDAR CADDESİ
Atik Ali Paşa Mosque
TÜRBEDAR SOKAĞI
Çemberlitaş Hamamı
ÇATAL ÇEŞME SOKAĞI
CAFERİYE SOK
Çemberlitaş
DİVANYOLU CADDESİ
Sultanahmet
PİYERLOTİ CAD
AYASOFYA MEYDANI
GEDİKPAŞA CAMİİ SOKAĞI
İMRAN ÖKTEM CADDESİ
9
ÜÇLER SOKAĞI
Kaiser Wilhelm Fountain
Sultanahmet Square
Museum of Turkish and Islamic Arts
KATİP SİNAN CAMİİ CADDESİ
TERZİHANE SOKAĞI
Hippodrome
KABASAKAL CAD
DİZDARİYE ÇEŞMESİ SOKAĞI
AT MEYDANI CADDESİ
Blue Mosque
Arasta Bazaar
ÖZBEKLER SOK
PAŞA YOK
MİMAR MEHMET AĞA CADDESİ
TORUN SOKAĞI
Sokollu Mehmet Paşa Mosque
Great Palace Mosaics Museum
10
G
H

J
K
0 metres
200
0 yards
200
N
7
8
9
10
GÜLHANE
PARKI
SOKAĞI
KENNEDY CADDESİ
Bosphorus
Gülhane Park
Topkapı Palace
Archaeological Museums
Darphane i Amire
Hagia Eirene
Soğukçeşme Sokağı
Hagia Sophia
Fountain of Ahmet III
İSHAK PAŞA CADDESİ
KENNEDY CADDESİ
SULTANAHMET
p84
SERAGLIO POINT

ARCHAEOLOGICAL MUSEUMS

ARKEOLOJI MÜZELERI

J8 Osman Hamdi Bey Yokuşu Gülhane 9am-6pm & 7-10pm daily
muze.gov.tr

From Phoenician tombs to Cypriot ceramics, the collections in these museums showcase treasures from across the Ottoman Empire, celebrating the rich history and heritage of the Middle East and eastern Mediterranean.

Although founded in the mid-19th century, this antiquities collection quickly expanded as provincial governors sent objects from across the Ottoman Empire. Today, it encompasses three museums – the Archaeological Museum (Arkeoloji Müzesi), the Ancient Orient Museum (Eski Şark Eserleri Müzesi) and Tiled Kiosk Museum (Çinili Köşk Müzesi). It has one of the world's richest collections of classical artifacts, and also includes treasures from the pre-classical world. The main building was erected under the directorship of Osman Hamdi Bey to house his finds. This archaeologist, painter and polymath discovered the exquisite sarcophagi in the royal necropolis at Sidon in present-day Lebanon.

↑ Stately façade of the building that houses the three archaeology museums

INSIDER TIP
Museum Pass

To skip the likely queues at the ticket office, it pays to buy the Museum Pass Istanbul *(muze.gen.tr)*, which is valid for five days after first use and gives access to 12 other museums across the city.

Treaty of Kadesh, a peace agreement between the Egyptians and Hittites ↑

← Sarcophagus of Sidamara, a highlight in the Classical Archaeology collection

↑ Exquisite pottery pieces in the Tiled Kiosk Museum

Exploring the Archaeological Museums

This vast collection, spanning 5,000 years, showcases a wide variety of beautiful artifacts, ranging from intricately crafted Mother Goddess figurines modelled in the 3rd millennium BCE to Turkish pottery thrown in the 19th century. To cover everything in one visit is impossible. Visitors with little time should not miss seeing the breathtaking sarcophagi from the royal necropolis at Sidon. The museum is currently undergoing renovations. While several galleries have reopened, the Thracian, Bithynian and Byzantine Collections, the "Istanbul Through the Ages" exhibit, the Tiled Kiosk Museum and the Ancient Orient Museum remain closed while work is completed.

Did You Know?

The Kadesh Treaty, dating to the 13th century BCE, is the world's oldest peace treaty.

HEINRICH SCHLIEMANN

German businessman Heinrich Schliemann (1822–90) turned to archaeology in the 1870s, starting with excavations across Greece and Turkey. A fan of Homer's *Iliad*, he was determined to prove that Troy and Hisarlik in Turkey were the same. Initially, Schliemann won praise for discovering "Priam's treasure" in Hisarlik. However, the amateur archaeologist later attracted criticism for ignoring permit rules, using dynamite to speed up work and illegally removing artifacts from the country without proper permission.

Beautiful marble statues in the Classical Archaeology section

Highlights

Classical Archaeology

This collection focuses on ancient Egyptian and Near Eastern art. Highlights include the sarcophagi unearthed in 1887 at Sidon (present-day Lebanon) – thought to have been made for a line of Phoenician kings (6th–4th centuries BCE) – which show the transition from Egyptian to Greek influence in the art of the Near East at that time. Rooms 14–20 contain some remarkable statues and realistic busts of Roman emperors.

Thracian, Bithynian and Byzantine Collections

The New Building's ground floor gallery features religious objects and artifacts from the ancient Thracian, Bithynian and Byzantine civilizations, including a statue of Emperor Valens. This section also covers ancient architecture.

Tiled Kiosk Museum

The Tiled Kiosk Museum features geometric and calligraphic tiles with a notable 15th-century tiled mihrab from central Anatolia. Rooms 3 and 4 display İznik tiles and mosque lamps while rooms 5 and 6 exhibit pieces from Kütahya, which became known for its high-quality ceramics when the popularity of İznik tiles declined in the late 16th century.

Anatolia and Troy

One side of this long hall traces Anatolian history from the Palaeolithic era to the Iron Age, ending with the Phrygian culture. The other side displays finds from Troy's excavations, spanning nine civilizations from 3000 BCE to the time of Christ.

Anatolia's Neighbouring Cultures

This gallery is split into two sections: Cyprus and Syria-Palestine. The Cypriot collection was assembled by the joint American and Russian consul to Cyprus, Luigi Palma di Cesnola, who looted its tombs from 1865–73. The Syrian exhibits include funerary reliefs, the Gezer Calendar (925 BCE) and a reconstructed mausoleum from Palmyra.

Ancient Orient Museum

This collection features rare antiquities from the Egyptian and Hittite cultures, as well as the early civilizations of Mesopotamia (present-day Iraq). Admire the monumental glazed brick friezes from Babylon's Ishtar Gate (605–562 BCE) and the Hittite copy of the famous Treaty of Kadesh here.

Istanbul through the Ages

Chronicling Istanbul's archaeological past from the Neolithic to the Byzantine period, this gallery includes exhibits such as the rare Mosaic Icon of the Presentation (c 600 CE) from the Kalenderhane Mosque *(p114)* and a section of the iron chains that the Byzantines hung across the Golden Horn *(p113)* to stop hostile ships.

2

TOPKAPı PALACE

TOPKAPı SARAYı

J8 Babıhümayun Cad Sultanahmet 9am-5pm Wed-Mon millisaraylar.gov.tr

A labyrinthine complex of opulent pavilions, Topkapı Palace was once the heart of the Ottoman Empire, serving as the home of sultans, their royal court and the seat of government. Today, it remains a grandiose reminder of Istanbul's powerful past.

Between 1459 and 1465, shortly after his conquest of Constantinople *(p53)*, Mehmet II built Topkapı Palace as his main residence. Rather than a single building, it was conceived as a series of pavilions contained by four enormous courtyards, a stone version of the tented encampments from which the nomadic Ottomans had emerged. Initially, the palace served as the seat of government and housed a school in which civil servants and soldiers were trained. In the 18th century, however, the government was moved to the Sublime Porte. Sultan Abdül Mecit I abandoned Topkapı in 1853 in favour of Dolmabahçe Palace *(p152)*. In 1924 Topkapı was opened to the public as a museum.

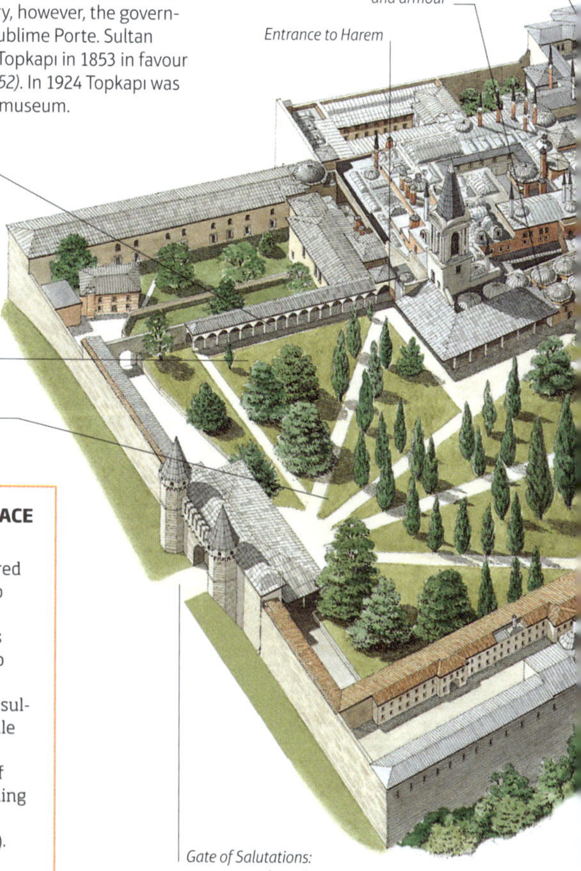

The Harem is a labyrinth of rooms where the sultan's wives and concubines lived.

Exhibition of arms and armour

Entrance to Harem

Harem ticket office

This chamber, known as the Divan, served as the meeting place for the viziers of the imperial council. These meetings were sometimes watched covertly by the sultan.

Second courtyard

Gate of Salutations: entrance to the palace

FEASTS AT THE PALACE

The Topkapı Palace's kitchen complex required a staff of around 800 to feed its population of 4,000. One section was exclusively reserved to prepare rich, fragrant meals intended for the sultan and his guests, while another was devoted solely to the creation of confectionaries, including sherbets, baklava and *lokum* (Turkish delight).

← Picturesque setting of the tiled 17th-century Baghdad Pavilion

GREAT VIEW
Topkapı's Fourth Courtyard

Head to the Marble Terrace's gilded canopy in the fourth courtyard to enjoy sweeping views across the confluence of the Bosphorus and Golden Horn.

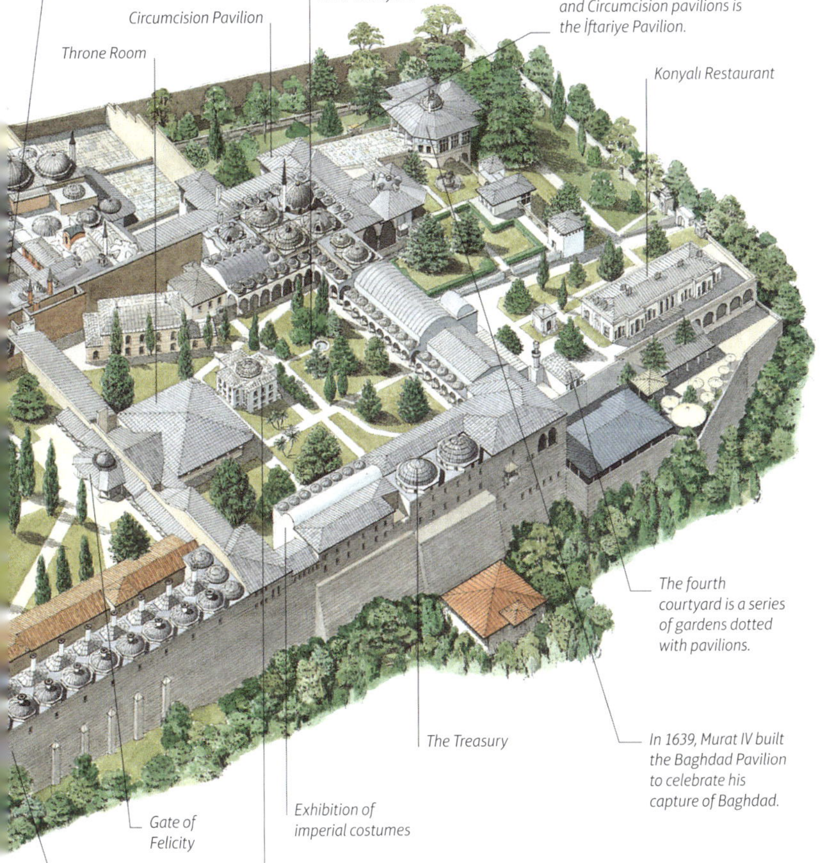

Exhibition of clocks

Circumcision Pavilion

Throne Room

Third courtyard

Standing between the Baghdad and Circumcision pavilions is the İftariye Pavilion.

Konyalı Restaurant

The fourth courtyard is a series of gardens dotted with pavilions.

The Treasury

In 1639, Murat IV built the Baghdad Pavilion to celebrate his capture of Baghdad.

Gate of Felicity

Exhibition of imperial costumes

The kitchens contain an exhibition of ceramics, glass and silverware.

Erected in 1719, the Library of Ahmet III is an elegant marble building.

↑ Illustration of the 15th-century Topkapı Palace complex

EXPLORING THE PALACE'S COLLECTIONS

During their 470-year reign, the Ottoman sultans amassed a glittering collection of treasures. After the foundation of the Turkish Republic in 1923, most of these artifacts were nationalized and put on display in the Topkapı Palace. The collection includes diplomatic gifts, pieces commissioned from the palace artisans and numerous items acquired as military "booty".

Ceramics, Glass and Silverware

The kitchens contain the palace's extensive collection of ceramics, glass and silverware.

Turkish and European pieces are overshadowed by the vast display of Chinese and some Japanese porcelain, which were brought to Turkey along the Silk Road. Topkapı's collection of Chinese porcelain, which spans four dynasties, from the 10th to the 20th century, is the best in the world outside of China. The Ottomans valued Celadon for its ability to neutralize poison in food. There are also several exquisite blue-and-white pieces, mostly dating from the 14th to 17th century.

Chinese aesthetics inspired Ottoman crafters, especially in developing the ceramics industry at İznik *(p186)*. Many of the tiles on the palace walls show the influence of designs common in Chinese blue-and-white porcelain, such as cloud scrolls and stylized flowers. Much of the later porcelain, particularly the Japanese Imari ware, was made for export.

The well-preserved old confectioners' pantry in the kitchens also has huge cauldrons and other utensils used by the palace's chefs to prepare meals for its 12,000 residents and guests.

↑ Pretty French-style dinnerware on display in the kitchens

Imperial Costumes

A collection of imperial costumes is displayed in the Hall of the Campaign Pages, whose task was to look after the royal wardrobe. It was a palace tradition that on the death of a sultan his clothes were carefully folded and placed in sealed bags. As a result, it is possible to see a perfectly preserved kaftan once worn by Mehmet the Conqueror *(p53)*. The reforms of Sultan Mahmut II included a revolution in the dress code. The end of an era came as plain grey serge replaced the earlier luxurious silken textiles.

Clocks

European clocks given to, or bought by, various sultans form the majority of this collection, despite the fact that there were makers of clocks and watches in Istanbul from the 17th century. The clocks range from simple, weight-driven 16th-century examples to an exquisite 18th-century English mechanism encased in mother-of-pearl and featuring a German organ which played tunes on the hour to the delight of the harem.

Interestingly, the only male European eyewitness accounts of life in the Harem were written by the mechanics sent to service these instruments.

The Library of Ahmet III with its beautiful tiled walls and marble columns

Did You Know?

The palace's Imperial Mint continued to produce Turkey's coinage right up until the 1960s.

Treasury

Of all the exhibitions in the palace, the Treasury's collection is the easiest to appreciate, dazzling with thousands of precious and semi-precious stones.

The first hall features a full, diamond-encrusted suit of chain mail, designed for Mustafa III for ceremonial use. Diplomatic gifts include a fine pearl statuette of a prince seated beneath a canopy, which was sent to Sultan Abdül Aziz from India. The greatest pieces are in the second hall. Foremost among these is the Topkapı dagger (1741). Alongside other exhibits here are a selection of the bejewelled aigrettes (plumes), which added splendour to imperial turbans.

In the third hall, the 86-carat Spoonmaker's diamond is said to have been discovered in a rubbish heap in Istanbul in the 17th century, and bought from a scrap merchant for three spoons. The gold-plated Bayram throne was given to Murat III by the Governor of Egypt in 1574 and used for state ceremonies until early this century.

It was the throne in the fourth hall, given by the Shah of Persia, which was to have been acknowledged by the equally magnificent gift of the Topkapı dagger. In a cabinet near the throne is an unusual relic: a case containing bones said to be from the hand of St John the Baptist.

Miniatures and Manuscripts

It is possible to display only a tiny fraction of Topkapı's total collection of over 13,000 miniatures and manuscripts at any one time. This section includes highlights such as scenes of nomadic life and depictions of demons and other fantastic creatures from the Topkapı Siyah-Qalam albums (Hazine 2153), attributed to Muhammad (Mehmed) Siyah Qalam and dated to the late 14th to early 15th century. It is from this Eastern tradition of miniature painting, which was also prevalent in Mogul India and Persia, that the Ottoman style of miniatures developed.

Also on show are some fine examples of calligraphy *(p116)*, including texts of the Koran, manuscripts in Turkish, Arabic, Persian, Latin, Hebrew and Greek, along with several *firmans*, or imperial decrees.

Pavilion of the Holy Mantle

Some of the holiest relics of Islam are displayed in these five domed rooms, which are a place of pilgrimage for Muslims. Most of these relics found their way to Istanbul as a result of the conquest by Selim "the Grim" of Egypt and the Arabian Peninsula, and his assumption of the caliphate (the leadership of Islam) in 1517.

The most sacred treasure is the mantle once worn by the Prophet Mohammed, which can only be viewed from an antechamber through an open doorway. Holy men continuously chant passages from the Koran over the gold chest in which the mantle is stored. A stand in front of the chest holds two of Mohammed's swords.

A glass cabinet in the anteroom contains hairs from the beard of the Prophet, a letter written by him and an impression of his footprint.

In the other rooms you can see some of the ornate locks and keys for the Kaaba *(p99)* which were sent to Mecca by successive sultans.

Arms and Armour

Taxes and tributes from all over the empire were once stored in the Inner Treasury. There is also a series of horsetail, which proclaimed the rank of their owners.

The weaponry includes ornately embellished swords and several bows made by sultans themselves (Beyazıt II was a particularly masterful craftsman). The bulky iron weaponry used by European crusaders looks rudimentary by comparison. Also on view are examples of 15th-century Ottoman chain mail and colourful shields.

Bronze armour in the Armoury

THE HAREM

A palace within a palace, the Harem was an opulently tiled maze, comprising over 300 rooms. Today, it gives a behind-the-scenes peek at the decadent but cloistered lifestyle of the sultan's family and the sultan's concubines.

The word harem derives from the Arabic for "forbidden". A harem was the residence of the sultan's wives, concubines and children, who were guarded by enslaved Black eunuchs. This role was the only opportunity for enslaved Africans in the Ottoman capital to achieve a high-ranking status within the palace hierarchy. The sultan and his sons were the only other men allowed access to the Harem, which also included the Cage, a set of rooms where the sultan's brothers were confined to avoid destabilizing succession contests. Topkapı's Harem was laid out by Sultan Murat III in the late 16th century and is a labyrinth of brilliantly tiled corridors and chambers.

Did You Know?

Upper-class Ottoman homes had their own harem, the private quarters for the family.

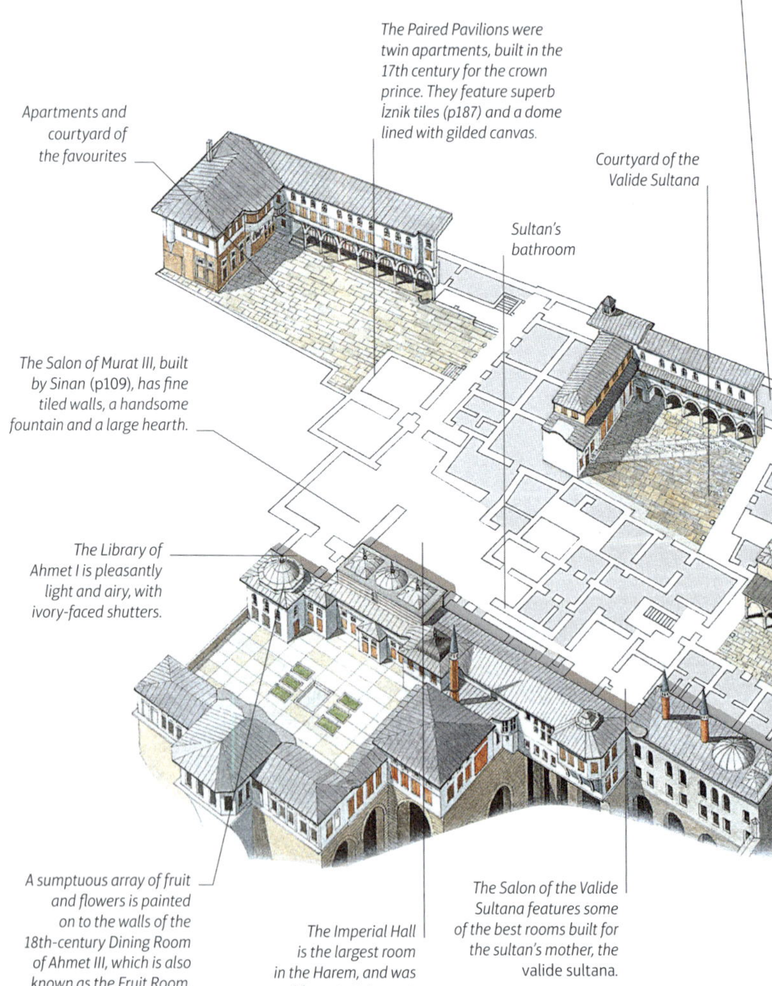

The Golden Way is so called because new sultans reputedly threw gold coins to their concubines here.

The Paired Pavilions were twin apartments, built in the 17th century for the crown prince. They feature superb İznik tiles (p187) and a dome lined with gilded canvas.

Apartments and courtyard of the favourites

Courtyard of the Valide Sultana

Sultan's bathroom

The Salon of Murat III, built by Sinan (p109), has fine tiled walls, a handsome fountain and a large hearth.

The Library of Ahmet I is pleasantly light and airy, with ivory-faced shutters.

A sumptuous array of fruit and flowers is painted on to the walls of the 18th-century Dining Room of Ahmet III, which is also known as the Fruit Room.

The Imperial Hall is the largest room in the Harem, and was used for entertainment.

The Salon of the Valide Sultana features some of the best rooms built for the sultan's mother, the valide sultana.

1 The Courtyard of the Favourites was where the sultan's favourite wives and concubines lived.

2 The grand Imperial Hall, built solely for entertainment, features a large throne from where the sultan would view the proceedings.

3 There are many arched doorways throughout the palace, all of them adorned with İznik tiles and elegant calligraphy.

The Tower of Justice offers a superb view of Topkapı's rooftops and beyond.

The Harem baths were where the concubines bathed and relaxed.

Marble columns line the Courtyard of the Black Eunuchs, which still has some old-fashioned, wrought-iron lamps.

Barracks of the Black eunuchs

Courtyard of the Concubines

Illustration of the Harem, set within the Topkapı Palace ↑

LIFE IN THE HAREM

The enslaved women of the Harem were gathered from the furthest corners of the Ottoman Empire and beyond. Some attempted to become a favourite of the sultan by bearing him a son, which on some occasions could lead to marriage. Competition was stiff, however; at its height the Harem contained over 1,000 concubines, many of whom never rose beyond the service of the other women in the harem. The last women eventually left in 1909.

EXPERIENCE MORE

Hagia Eirene

Aya İrini Kilisesi

J8 First courtyard of Topkapı Palace (0212) 522 17 50 Gülhane, Sultanahmet 9am-5pm Wed-Mon

The present church, dating from the 6th century, is the third structure built on what is thought to be Istanbul's oldest site of Christian worship. After the 1453 Muslim conquest *(p53)*, it became a part of the Topkapı Palace complex for use as an arsenal. Today, it is known for its excellent acoustics and hosts concerts during the Istanbul Music Festival *(p48)*.

Inside are three unique features that are not found in other Byzantine churches in the city. The *synthronon*, with five rows of built-in seats hugging the apse, was occupied by clergymen officiating during services. Above it looms a black mosaic cross on a gold background, which dates from the iconoclastic period (c 753 CE).

At the back of the church is a cloister-like courtyard where deceased Byzantine emperors were once laid in porphyry sarcophagi. Most of these have been moved to the Archaeological Museums *(p68)*.

Fountain of Ahmet III

Ahmet III Çeşmesi

J9 Junction of İshak Paşa Cad & Babıhümayun Cad Gülhane, Sultanahmet

Built in 1729, Istanbul's most beautiful fountains survived the violent deposition of Sultan Ahmet III two years later. Many of the other monuments constructed by the sultan were destroyed during his reign, which was known as the Tulip Period. Designed in delicate Turkish Rococo style, the fountain features five small domes, mihrab-shaped niches and intricate floral reliefs.

Ottoman "fountains" are ornate public taps, and often include a *sebil* for serving refreshments. Each of the fountain's four walls has a *çeşme* (tap) above a carved marble basin. Each tap is adorned with elaborate calligraphy by the 18th-century poet Seyit Vehbi Efendi, honouring the fountain and its founder. The four corners have a *sebil* with three windows covered by ornate marble grilles, offering sherbets and flavoured waters in silver goblets instead of iced water.

Soğukçeşme Sokağı

J8 Gülhane

Charming old wooden houses line this narrow, cobbled lane, known as "the street of the cold fountain",

OTTOMAN HOUSES

The typical 19th-century houses in Istanbul had a stone ground floor with one or two wooden upper storeys and a projecting section called a *çikma*. Originating from traditional Turkish balconies, the upper windows had wooden lattice covers *(kafesler)* for privacy. Despite legal protections against demolition, obtaining insurance for these homes remains difficult in a city prone to devastating fires. Today, few wooden houses remain. Their survival is largely due to tourism, and many have been restored as hotels.

between the outer walls of Topkapı Palace and Hagia Sophia's minarets. The traditional houses were built from the late 18th century onwards.

In the 1980s, the Turkish Touring and Automobile Club (TTOK) renovated the buildings in the lane. Nine of these became the Ayasofya Konakları, a series of attractive pastel-painted guesthouses popular with tourists. Another building has been converted by the TTOK into a library of historical writings on Istanbul and an archive of engravings and photographs of the city. A Roman cistern towards the bottom of the lane has been converted into the atmospheric Sarnıç restaurant *(sarnic restaurant.com/tr)*.

Cafer Ağa Courtyard

Cafer Ağa Medresesi

H8 Caferiye Sok
(0212) 513 18 43
Gülhane, Sultanahmet
8:30am-8pm daily

This peaceful courtyard at the end of an alley was built in 1559 by Sinan *(p109)* for the chief Black eunuch *(p76)* as a *medrese* (Islamic educational institution, *p33*). Sinan's bust presides over the café tables in the courtyard. The former students' lodgings are now used to display a variety of craft goods typically including jewellery, silk prints, ceramics and calligraphy, showcasing the rich artistic heritage of the region.

Gülhane Park

Gülhane Parkı

J8 Alemdar Cad
Gülhane 7am-10pm daily

Gülhane Park occupies what used to be the lower grounds of Topkapı Palace. Today, it is a well-maintained urban park, a pleasant shaded place to stroll and home to a couple of interesting landmarks.

The Alay Köşkü (Procession Kiosk), built into the Topkapı Palace complex, enabled sultans to keep an eye on who was coming out of and going into the Sublime Porte. At the far end of the park is the Goths' Column, a well-preserved 3rd-century victory monument, surrounded by clapboard teahouses. Its name comes from the Latin inscription on it which reads: "Fortune is restored to us because of victory over the Goths".

Across Kennedy Caddesi, the main road that runs along the northeast side of the park, there is a viewpoint over the busy waters where the Golden Horn meets the Bosphorus.

GÜLHANE PARK SIGHTS

Gülhane Cistern
An early Byzantine cistern in the park.

Alay Pavilion
The sultan would watch processions from this ornate pavilion.

Ahmet Hamdi Tanpınar Literature Museum Library
Dedicated to Turkish literature and writers.

Fountain of Ahmet III, adorned with floral reliefs and elegant calligraphy

An exhibit at the Istanbul History of Science and Technology in Islam Museum

8  

Istanbul History of Science and Technology in Islam Museum

Museum Istanbul Islam ve Teknoloji Tarihi Müzesi

H8 Gülhane Park Gülhane 9am-6pm daily

Housed in the former Topkapı Palace stables, this museum is home to scale models of some of the greatest inventions in the Islamic world, between the 8th and 16th centuries. The intricate models, which include a planetarium and water clock, were built in Frankfurt's Johann Wolfgang Goethe University.

9 

Sirkeci Station

Sirkeci Garı

H7 Sirkeci İstasyon Cad, Sirkeci (0212) 527 00 50 or 520 65 75 Sirkeci Daily

This magnificent railway station was built to receive the long-anticipated *Orient Express* from Europe. It was officially opened in 1890, even though the luxurious train had been running into Istanbul for a year by then. The design, by the German architect Jasmund, successfully incorporates features from the different architectural traditions of Istanbul. Byzantine alternating stone and brick courses are combined with a Seljuk-style monumental recessed portal and Muslim horseshoe arches around the windows.

The station is now closed to trains but is still a stop on the Marmaray Metro line, which links Europe with Asia via the Bosphorus tunnel. The station building houses a small, free railway museum, which is open from 9am to 5pm from Tuesday to Saturday.

THE FAMOUS ORIENT EXPRESS

This luxury train first ran from Paris to Istanbul in 1889, covering 2,900 km (1,800 miles) in three days. Sirkeci Station and Pera Palace Hotel *(p132)* were built to accommodate its distinguished passengers, including kings, politicians and celebrities. Known as "The Train of Kings, the King of Trains", it symbolized glamour and romance, inspiring 19 books, six films and a musical piece. Although the Cold War saw luxury travel decline, the train continued to run twice weekly until 1977.

10  

Cağaloğlu Baths

Cağaloğlu Hamamı

H8 Prof Kazım İsmail Gürkan Cad 34, Cağaloğlu Sultanahmet 9am-10pm daily (to 11pm Fri-Sun) cagalogluhamami.com.tr

Among the city's more sumptuous Turkish baths, the ones in Cağaloğlu were built by Sultan Mahmut I in 1741. The income from them was designated for the maintenance of Mahmut's library in the Hagia Sophia *(p88)*.

The city's smaller baths have different times at which men and women can use the same facilities. But in larger baths, such as this one, there are entirely separate sections. In the Cağaloğlu Baths the men's and women's sections are at right angles to one another and entered from different streets. Each consists of three parts: a *camekan*, a *soğukluk* and the main bath chamber or *hararet*, which centres on a massive octagonal massage slab.

The Cağaloğlu Baths are popular with foreign visitors because the staff are happy to explain the procedure. Even if you do not want to sweat it out, you can still take a look inside the entrance corridor and *camekan* of the men's section. Here you will find a small display of Ottoman bathing regalia, including precarious wooden clogs once worn by women on what would frequently be their only outing from the confines of the home. You can also sit and have a drink by the fountain in the peaceful *camekan*.

TURKISH BATHS

No trip to Istanbul is complete without a visit to a Turkish bath (hammam). Made for relaxation, Turkish baths resemble ancient Roman baths, except there is no pool of cold water to plunge into at the end.

A full service includes relaxing in a steam-filled hot room, followed by vigorous soaping and massaging. There is no time limit, but allow at least an hour and a half. Towels and soap are provided, but you can bring your own toiletries. Four historic baths located in the Old City - Çemberlitaş *(p120)*, Hürrem Sultan Hamamı *(p96)*, Cağaloğlu *(illustrated below)* and the Süleymaniye Hamamı - cater to tourists, while most luxury hotels have their own baths.

SEPARATE ENTRANCES

Larger Turkish baths, including the opulent, 18th-century baths at Cağaloğlu, have separate, identical sections for men and women.

CHOOSING A SERVICE

Services, detailed in a price list at the entrance, range from a self-service option to a luxury body scrub, shampoo and massage.

CHANGING CLOTHES

Before changing you will be given a cloth *(peştemal)*, to wrap around yourself, and slippers for walking on the hot, wet floor.

THE EXFOLIATING BODY SCRUB

In between steaming, you (or the staff at the baths) scrub your body briskly with a coarse, soapy mitt *(kese)*.

THE BODY MASSAGE

A marble plinth *(göbek taşı)* occupies the centre of the hot room. This is where you will have your pummelling full-body massage.

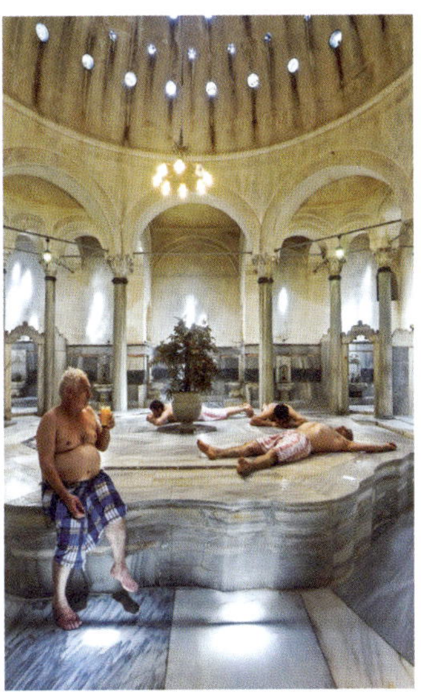

↑ *Hararet* of the Cağaloğlu Baths, with stunning marble interiors and a domed ceiling

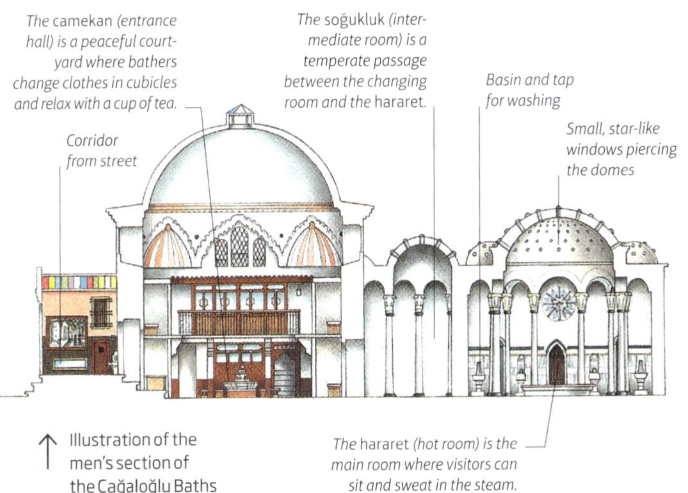

↑ Illustration of the men's section of the Cağaloğlu Baths

A SHORT WALK

THE FIRST COURTYARD OF TOPKAPı PALACE

Distance 1 km (half a mile) **Time** 20 minutes
Nearest tram Gülhane

Begin your exploration of Topkapı Palace in the First Courtyard, the outer precinct that once supported the palace's daily life. This was formerly a service area, housing the mint, a hospital, college and a bakery. It was also the mustering point of the Janissaries. Nowadays, the Cafer Ağa Courtyard and Büfe, just outside the courtyard wall, offer unusual settings for refreshments. If you wander a little further, you'll find yourself in Gülhane Park, one of the city's rare expanses of shade and greenery, a welcome retreat from Istanbul's dense tapestry of monuments.

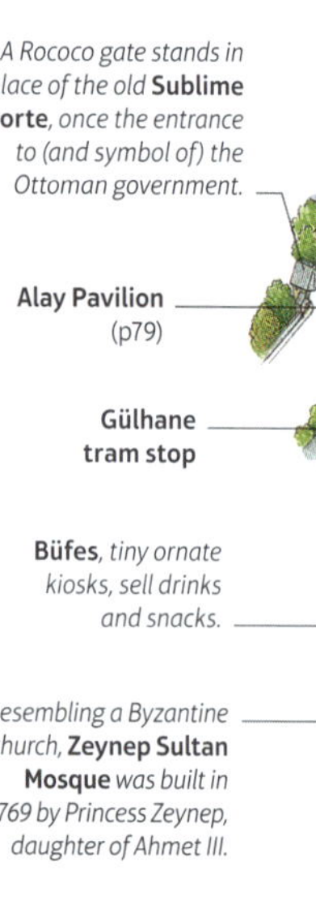

Once a rose garden in the outer grounds of Topkapı Palace, the wooded **Gülhane Park** (p79) *offers welcome shade to escape from the heat of the city.*

Entrance to **Gülhane Park**

A Rococo gate stands in place of the old **Sublime Porte**, *once the entrance to (and symbol of) the Ottoman government.*

Alay Pavilion (p79)

Gülhane tram stop

Büfes, *tiny ornate kiosks, sell drinks and snacks.*

Resembling a Byzantine church, **Zeynep Sultan Mosque** *was built in 1769 by Princess Zeynep, daughter of Ahmet III.*

Ancient Orient Museum

The cells of **Cafer Ağa Courtyard** (p79), *a former college, ranged round a tranquil courtyard café, are now occupied by jewellers, calligraphers and other artisans selling their wares.*

Soğukçeşme Sokağı (p78) *is a narrow street lined with traditional, painted wooden houses.*

Did You Know?

A colony of grey herons lives in Gülhane Park.

Locator Map
For more detail see p66

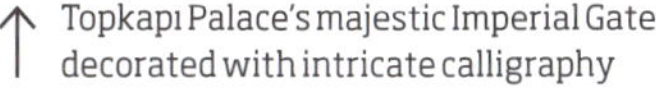
↑ Topkapı Palace's majestic Imperial Gate decorated with intricate calligraphy

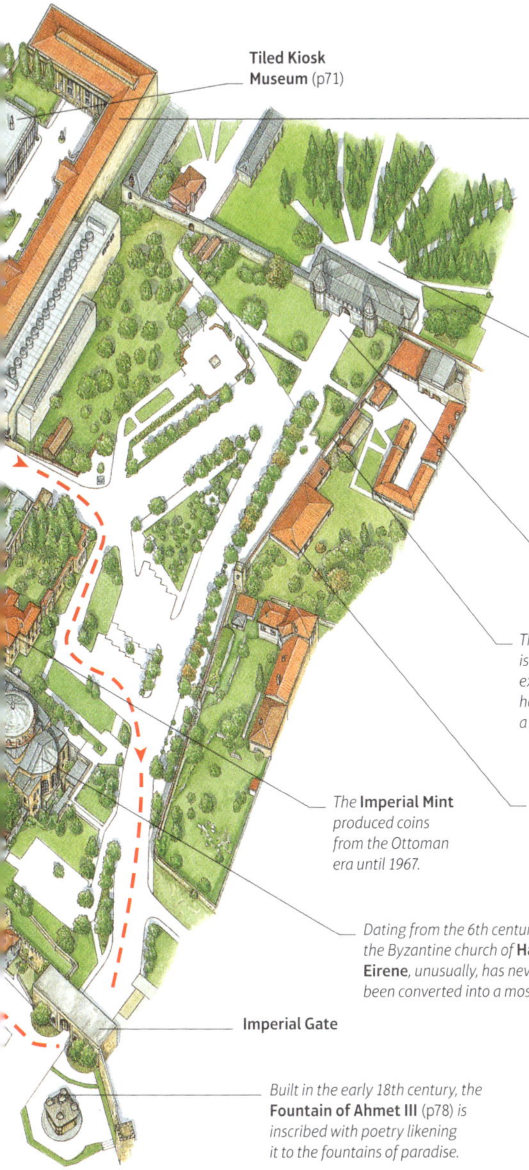

Tiled Kiosk Museum (p71)

Classical statues, dazzling carved sarcophagi, Turkish ceramics and other treasures from all over the Ottoman Empire make the **Archaeological Museums** *(p68) one of the world's great collections of antiquities.*

For 400 years, the Ottoman sultans ruled their empire from the vast **Topkapı Palace** *(p72). Its fine art collections, opulent rooms and leafy courtyards are among the highlights of a visit to Istanbul.*

Entrance to **Topkapı Palace**

The **Executioner's Fountain** *is so named because the executioner would wash his hands and sword here after a public beheading.*

The **Imperial Mint** *produced coins from the Ottoman era until 1967.*

Topkapı Palace *ticket office*

Dating from the 6th century, the Byzantine church of **Hagia Eirene**, *unusually, has never been converted into a mosque.*

Imperial Gate

Built in the early 18th century, the **Fountain of Ahmet III** *(p78) is inscribed with poetry likening it to the fountains of paradise.*

0 metres 75
0 yards 75
N ↑

Hagia Sophia and the Blue Mosque

SULTANAHMET

After his arrival in 324 CE, Constantine the Great transformed this focal area into the dazzling jewel of Constantinople, a new capital for the Roman Empire. The Hagia Sophia, an outstanding example of early Byzantine architecture, dates from this time, as does the Basilica Cistern and the scant remains of the Hippodrome, a huge chariot-racing stadium built by Emperor Septimus Severus and expanded by Constantine. Once the Ottomans seized power in 1453, they, too, stamped their authority – both religious and secular – on its buildings. Sultan Ahmet I, who lends his name to the district, built the sublime Blue Mosque in the early 1600s as a rival to the Hagia Sophia, which it still faces across an area of gardens known informally as Sultanahmet Square. Beyond here, the district slopes down to the Sea of Marmara in a jumble of alleyways, where traditional-style Ottoman wooden houses have been built over the remains of the Great Palace of the Byzantine emperors.

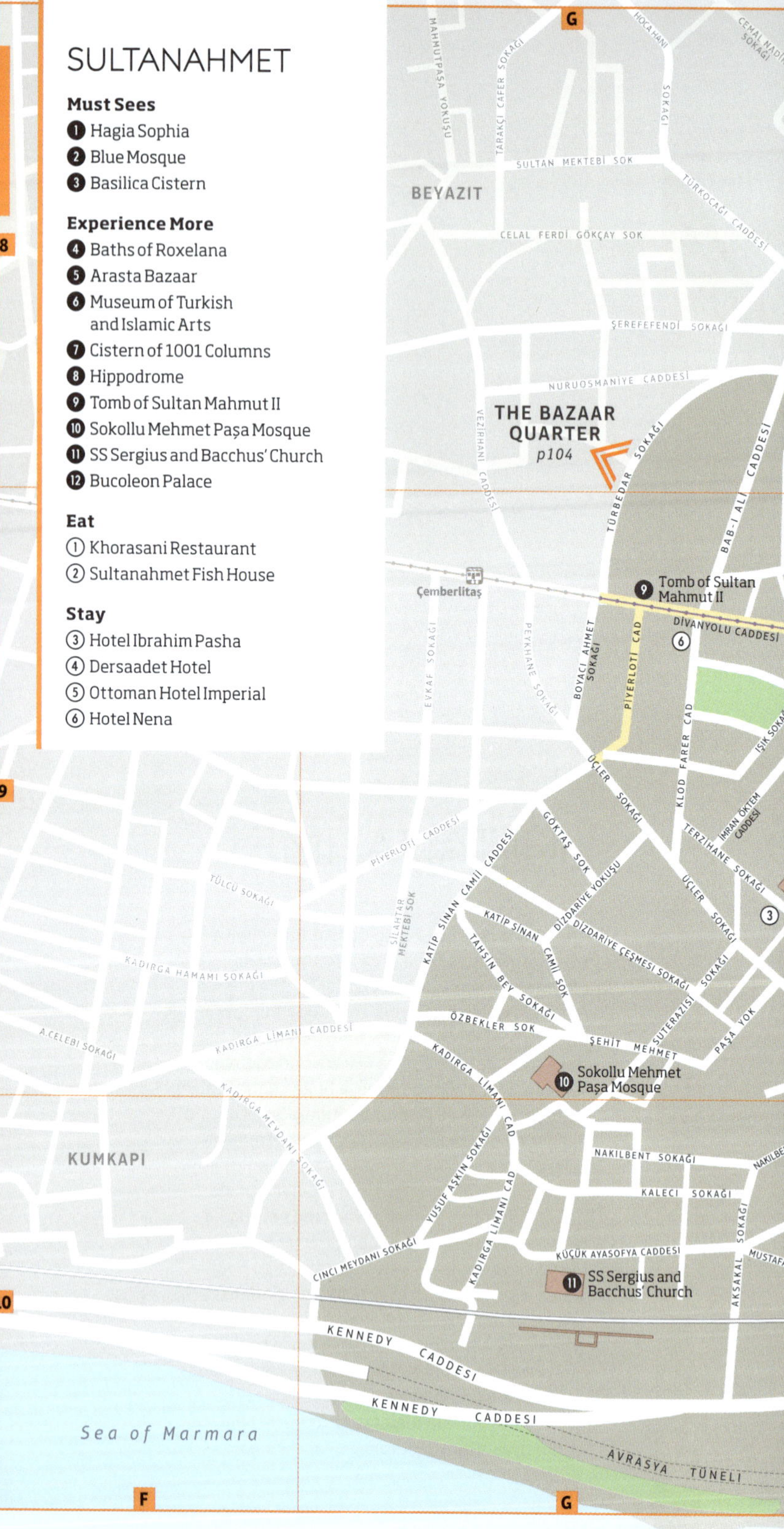

SULTANAHMET
Must Sees
1 Hagia Sophia
2 Blue Mosque
3 Basilica Cistern
Experience More
4 Baths of Roxelana
5 Arasta Bazaar
6 Museum of Turkish and Islamic Arts
7 Cistern of 1001 Columns
8 Hippodrome
9 Tomb of Sultan Mahmut II
10 Sokollu Mehmet Paşa Mosque
11 SS Sergius and Bacchus' Church
12 Bucoleon Palace
Eat
(1) Khorasani Restaurant
(2) Sultanahmet Fish House
Stay
(3) Hotel Ibrahim Pasha
(4) Dersaadet Hotel
(5) Ottoman Hotel Imperial
(6) Hotel Nena
G
F
8
9
10
BEYAZIT
THE BAZAAR QUARTER
p104
KUMKAPI
Sea of Marmara
Çemberlitaş
MAHMUTPAŞA YOKUŞU
TARAKÇI CAFER SOKAĞI
HOCA HANI SOKAĞI
CEMAL NADİR SOKAĞI
SULTAN MEKTEBİ SOK
TÜRKOCAĞI CADDESİ
CELAL FERDİ GÖKÇAY SOK
ŞEREFEFENDİ SOKAĞI
NURUOSMANİYE CADDESİ
VEZİRHANI CADDESİ
TÜRBEDAR SOKAĞI
BAB-I ALİ CADDESİ
Tomb of Sultan Mahmut II
DİVANYOLU CADDESİ
BOYACI AHMET SOKAĞI
PİYERLOTİ CAD
PEYKHANE SOKAĞI
EVKAF SOKAĞI
KLOD FARER CAD
IŞIK SOKAĞI
ÜÇLER SOKAĞI
İMRAN ÖKTEM CADDESİ
TERZİHANE SOKAĞI
GÖKTAŞ SOK
PİYERLOTİ CADDESİ
TÜLCÜ SOKAĞI
SİLAHTAR MEKTEBİ SOK
KATİP SİNAN CAMİİ CADDESİ
DİZDARİYE YOKUŞU
KATİP SİNAN CAMİİ SOK
DİZDARİYE ÇEŞMESİ SOKAĞI
TAHSİN BEY SOKAĞI
KADIRGA HAMAMI SOKAĞI
ÖZBEKLER SOK
SUTERAZİSİ SOKAĞI
PAŞA YOKUŞU
ŞEHİT MEHMET
A.ÇELEBİ SOKAĞI
KADIRGA LİMANI CADDESİ
KADIRGA LİMANI CAD
Sokollu Mehmet Paşa Mosque
KADIRGA MEYDANI SOKAĞI
NAKILBENT SOKAĞI
NAKILBENT
YUSUF AŞKIN SOKAĞI
KALECİ SOKAĞI
KÜÇÜK AYASOFYA CADDESİ
MUSTAFA
AKSAKAL SOKAĞI
CINCI MEYDANI SOKAĞI
SS Sergius and Bacchus' Church
KENNEDY CADDESİ
AVRASYA TÜNELİ

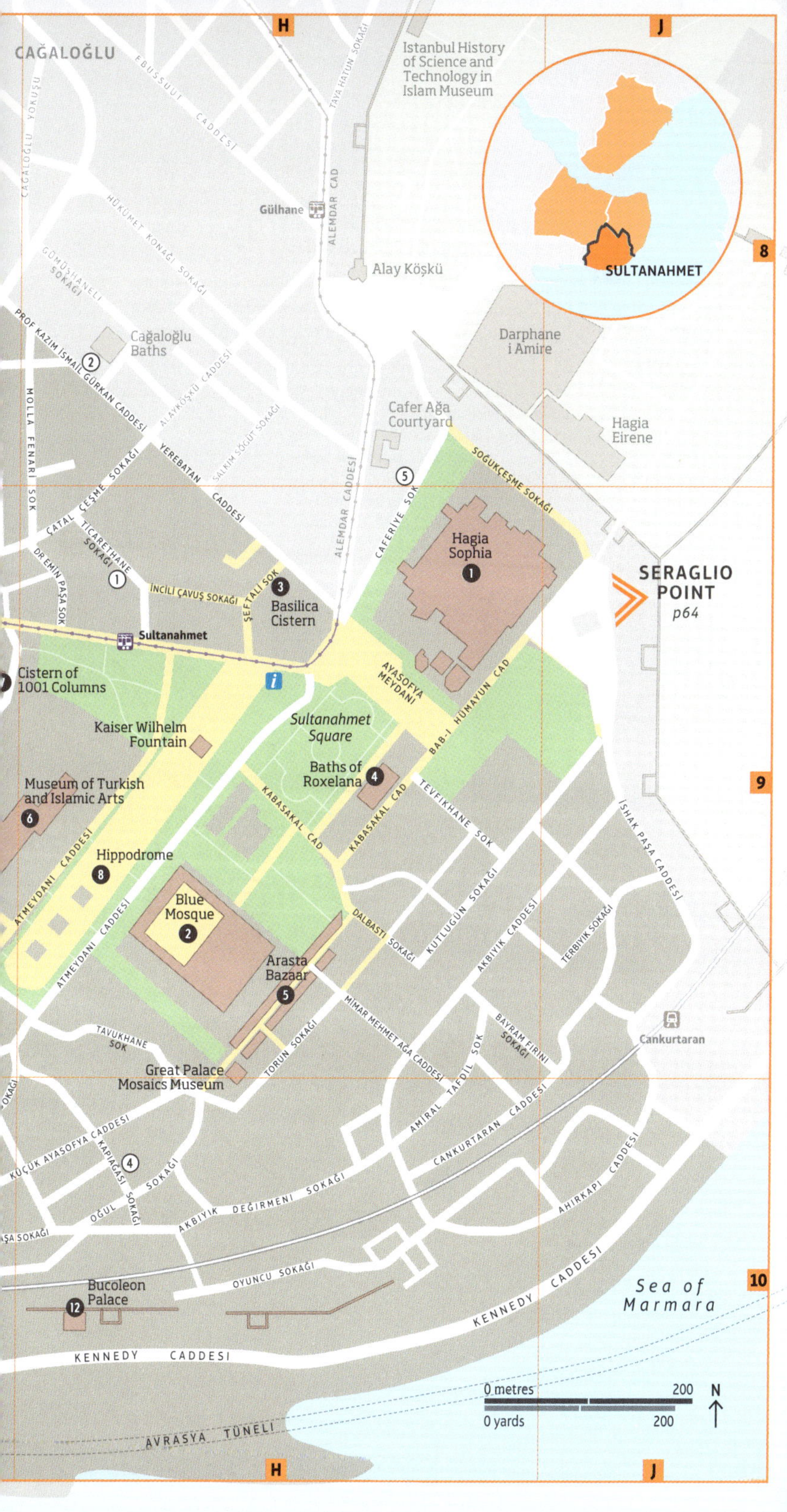

H
J
8
9
10
CAĞALOĞLU
Istanbul History of Science and Technology in Islam Museum
SULTANAHMET
Gülhane
Alay Köşkü
Darphane i Amire
Cağaloğlu Baths
Cafer Ağa Courtyard
Hagia Eirene
Hagia Sophia
SERAGLIO POINT
p64
Basilica Cistern
Sultanahmet
Cistern of 1001 Columns
Kaiser Wilhelm Fountain
Sultanahmet Square
Baths of Roxelana
Museum of Turkish and Islamic Arts
Hippodrome
Blue Mosque
Arasta Bazaar
Cankurtaran
Great Palace Mosaics Museum
Bucoleon Palace
Sea of Marmara
KENNEDY CADDESI
AVRASYA TÜNELI
0 metres 200
0 yards 200
N

HAGIA SOPHIA

AYA SOFYA CAMII

H9 Ayasofya Sultanahmet Meydanı 1 Sultanahmet 9am-7:30pm Sat-Thu, 9am-12:30pm & 2:30-7:30pm Fri muze.gen.tr

One of the oldest symbols of Istanbul, this iconic landmark is known for its colossal dome and marble-clad interior. From 1935 to 2020, it served as a museum, and is now a mosque, with its upper galleries open to tourists.

The "church of holy wisdom", Hagia Sophia is among the world's greatest architectural achievements. More than 1,400 years old, it stands as a testament to the sophistication of the 6th-century Byzantine capital. The vast edifice was built over two earlier churches and inaugurated by Emperor Justinian in 537. In the 15th century the Ottomans converted it into a mosque: the minarets, tombs and fountains date from this period. To help support the structure's great weight, the exterior has been buttressed on numerous occasions, which has partly obscured its original shape. Three mausoleums at the site are also open to the public.

Calligraphic roundel

The nave is covered by a huge dome reaching a height of 56 m (184 ft).

Kürsü

Imperial Gate

Buttresses

Among the ruins of the entrance to the earlier church is a Byzantine frieze of sheep, symbolizing the apostles.

Inner Narthex

Outer Narthex

The galleries were originally used by women during services.

Built around 1740, the Ablutions Fountain is an exquisite example of Turkish Rococo style.

Did You Know?

The dome has partially collapsed and been rebuilt three times (in 558, 989 and 1346).

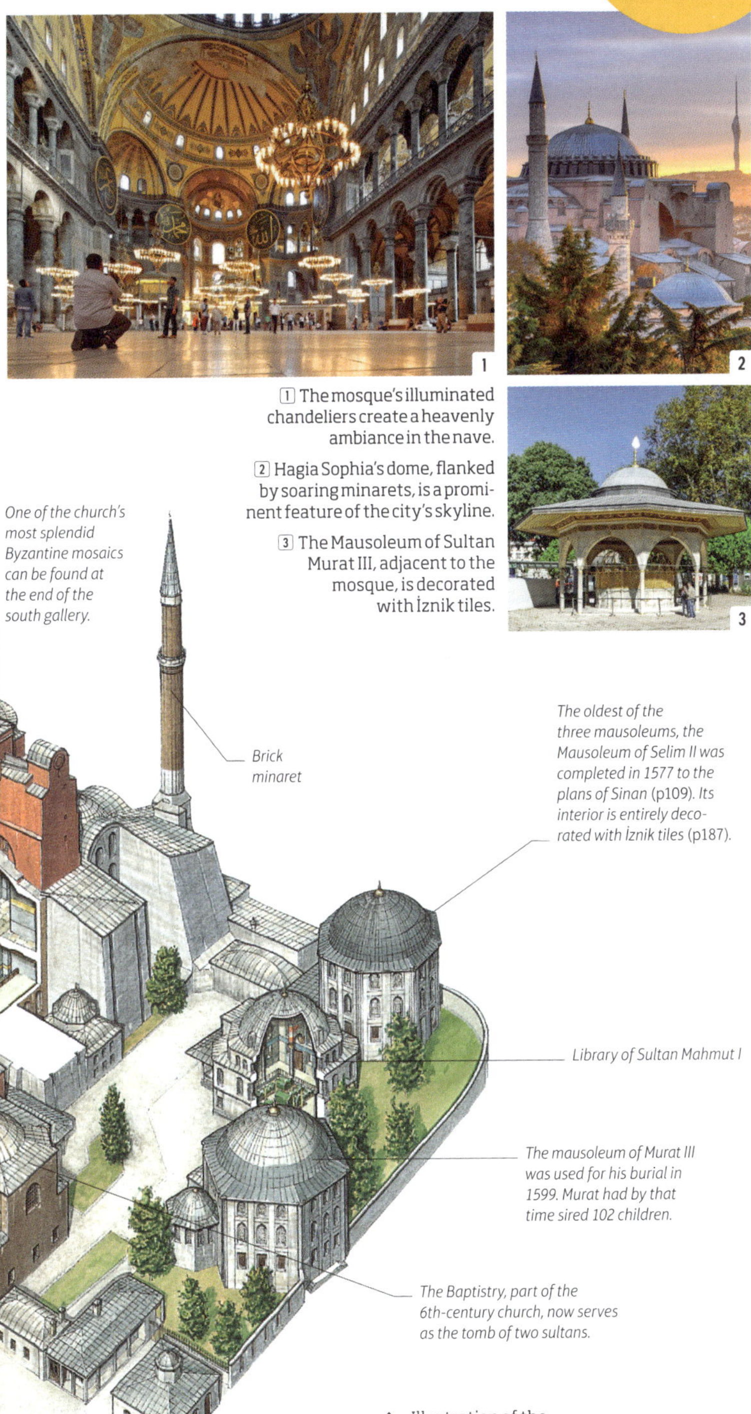

1 The mosque's illuminated chandeliers create a heavenly ambiance in the nave.

2 Hagia Sophia's dome, flanked by soaring minarets, is a prominent feature of the city's skyline.

3 The Mausoleum of Sultan Murat III, adjacent to the mosque, is decorated with İznik tiles.

↑ Illustration of the 6th-century complex of Hagia Sophia

↑ Dome, above the nave, decorated with stunning mosaics and calligraphy

EXPLORING HAGIA SOPHIA

Designed as an earthly mirror of the heavens, the interior of the Hagia Sophia is truly something to behold. Its artistic highlights include 9th-century mosaics, remnants of Byzantine art and elaborate 6th-century patterned ceilings. The latter are best seen in the outer narthex and the Vestibule of the Warriors, preserved from the building's original decoration.

INSIDER TIP
Mosque Etiquette

When visiting the Upper Galleries, visitors are expected to dress modestly, with clothing that covers both upper arms and legs. Women are required to wear a headscarf before entering.

Ground Floor

The first of the surviving Byzantine mosaics can be seen over the Imperial Gate. This is the main public entrance for Muslim worshippers into the mosque, although previously only the emperor and his entourage were allowed to pass through it. The mosaic shows Christ on a throne with an emperor kneeling beside him and has been dated to between 886 and 912. The emperor is thought to be Leo VI, the Wise.

The most conspicuous features at ground level in the nave are those added by the Ottoman sultans after the conquest of Istanbul (then Constantinople) in 1453, when the church was converted into a mosque.

Visible from the upper galleries, the mihrab was installed in the apse of the church directly opposite the entrance. The sultan's loge, on the left of the mihrab, was built by the Fossati brothers. These Italian-Swiss architects undertook a major restoration of Hagia Sophia for Sultan Abdül Mecit in 1847–9.

To the right of the mihrab is the *minber*, or pulpit, which was installed by Murat III. He also erected the four *müezzin mahfilis* *(p32)*, marble platforms for readers of the Koran. The largest of these is adjacent to the *minber*. The patterned marble coronation square next to it marks the supposed site of the Byzantine emperor's throne, or *omphalos* (centre of the world). The library of Mahmut I, which was built in 1739, can be seen from the ground floor near the south aisle and is entered via a decorative bronze door.

Across the nave, between two columns, is the 17th-century marble preacher's throne, the contribution of Murat IV. Behind it is one of

← The *minber* from where Muslim preachers would give sermons

several *maqsuras*. These low, fenced platforms were used by elders to sit and listen to or read the Koran.

In the northwestern and western corners of the mosque are two marble urns, thought to date from the Hellenistic or early Byzantine period. A rectangular pillar behind one of the urns, the pillar of St Gregory the Miracle-Worker, is believed to have healing powers.

Upper Galleries

The ramp up to the upper galleries leads on to the south gallery. Start by passing through the Gates of Heaven and Hell, a marble doorway.

Around the corner to the right is the Deësis Mosaic showing the Virgin Mary and John the Baptist with Christ Pantocrator (the All-Powerful). On the floor opposite is the tomb of Enrico Dandalo, the Doge of Venice, responsible for the sacking of Constantinople in 1204 *(p53)*.

In the last bay of the southern gallery there are two more mosaics. The right-hand one is of the Virgin holding Christ, flanked by Emperor John II Comnenus and Empress Irene. The other is of Christ with Emperor Constantine IX Monomachus and Empress Zoe.

Eight stunning wooden plaques bearing calligraphic inscriptions hang over the nave at the level of the gallery. An addition by the Fossati brothers, they bear the names of Allah, the Prophet Mohammed, the first four caliphs and Hasan and Hussein, two of the Prophet's grandsons who are revered as martyrs.

In the north gallery, on the eastern side of the great northwest pier, you will find the 10th-century mosaic of Emperor Alexander holding a skull. On the west face of the same pier is a medieval drawing of a galleon in full sail. The highlight in the western gallery is a green marble disk marking the location of the Byzantine Empress's throne.

HIDDEN MOSAICS

Since the Hagia Sophia's reconversion from a museum to a mosque in 2020, some of its famous artworks, now in the prayer hall, are hidden behind screens. The revised ground-floor restrictions also prevent non-worshippers from accessing the inner narthex's Christ as Pantocrator mosaic.

As you leave the mosque you will pass through the Vestibule of the Warriors, so called because the emperor's bodyguards would wait here for him when he came to worship. As you enter, look behind to see the wonderful mosaic of the Virgin with Constantine and Justinian above the door. It shows Mary seated on a throne holding the infant Jesus and flanked by two of the greatest emperors of the city. Constantine, on her left, presents her with the city of Constantinople, while Justinian offers her Hagia Sophia. This was made long after either of these two emperors lived, probably in the 10th century, during the reign of Basil II. Visitors exit the church by the door that was once reserved for the emperor due to its proximity to the Great Palace *(p100)*.

Upper Walls and Domes

The apse's large and striking mosaic showing the Virgin with the infant Jesus on her lap is usually kept covered these days. Two other mosaics in the apse show the archangels Gabriel and Michael, but only fragments of the latter now remain. The unveiling of these mosaics on Easter Sunday 867 was a triumphal event celebrating victory over the iconoclasts. Three mosaic portraits of saints adorn niches in the north tympanum and are visible from the south gallery.

In the four pendentives (the triangular, concave areas at the base of the dome) are mosaics of six-winged seraphim. The ones in the eastern pendentives date from 1346–55, but may be copies of much older ones. Those on the western side are 19th-century imitations that were added by the Fossati brothers.

The great dome is adorned with Koranic inscriptions. It was once covered in golden mosaic and the tinkling sound of pieces dropping to the ground was familiar to visitors until the building's 19th-century restoration.

↓ Mosaic of the Virgin Mary and John the Baptist with Christ Pantocrator

BLUE MOSQUE

SULTAN AHMET CAMII

H9 Atmeydanı Sok, Sultanahmet (0212) 458 07 76 Sultanahmet 8:30am-6:30pm daily (from 2:30pm Fri) Prayer times

Built to rival the neighbouring Hagia Sophia in beauty, the Blue Mosque features a façade made of cascading domes hemmed by six pencil-minarets. Inside, its soaring prayer hall is a showcase of Ottoman artistry, clad in a dizzying array of İznik tiles.

PICTURE PERFECT
Sultanahmet Park

Situated between the Blue Mosque and Hagia Sophia, this manicured park filled with tulip gardens and fountains offers photographers lovely vantage points for capturing both buildings.

The Blue Mosque, named for the stunning blue İznik tilework *(p187)* decorating its interior, is one of the world's most renowned religious structures. While its serene beauty captivates visitors at any time, it becomes truly magical when illuminated at night, with its towering minarets silhouetted against the sky, often with seagulls circling above. Despite being commissioned by Sultan Ahmet I during a period of declining Ottoman fortunes, the mosque was built between 1609–16 under the supervision of the imperial architect Mehmet Ağa. The splendour of the plans provoked great hostility at the time, especially because a mosque with six minarets was considered a sacrilegious attempt to rival the architecture of Mecca itself.

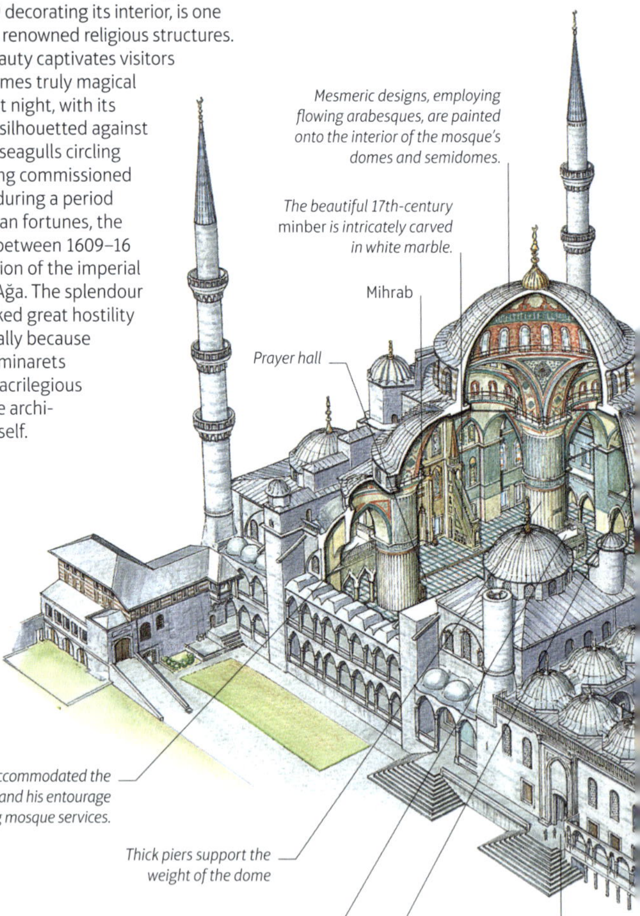

Mesmeric designs, employing flowing arabesques, are painted onto the interior of the mosque's domes and semidomes.

The beautiful 17th-century minber *is intricately carved in white marble.*

Mihrab

Prayer hall

The loge accommodated the sultan and his entourage during mosque services.

Thick piers support the weight of the dome

Müezzin mahfili

Over 250 windows allow light to flood into the mosque.

Entrance to courtyard

Cross-section of the Blue Mosque with its towering minarets ↑

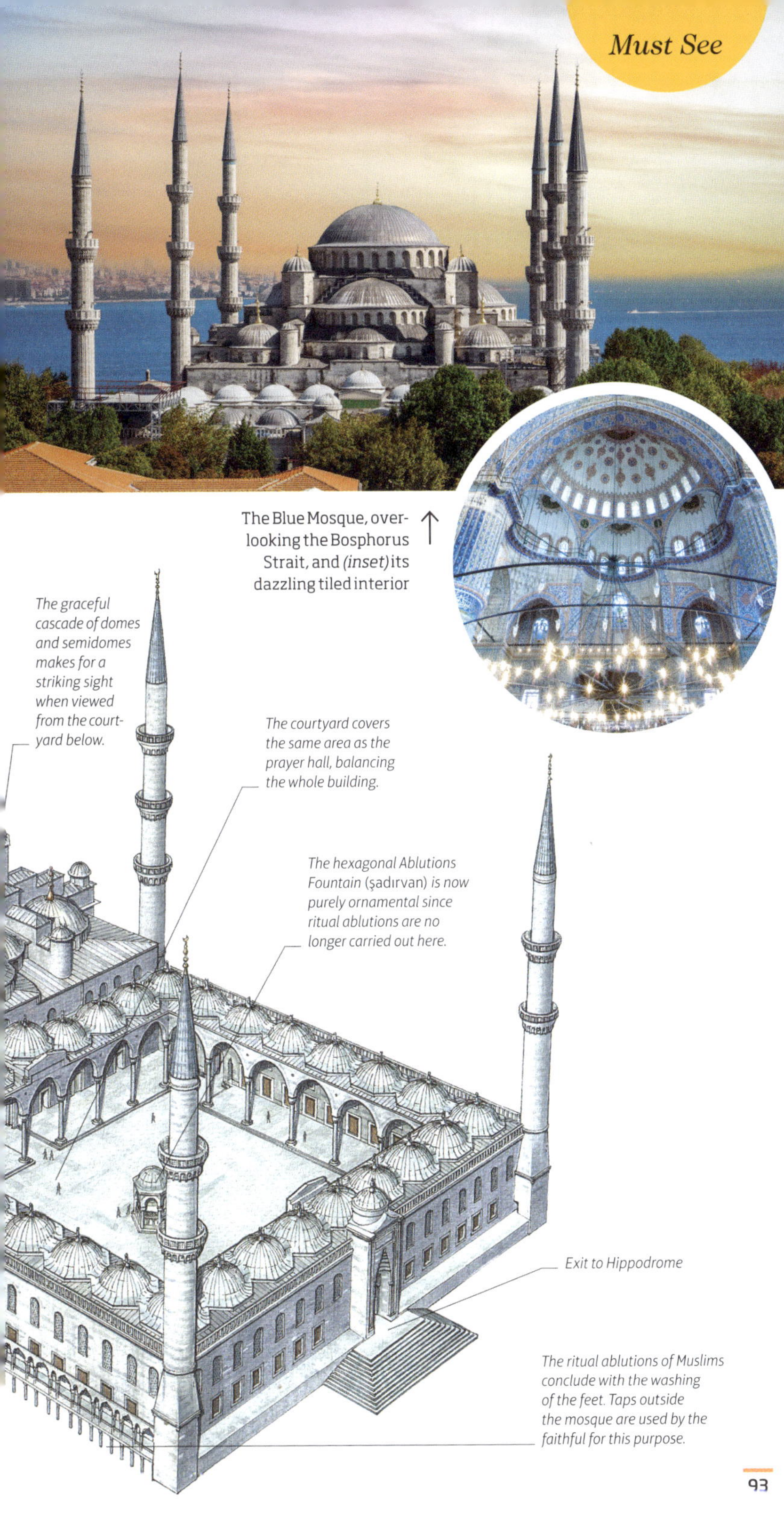

The Blue Mosque, over-looking the Bosphorus Strait, and *(inset)* its dazzling tiled interior ↑

3

BASILICA CISTERN

YEREBATAN SARNICI

H9 13 Yerebatan Cad, Sultanahmet Sultanahmet
9am-10pm daily yerebatan.com

Set close to Hagia Sophia, the Basilica Cistern is a magnificent underground chamber that once supplied water to the Great Palace of Constantinople. Its striking columns are just as impressive as its history.

This vast underground water cistern, a beautiful piece of Byzantine engineering, is the most unusual tourist attraction in the city. Although there may have been an earlier, smaller cistern here, this cavernous vault was laid out under Justinian in 532 CE, mainly to satisfy the growing demands of the Great Palace *(p100)* on the other side of the Hippodrome *(p98)*. For a century after the conquest *(p53)*, the Ottomans did not know of the cistern's existence. It was rediscovered after people were found to be collecting water, and even fish, by lowering buckets through holes in their basements.

Visitors tread walkways to the mixed sounds of classical music and dripping water. The cistern's roof is held up by 336 columns, each over 8 m (26 ft) high. The original structure covered a total area of 9,800 sq m (105,000 sq ft) but today only about two-thirds of it is visible, the rest having been bricked up in the 19th century. Water reached the cistern, which held about 100 million litres (22 million gallons), from the Belgrade Forest, 20 km (12 miles) north of Istanbul, via the Valens Aqueduct *(p114)*.

ISTANBUL'S HISTORIC WATER SYSTEM

Rapid population growth in late antiquity led to Constantinople's fresh water shortage, as the peninsula on which it was built lacked adequate fresh water. An estimated 550 km (342 miles) of aqueduct channels were built to transport water from the countryside to the city, where cisterns were constructed for storing it. The Basilica Cistern *(p94)* and the Valens Aqueduct *(p114)* are surviving parts of this project.

This marble Medusa head is one of two classical column bases found in the basilica ↑

Did You Know?

Parts of the 1963 James Bond film *From Russia With Love* were filmed inside the Basilica Cistern.

↑ Inside the Basilica Cistern, its columns beautifully reflected in the tranquil waters

Arasta Bazaar lined with colourful shops selling traditional handicrafts ↑

EXPERIENCE MORE

Baths of Roxelana

Hürrem Sultan Hamamı

H9 Ayasofya Meydanı Sultanahmet 8am-10pm daily hurremsultanhamami.com

These baths were built in 1556 for Süleyman the Magnificent *(p54)* by Sinan *(p109)*, and are named after Roxelana, the sultan's shrewd wife. They were constructed on the site of an earlier Roman-era public bathhouse. With the women's entrance at one end of the building and the men's at the other, their absolute symmetry makes them perhaps the most handsome baths in the city. The men's section of the baths faces Hagia Sophia and has a fine colonnaded portico, enhancing the architectural elegance of this historic site.

Each end of the baths starts with a *camekan*, a massive domed hall that would originally have been centred on a fountain. Next is a small *soğukluk*, or intermediate room, which opens into a *hararet*, or steam room. The octagonal massage slab in each *hararet*, the *göbek taşı*, is inlaid with coloured marbles, indicating that the baths are of imperial origin.

The baths functioned as a public bathhouse for over 350 years until 1910. After being used for other purposes over several decades, the bath-house underwent major restoration and reopened as a luxury hammam in 2012.

ROXELANA

Süleyman the Magnificent's ambitious wife Roxelana (1500-58, Hürrem Sultan), rose from being a concubine to become his chief wife, or first *kadın*. Believed to be of Russian origin, she was the first consort permitted to live within the Topkapı Palace *(p72)*. She convinced the sultan to have İbrahim Paşa strangled. Later, in 1553, she persuaded the sultan to have his popular heir, Mustafa, murdered by deaf mutes to clear the way for her own son Selim to inherit the throne.

Arasta Bazaar

Arasta Çarşısı

H9 Kabasakal Cad Sultanahmet 9am-7pm daily

Established in 1616, this historic shopping arcade is an integral part of the magnificent Blue Mosque complex *(p92)*. Its inclusion is a characteristic example of typical Ottoman mosque complexes, known as *külliyes*, which often incorporated public buildings, such as schools and an *arasta* (row of shops), alongside various charitable institutions like soup kitchens and hospitals, to serve the community and to generate funds for the mosque's upkeep.

The bazaar was severely damaged during a fire in 1912 and remained derelict for decades until it was restored in the 1980s. Today, the boutiques here primarily cater to tourists, with several shops selling fine tilework and ceramics, jewellery and high-quality hand-loomed *peştamals* (traditional Turkish hammam towels).

Each room of the musuem highlights a specific historical period or geographical area of the Islamic world.

6   

Museum of Turkish and Islamic Arts

Türk ve İslam Eserleri Müzesi

H9 Atmeydanı Sok Sultanahmet 9am-6pm & 7-10pm daily muze.gov.tr

Over 40,000 items are on display in the former palace of İbrahim Paşa (c 1493–1536), the most gifted of Süleyman's many grand viziers. İbrahim Paşa, who married the sultan's sister upon Süleyman's ascension to the throne, oversaw the establishment of this remarkable repository. The collection was begun in the 19th century and ranges from the earliest period of Islam, under the Umayyad caliphate (661–750), through to modern times.

Each room of the musuem highlights a specific historical period or geographical area of the Islamic world, featuring detailed explanations in both Turkish and English. The museum is especially celebrated for its remarkable collection of rugs, which spans from 13th-century Seljuk fragments to exquisite palatial Persian silks that adorn the walls from floor to ceiling in the palace's great hall.

The ground floor features an ethnographic section that showcases the diverse lifestyles of various Turkish peoples, with a particular focus on the nomads of central and eastern Anatolia. Highlights include beautifully crafted re-creations of a round felt *yurt* (Turkic nomadic tent) and a traditional brown tent.

7 

Cistern of 1001 Columns

Binbirdirek Sarnıcı

G9 Imran Okten Sok 4 Sultanahmet 9am-5pm daily binbirdirek.com

This cistern, dating back to the 4th century CE, is the second-largest underground Byzantine cistern in Istanbul after the Basilica Cistern *(p94)*. Spanning an area of 64 m (210 ft) by 56 m (184 ft), its herringbone brick roof vaults are supported by 264 marble columns – though its name, the "1,001 columns", is a poetic exaggeration. Until recently, the cistern was filled with rubble and primarily explored by adventurous visitors, but it has since undergone significant restoration.

← Pottery from the 13th century at the Museum of Turkish and Islamic Arts

STAY

Hotel İbrahim Pasha

Located in the heart of Istanbul's historic district, this stylish hotel offers a private bar, a well-stocked library and a rooftop terrace with iconic views of the Blue Mosque.

G9 Terzihane Sok 7 ibrahimpasha.com

Dersaadet Hotel

This Ottoman wooden mansion, now a boutique hotel, is known for its old-world ambiance. Its rooms are decorated in a charming late 19th-century style.

H10 Kapıağası Sok 5 hoteldersaadet.com

Ottoman Hotel Imperial

Once a school, this heritage hotel offers classically styled rooms. Its proximity to key sights like the Hagia Sophia makes it a popular choice.

H8 Caferiye Sok 6/1 ottomanhotel imperial.com

Hotel Nena

Nena offers sleek, contemporary rooms decorated in a minimalist style. Book a deluxe room with a balcony to watch the sunrise over the Blue Mosque.

G9 Klodfarer Cad 6 hotelnena.com

Hippodrome

At Meydanı

H9 Sultanahmet Sultanahmet

Little remains of the massive chariot-racing arena that once dominated the Byzantine city of Constantinople *(p51)*. Originally laid out by Emperor Septimus Severus in the 3rd century CE, it was later enlarged by Emperor Constantine *(p51)*, who connected its *kathisma*, or royal box, to the nearby Great Palace *(p100)*. It is believed that the arena could hold up to 100,000 spectators. Today, the site is an elongated public garden, At Meydanı or , Cavalry Square, which holds enough remains of the Hippodrome to convey its historical scale and significance.

The road around the square roughly follows the chariot-racing track, and visitors can also spot some of the arches of the *sphendrome* (the curved end of the Hippodrome) by walking a few steps down Nakilbent Sok. Constantine adorned the *spina*, the stadium's central line, with obelisks and columns from ancient Egypt and Greece. The four bronze horses that stood on the ruined entry gate were pillaged during the Fourth Crusade *(p53)* and taken to St Mark's in Venice. However, ancient monuments remain: the Egyptian Obelisk, which was built in 1500 BCE, stood at Karnak in Luxor until Constantine had it brought to his city, and the Serpentine Column, dating back to 479 BCE, was shipped here from Delphi.

Another obelisk, often called the Constantine Porphyrogenitus, is named after the emperor who restored it in the 10th century CE. Its dilapidated state owes much to the young Janissaries who routinely scaled it as a test of their bravery.

Domed Sokollu Mehmet Paşa Mosque, and *(inset)* its tiled interior

The only other structure in the Hippodrome is a domed fountain, which commemorates the visit of Kaiser Wilhelm II to Istanbul in 1898.

The Hippodrome was the scene of one of the bloodiest events in Istanbul's history. In 532 CE a brawl between rival chariot-racing teams developed into the Nika Revolt, during which much of the city was destroyed. The end of the revolt came when an army of mercenaries, under the command of Justinian's general Belisarius, massacred an estimated 30,000 people trapped in the Hippodrome.

CEREMONIES IN THE HIPPODROME

Inaugurated on 11 May 330, the Hippodrome *(p94)* served as the setting for Constantinople's most important public events for 1,300 years. Even after its decline into ruins post the Ottoman conquest *(p53)*, it remained a venue for major public occasions. This 16th-century illustration shows Sultan Murat III watching the 52-day-long festivities for his son Mehmet's circumcision.

9

Tomb of Sultan Mahmut II

Mahmut II Türbesi

G9 Divanyolu Cad, Çemberlitaş Çemberlitaş 9:30am-4:30pm daily

This large octagonal mausoleum is in the Empire style (modelled on Roman architecture) made popular by Napoleon. It was built in 1838, the year before Sultan Mahmut II's death and is shared by sultans Mahmut II, Abdül Aziz and Abdül Hamit II. Within, Corinthian pilasters divide up walls which groan with symbols of victory and prosperity. The huge tomb dominates a cemetery that has beautiful headstones, a fountain and a lovely café.

Sokollu Mehmet Paşa Mosque

Mosque Sokollu Mehmet Paşa Camii

G9 Şehit Çeşmesi Sok, Sultanahmet Çemberlitaş, Sultanahmet 8:30am-6:30pm daily (from 2:30pm Fri) Prayer times

Built by the architect Sinan *(p109)* in 1571–2, this mosque was commissioned by Sokollu Mehmet Paşa, grand vizier to Selim II. The simplicity of Sinan's design solution for the mosque's sloping site has been widely admired. A steep entrance stairway leads up to the mosque courtyard from the street, passing beneath the teaching hall of its *medrese (p33)*, which still functions as a college. Only the tiled lunettes above the windows in the portico give a hint of the jewelled mosque interior to come.

Inside, the far wall around the carved mihrab is entirely covered in İznik tiles *(p187)* of a sumptuous green-blue hue. This tile panel, designed specifically for the space, is complemented by six stained-glass windows. The "hat" of the *minber* is covered with the same tiles. Most of the mosque's other walls are of plain stone, but they are enlivened by a few more tile panels. Set into the wall over the entrance there is a small piece of greenish stone which is supposedly from the Kaaba, the holy stone at the centre of Mecca.

EAT

Khorasani Restaurant

This *ocakbaşı* (kebab house) serves excellent, classic Turkish kebabs.

H9 Ticaretine Sok 9/B khorasanikebab.com

Sultanahmet Fish House

A popular seafood restaurant, this spot offers fish dishes from Turkey's Aegean, Mediterranean and Black Sea regions.

H8 Prof Kazım İsmail Gürkan Cad 16 sultanahmetfishhouse.com

Impressive interior of the SS Sergius and Bacchus' Church

11

SS Sergius and Bacchus' Church

Küçük Ayasofya Camii

G10 Küçük Ayasofya Cad Çemberlitaş, Sultanahmet 8:30am-6:30pm daily (from 2:30pm Fri) Prayer times

Commonly referred to as "Little Hagia Sophia", this well-preserved church was built in 527, a few years before its namesake *(p88)*. It too was founded by Emperor Justinian, together with his empress, Theodora, at the beginning of his long reign. Ingenious and highly decorative, the mosque gives a somewhat higgledy-piggledy impression both inside and out, and is one of the most charming of all the city's architectural treasures.

Inside, an irregular octagon of columns on two floors supports a broad central dome composed of 16 vaults. The mosaic decoration that once adorned some of the walls has long since crumbled away. However, the green and red marble columns,

RECONSTRUCTION OF THE GREAT PALACE

In Byzantine times, Sultanahmet was the site of the Great Palace, which, in its heyday, had no equal in Europe and dazzled medieval visitors with its opulence. This great complex of buildings - including royal apartments, state rooms, churches, courtyards and gardens - extended over a sloping, terraced site from the Hippodrome to the imperial harbour on the shore of the Sea of Marmara. The palace was built in stages, beginning under Constantine in the 4th century. It was enlarged by Justinian following the fire caused by the Nika Revolt in 532. Later emperors, especially the 9th-century Basil I, extended it further. After several hundred years of occupation, it was finally abandoned in the second half of the 13th century in favour of Blachernae Palace.

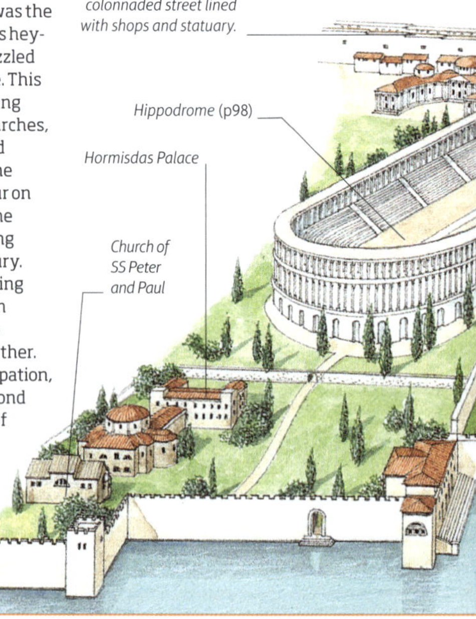

Illustration of the Great Palace after its reconstructon

INSIDER TIP
Tea Break

For a tranquil tea break in Sultanahmet, the shaded garden café in the courtyard across from the entrance of the SS Sergius and Bacchus' Church is simply unbeatable.

the delicate tracery of the capitals, and the carved frieze running above the columns are original features of the building.

The inscription on this frieze, in boldly carved Greek script, mentions the founders of the church and St Sergius, but not St Bacchus. The two saints were Roman centurions who converted to Christianity and were martyred. Justinian credited them with saving his life when, as a young man, he was implicated in a plot to kill his uncle, Justin I. The saints supposedly appeared to Justin in a dream and told him to release his nephew.

The SS Sergius and Bacchus' Church was built between two important edifices to which it was connected, the Palace of Hormisdas and the Church of SS Peter and Paul, but has outlived them both. After the conquest of Istanbul in 1453 *(p53)* it was converted into a mosque.

Bucoleon Palace

Bukoleon Sarayı

H10 Kennedy Cad
Sultanahmet

The Bucoleon Palace (the Boukoleon) is a fragmentary maritime wing of Constantine's Great Palace complex, the main residence of Byzantine emperors from the 4th to the 11th century CE. Its remnants are still visible, clinging to the ancient sea walls that once protected the city along the Sea of Marmara. Today, only a creeper-clad stretch of weathered stonework remains, notable for three large, marble-framed windows that offer a glimpse into its past splendour. This is all that survives of what was once an opulent emperor's waterfront residence, which featured its own harbour and a dedicated set of steps for the imperial caïques (ceremonial boats used by the Byzantine emperors). Visitors should note that the site is currently undergoing a multi-year restoration project, so parts of the ruins may be obscured by scaffolding.

Just to the east of these ruins stands the tower that served as the Byzantine Pharos (lighthouse), which guided ships safely to the bustling harbour. The entire site is located next to the modern thoroughfare of, Kennedy Caddesi, and is close to the historic SS Sergius and Bacchus' Church.

The Kathisma was the imperial box of the Hippodrome.

Hagia Sophia (p88)

The Milion was the point from which road distances were measured.

The Augusteum was a porticoed public square.

Magnaura Palace

Chalke Gate was the main entrance to the palace.

The Nea Ekklesia, erected by Basil I, set the style for all subsequent Byzantine churches.

Lighthouse

Daphne Palace

The Bucoleon Palace had a façade looking out over the sea.

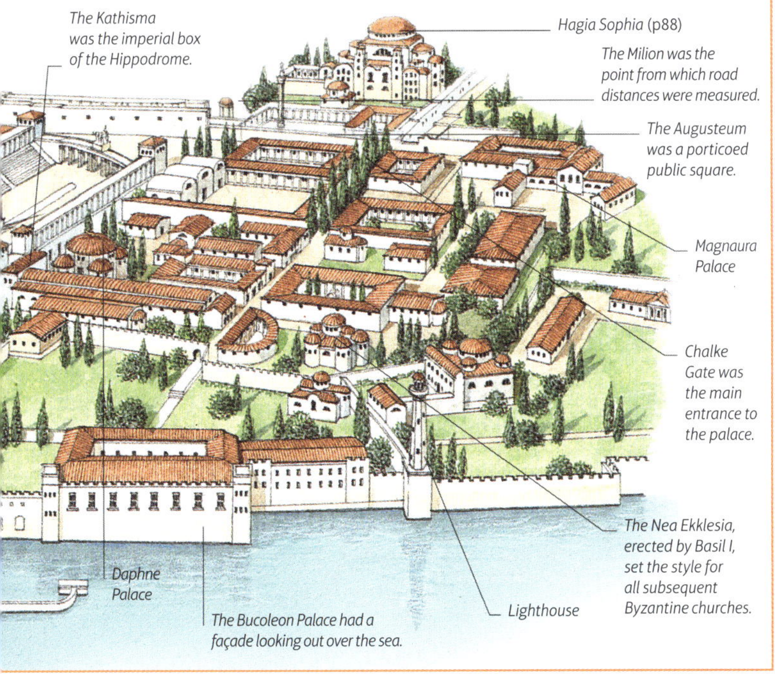

A SHORT WALK
SULTANAHMET SQUARE

Distance 1.5 km (1 mile) **Time** 25 minutes
Nearest tram Sultanahmet

Start your stroll in the heart of Istanbul's historic peninsula, where two of the city's most iconic landmarks – the Blue Mosque and Hagia Sophia – stand facing each other across leafy Sultanahmet Square (Sultanahmet Meydanı), next to the Hippodrome of Byzantium. Also in this historic quarter are a few museums, including the Great Palace Mosaics Museum, built over part of the old Byzantine Great Palace *(p100)*, and the Museum of Turkish and Islamic Arts. No less diverting than the cultural sights of this pedestrianized area are the cries of the *simit* (bagel) hawkers and carpet sellers, and the chatter of children selling postcards.

Stunning 17th-century İznik tiles (p187) adorn the interior of the **Tomb of Sultan Ahmet I**, *which is part of the outer complex of the Blue Mosque (p92).*

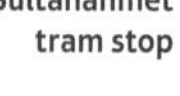

Sultanahmet tram stop

Firuz Ağa Mosque

Fountain of Kaiser Wilhelm II

DIVAN

Egyptian Obelisk

Yurts, traditionally used by Turkey's nomadic peoples, and rugs are on display in the **Museum of Turkish and Islamic Arts** (p97).

ATMEYDANI SOK

Brazen Column

ATMEYDANI SOK

START

FINISH

The **Hippodrome** (p98) *is a stadium that was the city's focal point for more than 1,000 years before it fell into ruin. Only a few sections, such as the central line of monuments, remain.*

TAVUKHANE SOK

Serpentine Column

TORUN SOK

Towering above Sultanahmet Square are the six beautiful minarets of the world-famous **Blue Mosque** (p92), *which was built in the early 17th century for Ahmet I.*

Hunting scenes are common in the mosaics displayed in the **Great Palace Mosaics Museum**, *currently closed for restoration.*

Did You Know?

The ruins in the park next to Firuz Ağa Mosque are from the 5th-century Palace of Antiochus.

The iconic Hagia Sophia, on one side of Sultanahmet Square

Özer

Shopping in the Spice Bazaar

THE BAZAAR QUARTER

In 1453, after his conquest of Constantinople, Sultan Mehmet II chose this area, close to the Graeco-Roman Forum of the Bulls, as the place to begin construction of a model city based on Islamic principles. The key elements were mosques and *medreses* (religious schools), charitable institutions, accommodation for travellers and a Grand Bazaar – the latter funding all the others and a great deal more besides. The Süleymaniye Mosque, a glorious expression of 16th-century Ottoman culture, is just one of numerous beautiful mosques the Ottomans consequently bestowed on this area, while the labyrinthine Grand Bazaar, with its seemingly limitless range of goods, remains at the centre of the district's commercial activity. Trade has always been important in a city that straddles the continents of Asia and Europe, and beyond the Grand Bazaar itself lies a warren of streets with goods tumbling out of shops and onto the pavement. Look through any of the archways in between these shops today and you will see hidden courtyards or *hans (p119)*, containing feverishly industrious workshops.

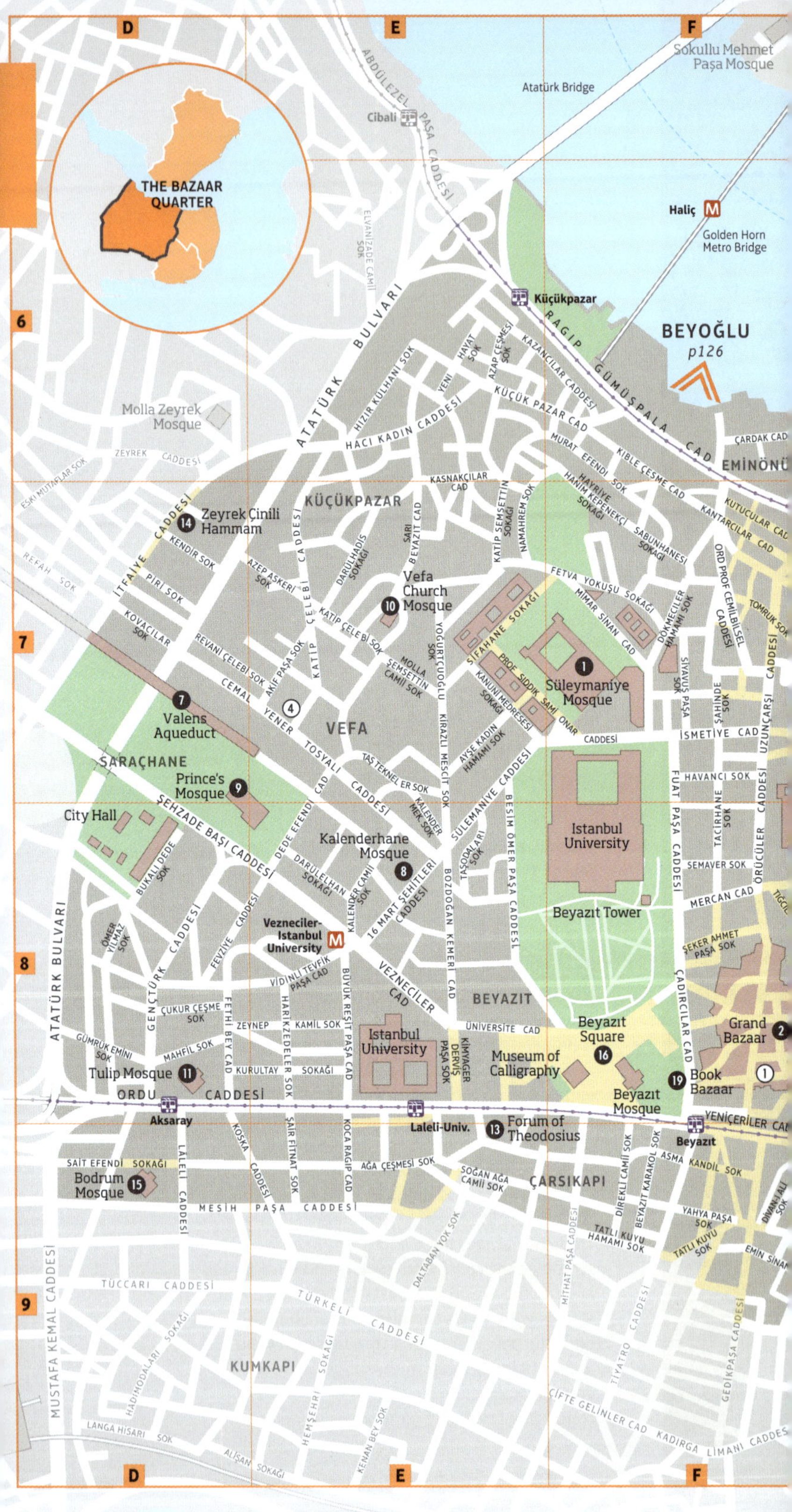

THE BAZAAR QUARTER
Sokullu Mehmet Paşa Mosque
Atatürk Bridge
Cibali
Haliç
Golden Horn Metro Bridge
Küçükpazar
BEYOĞLU
p126
EMİNÖNÜ
Molla Zeyrek Mosque
KÜÇÜKPAZAR
Zeyrek Çinili Hammam
Vefa Church Mosque
Süleymaniye Mosque
Valens Aqueduct
VEFA
ŞARAÇHANE
Prince's Mosque
City Hall
Istanbul University
Kalenderhane Mosque
Beyazıt Tower
Vezneciler-Istanbul University
BEYAZIT
Beyazıt Square
Museum of Calligraphy
Grand Bazaar
Istanbul University
Tulip Mosque
Book Bazaar
Beyazıt Mosque
Aksaray
Laleli-Univ.
Forum of Theodosius
Beyazıt
Bodrum Mosque
ÇARSIKAPI
KUMKAPI
ATATÜRK BULVARI
ORDU CADDESİ
MUSTAFA KEMAL CADDESİ
ŞEHZADE BAŞI CADDESİ

THE BAZAAR QUARTER
Must Sees
1 Süleymaniye Mosque
2 Grand Bazaar
Experience More
3 Spice Bazaar
4 New Mosque
5 Rüstem Paşa Mosque
6 Golden Horn
7 Valens Aqueduct
8 Kalenderhane Mosque
9 Prince's Mosque
10 Vefa Church Mosque
11 Tulip Mosque
12 Barin Han
13 Forum of Theodosius
14 Zeyrek Çinili Hammam
15 Bodrum Mosque
16 Beyazıt Square
17 Çorlulu Ali Paşa Courtyard
18 Valide Han
19 Book Bazaar
20 Çemberlitaş Hamamı
21 Atik Ali Paşa Mosque
22 Constantine's Column
23 Nuruosmaniye Mosque
24 Mahmut Paşa Mosque
Eat
1 Saaf-I Kebap Salonu
2 Aslan Restaurant
3 Aynen Dürüm
Drink
4 Vefa Bozacısı
G
H
J
9
SALT Galata/Ottoman Bank Museum
KARAKÖY
Karaköy
Golden Horn
Galata Bridge
Eminönü
Sirkeci
Rüstem Paşa Mosque
New Mosque
Spice Bazaar
SİRKECİ
Valide Han
Istanbul Erkek High School
Mahmut Paşa Mosque
Nuruosmaniye Mosque
CAĞALOĞLU
Çorlulu Ali Paşa Courtyard
Atik Ali Paşa Mosque
Constantine's Column
Çemberlitaş Hamamı
Barın Han
Çemberlitaş
Sultanahmet
Basilica Cistern
Hagia Eirene
Hagia Sophia
Sultanahmet Square
Baths of Roxelana
Museum of Turkish and Islamic Arts
Blue Mosque
Arasta Bazaar
Great Palace Mosaics Museum
SERAGLIO POINT p64
SULTANAHMET p84
0 metres 250
0 yards 250
N

1

SÜLEYMANIYE MOSQUE

SÜLEYMANIYE CAMII

F7 Prof Siddik Sami Onar Caddesi, Vefa Vezneciler Vezneciler Beyazıt, Laleli, Eminönü then 10 mins walk (0212) 522 02 98 9am-6:30pm daily (from 2:30pm Fri) Prayer times

Dominating the skyline of the Golden Horn, this vast mosque is perched upon the historic district's highest hill. It is one of Istanbul's finest examples of imperial mosque architecture – the elegant symmetry of its prayer hall is especially breathtaking.

Istanbul's most important mosque is both a tribute to its brilliant architect, the renowned Sinan, and serves as a fitting memorial to its illustrious founder, Süleyman the Magnificent *(p54)*. It was built between 1550 and 1557 above the Golden Horn in the grounds of the old palace, Eski Saray *(p118)*. Like the city's other imperial mosques, the Süleymaniye Mosque transcends its role as a mere place of worship; it is also a charitable foundation, or *külliye (p33)*. The mosque is surrounded by its former hospital, soup kitchen, schools, caravanserai and bathhouse. This complex provided a welfare system, which fed over 1,000 of the city's poor – Muslims, Christians and Jews alike – every day.

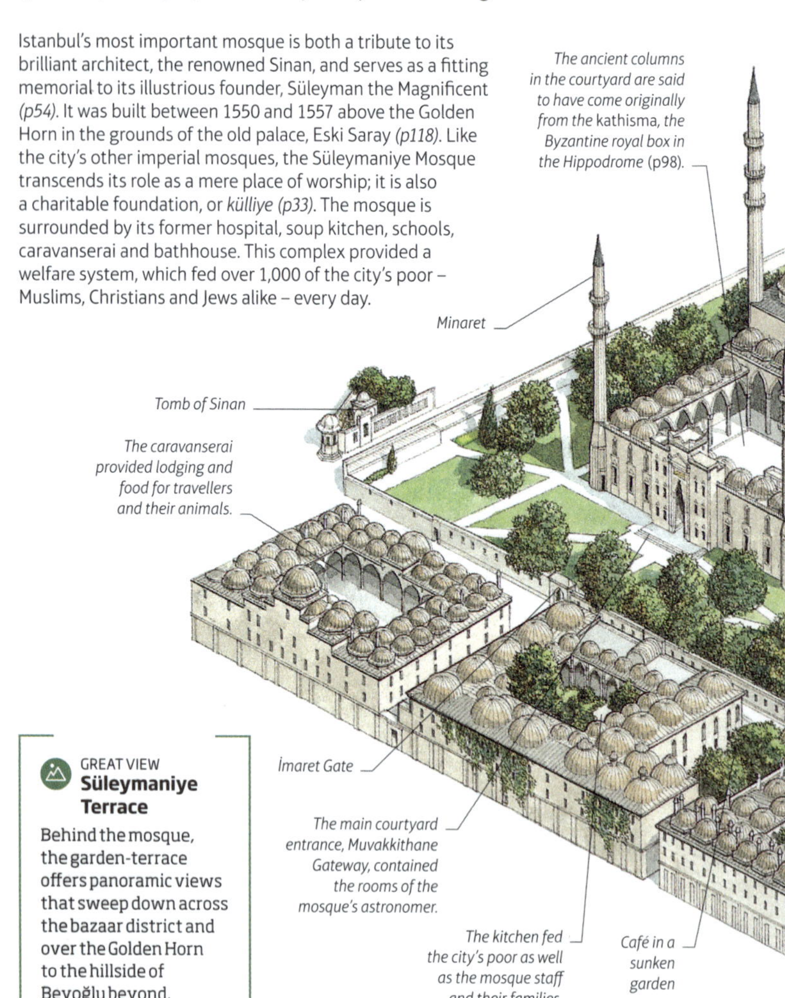

GREAT VIEW
Süleymaniye Terrace

Behind the mosque, the garden-terrace offers panoramic views that sweep down across the bazaar district and over the Golden Horn to the hillside of Beyoğlu beyond.

Süleymaniye Mosque's central courtyard surrounded by ancient columns ↑

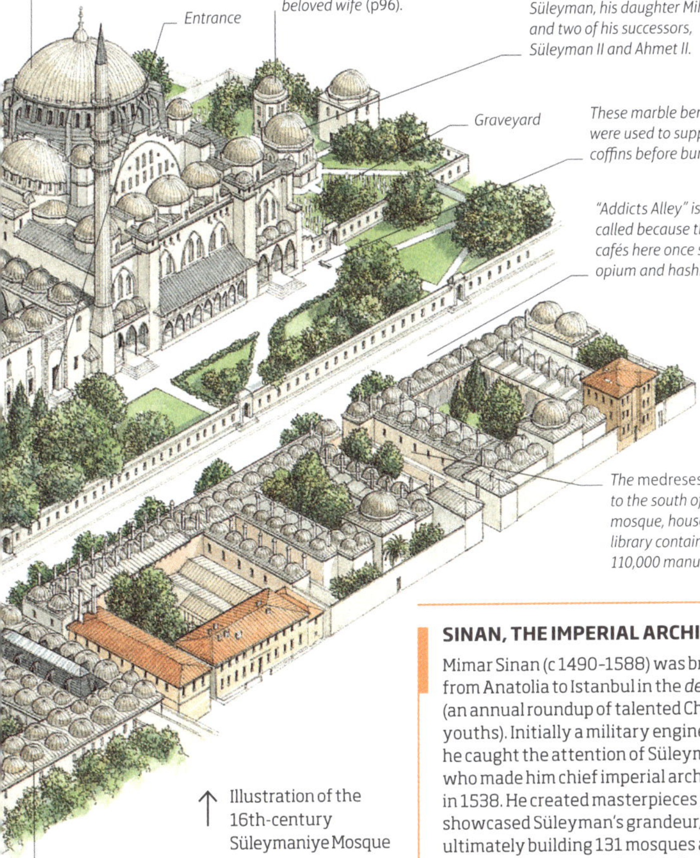

A sense of soaring space and calm strikes you as you enter the mosque.

Entrance

The Tomb of Roxelana contains Süleyman's beloved wife (p96).

In the Tomb of Süleyman, it is said that ceramic stars set with emeralds sparkle above the coffins of Süleyman, his daughter Mihrimah and two of his successors, Süleyman II and Ahmet II.

Graveyard

These marble benches were used to support coffins before burial.

"Addicts Alley" is so called because the cafés here once sold opium and hashish.

The medreses (p33), *to the south of the mosque, house a library containing 110,000 manuscripts.*

Former hospital and asylum

↑ Illustration of the 16th-century Süleymaniye Mosque

SINAN, THE IMPERIAL ARCHITECT

Mimar Sinan (c 1490–1588) was brought from Anatolia to Istanbul in the *devşirme* (an annual roundup of talented Christian youths). Initially a military engineer, he caught the attention of Süleyman I, who made him chief imperial architect in 1538. He created masterpieces that showcased Süleyman's grandeur, ultimately building 131 mosques and 200 other buildings before his death.

GRAND BAZAAR

KAPALI ÇARŞI

F8 Çarşıkapı Cad, Beyazıt Beyazıt (for Çarşıkapı Gate), Çemberlitaş (for Nuruosmaniye Gate) 61B 8:30am-7pm Mon-Sat

Much like a 600-year-old shopping mall, this city-within-a-city sprawl of *hans* (caravanserais) and *bedestens* (market halls) has been a bustling hub of commerce and trade since the 15th century. This labyrinth of streets, covered by painted vaults, is lined with thousands of booth-like shops, whose wares spill out attracting visitors and locals alike.

İç Bedesten

Also known as Cevahir Bedesteni, this is the oldest section of the bazaar. The structure is said to have been commissioned by Mehmet the Conqueror in 1460 to generate revenue for the Hagia Sophia. Initially, it functioned as a locked warehouse, but later it transformed into a specialized marketplace where jewellers could make and sell their wares.

Zincirli Han

Widely regarded as one of the prettiest *hans* in the bustling bazaar, Zincirli Han stands as a testament to remarkable craftsmanship. It is an exceptional spot for those seeking unique and personalized adornments. Here, discerning patrons have the unique opportunity to commission bespoke pieces of jewellery, crafted precisely to their individual design specifications.

Oriental Kiosk

Originally built as a vibrant coffee house in the 17th century, the Oriental Kiosk was a popular social hub. Over the centuries, the building has undergone significant transformation. Today, it houses a jewellery shop, offering a modern commercial function while still preserving its historical essence.

↑ The Oriental Kiosk, now housing a unique jewellery shop

↑ Browsing wares in the colourful shops of the Grand Bazaar

INSIDER TIP
Navigating the Bazaar

To most easily navigate the bazaar, enter through the southeast Nuruosmaniye Gate, which will lead to the main thoroughfare of Kalpakçılar Caddesi, from which you should veer north to reach the core.

Gateway to the İç Bedesten

The eagle depicted on the gateway to the İç Bedesten, while a recognizable symbol associated with the Byzantine emperors, is in fact, much like the bazaar itself, a later addition that postdates the Byzantine era.

Sandal Bedesteni

A remarkable example of 16th-century Ottoman architecture, the Sandal Bedesteni features a distinctive roof that is characterized by 20 brick domes. These domes are expertly supported on a series of robust piers, which evenly distribute the weight and stress. This structural design allows for the creation of a vast, open interior space that was likely utilized for various commercial or public functions.

⑥

Kalpakçılar Caddesi

The thoroughfare in the bazaar, Kalpakçılar Caddesi offers a dazzling spectacle. Along its length, the street is flanked by an array of jewellery shops, featuring sparkling and gleaming windows with a wide range of precious metals and gemstones.

Marble Fountain

Located in the centre of the bazaar are two magnificent marble fountains. These ornate structures feature a delicate interplay of copper and marble, and were once essential conduits for fresh, cool water, making them the lifeblood of the vibrant marketplace.

TOP 5 SOUVENIRS TO BUY

Carpets, Kilims and Cicims
Shop for carpets, *kilims* (flat-weaves) and *cicims* (embroidery-like tapestry weaves).

Peştamals
Traditional *peştamals* (handwoven hammam towels) made from high-quality cotton.

Tea and Coffee Sets
Consider purchasing the engraved metal cup-holders, which often include a *cezve* (Turkish coffee pot).

Jewellery
Buy silver and gold pieces that incorporate Ottoman designs or Anatolian motifs.

Textiles
Embroidered Uzbek Suzani textiles are precious finds.

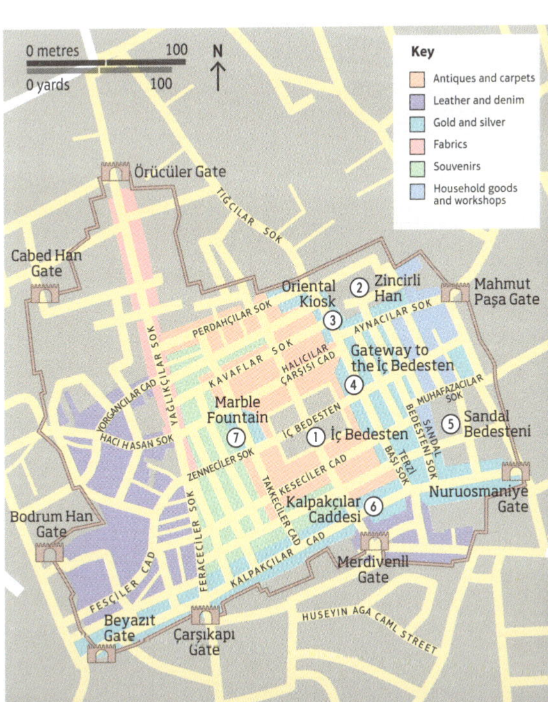

EXPERIENCE MORE

↑ A wide variety of spices and condiments on sale at the Spice Bazaar

Spice Bazaar

Mısır Çarşısı

G7 Cami Meydanı Sok Eminönü 8am-7pm Mon-Sat

This cavernous, L-shaped market was built in the early 17th century as an extension of the New Mosque complex. Its revenues once helped maintain the mosque's philanthropic institutions.

In Turkish the market is named the Mısır Çarşısı – the Egyptian Bazaar – because it was built with money paid as duty on Egyptian imports. In English it is usually known as the Spice Bazaar. From medieval times spices were a vital and expensive part of cooking and they became the market's main produce. The bazaar came to specialize in spices from Asia, taking advantage of Istanbul's site on the trade route between the East (where most spices were grown) and Europe.

Stalls in the bazaar stock spices, herbs and other foods such as honey, nuts, sweetmeats and *pastirma* (cured beef). Today's expensive Eastern commodity, caviar, is also available, the best variety being Iranian. Nowadays, an eclectic range of other items can be found in the Spice Bazaar, including everything from household goods, toys and clothes to surprising aphrodisiacs. The square between the two arms of the bazaar is full of commercial activity, with cafés, and stalls selling plants and pets.

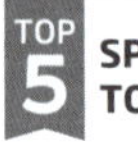

SPICES TO BUY

Aleppo Pepper Flakes (Pul Biber)
Seasoning made from red Aleppo pepper.

Sumac (Sumak)
A sour spice made from the wild sumac shrub.

Kofta Spice-Blend (Köfte Baharatı)
Savoury blend of five or six spices.

Urfa Pepper Flakes (Isot)
Smokey, maroon-black dried red pepper flakes.

Nigella Seeds (Çörek Otu)
Onion-flavoured seeds.

New Mosque

Yeni Cami

G7 Yeni Cami Meydanı, Eminönü Eminönü 9am-6:30pm daily (from 2:30pm Fri) Prayer times

Situated at the southern end of Galata Bridge, the New Mosque is one of the most prominent mosques in the city. It dates from the time when a few women from the harem became powerful enough to dictate the policies of the Ottoman sultans. The mosque was started in 1597 by Safiye, mother of Mehmet III, but building was suspended on the sultan's death as his mother then lost her position. It was not completed until 1663, after Turhan Hatice, mother of Mehmet IV, took up the project.

Though the mosque was built after the classical period of Ottoman architecture, it shares many traits with earlier imperial foundations, including a monumental courtyard. The mosque once had a hospital, school and public baths.

The turquoise, blue and white floral tiles decorating the interior are from İznik *(p186)* and date from the mid-17th century, though by this time the quality of the tiles produced there was already in decline. More striking are the tiled lunettes and bold Koranic frieze decorating the porch between the courtyard and the prayer hall.

At the far left-hand corner of the upper gallery is the sultan's loge, which is directly linked to his personal suite of rooms.

Did You Know?

There are more than 100 different tulip and carnation motifs on the tiles in Rüstem Paşa Mosque.

Rüstem Paşa Mosque

Rüstem Paşa Camii

F7 Hasırcılar Cad, Eminönü Eminönü 9am-6pm daily (from 2:30pm Fri) Prayer times

Raised above the busy shops and warehouses around the Spice Bazaar, this mosque was built in 1561 by the great architect Sinan *(p109)* for Rüstem Paşa, son-in-law of and grand vizier to Süleyman I *(p54)*. Rents from the businesses in the bazaar were intended to pay for the upkeep of the mosque.

The wealth of its decoration says something about the amount of money that the corrupt Rüstem managed to salt away during his career. Most of the interior is covered in İznik tiles of the very highest quality.

The four piers are adorned with tiles of one design but the rest of the prayer hall is a riot of different patterns, from abstract to floral. Some of the finest tiles are found on the galleries. No other mosque in the city is adorned with such a magnificent blanket of tiles.

The mosque is also notable for its numerous windows: it was built with as many as the structure would allow.

Golden Horn

Haliç

G6 Eminönü 55T, 99A

Known as the world's greatest natural harbour, the Golden Horn is a flooded river valley, which flows southwest into the Bosphorus. The estuary attracted settlers to its shores in the 7th century BCE and later enabled Constantinople to become a major port. According to legend, the Byzantines threw so many valuables into it during the Ottoman conquest *(p53)*, that the waters glistened with gold. Heavily polluted until recently, the waters today are clean enough to support fish and cormorants. There are plans to turn a part of it into a marina.

For hundreds of years the city's trade was conducted by ships that off-loaded their goods into warehouses lining the Golden Horn. Nowadays, though, the great container ships coming to Istanbul use ports on the Sea of Marmara. Spanning the mouth of the Horn is the Galata Bridge, which joins Eminönü to Galata. The bridge, built in 1994, opens in the middle to allow access for tall ships. It is a good place from which to view the complex geography of the city and admire the minaret-filled skyline.

To the north of Galata Bridge lies the Haliç Bridge. It was opened in 2013 amid controversy as its prominent profile interrupts views of the Old City's famous skyline. The bridge carries the M2 Metro line across the Golden Horn, linking the Old City with Beyoğlu. Beyond it lies the Atatürk (Unkapanı) Bridge. There is also a motorway bridge across the estuary near the terminus of the Theodisian Walls, much further up the Horn. The T5 tram route runs along the Golden Horn's southern shore between Eminönü and Eyüp.

Exquisite tiles of the Rüstem Paşa Mosque, and *(inset)* its distinctive dome and minaret ↓

Valens Aqueduct

Bozdoğan Kemeri

D7 Atatürk Bulvarı, Saraçhane M Vezneciler Laleli 28, 61B, 87

Emperor Valens built this mighty aqueduct, supported by two imposing rows of arches, in the late 4th century CE. Part of the elaborate water system feeding the palaces and fountains of the Byzantine capital, it brought water from the Belgrade Forest as well as mountains over 200 km (125 miles) away to a vast cistern, which stood in the vicinity of what is now Beyazıt Square *(p118)*.

The aqueduct supplied the city's water until the late 19th century, when it was made obsolete by a modern water distribution network. The original open channels, however, had by this stage already been replaced first by clay pipes and then by iron ones.

The structure was repaired many times during its history, latterly by sultans Mustafa II (1695–1703) and Ahmet III. It was originally 1,000 m (3,300 ft) long, of which 625 m (2,050 ft) remain.

INSIDER TIP
Foodies' Paradise

Kadınlar Pazarı, which is located underneath the aqueduct, is popular for restaurants specializing in meat dishes from Turkey's southeast, and shops selling local cheeses and honey, dried fruits, nuts and olives.

Kalenderhane Mosque

Kalenderhane Camii

E8 16 Mart Şehitleri Cad, Saraçhane M Vezneciler Laleli/Üniversite 9am-6:30pm daily (from 2:30pm Fri) Prayer times

Sitting in the lee of the Valens Aqueduct, this Byzantine church has a chequered history. It was built and rebuilt several times between the 6th and 12th centuries, before being converted into a mosque shortly after the conquest in 1453 *(53)*. It is named after the Kalender brotherhood of dervishes, who occupied it for some years following the conquest.

The building has the cruciform layout characteristic of Byzantine churches of the period. Some of the decoration remaining from its last incarnation, as the Church of Theotokos Kyriotissa (her Ladyship Mary, Mother of God), also survives in the prayer hall with its marble panelling and in the fragments of fresco in the narthex (entrance hall). A series of frescoes depicting the life of St Francis of Assisi were removed in the 1970s. Fragments can be seen in the Archaeological Museums *(p64)*,

↑ The impressive Valens Aqueduct crossing Atatürk Bulvarı

Each tomb has beautiful İznik tiles and lustrous original stained glass. That of Şehzade Mehmet also features the finest painted dome in Istanbul.

as can the only iconoclastic figurative mosaic to have survived in the city, the Icon of the Presentation *(p71)*.

Prince's Mosque

Şehzade Camii

D7 Şehzade Başı Cad 70, Saraçhane Vezneciler Laleli/Üniversite 9am-6:30pm daily (from 2:30pm Fri); tombs: 9am-5pm Tue-Sun Prayer times

This mosque complex was erected by Süleyman the Magnificent *(p54)* in memory of his eldest son by Roxelana *(p96)*, Şehzade (Prince) Mehmet, who died of smallpox at the age of 21. The building was Sinan's *(p109)* first major imperial commission and was completed in 1548. The architect used a decorative style in designing this mosque before abandoning it in favour of the classical austerity that characterizes his later work. The mosque is approached through an elegant porticoed inner courtyard, while the other institutions making up the mosque complex, including a *medresa (p37)*, are enclosed within an outer courtyard.

The interior of the mosque is unusual and was something of an experiment in that it is symmetrical, having a semi-dome on each of its four sides.

The three tombs located to the rear of the mosque, belonging to Şehzade Mehmet himself and grand viziers İbrahim Paşa and Rüstem Paşa, are the finest in the city. Each has beautiful İznik tiles *(p187)* and lustrous original stained glass. That of Şehzade Mehmet also features the finest painted dome in Istanbul.

On Fridays you will notice women flocking to another tomb within the complex, that of Helvacı Baba, as they have done for over 400 years. Helvacı Baba is said to miraculously cure illness, solve fertility problems and find husbands or accommodation for those who beseech him.

Vefa Church Mosque

Molla Gürani Camii

E7 Vefa Cad, Cami Sok, Vefa Vezneciler 28, 61B, 87 Prayer times only

The elaborate Byzantine Church of St Theodore was built between the 12th and 14th centuries, which was the last great era of Byzantine construction. It was converted into a mosque following the Ottoman conquest of the city in 1453 *(p53)*. Today, it is known as Molla Gürani Mosque. Its attractive brick exterior is admirable. The mosque reopened after restoration in 2021, but is usually shut outside of prayer time. The best way to see its interior is at the end of prayer time when there is usually a 30-minute window before the caretaker locks the door again.

DRINK

Vefa Bozacısı

Since 1876, this historic, wood-lined bar-shop has been serving traditional Turkish *boza*, a drink made from fermented barley and dusted with cinnamon.

E7 Vefa Cad 66
vefa.com.tr

Red-brick exterior of the sprawling Vefa Church Mosque

Striking marble interior, with stained-glass windows, of the Tulip Mosque

Tulip Mosque

Lâleli Camii

D8 Ordu Cad, Lâleli M Vezneciler Lâleli/Üniversite 9am-6pm daily (from 2:30pm Fri) Prayer times

Built from 1760–64, this mosque complex is the finest example of Baroque style in the city. It was designed by the renowned architect Mehmet Tahir Ağa. Inside the mosque, a variety of gaudy, coloured marble covers all of its surfaces.

More fascinating is the area underneath the main body of the mosque. This is a great hall supported on eight piers, with a fountain in the middle. The hall is now used as a popular subterranean clothing marketplace that's a favourite haunt for wholesale traders from Central Asia and Eastern Europe.

The nearby Büyük Taş Han, or Big Stone Han, is likely to have been part of the mosque's original complex but now houses a number of leather shops and a restaurant.

Barın Han

G9 Boyacı Ahmet Sok 4, Bindirdirek Çemberlitaş 10am-6pm Tue-Sun w barinhan.com

This building was once the studio and workshop of Istanbul-born Emin Barın (1913–87). One of the 20th century's most acclaimed Turkish decorative artists, Barın was best known for his calligraphy and bookbinding. Today, the structure hosts a permanent exhibition of his life and work, featuring prints of his calligraphy, as well as various temporary art exhibitions by local artists. It also serves as a studio space for local creatives.

Forum of Theodosius

Theodosius Forumu

E9 Ordu Cad, Beyazıt Laleli/Üniversite, Beyazıt

Constantinople featured several public squares, with the largest at present-day Beyazıt Square *(p114)*. It was originally called the Forum Tauri (the Forum of the Bull), due to the huge bronze bull in its centre, where sacrificial animals and, sometimes, criminals were roasted.

After Theodosius the Great enlarged it in the late 4th century, the forum was named in his honour. Relics of the triumphal arch and other structures can be found on either side of the tram tracks along Ordu Caddesi. The huge columns, with striking peacock-tail motifs, were reused all over the city once the forum had become derelict. Some can be seen in the Basilica Cistern *(p94)*. Other fragments from the forum were built into Beyazıt Hamamı, a Turkish bath further west down Ordu.

CALIGRAPHY

Calligraphy is a revered Islamic art, passed from expert to apprentice, with the aim of the pupil being able to replicate perfectly the hand of their teacher. In Ottoman Turkey, calligraphy was used to ornament *firmans* (imperial decrees), poetry and the Koran. However, many examples are also to be found on buildings, carved in wood and applied to architectural ceramics. The art of the calligrapher was to beautify the writing without altering the sense of the text, especially for the Koran. With the text of a *firman*, made to impress as much as to be read, the calligrapher could afford to add more flourishes.

HIDDEN GEM

Hammam History

Located on Beyazıt Square, Gedikpaşa Hamamı *(gedikpasa hamami.com)* was once the largest in Istanbul. It is now a museum dedicated to the history and culture of the Turkish bath.

Zeyrek Çinili Hammam

D7 İtfaiye Cad 44, Zeyrek M Vezneciler 8am-10pm Tue-Sun (museum: to 6pm) zeyrekcinilihamam.com

This 16th-century hammam, commissioned by Ottoman navy admiral Barbaros Hayreddin Paşa and designed by the imperial architect Sinan, was abandoned for decades before reopening in 2023, following a 13-year renovation.

Visitors can indulge in luxury scrubs, soaks and foam-massage rituals in the separate male and female bathing areas that retain their original layout. Its marbled rooms are studded with alcoves, topped by *muqarna* (honeycomb vaulting) and decorative flourishes, while light streams down from the star-shaped oculi windows in the domed ceiling.

Separate from the bathing rooms, the hammam complex also houses a museum displaying artifacts unearthed during the restoration, including fragments of the İznik tiles that once lined the interior walls, while the cistern beneath the hammam hosts a rotating programme of exhibitions. English guided tours of the museum are available every Wednesday at 11am; museum admission is free every Thursday.

Bodrum Mosque

Bodrum Cami

D9 Sait Efendi Sok, Laleli M Vezneciler Laleli/Üniversite 9am-6pm daily (from 2:30pm Fri) Prayer times

Narrow courses of brick forming the outside walls, and a window-pierced dome, betray the early origins of this mosque as a Byzantine church. It was built in the early 10th century by co-Emperor Romanus I Lacapenus (r 919–44) as part of the Monastery of Myrelaion and adjoined a small palace. The palace was later converted into a nunnery where the emperor's widow, Theophano, lived out her final years. She was eventually buried in a sanctuary chapel beneath the church, which is closed to the public. In the late 15th century, the church was converted into a mosque by Mesih Paşa, a descendant of the Palaeologus family, the last dynasty to rule Byzantium. The building was gutted by fire several times and nothing remains of its internal decoration. Today, it is still a working mosque and is accessed via a stairway that leads up to a piazza filled with coat stalls.

↓ Immaculate interior of the bathhouse Zeyrek Çinili Hammam

Beyazıt Square

Beyazıt Meydanı

F8 Ordu Cad, Beyazıt Beyazıt

Beyazıt Square is the most vibrant area in the city's old quarter. It hosts a weekly flea market, offering carpets, Central Asian silks and general bric-a-brac. When you are tired of rummaging, head to one of the many cafés here.

On the northern side of the square is the Moorish-style gateway of the **Istanbul University**. The university's 19th-century main building was once the Ministry of War. Within the campus's wooded grounds is the Beyazıt Tower, a marble fire-watching station built in 1828 on the site of Eski Saray, the first palace of Mehmet the Conqueror *(p53)*. Two of its original timber towers were destroyed by fire. The tower is illuminated to indicate weather conditions by using different lights.

On the square's eastern side is **Beyazıt Mosque**, commissioned by Beyazıt II and completed in 1506, making it the oldest surviving imperial mosque in the city. Behind its grand portal lies a harmonious courtyard with an elegant domed fountain, surrounded by columns of granite and green and red Egyptian porphyry, as well as a multi-coloured marble pavement. The mosque's interior is inspired by the Hagia Sophia *(p88)*.

Did You Know?

The Beyazıt Tower is lit in different colours to indicate the current weather forecast.

Istanbul University
Beyazıt, 34452 Fatih

Beyazıt Mosque
Yeniçeriler Cd 9am-6pm daily (from 2:30pm Fri) Prayer times

Çorlulu Ali Paşa Courtyard

Çorlulu Ali Paşa Külliyesi

F9 Yeniçeriler Cad, Beyazıt Beyazıt Daily

Like many others in the city, the *medrese (p33)* of this mosque complex outside the Grand Bazaar has become the setting for a group of outdoor cafés. It was built for Çorlulu Ali Paşa, son-in-law of Mustafa II, who served as grand vizier under Ahmet III. Ahmet later exiled him to the island of Lésbos and had him executed there in 1711. Some years later his family smuggled his head back to Istanbul and interred it in the tomb built for him. The complex is entered from Yeniçeriler Caddesi by two alleyways. Several carpet shops now inhabit the *medrese* and rugs are hung and spread all around, waiting for prospective buyers. The carpet shops share the *medrese* with a *kahvehanes* (traditional cafés; open 9am to 2am), which circle the courtyard and have seating under the arcades. They are popular with locals and students from the nearby university. Here you can sit and drink tea, and perhaps smoke a *nargile* (shisha pipe), while deciding which carpet to buy.

Situated across Bileyciler Sokak, an alleyway off Çorlulu Ali Paşa Courtyard, is the Koca Sinan Paşa tomb complex, the courtyard of which is another

Moorish-style gate to Istanbul University, Beyazıt Square

HIDDEN GEM
Historical Baths

Just off the other side of Yeniçeriler Caddesi is Gedikpaşa Hamamı *(gedikpasa hamami.com)*, thought to be the oldest working Turkish baths in the city.

tea garden. The charming *medrese*, mausoleum and *sebil* (a fountain where water was handed out to passers-by) were built in 1593 by Davut Ağa, who succeeded Sinan *(p109)* as chief architect of the empire. The tomb of Koca Sinan Paşa, grand vizier under Murat III and Mehmet III, is a striking 16-sided structure.

Valide Han

Valide Han

F8 Junction of Tarakçılar Sok & Çakmakçılar Yokuşu, Beyazıt Beyazıt, then 10 mins walk 9:30am-5pm Mon-Sat

If the Grand Bazaar *(p110)* seems large, it is sobering to realize that it is only the covered part of a huge area of seething commercial activity, which reaches all the way to the Golden Horn *(p113)*. As in the Grand Bazaar, most manufacturing and trade takes place in *hans*, courtyards hidden away from the street behind shaded gateways.

The largest *han* in Istanbul is Valide Han. It was built in 1651 by Kösem, the mother of Sultan Murat IV. You enter it from Çakmakçılar Yokuşu through a massive portal. After passing through an irregularly shaped forecourt, you come out into a large courtyard centring on a Shiite mosque. This was built when the *han* became the centre of Iranian trade in the city. Today, the *han* throbs to the rhythm of hundreds of weaving looms. In the courtyard, if you turn right and take the steps leading upstairs through the *han's* dilapidated upper storey, you'll find a hidden café with rooftop views of the old city.

A short walk further down Çakmakçılar Yokuşu is Büyük Yeni Han, hidden behind another impressive doorway. This Baroque *han*, built in 1764, has three arcaded levels. The entrance is on the top level, where distinctive bird cages are among the wares.

In the labyrinth of narrow streets around these *hans*, artisans are grouped according to their wares: on Bakırcılar Caddesi, for instance, you will find metalworkers, while the crafters of Uzunçarşı Caddesi make wooden items.

HANS OF ISTANBUL

The innumerable *hans* in central Istanbul were originally constructed to provide temporary accommodation for travelling traders and their livestock. Typically built as part of a mosque complex *(p33)*, a *han* consists of two- or three-storey buildings around a courtyard, accessed via a large, secured gateway. With the advent of vans and lorries, many hans were converted into small factories and workshops. Although often in disrepair, the bustling activity within these working hans ensure the continuation of the buildings' rich trading heritage.

Customers browsing the bookstores in the Book Bazaar

Book Bazaar

Çarşisi

F8 Sahaflar Çarşısı Sok, Beyazıt Laleli/Üniversite 8am-8pm Mon-Sat

This charming booksellers' courtyard, on the site of the Byzantine book and paper market, can be entered either from Beyazıt Square or from inside the Grand Bazaar *(p110)*. Racks are laden with all sorts of books, from tourist guides to academic tomes.

During the early Ottoman period *(p54)*, printed books were seen as a corrupting European influence and were banned in Turkey. As a result, the bazaar only sold manuscripts. Then on 31 January 1729 İbrahim Müteferrika (1674–1745) produced the first printed book in the Turkish language, an Arabic dictionary. His bust stands in the centre of the market today. Note that book prices are fixed and cannot be haggled over.

Çemberlitaş Hamamı

G9 Vezirhan Cad 8, Çemberlitaş Çemberlitaş 6am-midnight daily cemberlitashamami.com

Unlike most hammams in and around Istanbul's historic peninsula, which are known for their luxury services, the Çemberlitas Hamamı still offers a traditional and authentic Turkish bath experience. Visitors have the option of a full treatment with a professional attendant on standby, or they can enjoy a do-it-yourself traditional scrub and soak. The latter, though not cheap, is still affordable. Many locals and tourists alike praise its historic charm.

This beautiful hammam building, commissioned by Sultan Selim II's powerful and influential chief consort, Nurbanu, and designed by the Ottoman chief architect Sinan, has been providing customers with a steaming, exfoliating cleanse since 1584. After being handed the *peştamal* (hammam towel), soap and *kese* (exfoliating glove), visitors head to the *Sıcaklık* (hot room) to sweat on the *göbektaşı* (heated marble platform). Once finished – there's no time limit – marble basins are used to soap up and scrub down.

Set within a serene small garden, the mosque features a simple rectangular structure accessed through a deep stone porch.

Atik Ali Paşa Mosque

Atik Ali Paşa Camii

G9 Yeniçeriler Cad, Beyazıt Çemberlitaş 9am-6:30pm daily (from 2:30pm Fri) Prayer times

Hidden behind the walls in the tranquil area south of the Grand Bazaar, this mosque is one of the oldest in the city, offering a glimpse into Istanbul's rich history. Constructed in 1496 during the reign of Beyazıt II, the successor of Mehmet the Conqueror, it was commissioned by his eunuch grand vizier, Atik Ali Paşa. The mosque is set within a serene and small garden that provides a peaceful escape from the hustle and bustle of its surroundings. Its architectural design is characterized by a simple rectangular structure accessed through a deep stone porch that adds to its charm.

A distinctive feature is its mihrab, which is uniquely housed in a kind of apse, setting it apart from other mosques of the era. Unfortunately, most of the other buildings that were part of the original mosque complex, including the *imaret* (kitchen), *medrese* (Islamic educational institution) and *tekke* (Sufi monastery), have largely disappeared due to the expansion of the busy Yeniçeriler Caddesi.

Constantine's Column

Çemberlitaş

G9 Yeniçeriler Cad, Çemberlitaş Çemberlitaş

A resilient survivor of both storm and fire, this impressive 35-m- (115-ft-) high column was constructed in 330 CE to commemorate the inauguration of Constantinople as the new Byzantine capital

Beautiful Atik Ali Paşa Mosque and its surrounding garden

Constantine's Column towering over the street

(p51). Once a dominant feature of the magnificent Forum of Constantine, the column is made of striking porphyry, a material brought from Heliopolis in Egypt. It was originally surmounted by a Corinthian capital bearing a statue of Emperor Constantine dressed as Apollo, which was lost in a storm in 1106.

Despite its relatively unimposing appearance, it has been carefully preserved over the centuries. In 416 CE, the ten stone drums that make up the column were reinforced with metal rings to enhance stability. These rings were renewed in 1701 by Sultan Mustafa II, leading to its Turkish name, Çemberlitaş (meaning the "Hooped Column"). In English it is sometimes referred to as the Burnt Column because it was damaged by several fires, especially one in 1779, which decimated the Grand Bazaar *(p110)*.

A variety of fantastical holy relics were supposedly entombed in the base of the column, which has since been encased in stone to strengthen it. These included the axe that Noah used to build the ark, Mary Magdalen's flask of anointing oil, and remains of the loaves of bread with which Christ fed the multitude.

Nuruosmaniye Mosque

Nuruosmaniye Camii

G8 Vezirhanı Cad, Beyazıt Çemberlitaş 8:30am-6:30pm daily (from 2:30pm Fri) Prayer times

Nuruosmaniye Caddesi, a street lined with carpet and antique shops, leads to the gateway of the mosque from which it gets its name. Commissioned by Sultan Mahmut I in 1748, and completed by his brother, Osman III, in 1755, this mosque is a perfect example of early Baroque architecture. It is distinguished by its massive cornices and elaborate ornamentation. Its most striking features, however, are the enormous unconcealed arches supporting the dome, each pierced by a mass of windows. Light floods into the plain square prayer hall, allowing you to see the finely carved wooden calligraphic frieze that runs around the walls above the gallery.

On the other side of the mosque complex is the Nuruosmaniye Gate. This leads into Kalpakçılar Caddesi, the Grand Bazaar's street of jewellery shops *(p111)*.

Mahmut Paşa Mosque

Mahmut Paşa Camii

G8 Vezirhanı Cad, Beyazıt Çemberlitaş 61B 8:30am-6:30pm daily (from 2:30pm Fri) Prayer times

Built in 1462, just nine years after the Ottomans took over Istanbul, this mosque holds the distinction of being the first large mosque constructed within the city walls. Unfortunately, some of its original charm has been lost due to overzealous restoration efforts, but it still attracts many history buffs. It was originally commissioned by Mahmut Paşa, a Byzantine aristocrat who converted to Islam and rose to the position of grand vizier under Mehmet the Conqueror.

In 1474 Paşa's disastrous military leadership incurred the sultan's fury, and he was executed. His tomb, located behind the mosque, is notable for its unique Moorish-style decoration, with intricate small tiles in shades of blue, black, turquoise and green arranged in swirling geometric patterns.

EAT

Saaf-İ Kebap Salonu

An excellent-value-for-money spot, the Saaf-İ Kebap Salonu serves traditional kebab plates.

F8 İskender Boğazı Sok 17/1, Çemberlıtaş 0212 512 2626

Aslan Restaurant

Enjoy *lokanta*-style (traditional Turkish restaurant) dishes here.

G8 Vezirhan Cad 66, Çemberlıtaş 0212 513 7610 Sun

Aynen Dürüm

Aynen Dürüm offers the best *dürüm* (döner kebab wrap) in the Grand Bazaar.

G8 Muhafazacılar Sok 29/B, Kapalı Çarşı 0212 527 4728 Sun

A SHORT WALK
AROUND THE SPICE BAZAAR

Distance 1.5 km (1 mile) **Time** 25 minutes
Nearest tram Eminönü

The narrow streets around the Spice Bazaar encapsulate the spirit of old Istanbul. From here buses, taxis and trams head off across the Galata Bridge and into the interior of the city. The blast of ships' horns signals the departure of ferries from Eminönü to Asian Istanbul. It is the quarter's shops and markets, though, that are the focus of attention for the eager shoppers who crowd the Spice Bazaar and the streets around it, sometimes breaking for a leisurely tea beneath the trees in its courtyard. Across the way, and entirely aloof from the bustle, rise the domes of the New Mosque. On one of the commercial alleyways that radiate out from the mosque, an inconspicuous doorway leads upstairs to the terrace of the serene, tile-covered Rüstem Paşa Mosque.

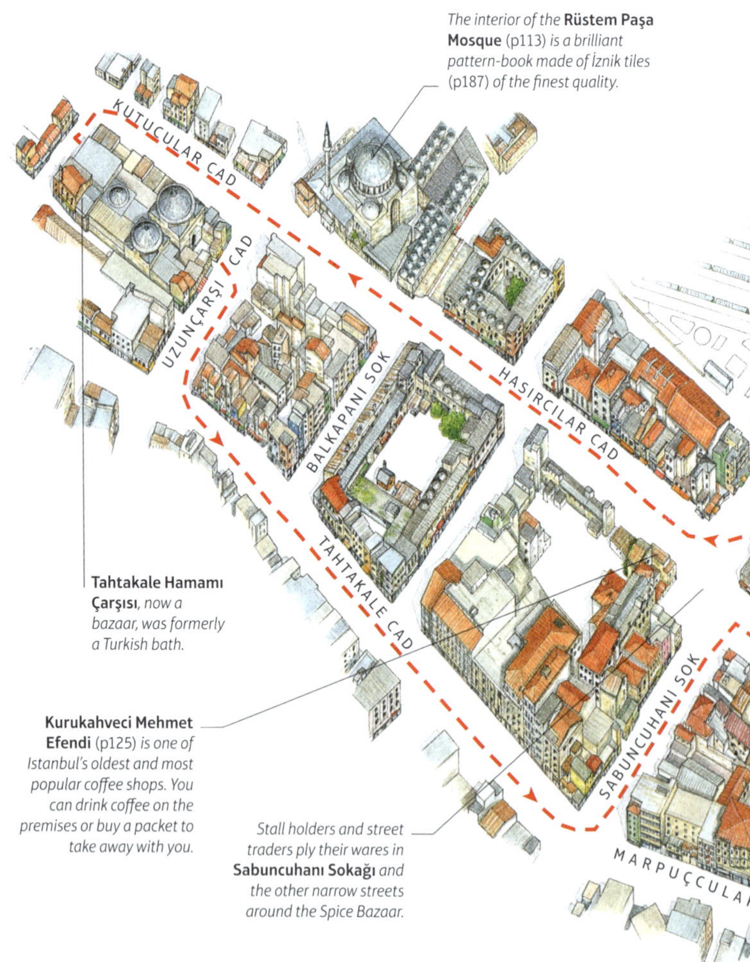

The interior of the **Rüstem Paşa Mosque** (p113) *is a brilliant pattern-book made of İznik tiles* (p187) *of the finest quality.*

Tahtakale Hamamı Çarşısı, *now a bazaar, was formerly a Turkish bath.*

Kurukahveci Mehmet Efendi (p125) *is one of Istanbul's oldest and most popular coffee shops. You can drink coffee on the premises or buy a packet to take away with you.*

Stall holders and street traders ply their wares in **Sabuncuhanı Sokağı** *and the other narrow streets around the Spice Bazaar.*

Malatya Pazarı

Around the Spice Bazaar
THE BAZAAR QUARTER

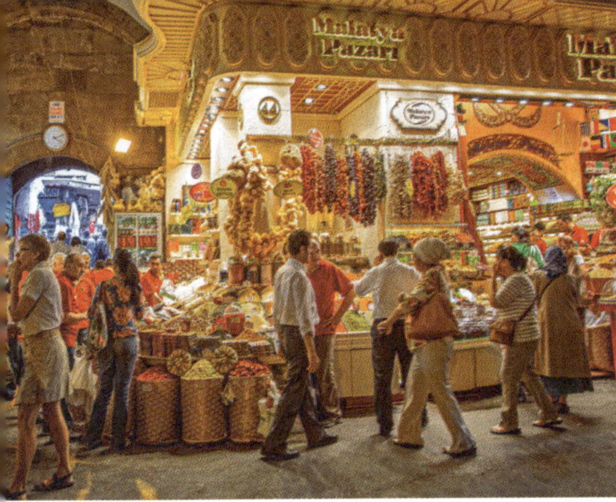

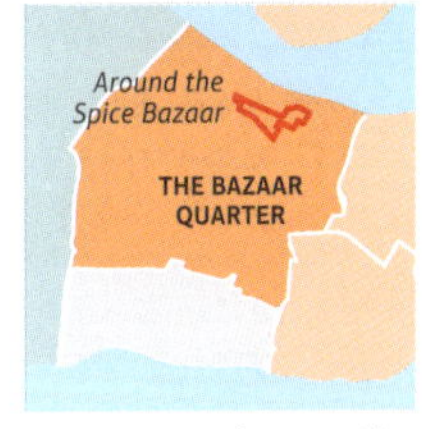

Locator Map
For more detail see p106

↑ Wide range of colourful items for sale at Istanbul's Spice Bazaar

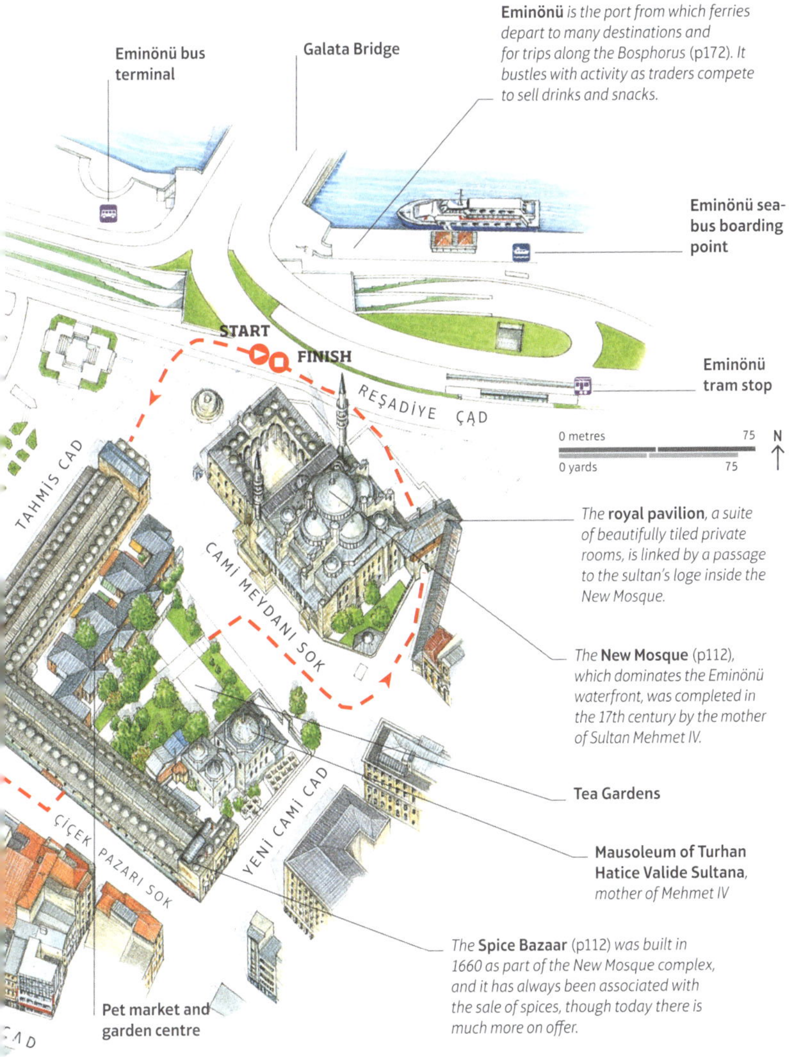

Eminönü bus terminal
Galata Bridge
Eminönü *is the port from which ferries depart to many destinations and for trips along the Bosphorus (p172). It bustles with activity as traders compete to sell drinks and snacks.*
Eminönü sea-bus boarding point
START
FINISH
Eminönü tram stop
REŞADİYE ÇAD
TAHMİS CAD
CAMİ MEYDANI SOK
ÇİÇEK PAZARI SOK
YENİ CAMİ CAD
0 metres 75
0 yards 75
N
The **royal pavilion**, *a suite of beautifully tiled private rooms, is linked by a passage to the sultan's loge inside the New Mosque.*
The **New Mosque** (p112), *which dominates the Eminönü waterfront, was completed in the 17th century by the mother of Sultan Mehmet IV.*
Tea Gardens
Mausoleum of Turhan Hatice Valide Sultana, *mother of Mehmet IV*
The **Spice Bazaar** (p112) *was built in 1660 as part of the New Mosque complex, and it has always been associated with the sale of spices, though today there is much more on offer.*
Pet market and garden centre

A LONG WALK BEYAZIT TO GALATA

Distance 4 km (2.5 miles) **Time** 1 hour 30 minutes **Nearest Metro** Vezneciler **Stopping-off points** Cafés or bars on Galata Bridge

Istanbul is a seductive mix of ancient and modern, religious and secular, and this captivating walk offers a flavour of all four. Starting at the magnificent Kalenderhane Mosque, nestled in the city's historic quarter, the route winds through a labyrinth of narrow shopping streets brimming with energy. It then leads to the Galata Bridge with its stunning views of the Bosphorus. After crossing the bridge, visitors will arrive at the trendy Beyoğlu district *(p126)*, whose shops, bars and cafés lend Istanbul its chic reputation.

Kurukahreci Mehmet Efendi, bustling with customers

Hasırcılar Caddesi *is famed for its spice shops, coffee stalls and delis.*

At the end of **Mimar Sinan Caddesi** *is the tomb of the famous architect Mimar Sinan* (p109).

Şifahane Sokak *helps visitors understand how Ottoman mosques were built as the central feature of a much larger complex.*

Süleymaniye Mosque (p108) *was completed in 1557 by architect Mimar Sinan.*

Süleymaniye Square *has a small fountain.*

Start your walk from the **Kalenderhane Mosque** (p114), *which was once a Byzantine church.*

Tünel Geçidi *is an open-air passage lined with late 19th-century European-style buildings.*

The **Quincentennial Foundation Museum of Turkish Jews** (muze500.com) *has a collection of old photographs, documents and religious objects relating to the city's Jewish population.*

The **Galata Tower** (p133) *is the district's focal point, offering panoramic views of the city from its 360 degree viewing deck.*

Featuring a Gothic façade, the **Beyoğlu Hospital** *was built in 1904 as a British naval hospital.*

Yüksek Kaldırım Caddesi *is a cobblestoned street lined with music shops selling traditional and hi-tech instruments.*

Karaköy fish market *has cafés serving delicious, affordably priced fish meals and sandwiches.*

Galata Bridge *offers stunning city views and features cafés, bars and restaurants on its lower deck.*

Kurukahveci Mehmet Efendi *is a traditional coffee shop, opened in 1871, famous for its range of blends.*

→

Imposing Galata Tower, dominating the city skyline

Galata Tower at sunset

BEYOĞLU

Set on a steep hill north of the Golden Horn, facing Istanbul's historic peninsula, is the "new town" of Beyoğlu, previously known as Pera – simply, "the other side". The area is hardly "new", though; there has been a settlement here for nearly 2,000 years. For centuries, it was home to the city's foreign residents. First to arrive here were the Genoese. As a reward for their help in the reconquest of the city from the Latins in 1261, they were given the Galata area, which is now dominated by the Galata Tower. During the Ottoman period, Jews from Spain, Arabs, Greeks and Armenians settled in communities here. From the 16th century, Pera became the commercial centre of Istanbul after the great European powers established embassies in the area to further their own interests within the lucrative territories of the Ottoman Empire. The district has not changed much in character since, and today Beyoğlu is the heart of modern European Istanbul, its streets (such as the main thoroughfare of İstiklal Caddesi) lined with consulates, churches, stylish bars and the latest shops selling the popular brands.

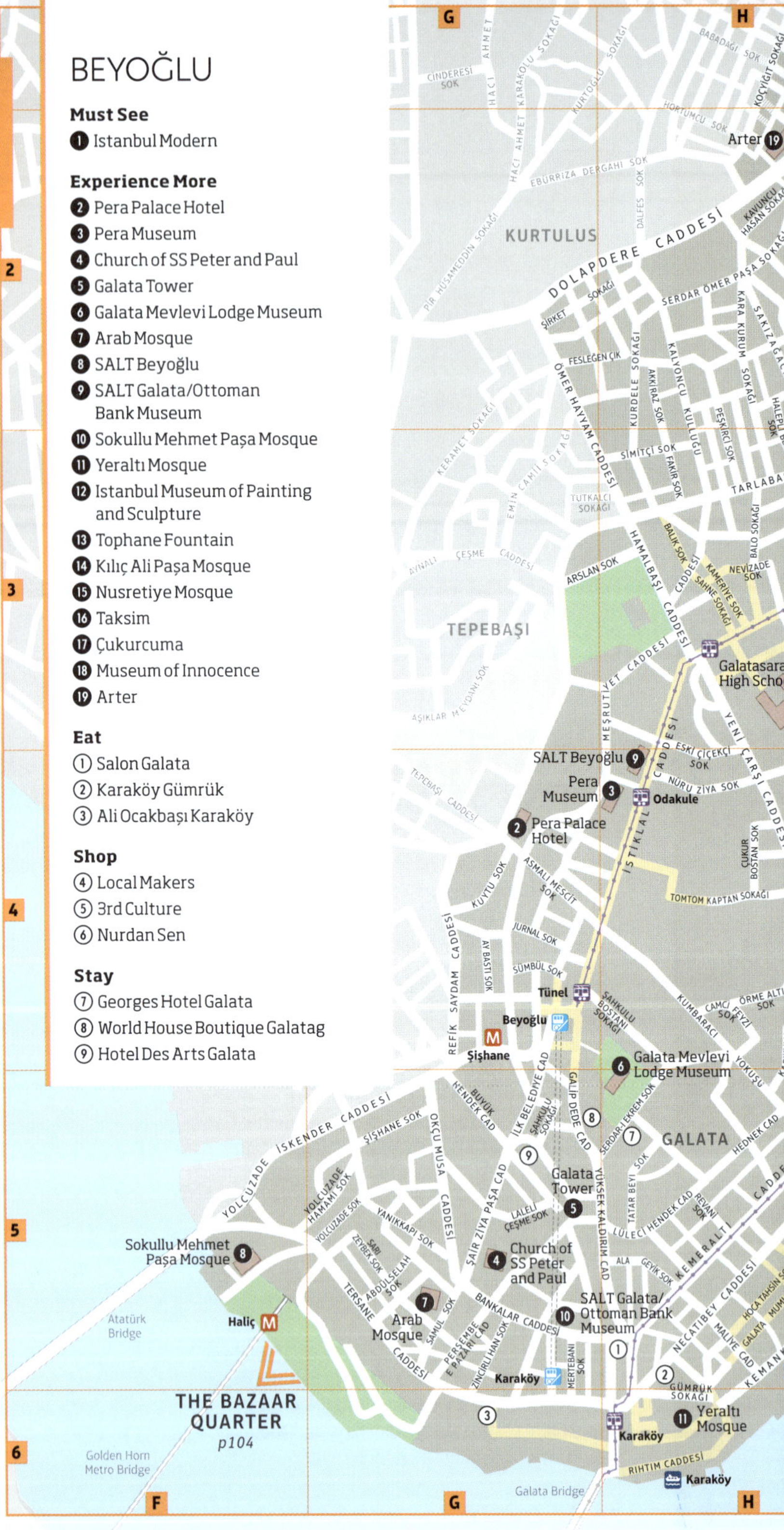

BEYOĞLU
Must See
1 Istanbul Modern
Experience More
2 Pera Palace Hotel
3 Pera Museum
4 Church of SS Peter and Paul
5 Galata Tower
6 Galata Mevlevi Lodge Museum
7 Arab Mosque
8 SALT Beyoğlu
9 SALT Galata/Ottoman Bank Museum
10 Sokullu Mehmet Paşa Mosque
11 Yeraltı Mosque
12 Istanbul Museum of Painting and Sculpture
13 Tophane Fountain
14 Kılıç Ali Paşa Mosque
15 Nusretiye Mosque
16 Taksim
17 Çukurcuma
18 Museum of Innocence
19 Arter
Eat
① Salon Galata
② Karaköy Gümrük
③ Ali Ocakbaşı Karaköy
Shop
④ Local Makers
⑤ 3rd Culture
⑥ Nurdan Sen
Stay
⑦ Georges Hotel Galata
⑧ World House Boutique Galatag
⑨ Hotel Des Arts Galata
G
H
F
2
3
4
5
6
KURTULUS
TEPEBAŞI
GALATA
DOLAPDERE CADDESİ
ÖMER HAYYAM CADDESİ
TARLABAŞI
İSTİKLAL CADDESİ
MEŞRUTİYET CADDESİ
YOLCUZADE İSKENDER CADDESİ
Arter
Galatasaray High School
SALT Beyoğlu
Pera Museum
Odakule
Pera Palace Hotel
Tünel
Beyoğlu
Şişhane
Galata Mevlevi Lodge Museum
Galata Tower
Church of SS Peter and Paul
SALT Galata/ Ottoman Bank Museum
Sokullu Mehmet Paşa Mosque
Arab Mosque
Yeraltı Mosque
Karaköy
Haliç
Atatürk Bridge
Golden Horn Metro Bridge
Galata Bridge
RIHTIM CADDESİ
THE BAZAAR QUARTER p104

J
K
L
1
2
3
4
5
6
Istanbul Technical University Faculty of Architecture
Divan Hotel
Maçka Park
Beşiktaş Stadium
Inter-Continental Hotel
Gezi Park
Taksim
Taksim Square
Istanbul Technical University
Dolmabahçe Mosque
Atatürk Cultural Centre
Marmara Hotel
Hüseyin Ağa Camii
KABATAŞ
Kabataş
GALATASARAY
Fındıklı
Mimar Sinan University
Çukurcuma
BEYOĞLU
Museum of Innocence
TOPHANE
Tophane
Istanbul Museum of Painting and Sculpture
Nusretiye Mosque
Tophane Fountain
Kılıç Ali Paşa Mosque
Istanbul Modern
Bosphorus
BEYOĞLU
0 metres 300
0 yards 300
N

1

ISTANBUL MODERN

J5 Tophane Iskele Cad, Galataport Tophane 56 10am-6pm Tue-Thu, Sat & Sun; 10am-8pm Fri istanbulmodern.org

Turkey's first dedicated museum for contemporary art, Istanbul Modern is now a premier venue. Housed in an impressive five-storey building with a view of Galataport's waterfront, this art museum celebrates both the local and international modern-art scene.

INSIDER TIP
Cinema Screenings

Istanbul Modern's cinema hosts a thematic monthly programme of art-film screenings. Tickets can be pre-booked online or purchased on the day at the museum.

Istanbul Modern is the most upbeat and thoroughly contemporary museum in Turkey. It houses both permanent collections and temporary exhibitions, providing a showcase for many of the eccentric and talented personalities who have shaped modern art in Turkey from the early 20th century to the present day. Many of the works are from the private collection of the Eczacıbaşı family, who founded the museum. Exhibits include abstract art, landscapes and watercolours as well as a sculpture garden and a stunning display of black-and-white photography. Workshops run by artists are also held for both children and adults, with a focus on eco-friendly art and upcycling. Weekend workshops in Turkish are also available for children aged 7–14.

1 The interior is graced by a sculpture by Olafur Eliasson.

2 The dynamic exterior of Istanbul Modern.

3 The *Chiharu Shiota: Between Worlds* exhibition at Istanbul Modern.

Explore the "Floating Island" exhibit in the new building

TOP 3 TURKISH ARTISTS

Ara Güler (1928-2018)
A renowned photojournalist, Güler is best known for his black-and-white street-life pictures from the 1950s and 60s.

Fahrelnissa Zeid (1901-91)
Zeid's photography is characterized by her bold abstract geometric works and expressionist portraiture.

Bedri Rahmi Eyüboğlu (1911-75)
Many of Eyüboglu's paintings and murals feature Anatolian folklore motifs and village life scenes.

EXPERIENCE MORE

Pera Palace Hotel

Pera Palas Oteli

G4 Meşrutiyet Cad 98-100, Tepebaşı Şişhane Tünel Beyoğlu pera palace.com

Opened in 1892 and recently renovated for £20 million renovation, the Pera Palace Hotel is a legendary establishment. It was the Ottoman Empire's first luxury hotel and the final stop for the *Orient Express (p80)*. Famous guests, such as Agatha Christie, Ernest Hemingway, Mata Hari, Greta Garbo, Jackie Kennedy Onassis and Alfred Hitchcock, are honoured with named guestrooms.

Non-guests can also enjoy the hotel's grandeur with an afternoon tea in the Kubbeli Lounge, sipping on cocktails in the Orient Bar or dining at the Agatha Restaurant. Atatürk's *(p55)* former room has now been converted into a museum, which requires advance booking due to a daily limit of 50 visitors.

Pera Museum

Pera Müzesi

H4 Meşrutiyet Cad 141, Tepebaşı Şişhane Tünel Beyoğlu Hours vary, check website 1 Jan, first day of religious hols peramuseum.org

Opened in June 2005 by the Suna and İnan Kıraç Foundation, this museum serves as a cultural centre. It is housed in a historic building that was once home to the Hotel Bristol. Notable collections include Ottoman weights and measures, over 400 examples of 18th-century Kütahya tiles and ceramics and the Suna and İnan Kıraç Foundation's exhibition of Orientalist art. This collection brings together works by Ottoman and European artists inspired by the Ottoman world from the 17th century to the early 19th century. The most famous painting is the *Tortoise Trainer* by Osman Hamdi Bey, the late Ottoman noble who set up Istanbul's excellent Archaeology Museum.

This museum also covers the last two centuries of the Ottoman Empire and provides an insight into the lives of the upper class. It also provides spaces for modern art exhibitions. Past shows have included works by American artist Andy Warhol and Spanish painter Miró. There is also an in-house arts cinema.

INSIDER TIP

Free Friday Nights

For a budget-friendly Friday evening cultural outing, visit the Pera Museum. Admission is free for all visitors every Friday between 6pm and 10pm.

Church of SS Peter and Paul

Aziz Peter ve Aziz Paul Kilisesi

G5 Galata Kulesi Sok 44, Karaköy Karaköy Tünel 2:30-5:30pm Fri & Sat; Mass: 8am Mon-Fri, 7pm Sat senpiyer.org

When their original church was requisitioned as a mosque (to become the nearby Arab Mosque) in the early 16th century, the Dominican brothers of Galata relocated to this site. The present building, dating from 1841, was designed by the Fossati brothers, renowned architects of Italian-Swiss origin who also worked on the restoration of the Hagia Sophia *(p88)*.

Opulent interior featuring period furnishings at the Pera Palace Hotel

Galata Tower, rising above the narrow cobbled streets of the Galata district, and *(inset)* stairs leading up to the top of the tower

According to Ottoman regulations, the main façade of the building could not be directly on a road, so the church is reached through a courtyard, the entrance to which is via a tiny door on the street. Ring the bell to gain admittance.

The church is built in the style of a basilica, with four side altars. The cupola over the choir is sky blue, studded with gold stars. Mass is said here in Italian on weekday mornings and on Saturday evening; there is no Sunday service.

Galata Tower

Galata Kulesi

G5 Büyük Hendek Sok, Beyoğlu Şişhane Tünel Beyoğlu 8:30am-6:15pm & 7-10pm daily muze.gov.tr

An iconic, conical-topped landmark, the Galata Tower dominates the skyline of the Golden Horn. Constructed by the Genoese in 1348, this stone edifice stands majestically at 60 m (196 ft) and originally served as a watchtower, providing a strategic vantage point over the bustling harbour and its surrounding areas. In the 18th century, the tower became famous when aviation pioneer, Hezarfen Ahmet Çelebi reportedly attached wings to his arms and leaped from here, and glided over the Bosphorus to land in Üsküdar.

Following a restoration in 2020, visitors can now explore a small exhibition space on the lower level that traces Istanbul's history. An elevator takes visitors up to the 7th floor, from where two further flights of a spiral staircase lead to the observation deck. The unmissable view from the top encompasses the city's skyline and beyond as far as the Princes' Islands *(p194)*.

STAY

Georges Hotel Galata

This luxury boutique hotel features elegant rooms and a rooftop bar and restaurant.

H5 Serdar-ı Ekrem Cad 24 georges.com

World House Boutique Galata

This 130-year-old building with exposed-brick detailing offers 15 rooms and an on-site café.

G5 Galip Dede Cad 85/A worldhouse bh.com

Hotel Des Arts Galata

Book a balcony room overlooking the Galata Tower to fully enjoy this boutique's prime location.

G5 Küçük Hendek Cad 11 hoteldes artsgalata.com

Sema, a traditional Sufi performance, at the Galata Mevlevi Lodge Museum

Galata Mevlevi Lodge Museum

Galata Mevlevihanesi Müzesi

H5 Galip Dede Cad 15, Beyoğlu Şişhane Tünel Beyoğlu 9am-6pm Tue-Sun muze.gov.tr

Tucked away off a street named after the great poet, Galip Dede, this museum is housed in an 18th-century lodge that once belonged to the most famous Sufi sect, the Whirling Dervishes. The original dervishes were disciples of the mystical poet and great Sufi master "Mevlâna" (Our Leader) Celaleddin Rumi, who died in Konya, in central Anatolia in 1273.

Downstairs are a series of rooms that display well-labelled objects used by the sect, from begging bowls to musical instruments and calligraphy pens. The *semahane*, or ritual dance floor, lies upstairs. Due to ongoing restoration, access may be restricted to certain interior sections of the building. Outside, in the calm, terraced garden, stand the ornate tombstones of ordinary sect members and prominent sheikhs (leaders).

Arab Mosque

Arap Camii

G5 Kalyon Sok 1, Galata Karaköy Tünel 9am-6pm daily (from 2:30pm Fri) Prayer times

Named after the Muslim refugees who settled in Galata following their expulsion from Andalucía after the fall of Granada in 1492, this mosque was originally the Church of SS Peter and Paul. Built in the first half of the 14th century by Dominican monks, the building was later given to the settlers for use as a mosque. It is an unusual building for Istanbul: a vast, strikingly rectangular Gothic church with a tall square belfry, which now acts as a minaret. The building has been restored several times.

Sokullu Mehmet Paşa Mosque

Sokullu Mehmet Paşa Camii

F5 Tersane Cad, Azapkapı Haliç 46H, 61B Prayer times only

Delightful though they are, this little mosque complex and fountain are somewhat overshadowed by the stream of traffic thundering over the adjacent Atatürk Bridge. The trees surrounding the mosque, however, help to screen it from the noise. It was built in 1577–8 by the master architect Sinan *(p106)* for the Grand Vizier Sokullu Mehmet Paşa and is considered to be one of Sinan's more attractive mosques.

SUFISM AND THE WHIRLING DERVISHES

Sufism is the mystical branch of Islam. The name comes from *suf*, the Arabic for wool, for Sufis were originally associated with poverty and self-denial, and often wore rough woollen clothes next to the skin. Sufis aspire to a personal experience of the divine. This takes the form of meditative rituals, involving recitation, dance and music, to bring the practitioner into direct, ecstatic communion with Allah. There are several sects of Sufis, the most famous of which are the Mevlevi *(p288)*, better known as the Whirling Dervishes on account of their ritual spinning dance.

Neo-Classical interior of the SALT Galata/ Ottoman Bank Museum

Housed in a stylish former 19th-century apartment block, SALT Beyoglu is one of Istanbul's leading cultural institutions.

9 SALT Beyoğlu

H4 İstiklal Cad 136 Şişhane Odakule Beyoğlu Tünel 11am-7pm Tue-Sat, 11am-6pm Sun saltonline.org

Housed in a stylish 19th-century former apartment block, SALT Beyoglu is one of Istanbul's leading cultural institutions. It hosts a variety of events, including exhibitions, lectures, film screenings and workshops focused on art, design, architecture and the social history of Turkey and the wider eastern Mediterranean region. On the ground floor, SALT's Walk-In Cinema is used to host film screenings, performances and talks. Art exhibitions are held on the ground, second and third floors, while the fourth floor has an enclosed greenhouse garden. Beyoğlu's beloved Robinson Crusoe 389 Bookshop, which stocks a wide range of English-language books, is located on the first floor. Admission, and entry to all events, is free.

10 SALT Galata/Ottoman Bank Museum

SALT Galata/Osmanlı Bankası Müzesi

G5 Bankalar Cad 11, Karaköy Karaköy 25E, 56 Tünel, Karaköy 11am-7pm Tue-Sat, 11am-6pm Sun saltonline.org; obmuze.com

This vibrant cultural centre is set in a former 19th-century bank building, with a beautiful Neo-Classical interior. Much like its nearby counterpart, SALT Beyoğlu, it offers an exciting calendar of thought-provoking temporary art exhibitions and installations.

The same building also hosts the Ottoman Bank Museum. Established in 2002, this museum features exhibits of Ottoman-era banknotes, promissory notes from imperial palace officials (a kind of legal "I Owe You"), and a comprehensive collection of 6,000 photographs of the bank's employees.

HIDDEN GEM

Pera Glass Studio

Located close to SALT Galata/Ottoman Bank Museum is the Pera Glass Museum *(Camekan Sok 1)*. See glassworks or try glass shaping and stained-glass painting at a workshop.

EAT

Salon Galata
Expect bistro-cooking with a unique Turkish twist at this modern café-restaurant.

H5 Bankalar Cad 3
0212 252 7256

Karaköy Gümrük
This cosy, art-filled café-restaurant serves European steak and pasta, alongside Turkish-inspired dishes.

H5 Gümrük Sok 4
karakoygumruk.com

Ali Ocakbaşı Karaköy
Feast on fine-dining versions of classic kebab dishes here.

G6 Grifin Han, Kardeşim Sok 45
aliocakbasi.com

Yeraltı Mosque

Yeraltı Camii

H6 Karantina Sok, Karaköy Karaköy 9am-6:30pm daily (from 2:30pm Fri) Prayer times

This mosque, literally "the underground mosque", contains the shrines of two Muslim saints, Abu Sufyan and Amiri Wahibi, who died during the first Arab siege of the city in the 7th century. It was the discovery of their bodies in the cellar of an ancient Byzantine fortification in 1640 that led to the creation of a shrine on the site and later, in 1757, a mosque.

Modern exterior of the Istanbul Museum of Painting and Sculpture

Istanbul Museum of Painting and Sculpture

İstanbul Resim ve Heykel Müzesi

J5 Meclis-i Mebusan Cad 6, Galataport Karaköy Odakule 26, 26A, 28 10am-5pm Wed-Sun, 10am-8pm Tue irhm.msgsu.edu.tr

This art-museum is home to Istanbul's largest collection of paintings, sculpture, ceramic art and calligraphy from the 19th and 20th centuries. The permanent collection includes important worksby late-Ottoman artists and traces the development of art movements such as Cubism, Art Deco and abstract art in Turkey during the 20th century.

In the painting galleries, notable artworks include pieces by Ottoman-era painters such as Osman Hamdi Bey, the founder of Istanbul's Mimar Sinan Fine Arts University, and Impressionist Ömer Adil. Influential works of the mid-20th century also include Neşet Günal's narrative-figurative paintings, which are heavily influenced by central Anatolia, and Bedri Rahmi Eyüboğlu's abstract pieces.

The sculpture, ceramic and calligraphy galleries highlight a range of prominent Turkish artists who have championed these art forms by blending both traditional and contemporary interpretations. The museum also regularly hosts temporary exhibitions focusing on the work of individual Turkish artists.

Tophane Fountain

Tophane Çeşmes

J5 Tophane İskele Cad, Tophane 25E, 56 Tophane

Beside Kılıç Ali Paşa Mosque stands a beautiful but abandoned Baroque fountain, built in 1732 by Mahmut I. With its elegant roof and dome, it resembles the fountain of Ahmet III *(p78)*. Each of the four walls is entirely covered in low-relief floral carving.

The name, meaning "cannon foundry fountain", comes from the brick and

HIDDEN GEM
Tophane-İ Amire Culture and Art Center
Located across the road from the Tophane Fountain, this grand brick building, originally an Ottoman cannon-foundry, is now a venue for art exhibitions.

stone foundry building on the hill nearby. Established in 1453 by Mehmet the Conqueror *(p53)* and rebuilt several times, the foundry is now home to the Tophane-İ Amire Culture and Art Center.

Kılıç Ali Paşa Mosque

Kılıç Ali Paşa Camii

H5 Necatibey Cad, Tophane Tophane 25E, 56 9am-6:30pm daily (from 2:30pm Fri) Prayer times

This mosque was built in 1580 by Sinan, who was by then in his 90s. The church of Hagia Sophia *(p88)* provided the architect with his inspiration. İznik tiles adorn the mihrab and there is a delightful deep porch before the main door.

Above the entrance portal is an inscription giving the date when the mosque was established.

Kılıç Ali Paşa, who commissioned the mosque, had a colourful life. Born in Italy, he was captured by Muslim pirates and later converted to Islam in the service of Süleyman the Magnificent (r 1520–66). He served as a naval commander under three sultans and after retiring asked Murat III where to build his mosque. The sultan is said to have replied "in the admiral's domain, the sea". Taking him at his word, Kılıç Ali Paşa reclaimed part of the Bosphorus for his complex.

The **Kılıç Ali Paşa Hamamı** attached to the mosque has undergone careful restoration, it provides a wonderful alternative to the bathhouses in the Old City, especially for those in search of a quieter and more traditional hammam experience.

Kılıç Ali Paşa Hamamı

Women: 8am-4pm daily; men: 4:45-11:30pm daily kilicalipasahamami.com

Nusretiye Mosque

Nusretiye Camii

J5 Meclis-i Mebusan Cad, Tophane 25E, 56 9am-6:30pm daily (from 2:30pm Fri) Prayer times

The Baroque "Mosque of Victory" was built in the 1820s by Kirkor Balyan, who went on to found a dynasty of architects.

Commissioned by Mahmut II to commemorate his abolition of the Janissary corps in 1826, it faces the Selimiye Barracks *(p168)*, across the Bosphorus, which housed the New Army that replaced the Janissaries. The Empire-style swags and embellishments celebrate the sultan's victory. The marble panel of calligraphy around the interior of the mosque is particularly fine, as is the pair of *sebils* (kiosks for serving drinks) outside.

← Baroque prayer hall of the Nusretiye Mosque, and *(inset)* the mosque and clock tower in Tophane Square

16

Taksim Square

J2 Taksim

Taksim Square is the focal point of Republican Istanbul. In 2013, Gezi Park, located close to Taksim Square, became the centre of anti-government protests. Taksim means "water distribution centre"; from the early 1700s, it was from this site that water from the Belgrade Forest was distributed in the city. The original stone reservoir, built in 1732 by Mahmut I, still stands at the top of İstiklal Caddesi. In the southwest of the square is the 1928 Monument of Independence, by the Italian artist Canonica. It shows Atatürk *(p55)* and the other founding fathers of the modern Turkish Republic.

Near the entrance to İstiklal Caddesi is the **Republic Museum** (İBB Cumhuriyet Müzesi). Housed in a historic building that once served as a school, it displays exhibits that trace the founding of the Republic of Turkey.

Republic Museum
İstiklal Cad 2, Taksim
10am-7pm Tue-Sun

↑ Relaxing at one of the many charming cafés in Çukurcuma

Çukurcuma

H4 Taksim

This charming old quarter has become an important centre for Istanbul's furnishings and antiques trades. The old warehouses and houses in this district have been converted into shops and showrooms, where modern upholstery materials are piled up in carved marble basins and antique cabinets. Visitors can find hidden treasures, ranging from valuable paintings and prints and 19th-century Ottoman embroidery to 1950s biscuit boxes.

Republic Monument symbolizing Turkey's path to independence, Taksim Square

Museum of Innocence

Masumiyet Müzesi

H4 Çukurcuma Cad & Dalgıç Çıkmazı Şişhane Taksim Beyoğlu Tünel 10am-6pm Tue-Sun masumiyetmuzesi.org

Established by Nobel-prize winning Turkish author Orhan Pamuk, this fascinating museum brings to life the world of his acclaimed 2008 novel, *The Museum of Innocence*. Located in the city centre, this museum is set within a beautifully preserved 19th-century wooden house, which itself serves as a testament to the rich architectural heritage of the city.

The museum's eclectic collection features a diverse array of artifacts that reflect the lives and experiences of the novel's characters. Visitors will find cupboards brimming with curiosities and trinkets that evoke a sense of nostalgia, as well as meticulously curated displays of everyday household items that would have been common in Turkish homes during the late 20th century, the period in which the novel is set. These items include vintage photographs, ornate glassware and traditional textiles, each telling a story of a bygone era.

Among the museum's most striking features is a thought-provoking art installation consisting of 4,213 cigarette butts, which challenges visitors to reflect on themes of loss and longing, central to Pamuk's narrative.

The museum's audioguide, which features commentary from Pamuk himself, is particularly useful for those who wish to gain deeper insights of the museum's exhibits.

Arter

H3 Irmak Cad 13, Dolapdere M Taksim 70D 11am-7pm Tue, Wed & Fri-Sun, 11am-8pm Thu arter.org.tr

Opened in 2019, Arter is a distinctive, ultra-contemporary building that houses the modern art collection of the Vehbi Koç Foundation, a major philanthropic organization set up by billionaire industrialist Vehbi Koç. Its architectural design is characterized by clean lines, expansive glass façades and innovative use of space, enabling works by artists such as Mona Hatoum to shine. Featuring over 1,400 works by Turkish and international artists from the 1960s to the present day, Arter's galleries showcase a diverse array of contemporary art forms, including painting, photography, sculpture and cutting-edge multimedia installations.

Throughout the year, Arter hosts a vibrant programme of temporary exhibitions, often highlighting individual artists or thematic explorations like personal histories, urban life, and migration. These exhibitions are complemented by a wide-ranging events calendar that celebrates the performing arts. Visitors can enjoy an eclectic mix of classical chamber music concerts, electronic music performances, modern dance showcases, experimental theatre and film screenings.

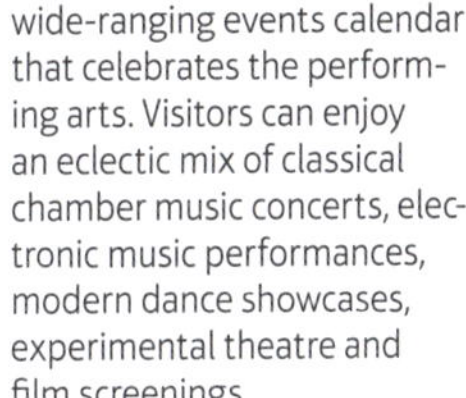

Guided tours of the exhibition galleries are offered twice daily from Tuesday to Friday, and three times daily on weekends. These tours provide an insight into the artworks on display, as well as the artists' intentions and their techniques. Admission to the galleries is free on Thursdays.

INSIDER TIP
Free Transport

Prefer not to walk from the metro? A free shuttle-bus service runs every 30 minutes between the Taksim metro station and Arter during the museum's opening hours.

The sleek and modern exterior of Arter Contemporary Art Museum

SHOP

Local Makers

Shop a wide selection of modern, handcrafted local ceramics, textiles and jewellery here.

H4 Çukurcuma Cad 27/B localmakers.com.tr

3rd Culture

3rd Culture is known for its contemporary furniture, soft furnishings and stylish homeware that blends global style influences with Turkey's long tradition of local artisan craftwork.

H4 Çukurcuma Cad 38 3rdcultureproject.com

Nurdan Sen

From bold abstract statement necklaces and bracelets to subtle earrings, Nurdan Sen often incorporates Anatolian motifs into individual pieces.

H3 Turnacıbaşı Cad 35/A (0212) 251 3116

A SHORT WALK
İSTIKLAL CADDESI

Distance 1.5 km (1 mile) **Time** 25 minutes
Nearest tram Tünel Square

The pedestrianized İstiklal Caddesi is Beyoğlu's main street. Once known as the Grande Rue de Pera, it is lined by late 19th-century apartment blocks and European embassy buildings whose grandiose gates and façades belie their use as mere consulates since Ankara became the Turkish capital in 1923 *(p276)*. Hidden from view stand the churches that used to serve the foreign communities of Pera (as this area was formerly called), some still buzzing with worshippers, others just quiet echoes of a bygone era. The once seedy backstreets of Beyoğlu, off İstiklal Caddesi, are now filled with trendy jazz bars, shops selling handcrafted jewellery, furniture and the like. Crowds are also drawn by the area's cinemas and numerous stylish restaurants. A red period tram rumbles up and down İstiklal Caddesi, linking Tünel Square with Taksim Square.

GREAT VIEW
Büyük Londra

The rooftop bar at the Buyuk Londra hotel *(Meşrutiyet Cad 53)* is a fantastic spot to take in sweeping panoramic views. From here, you can gaze across Beyoğlu and the Golden Horn to the minaret-punctured skyline of Istanbul's historic peninsula.

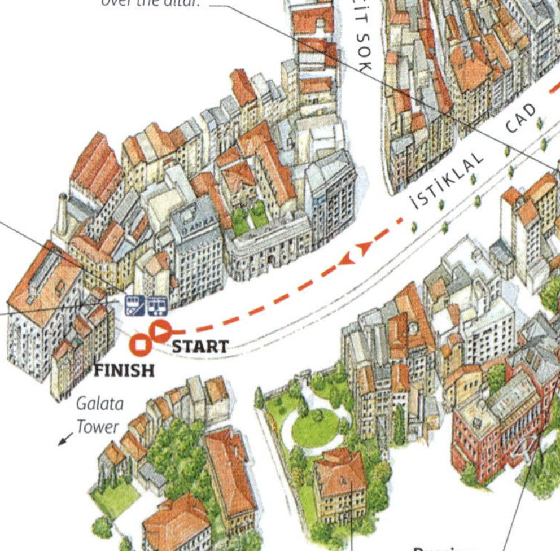

The **Pera Palace Hotel** (p132) *is an atmospheric period piece. Many famous guests, including Agatha Christie, Ernest Hemingway and Alfred Hitchcock, have stayed here since it opened in 1892.*

St Mary Draperis *is a Franciscan church dating from 1789. A small statue of the Virgin stands above the entrance from the street. The vaulted interior of the church is colourfully decorated. An icon of the Virgin, said to perform miracles, hangs over the altar.*

Tünel *underground funicular to Karaköy*

Tünel Square

Galata Tower

A peaceful garden surrounds the **Galata Mevlevi Lodge Museum** (p134). *On the last Sunday of every month visitors can see dervishes perform their famous swirling dance.*

Swedish Consulate

Russian Consulate

Galatasaray Fish Market *(Balık Pazarı) mainly sells fresh fish, but visitors will also find delicatessens offering everything from meats and cheeses through to delicious sweetmeats and pickles.*

BEYOGLU

İstiklâl Caddesi

Locator Map

For more detail see p128

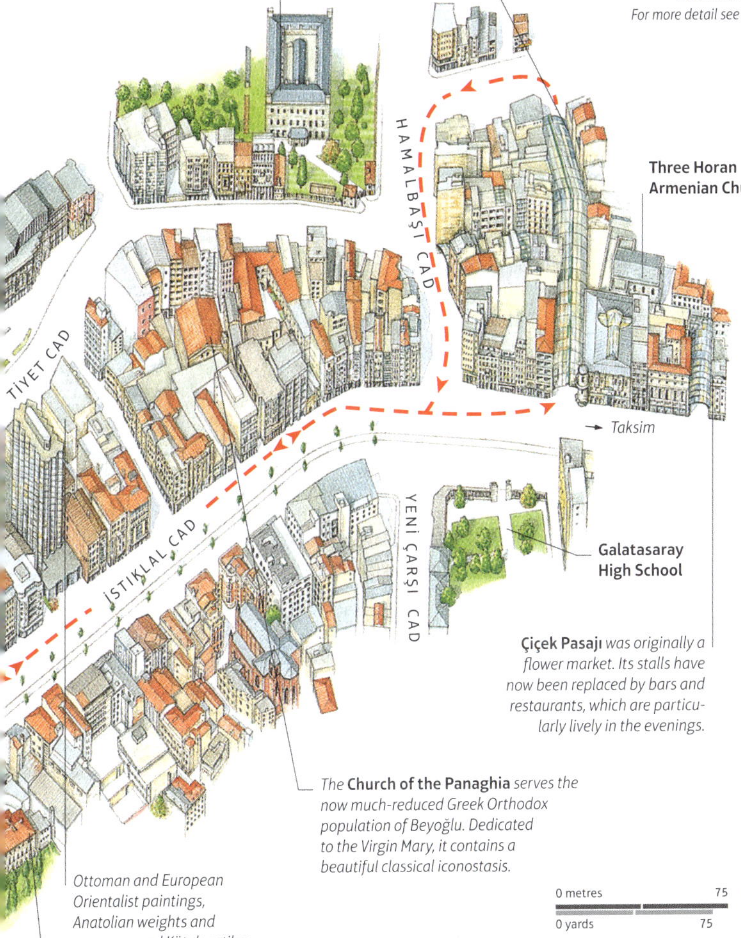

British Consulate

HAMALBAŞI CAD

Three Horan Armenian Church

TİYET CAD

→ *Taksim*

İSTIKLAL CAD

YENİ ÇARŞI CAD

Galatasaray High School

Çiçek Pasajı *was originally a flower market. Its stalls have now been replaced by bars and restaurants, which are particularly lively in the evenings.*

The **Church of the Panaghia** *serves the now much-reduced Greek Orthodox population of Beyoğlu. Dedicated to the Virgin Mary, it contains a beautiful classical iconostasis.*

Ottoman and European Orientalist paintings, Anatolian weights and measures and Kütahya tiles and ceramics are part of the collection at the **Pera Museum** (p132).

0 metres 75

0 yards 75

N

Dutch Consulate

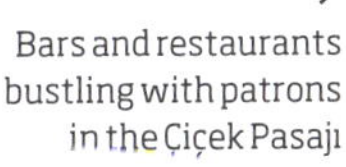

Bars and restaurants bustling with patrons in the Çiçek Pasajı

A LONG WALK

TAKSIM SQUARE TO ISTANBUL MODERN

Distance 2.5 km (1.5 miles) **Time** 1 hour 30 minutes **Nearest metro** Taksim **Stopping-off points** Fransız Sokagı, for a coffee or a glass of Turkish tea.

It was in the Pera district, where the embassies and palatial residences mirrored the lifestyle of Topkapı Palace, on the opposite side of the Golden Horn, that Constantinople's cosmopolitan population lived and worked in the 19th century. Once known as the "Paris of the East", life centred on the Grand Rue de Pera, today's İstiklal Caddesi. Even today the Avrupa Pasajı and Çiçek Pasajı are reminders of this area's history, especially when contrasted with the remarkable Pera Museum and sophisticated Istanbul Modern.

The former flower market, ***Çiçek Pasajı*** *was built by Italian architect Michel Capello in 1856. Today, it is home to numerous restaurants.*

The old ***Fish market*** *(or Balık Pazar) is still home to some stores selling fresh fish.*

British Consulate General

Avrupa Pasajı *is a shopping arcade featuring Neo-Renaissance interiors, with marble floors and classical statues.*

In 1905, a group of students got together at the ***Galatasaray High School*** *to form one of Turkey's leading football clubs.*

The philanthropic Suna and İnan Kiraç Foundation exhibits its art collection and Turkish tiles at the ***Pera Museum*** *(p132).*

Galatasaray Hammam *is home to Turkish baths built in 1481 and in use ever since.*

Fransız Sokağı *is home to numerous French-style cafés.*

Tomtom Kaptan Mosque *has a pretty 17th-century fountain.*

Balık Pazar
Çiçek Pasajı
Avrupa Pasajı
British Consulate General
Galatasaray Lisesi
Galatasaray High School
Galatasaray Hammam
Pera Museum
Odakule
Tomtom Kaptan Mosque
BALO SOKAĞI
BÜYÜK BAYRAM SOK
HAMALBAŞI CAD
ARSLAN SOK
SAHNE SOK
TURNACIBAŞI SOKAĞI
MEŞRUTIYET CADDESİ
YENİ ÇARŞI CADDESİ
NÜRU ZİYA SOK
FRANSIZ SOKAĞI
İSTİKLAL CADDESİ
ASMALI MESCİT SOK
PİREMECİ SOKAĞI
BOĞAZKESEN CADDESİ
ÖRME ALTI SOK
KUMBARACI YOKUŞU
KAPIKULU SOK
KARABAŞ CADDESİ

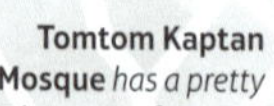

The arcaded Avrupa Pasajı, lined with shops selling textiles and ceramics

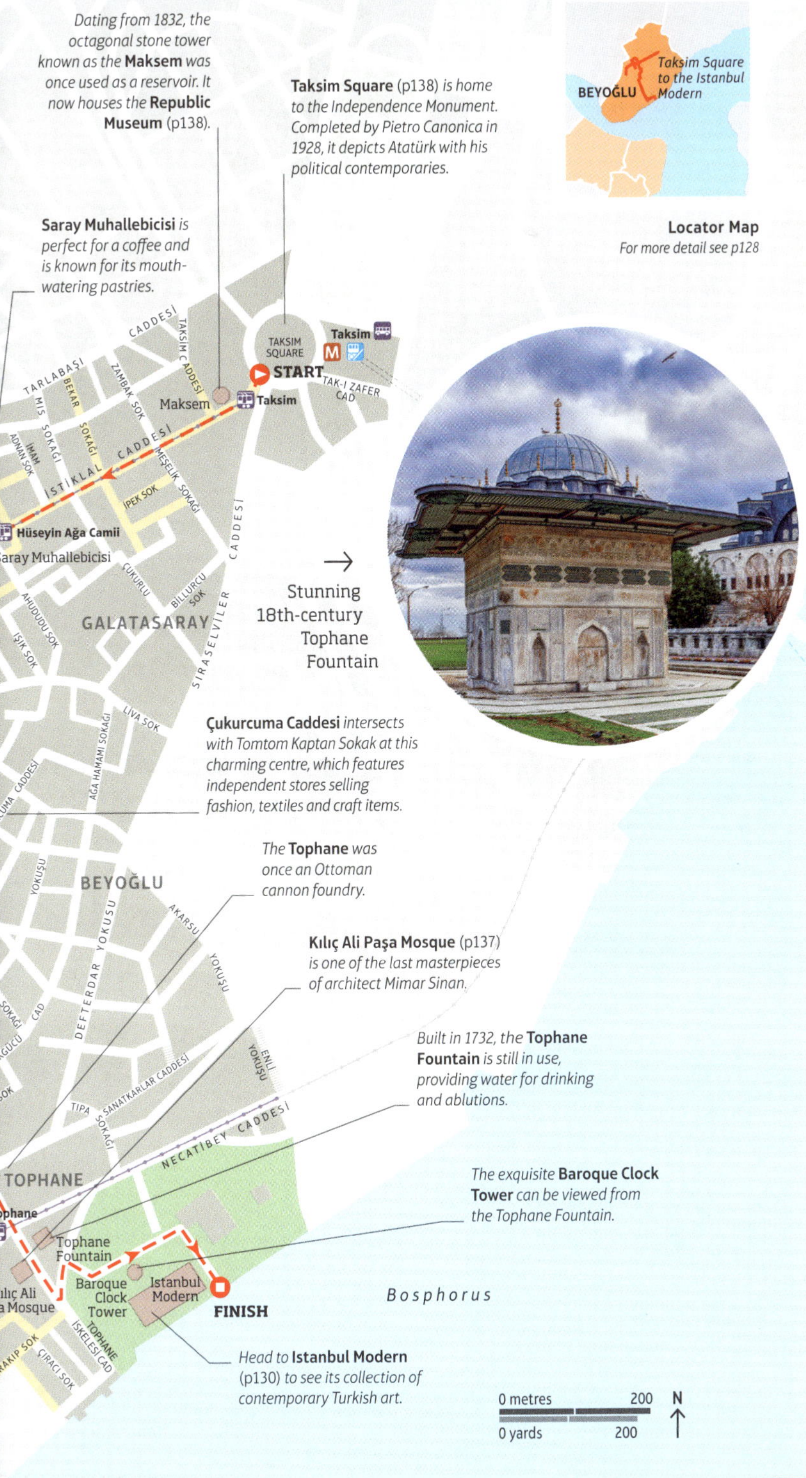
Dating from 1832, the octagonal stone tower known as the **Maksem** was once used as a reservoir. It now houses the **Republic Museum** (p138).
Taksim Square (p138) is home to the Independence Monument. Completed by Pietro Canonica in 1928, it depicts Atatürk with his political contemporaries.
Taksim Square to the Istanbul Modern
BEYOĞLU
Locator Map
For more detail see p128
Saray Muhallebicisi is perfect for a coffee and is known for its mouth-watering pastries.
TAKSIM SQUARE
Taksim
START
TAK-I ZAFER CAD
Maksem
Taksim
Hüseyin Ağa Camii
Saray Muhallebicisi
GALATASARAY
Stunning 18th-century Tophane Fountain
Çukurcuma Caddesi intersects with Tomtom Kaptan Sokak at this charming centre, which features independent stores selling fashion, textiles and craft items.
The **Tophane** was once an Ottoman cannon foundry.
BEYOĞLU
Kılıç Ali Paşa Mosque (p137) is one of the last masterpieces of architect Mimar Sinan.
Built in 1732, the **Tophane Fountain** is still in use, providing water for drinking and ablutions.
TOPHANE
NECATİBEY CADDESİ
The exquisite **Baroque Clock Tower** can be viewed from the Tophane Fountain.
Tophane Fountain
Baroque Clock Tower
Istanbul Modern
FINISH
Bosphorus
Head to **Istanbul Modern** (p130) to see its collection of contemporary Turkish art.
0 metres 200
0 yards 200
N

Outside Beşiktaş's ornate Dolmabahçe Palace

FURTHER AFIELD

Away from Istanbul's centre, the city's ancient origins and path of expansion can be traced. The districts of Fener and Balat only began to be developed after the Roman Emperor Theodosius II extended Constantinople's city limits west in the 5th century CE when he built the Theodosian walls, incorporating this previously rural area. Throughout the Ottoman period, both neighbourhoods were multicultural, with Fener the seat of the Greek Patriachate and Balat home to a large Jewish community. Further west, Eyüp became Istanbul's most important Islamic pilgrimage destination.

In the late-Ottoman era, the villages scattered across the nearby Asian and Bosphorus coasts became part of the city proper. Ottoman sultans had summer palaces built along the Bosphorus's forested shoreline, culminating in Sultan Abdül Mecit I building Dolmabahçe Palace in Beşiktaş in 1856 and transferring the seat of the empire here. More of the city's elite followed suit, moving out of the centre to be near the new power base.

Istanbul eventually lost its status as capital in 1923, but the continued village-to-city migration throughout the 20th century meant that it remained Turkey's largest city. Its urban sprawl extends along the European and Asian shores of both the Bosphorus Strait and the Sea of Marmara.

FURTHER AFIELD

Must Sees

1 Kariye Mosque
2 Theodosian Walls
3 Dolmabahçe Palace
4 Yıldız Park

Experience More

5 Ahrida Synagogue
6 Fethiye Mosque
7 Church of St Stephen of the Bulgars
8 Church of St Mary of the Mongols
9 Greek Orthodox Patriarchate
10 Mosque of Selim I
11 Mosque of the Holy Mantle
12 Fatih Mosque
13 Bulgur Palace
14 Molla Zeyrek Mosque
15 Yedikule Fortress
16 Panorama 1453 History Museum
17 Shrine of Zoodochus Pege
18 Palace of the Porphyrogenitus
19 Gazi Ahmet Paşa Mosque
20 Eyüp Sultan Mosque
21 Complex of Valide Sultan Mihrişah
22 Pierre Loti Café
23 Rahmi M. Koç Industrial Museum
24 Naval Museum
25 Maiden's Tower
26 Military Museum
27 Mihrimah Sultan Mosque
28 Atik Valide Mosque
29 Selimiye Barracks
30 Haydarpaşa Station
31 Ortaköy
32 Bosphorus Bridge
33 Sakıp Sabancı Museum
34 Fortress of Europe
35 Beylerbeyi Palace

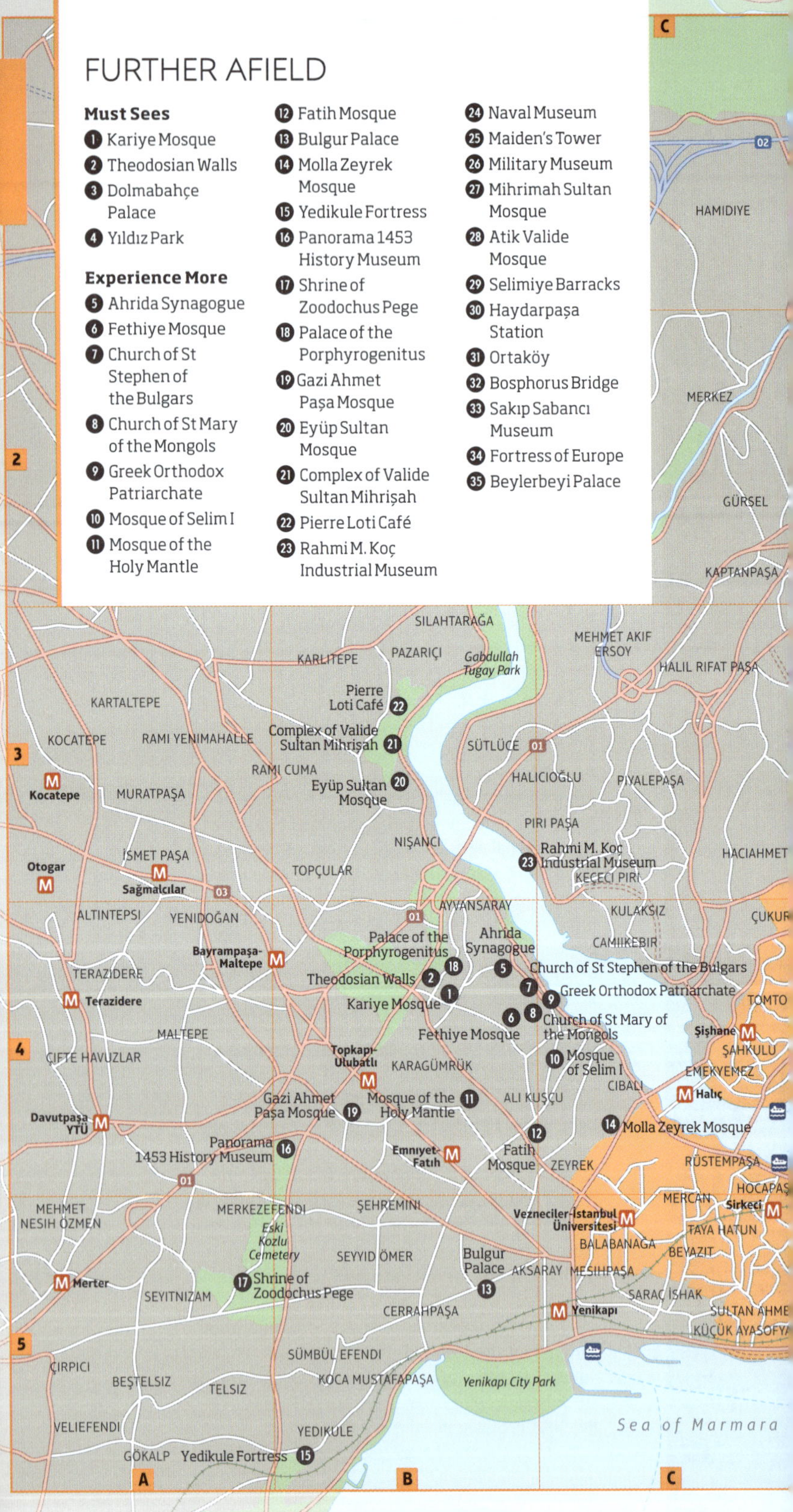

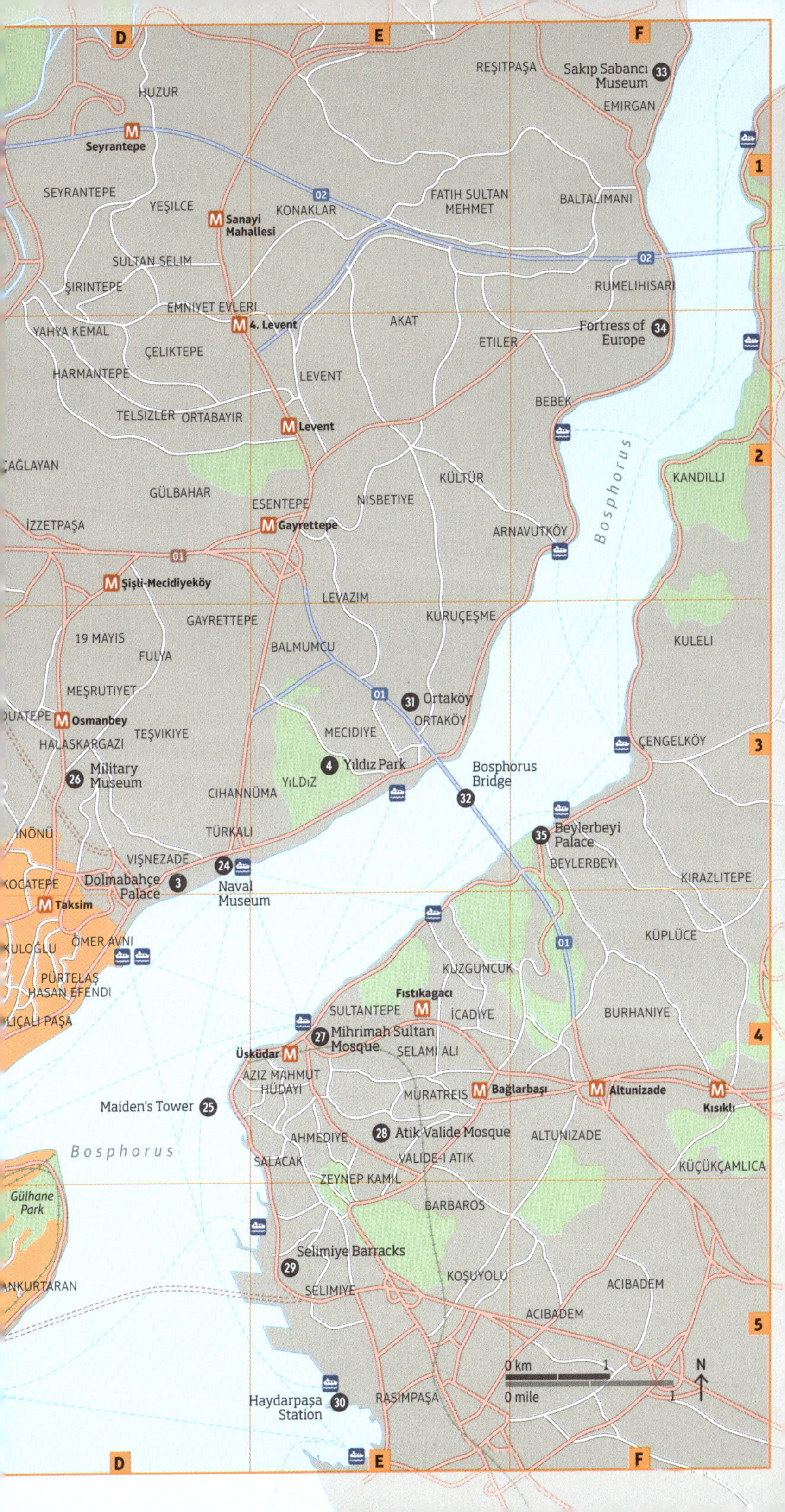
D
E
F
1
2
3
4
5
HUZUR
Seyrantepe
SEYRANTEPE
YEŞILCE
Sanayi Mahallesi
KONAKLAR
RESITPAŞA
Sakıp Sabancı Museum
33
EMIRGAN
FATIH SULTAN MEHMET
BALTALIMANI
SULTAN SELIM
ŞIRINTEPE
EMNIYET EVLERI
4. Levent
RUMELIHISARI
YAHYA KEMAL
ÇELIKTEPE
AKAT
ETILER
Fortress of Europe
34
HARMANTEPE
LEVENT
TELSIZLER
ORTABAYIR
Levent
BEBEK
ÇAĞLAYAN
KÜLTÜR
KANDILLI
GÜLBAHAR
ESENTEPE
NISBETIYE
Bosphorus
İZZETPAŞA
Gayrettepe
ARNAVUTKÖY
Şişli-Mecidiyeköy
LEVAZIM
KURUÇEŞME
GAYRETTEPE
19 MAYIS
KULELI
FULYA
BALMUMCU
MEŞRUTIYET
Ortaköy
31
ORTAKÖY
Osmanbey
TEŞVIKIYE
MECIDIYE
HALASKARGAZI
ÇENGELKÖY
Military Museum
26
Yıldız Park
4
Bosphorus Bridge
32
YILDIZ
CIHANNÜMA
İNÖNÜ
TÜRKALI
Beylerbeyi Palace
35
BEYLERBEYI
VIŞNEZADE
KIRAZLITEPE
KOCATEPE
Dolmabahçe Palace
3
24
Naval Museum
Taksim
KÜPLÜCE
ÖMER AVNI
KUZGUNCUK
PÜRTELAŞ HASAN EFENDI
Fıstıkagacı
SULTANTEPE
İCADIYE
BURHANIYE
27
Mihrimah Sultan Mosque
Üsküdar
SELAMI ALI
AZIZ MAHMUT HÜDAYI
MURATREIS
Bağlarbaşı
Altunizade
Kısıklı
Maiden's Tower
25
AHMEDIYE
28
Atik Valide Mosque
ALTUNIZADE
Bosphorus
SALACAK
VALIDE-I ATIK
KÜÇÜKÇAMLICA
ZEYNEP KAMIL
Gülhane Park
BARBAROS
Selimiye Barracks
29
KOŞUYOLU
ACIBADEM
SELIMIYE
ACIBADEM
0 km
1
0 mile
1
N
Haydarpaşa Station
30
RASIMPAŞA
02
01

Admiring the beautiful mosaics in the Kariye Mosque ↑

KARIYE MOSQUE

KARIYE CAMII

B4 Kariye Camii Sok, Edirnekapı (0212) 631 92 41 Edirnekapı 28, 86 or 90, then 5 minutes' walk 9am-6pm Mon-Thu, Sat & Sun Prayer times

Formerly a church in a monastery complex, the Kariye Mosque is a perfect example of exuberant and lavish Late Byzantine art. It is famed for the dazzling interior mosaics and frescoes that adorn its narthexes and side chapel.

The most exquisite Byzantine mosaics and frescoes found in this mosque were originally part of the Church of St Saviour in Chora. Little is known of the early history of the church, although its name "in Chora", which means "in the country", suggests that the church originally stood in a rural setting. The present architectural marvel dates back to the 11th century. Between 1315 and 1321 it underwent a huge transformation under the patronage of Theodore Metochites – a theologian, philosopher and one of the elite Byzantine officials of his time – who oversaw a grand remodelling that introduced breathtaking mosaics and intricate frescoes depicting scenes from the New Testament, including the *Annunciation*, the *Nativity* and the *Last Judgment*.

Did You Know?

Theodore Metochites is depicted, kneeling before Christ, in a panel over the doorway to the inner narthex.

Mosque Highlights

The Genealogy of Christ

▷ Theodore Metochites, who restored St Saviour, wrote that his mission was to relate how "the Lord himself became a mortal on our behalf". He takes the *Genealogy of Christ* as his starting point: the mosaics in the two domes of the inner narthex portray 66 of Christ's forebears. The crown of the southern dome is occupied by a figure of Christ. In the dome's flutes are two rows of his ancestors: Adam to Jacob ranged above the 12 sons of Jacob. In the northern dome, there is a central image of the Virgin and Child, with the kings of the House of David in the upper row and lesser ancestors of Christ in the lower row.

The Life of the Virgin

▽ All but one of the 20 mosaics in the inner narthex depicting the *Life of the Virgin* are well preserved. This cycle is based mainly on the apocryphal Gospel of St James, written in the 2nd century, which gives an account of the Virgin's life. Among the events shown are the first seven steps of the Virgin, the Virgin entrusted to Joseph and the Virgin receiving bread from an angel.

The Infancy of Christ

Scenes from the *Infancy of Christ*, based largely on the New Testament, occupy the semicircular panels of the outer narthex. They begin on the north wall of the outer narthex with a scene of Joseph being visited by an angel in a dream. Subsequent panels include Mary and Joseph's *Journey to Bethlehem*, their *Enrolment for Taxation*, the *Nativity of Christ* and, finally, Herod ordering the *Massacre of the Innocents*.

Other Mosaics

Devotional panels in the two narthexes include one, on the east wall of the south bay of the inner narthex, of the Deësis, depicting Christ with the Virgin Mary and, unusually, without St John. Another, in the inner narthex over the door into the nave, is of Theodore Metochites himself, shown wearing a large turban, and humbly presenting the restored church as an offering to Christ. The building's original nave (now the mosque's prayer hall) once held three panels, including the *Dormition of the Virgin*, but these are now covered up and cannot be viewed.

↑ Distinctive domes and tower of the Kariye Mosque

Frescoes

▷ The frescoes in the parecclesion (side chapel) are thought to have been painted just after the mosaics were completed (c 1320). The most engaging of the frescoes - which reflect the purpose of the parecclesion as a place of burial - is the *Anastasis*, in the semidome above the apse. In it, the central figure of Christ, the vanquisher of death, is shown dragging Adam and Eve out of their tombs. Under Christ's feet are the gates of hell, while Satan lies before him. The fresco in the vault overhead depicts the *Last Judgment*.

2

THEODOSIAN WALLS

TEODOS II SURLARI

B4 From Yedikule to Ayvansaray Kazlıçeşme, Topkapı-Ulubatlı Yedikule

Considered one of the greatest fortifications ever built, the surviving fragments of Emperor Theodosius's land walls were once part of an elaborate defensive system. For 800 years, these walls successfully repelled attackers until Ottoman cannon firepower finally breached them in 1453.

The impressive double walls of Constantinople, featuring 11 fortified gates and 192 towers, protected the city's landward side for over a thousand years. These walls, extending 6.5 km (4 miles) from the Sea of Marmara to the Golden Horn, were built with alternating layers of red tile and limestone blocks. Visitors can access different sections by metro, tram, taxi or bus, with the northern section being the easiest section to walk along.

Built between 412 and 422 CE during the reign of Theodosius II, the walls were initially damaged by an earthquake in 447 but were quickly rebuilt due to the looming threat from Attila the Hun. They withstood sieges by Arabs, Bulgarians, Russians and Turks, and even the Fourth Crusade *(p53)* only managed to storm the ramparts along the Golden Horn. The walls were finally breached by Mehmet the Conqueror in May 1453 *(p53)*.

Ottoman sultans continued to maintain the walls until the late 17th century, and while many sections, particularly around Belgrade Gate (Belgratkapı), have been rebuilt, the use of modern building materials has drawn criticism. Many gateways, including the Charsius Gate (now Edirnekapı) and Yedikule Gate (which stands beside the fortress of the same name), remain intact, with the latter featuring an imperial Byzantine eagle carved above its main archway. Unfortunately, a section near the Topkapı Gate was demolished in the 1950s for road construction.

INSIDER TIP
Exploring the Walls

The restored Mevlana Gate (Mevlanakapı), also known as the Rhesian Gate during the Byzantine era, grants visitors access to the top of the walls. Access is also available at the striking Yedikule Fortress *(p161)*.

DEFENDING THE THEODOSIAN WALLS

The double walls, towers and moat managed to thwart attackers for almost 1,000 years.

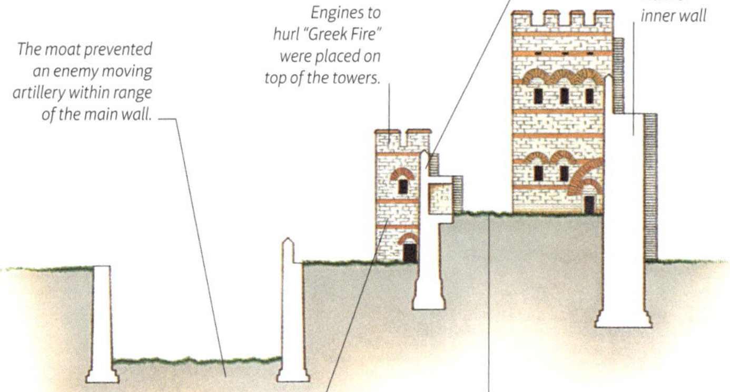

Outer wall

Main or inner wall

Engines to hurl "Greek Fire" were placed on top of the towers.

The moat prevented an enemy moving artillery within range of the main wall.

The towers of the outer wall alternate with those of the inner wall to create a continuous line of defence.

The peribolos, a road, was used for troop movements.

Cross-section of the Theodosian Walls and their moat

The walls withstood sieges by Arabs, Bulgarians, Russians and Turks, and even the Fourth Crusade.

The Theodosian Walls, which protected the city for almost 1,000 years, and *(inset)* taking in the views

3

DOLMABAHÇE PALACE

DOLMABAHÇE SARAYI

D3 Dolmabahçe Cad, Beşiktaş Kabataş 25E, 40 9am-5pm Tue-Sun First day of religious festivals millisaraylar.gov.tr

This magnificent palace, overlooking the Bosphorus, is renowned for its Baroque and Rococo interiors. Its European-style design made it distinct from the Topkapı Palace *(p72)* and revolutionized imperial architecture.

In 1856, Sultan Abdül Mecit built Dolmabahçe Palace. As its designers he employed Karabet Balyan and his son Nikoğos, members of the famous family of Armenian architects. This opulent palace, one of many of their creations lining the Bosphorus in the 19th century *(p172)*, belies the fact that it was built when the Ottoman Empire was in decline. The sultan financed the palace with loans from foreign banks. The palace was divided into two main sections: the Selamlık (or Mabeyn-i Hümayun), which housed the state rooms and the enormous Ceremonial Hall, was reserved for men, while the Harem served as the living quarters for the sultan and his entourage.

Did You Know?

The Ceremonial Hall's crystal chandelier is reputedly the heaviest in the world.

This crystal staircase, built in a double horseshoe shape, is made of Baccarat crystal and brass, featuring a polished mahogany rail.

The Süfera Salon, where ambassadors awaited the sultan, is one of the palace's most luxurious rooms.

Once used only by the sultan and his ministers, the Imperial Gate is now the palace's main entrance. The Mehter, or Janissary, Band performs in front of the gate on Tuesdays at 11am in summer.

The Swan Fountain is located in the Imperial Garden, originally a 16th-century garden re-created from recovered land, giving Dolmabahçe its name, meaning "Filled-in Garden".

Entrance

Selamlık

The Red Room was used by the sultan to receive ambassadors.

COMMEMORATING ATATÜRK'S DEATH

Mustafa Kemal Atatürk, the founder and first president of the Turkish Republic, passed away at 9:05am on 10 November 1938, in the palace. This day is commemorated throughout Turkey to honour his legacy. Every year, at 9:05am, Istanbul comes to a standstill: sirens blare, ships on the Bosphorus blast their horns, traffic stops and people on the streets pause to remember Turkey's founding father and pay their respects.

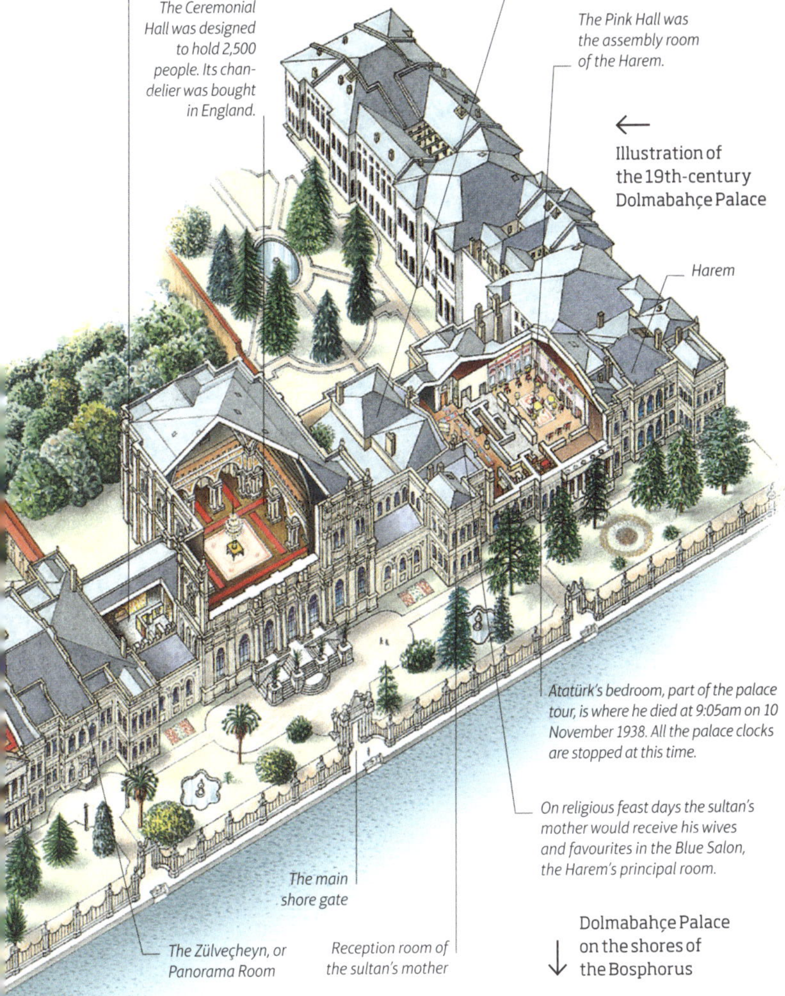

The walls of the main bathroom are revetted in finest Egyptian alabaster, while the taps are solid silver. The brass-framed bathroom windows afford stunning views across the Bosphorus.

Sultan Abdül Aziz's bedroom had to accommodate a huge bed built especially for the 150-kg (23-stone) amateur wrestler.

The Ceremonial Hall was designed to hold 2,500 people. Its chandelier was bought in England.

The Pink Hall was the assembly room of the Harem.

← Illustration of the 19th-century Dolmabahçe Palace

Harem

Atatürk's bedroom, part of the palace tour, is where he died at 9:05am on 10 November 1938. All the palace clocks are stopped at this time.

On religious feast days the sultan's mother would receive his wives and favourites in the Blue Salon, the Harem's principal room.

The main shore gate

The Zülveçheyn, or Panorama Room

Reception room of the sultan's mother

↓ Dolmabahçe Palace on the shores of the Bosphorus

YıLDıZ PARK

YıLDıZ PARKı

E3 Çırağan Cad, Beşiktaş Yıldız 25E, 40, 56 9am-5pm Thu-Tue Şale, Malta and Çadır Pavilions: for restoration millisaraylar.gov.tr

This forested hillside, a favoured hunting ground for the Ottoman sultans from the 16th century onwards, is now one of the few large green spaces in the inner city.

Originally the garden of the first Çırağan Palace *(p167)*, Yıldız Park now encompasses the grounds of Yıldız Palace, featuring buildings from various eras. The park is a popular picnic spot with its ancient trees and diverse flora. Located on a steep hill, it is best accessed by walking downhill from the Yıldız metro stop.

Yıldız Palace

The palace is a remarkable collection of pavilions and villas from the 19th and 20th centuries, primarily commissioned by the eccentric Sultan Abdül Hamit II (1876–1909). Its courtyard features the State Apartments (Büyük Mabeyn), dating back to Sultan Selim III's reign (1789–1807); they are currently not open to the public. Nearby, the City Museum (Şehir Müzesi) showcases Yıldız porcelain, while the nearby Italianate building serves as the former armoury, or Silahhane. Next to the museum, the Yıldız Palace Museum occupies Abdül Hamit's former carpentry workshop, displaying a changing collection of art and objects from the palace. Further on is the Yıldız Palace Theatre, completed in 1889 by Abdül Hamit. The interior is mainly blue and gold and the stars on the domed ceiling are a reference to the name of the palace: yıldız means "star" in Turkish.

Strolling along a tranquil path at Yıldız Park ↑

Elegant floral motifs above the main staircase at the Malta Pavilion

Yıldız Park Pavilions

With the main palace complex of Yıldız Palace now fully restored and reopened, efforts have shifted to the restoration of the park's other royal buildings. As a result, the following structures are presently closed.

Şale Pavilion

The Şale Pavilion (Şale Köşkü), the park's most impressive structure, was built in three stages by Abdül Hamit II. Originally resembling a Swiss chalet, it hosted figures like Winston Churchill, Charles de Gaulle and Nicolae Ceauşescu. A second section was added in 1889, to accommodate Kaiser Wilhelm II on the first ever state visit of a foreign monarch to the Ottoman capital.

Malta and Çadır Pavilions

Built during Abdül Aziz's reign (1861–76), these charming pavilions once served as prisons and later as cafés. Mithat Paşa, reformist and architect of the constitution, was imprisoned in Çadır Pavilion, while Murat V and his mother were confined in Malta Pavilion for 27 years.

Imperial Porcelain Factory

Opened in 1895, this factory, designed to look like a medieval castle, catered to the upper classes' demand for European-style ceramics. Its original pieces, depicting idealized scenes of the Bosphorus, are displayed in museums, with plans to open the factory to tourist visits.

The 19th-century Turkish Ottoman Yıldız Palace

INSIDER TIP

Park Access

Yıldız Palace can be accessed through the gate on Yıldız Caddesi, off Barbaros Bulvarı. To enter the park, use the gate on Palanga Caddesi or, take an uphill route from Çırağan Caddesi.

Wooden, boat-shaped *tevah* (pulpit) inside Ahrida Synagogue

EXPERIENCE MORE

Ahrida Synagogue

Ahrida Sinagogu

B4 Kürkçü Çeşmesi Sok, Balat (0212) 243 51 66 Balat 55T, 99A By appt, call ahead

The oldest and most beautiful synagogue in Istanbul is named after Ohrid, the city in North Macedonia from where its congregation came.

Founded before the Muslim conquest of Istanbul in 1453, it has been in constant use ever since. The painted walls and ceilings, dating from the late 17th century, have been restored to their Baroque glory. Pride of place is the central Holy Ark, which is covered in rich tapestries.

In the 17th century, the religious leader Shabbetai Zevi (1629–76), a self-proclaimed messiah, started preaching at this synagogue. He was later banished and converted to Islam, though his followers, the Sabbatians, believed this conversion was a ruse, and their movement exists to this day.

Visits to the synagogue are possible by prior arrangement through the Chief Rabbinate. Donation is mandatory.

Fethiye Mosque

Fethiye Camii

B4 Fethiye Kapısı Sok, Fatih Fener 90, 90B Prayer times only

Despite the important role this building has played in the history of the city, it is rarely visited. Originally the Church of the Pammakaristos for over 100 years after the Ottoman conquest, it housed the Greek Orthodox Patriarchate, but was converted into a mosque in the late 16th century by Sultan Murat III to commemorate his conquests of Georgia and Azerbaijan.

The charming exterior is obviously Byzantine, with its alternating stone and brick courses and finely carved marble details. The main body of the building is the working mosque, but the principal draw here are the stunning mosaics found in the building's side chapel, now known as the **Fethiye Museum**, although it is presently undergoing a years-long renovation. The interiors of the main church itself once housed Byzantine mosaics and frescoes, but these were plastered over during renovation work.

> **Founded before the Muslim conquest of Istanbul in 1453, the Ahrida Synagogue has been in constant use ever since. The painted walls and ceilings have been restored to their Baroque glory.**

What remains is the cleanly pointed brickwork, an example of Byzantine stonework. The windows set beneath the dome are patterned with glass panels, while the dome is decorated in two distinct styles: European floral embellishments on one half, and a traditional Islamic style of repeating patterns on the other.

Fethiye Museum
For renovation
muze.gov.tr

Church of St Stephen of the Bulgars

Sveti Stefan Kilisesi

B4 85 Mürsel Paşa Cad, Balat Balat, Fener 55T, 99A Ayvansaray 9am-5pm daily

Astonishingly, this entire church was cast in iron, even the internal columns and galleries. It was created in Vienna in 1871, before being shipped all the way to the Golden Horn *(p113)* and assembled on its shore. The church was built for the local Bulgarian community who had broken away from the authority of the Greek Orthodox Patriarchate *(p158)* just up the hill. It replaced an earlier church on the same spot, which was damaged during a fire

Today, it is still used by this community, who ensure that the marble tombs of the first Bulgarian patriarchs remain permanently decorated with flowers. The church itself is located in a pretty little park dotted with trees, and which runs down to the edge of the Golden Horn.

HIDDEN GEM
Haliç Sanat 3

A short stroll south from the Church of St Stephen of the Bulgars is Haliç Sanat 3 *(Mürselpaşa Cad 4)*, a restored 18th-century tower-house that hosts contemporary art exhibitions.

Ornate interior of the Church of St Stephen of the Bulgars, and *(inset)* its façade ↓

Church of St Mary of the Mongols

Meryem Ana Rum Ortodoks Kilisesi

B4 Tevkii Cafer Mektebi Sok, Fener 55T, 99A (0212) 521 71 39 Fener By appt

Consecrated in the late 13th century, the Church of St Mary of the Mongols is the only Greek Orthodox church in Istanbul to have remained continuously in the hands of the Greek community since the Byzantine era. Its immunity from conversion into a mosque was decreed in an order signed by Mehmet the Conqueror *(p53)*. A copy of this is kept by the church to this day. The church gets its name from the woman who founded it, Maria Palaeologina, an illegitimate Byzantine princess who was married off to a Mongol khan, Abagu, and lived piously with him in Persia for 15 years. After her husband's assassination, Princess Palaeologina returned to Constantinople, built this church and lived out her days here as a nun. Ring the bell of the compound to gain entry; the caretakers, a family from Antakya, are usually around. Donations are appreciated.

Greek Orthodox Patriarchate

Ortodoks Patrikhanesi

C4 Dr Sadık Ahmet Cad 19, Fener Fener 55T, 99A 8am-4pm daily (to 4:30pm Mon-Fri) ec-patr.org

This walled complex has served as the seat of the patriarch of the Greek Orthodox Church since the early 17th century. Though nominally head of the whole church, the patriarch is now shepherd to a diminishing but passionate flock in and around Istanbul.

As you walk up the steps to enter the patriarchate through a side door, you will see the main door that has been welded shut. This door has been built as a memorial to Patriarch Gregory V, who was hanged here for treason in 1821 after encouraging the Greeks to throw off Ottoman rule at the start of the Greek War of Independence (1821–32). The period after this saw a significant escalation in tensions between the Turkish and Greek communities. This antagonism was further inflamed by the Greek occupation of parts of Turkey in the 1920s, anti-Greek riots in 1955, and the expulsion of Greek residents in the mid-1960s. Today, the clergy at the Patriarchate are protected by a metal detector at the entrance.

The Patriarchate centres on the basilica-style Church of St George, dating back to 1720, yet the church contains much older relics and furniture. The patriarch's throne is thought to be Byzantine, while the pulpit is adorned with fine Eastern wooden inlay and several Orthodox icons.

GREAT VIEW

Terrace Vista

From the elevated garden-terrace of the Mosque of Selim I, which is perched on a hilltop, visitors can admire panoramic views across the Fener rooftops to the boats bobbing on the Golden Horn below.

Bowing in front of the iconostasis in the Church of St Mary of the Mongols

Spacious inner courtyard of the Mosque of Selim I, enclosed by pillars

10

Mosque of Selim I

Yavuz Sultan Selim Camii

C4 Yavuz Selim Cad, Fener 55T, 90, 90B, 99A Fener 9am-6:30pm daily (from 2:30pm Fri) Prayer times

This much-admired mosque is named for the infamous Selim I, whose nickname was Yavuz, "the Grim". It is idyllic in a rather offbeat way, which does seem at odds with Selim's barbaric reputation. The mosque, built between 1522 and 1529, sits alone on a hill beside what is now a vast sunken park area, once the Byzantine Cistern of Aspar. Beautifully restored, it is one of the most impressive mosques in Istanbul, with a shallow dome covering an austere prayer hall.

The windows set into the porticoes in the courtyard are capped by early İznik tiles *(p187)* made by the *cuerda seca* technique, whereby each colour is separated during the firing process, affording the patterns greater definition. Similar tiles lend decorative effect to the simple prayer hall, with its fine mosque furniture and original, carefully painted woodwork.

11

Mosque of the Holy Mantle

Hırka-i Şerif Camii

B4 Keçeciler Cad, Karagümrük Emniyet Vatan 28, 87, 90, 91 9am-6pm daily (from 2:30pm Fri) Prayer times

Constructed in 1850 in the opulent Empire style, this mosque was designed to safeguard a highly revered relic: a *hırka* (cloak) from the imperial collection, believed to have once belonged to and been worn by the Prophet Mohammed himself. This sacred garment is enshrined in a dedicated sanctuary positioned directly behind the mihrab, the prayer niche indicating the direction of Mecca, thus making it a focal point of the mosque's spiritual significance.

The mosque's minarets are in the style of Classical columns, and the features of its balconies are reminiscent of Corinthian capitals. The interior of the octagonal prayer hall, meanwhile, is full of decorative marble. Abdül Mecit I, the mosque's patron, was jointly responsible for the design of its calligraphic frieze.

EAT

Al Muallim

Savour classic Levantine dishes, including the *mansaf*, a Bedouin speciality featuring slow-cooked lamb, at this restaurant.

B4 Hüsrevpaşa Sok 50/5, Fatih
0554 189 9981

Beit Ward

This spot serves Arabian specialities such as *molokhiya* (jute-leaf stew) and *mahshi* (stuffed vegetables), as well as hummus.

B4 Mütercim Asım Sok 11, Fatih
0554 189 9981

12 Fatih Mosque

Fatih Camii

B4 Macar Kardeşler Cad, Fatih Emniyet 28, 87, 90 8am-6:30pm daily (from 2:30pm Fri) Prayer times

A spacious outer courtyard surrounds this Baroque mosque, the third major structure on this site. The first was the Church of the Holy Apostles, the burial place of most of the Byzantine emperors. Most of what you see today was the work of Mehmet Tahir Ağa, the chief imperial architect under Mustafa III. Many of the buildings he constructed around the prayer hall, including eight *medreses* (Islamic institutions of learning) and a hospice, still stand. The only surviving parts of Mehmet the Conqueror's mosque are the three porticoes of the courtyard, the ablutions fountain, the main gate into the prayer hall and, inside, the mihrab. Two exquisite forms of 15th-century decoration can be seen over the windows in the porticoes: İznik tiles and lunettes adorned with calligraphic marble inlay. Stencilled patterns decorate the domes of the prayer hall, and parts of the walls are covered with beautiful tiles.

The tomb of Mehmet the Conqueror stands behind the prayer hall, near that of his consort, Gülbahar. His sarcophagus and the turban decorating it are both appropriately large. It is a place of enormous gravity, always busy with supplicants.

INSIDER TIP
Wednesday Market

Every Wednesday, the streets east of the Fatih Mosque transform into the bustling Fatih Çarsamba Pazarı bazaar, selling items such as cheeses, olives, clothing and household goods.

13 Bulgur Palace

Bulgur Palas

B5 Aksaray, Kargı Çıkmazı 3, Fatih Aksaray Yusufpaşa 10am-7pm Tue-Sun

Neglected for many years, the five-storey Bulgur Palace has now been restored to its former glory. It is a prime example of the Turkish First National Architecture Movement *(p30)*. The palace was named after its original owner, Mehmet Habib Bey, a soldier and member of parliament who made his fortune selling wheat, barley and bulgur. Although Italian architect Giulio Mongeri is often credited with its 1912 design, evidence is lacking, despite its characteristic Mongeri flair. In 2024, the palace reopened as a library and culture centre, featuring a spiral staircase, workstations, marble columns, reading nooks, a café and a tower offering sweeping city views.

14 Molla Zeyrek Mosque

Molla Zeyrek Camii

C4 İbadethane Sok, Küçükpazar 28T, 30D, 78, 97GE 9am-6pm daily (from 2:30pm Fri) Prayer times

This building was a church in the Byzantine period,

Ancient walls of Yedikule Fortress, by the Sea of Marmara

←

Pink-hued exterior and lovely garden of the Molla Zeyrek Mosque

founded by Empress Irene, and was known as the Church of the Pantocrator ("Christ the Almighty") during the 12th century. It was once the centrepiece of one of Istanbul's most important religious foundations, the Monastery of the Pantocrator. The complex included an asylum, a hospice and a hospital. Converted into a mosque after the Ottoman conquest, it has a magnificent figurative marble floor and is composed of three interlinked chapels. Closed for restoration for many years, the mosque reopened in late 2014.

15

Yedikule Fortress

Yedikule Hisarı

B5 Yedikule Meydanı Sok 9, Yedikule (0212) 585 89 33 Kazlıçeşme, Yedikule 31, 28T, 93 or T6 9am-6pm Tue-Sun

Yedikule, the "Fortress of Seven Towers", was built in 1455 against the southern section of the Theodosian Walls *(p150)*. It displays both Byzantine and Ottoman features, being built in stages over a long period. Its seven towers are joined by thick walls to make a five-sided fortification. The two square marble towers built into the great land walls once flanked the Golden Gate (now blocked), which consisted of three magnificent golden portals. The gate was built by Emperor Theodosius I in 390 CE as the triumphal entrance into the thriving medieval city of Byzantium.

In the 15th century, Sultan Mehmet II (the Conqueror) completed Yedikule by adding three round towers and connecting curtain walls. After viewing the exterior, you can enter through a doorway in the northeastern wall. The tower to your left as you enter is the *yazılı kule*, "the tower with inscriptions". It was used as a prison for foreign envoys and others who fell out of favour with the sultan. Its name is derived from the names and epitaphs which many of these doomed individuals carved into the walls. Some of these morbid inscriptions are still visible.

There are two towers flanking the Golden Gate. The north tower was a place of execution. Among those who met their end here was the 17-year-old Sultan Osman II, who was dragged off to Yedikule by his own Janissaries in 1622, after four years of misrule. The walkway around the ramparts is accessible via a steep flight of stone steps and offers good views of the land walls, the southern marble tower and the market garden allotments.

DRINK

Zeyrekhane

Sip tea at this municipality-run café adjacent to the Molla Zeyrek Mosque's bulky pink structure, and enjoy Golden Horn views from the garden.

C4 Ibadethane Arkası Sok 10, Zeyrek (0212) 534 65 20

The Fall of Constantinople in 1453 at the Panorama 1453 History Museum

16 Panorama 1453 History Museum

Panoramik 1453 Tarihi Müzesi

B4 Topkapı Kültür Parkı Topkapı 8am-6:30pm daily panoramikmuze.com

The inside of the dome of this modern building has been decorated with a brilliant panoramic painting depicting the siege of Constantinople by the Ottoman Turks in 1453. The museum is located right opposite the section of the Theodosian Walls *(p150)* where Mehmet the Conqueror positioned his best troops and mightiest cannon. The magnificence of the painting, with over ten thousand figures, is heightened by sound effects inspired by the conquest. An informative audio guide is available in Turkish.

17 Shrine of Zoodochus Pege

Balıklı Meryem Ana Rum Ortodoks Manastırı

A5 3 Balıklı Seyit Nizam Cad, Silivrikapı (0212) 582 30 81 Zeytinburnu Seyitnizam-Akşemsettın 93T 8:30am-4pm daily

The Fountain of Zoodochus Pege ("Life-Giving Spring") is built over Istanbul's most famous sacred spring, which is believed to have miraculous powers. Legend has it that the fish swimming in the spring miraculously leapt into the water from a monk's frying pan just before the fall of Constantinople *(p53)*, in response to his declaration that a Turkish invasion of the fortified town was as likely as fish coming back to life.

Originally thought to be the site of an ancient sanctuary of the Greek goddess Artemis, it later became home to a church dedicated to the Virgin Mary. The spring was popular throughout the Byzantine era, especially on Ascension Day, when the emperor would visit. The church was destroyed and rebuilt several times, and the present structure dates from 1833. Its inner courtyard is filled with the tombs of bishops and patriarchs of the Greek Orthodox Church.

HIDDEN GEM
Medicinal Oasis

A short stroll north from the Shrine of Zoodochus Pege is Zeytinburnu Medicinal Plant Garden *(ztbb.org)*, a landscaped botanical garden featuring walking trails and over 700 medicinal plant species.

18 Palace of the Porphyrogenitus

Tekfur Sarayı

B4 Şişehane Cad, Edirnekapı (0212) 525 61 30 Ayvansaray Balat 87, 336E 10am-6pm Tue-Sun

The former Palace of the Porphyrogenitus has a three-storey façade in typically Byzantine style. It was most likely built in the late Byzantine era as an annexe of the Blachernae Palace. These palaces became the principal residences of the imperial sovereigns during the last two centuries before the fall of Constantinople to the Ottomans in 1453. During the reign of Ahmet III

Did You Know?

"Porphyrogenitus", meaning "born to the purple", refers to a son of a reigning Byzantine emperor.

(1703–30), the last remaining İznik potters *(p187)* moved to the palace and it became a centre for tile production.

It now houses a museum containing a rich collection of ceramic, glass and crockery items such as delicate coffee cup sets and tile panels depicting cityscapes – Cezri Kasım Paşa Mosque in Eyüp also has some fine examples of these tiles. Other notable pieces in the palace include a ceramic mihrab, relocated from an Istanbul mosque.

The roof of the palace has been converted into a platform offering views all the way up the Golden Horn and over to Beyoğlu and the Galata Tower on the other side.

Gazi Ahmet Paşa Mosque

Gazi Ahmet Paşa Camii

B4 Bican Bağcıoğlu Ykş 56 Topkapı-Ulubatlı Fetıhkapı 28T, 73, 93 8:30am-6pm daily (from 2:30pm Fri) Prayer times

A worthwhile detour along the city walls is the Gazi Ahmet Paşa Mosque. This lovely building, with its peaceful leafy courtyard and graceful proportions, is one of the imperial architect Sinan's *(p109)* lesser-known achievements, which he built in 1554 for Kara Ahmet Paşa, a grand vizier of Süleyman the Magnificent *(p54)*.

The courtyard is surrounded by the cells of a *medrese* and a *dershane*, or main classroom. Attractive apple-green and yellow İznik tiles dating from the mid-1500s grace the porch, with blue-and-white tiles on the east wall of the prayer hall.

Inside the Palace of the Porphyrogenitus, and *(inset)* its stately façade ↓

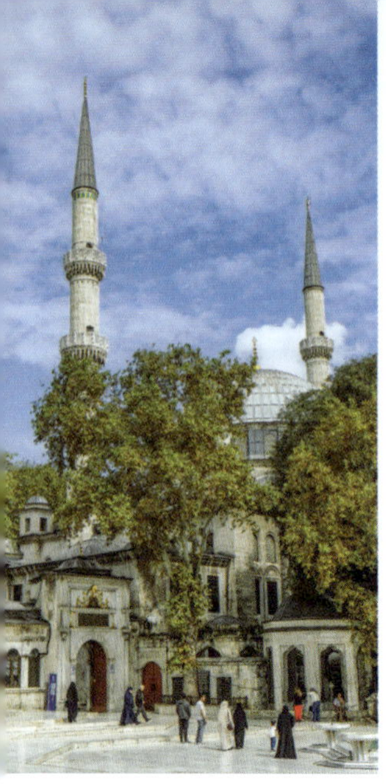

↑ Towering minarets of the beautiful Eyüp Sultan Mosque

Eyüp Sultan Mosque

Eyüp Sultan Camii

B3 Camii Kebir Sok (0212) 564 73 68 Eyüp Feshane 55T, 99A 9am-6:30pm daily (from 2:30pm Fri) Prayer times

Mehmet the Conqueror built the original mosque on this site in 1458, five years after his conquest of Istanbul, in honour of Eyüp Ensari. That building fell into ruins and the present mosque was completed in 1800, by Selim III.

The mosque's delightful inner courtyard features two huge plane trees on a platform. This was the setting for the Girding of the Sword of Osman, part of a sultan's inauguration in the days of Mehmet the Conqueror.

Opposite the mosque is the tomb of Eyüp Ensari himself, said to have been killed during the first Arab siege of Constantinople in the 7th century. The tomb dates from the same period as the mosque and its decoration is in the Ottoman Baroque style.

Complex of Valide Sultan Mihrişah

Mihrişah Valide Sultan Külliyesi

B3 Seyit Reşat Cad Feshane 39, 55T, 99A

Most of the northern side of the street leading from Eyüp Mosque's northern gate is occupied by the largest Baroque *külliye* *(p33)* in Istanbul, although unusually it is not centred on a mosque. Built in 1791, this historical complex is dedicated to Mihrişah, the mother of Selim III.

The complex includes the ornate marble tomb of Mihrişah and a soup kitchen, which is still in use today. There is also a beautifully designed *sebil* (grilled fountain), which once served as a refreshing oasis to passers-by, where an attendant offered water and sweet, flavourful sherbet.

Pierre Loti Café

Piyer Loti Kahvehanesi

B3 İdris Köşkü Cad, Eyüpsultan Eyüp Pierre Loti Teleferiği (TF2) 39, 55T, 99A 8:30am-midnight daily pierrelotitepesi.com

This famous café stands at the top of the hill in Eyüp Cemetery, a 20-minute walk up Karyağdı Sokağı from Eyüp Mosque. It is named after the French novelist Julien Viaud, a French naval officer, popularly known as Pierre Loti, who frequented the café during his stay here in 1876. Loti defiantly fell in love with a married Turkish woman and wrote an autobiographical novel,

EYÜP CEMETERY

Ottoman graveyards like Eyüp Cemetery, crowned by the Pierre Loti Café, were a garden of the dead, where the living happily strolled without morbid inhibitions. Gravestones were often lavishly symbolic: from their decoration, you can tell the occupation, rank and number of children of the deceased. The fez appears only on men's gravestones that were erected after 1829, when the turban was banned.

→ Patrons enjoying a meal at the popular Pierre Loti Café

Most of the northern side of the street leading from Eyüp Mosque's northern gate is occupied by the largest Baroque *külliye* in Istanbul.

Aziyade, about their affair. The café is prettily decked out with 19th-century furniture and the waiters wear period outfits.

Rahmi M. Koç Industrial Museum

Rahmi M. Koç Müzesi

B3 Rahmi M. Koç Cad 3, Hasköy (0212) 369 66 00 9:30am-5pm Tue-Fri, 10am-6pm Sat & Sun (Apr-Sep: to 8pm daily)

Vintage cars on display at the Rahmi M. Koç Industrial Museum

This is Turkey's best industrial museum, which was formerly a factory producing anchors, chains and other similar goods for the shipping industry. Well located on the banks of the Golden Horn, the museum can be easily reached by ferry from Eminönü. The exhibits here range from amphicars to penny farthings. Visitors will also find Royal Enfield motorcycles, Trabants, old steam ships, a Douglas DC-3 Dakota, a working railway and a submarine. For those weary after exploring the extensive collection, the museum also has a good on-site restaurant and three cafés worth checking out for their décor alone.

INSIDER TIP

Adventure by Boat

The Haliç Hattı ferry line from Karaköy is the most scenic route to reach key historical and cultural sites in Hasköy, home to the Rahmi M. Koç Industrial Museum, and the district of Eyüp.

Admiring the caïques on display at the Naval Museum

Naval Museum

Deniz Müzesi

D3 Sinanpaşa, Beşiktaş Cad 6, Beşiktaş Beşiktaş Kabataş 22, 22RE, 28 9am-4pm Tue-Fri, 10am-5pm Sat & Sun denizmuzeleri.dzkk.tsk.tr

The Naval Museum opened in 2013 after several years of restoration. Housed in a state-of-the-art complex on the seafront, it offers superb views of the Bosphorus Strait. The exhibits at the museum include a beautifully renovated series of imperial caïques. These were long, narrow rowing boats that once took the sultans and their entourages up and down the waterways around the city. Among these magnificent vessels, the largest caïque, measuring 40 m (130 ft) long, was once used by Mehmet IV and required a huge crew of 144 oarsmen to operate.

Did You Know?

Opposite the Naval Museum is a statue of Ottoman admiral Barbarossa, a 16th-century leader.

The museum also has a good bistro, ideal for lunch.

Maiden's Tower

Kız Kulesi

D4 Üsküdar Üsküdar kizkulesi.com.tr

Located on a tiny islet offshore from Üsküdar, the 18th-century Maiden's Tower is a well-known Bosphorus landmark. The tower once served as a quarantine centre during a cholera outbreak, as a lighthouse, a customs control point and a maritime tollgate. It is now home to a small café. The tower's Turkish name, Kız Kulesi (Maiden's Tower), comes from a legendary princess who was confined here after a prophet foretold that she would die of a snakebite. The tower's former English name, Leander's Tower, derived from the Greek myth of Leander, who swam the Hellespont (modern-day Dardanelles) to see his lover, priestess Hero.

Military Museum

Harbiye Askeri Müzesi

D3 Vali Konağı Cad, Harbiye (0212) 233 27 20 25G, 46T, 55T 9am-4:30pm Tue-Sun; Mehter Band performances: 3-3:30pm Tue-Thu, Sat & Sun, 11-11:30am & 3-3:30pm Fri

The impressive collection of the Harbiye Military Museum and Cultural Site Command, better known as the Military Museum, chronicles Turkey's conflicts

STAY

Çırağan Palace Kempenski

Housed in a former imperial palace, this luxury hotel offers spacious rooms and suites.

E3 Çırağan Cad 32, Beşiktaş kempinski.com/en/ciragan-palace

from the 1453 conquest of Constantinople *(p53)* to modern warfare. The building once served as the military academy where Atatürk studied from 1899 to 1905.

This museum is also the main location for performances by the Mehter Band, formed in the 14th century under Osman I. Until the 19th century the musicians were Janissaries, who accompanied the sultan into battle, performing songs about hero-ancestors and battle victories. The band significantly influenced composers like Mozart and Beethoven.

Some of the most striking weapons are displayed on the ground floor, including 15th-century curved daggers *(cembiyes)* carried at the waist by foot soldiers. These are ornamented with plant, flower and geometric motifs in relief and silver filigree. Other exhibits include 17th-century copper head armour for horses and Ottoman shields made from cane and willow covered in silk thread.

A moving portrayal of trench warfare is included in the section concerned with the ANZAC landings of 1915 at Chunuk Bair on the Gallipoli Peninsula *(p220)*, and upstairs is a spectacular exhibit of the tents used by sultans on their campaigns.

Just a short walk away from the Hasköy station on Taşkışla Caddesi you can take the cable car across Maçka Park to Abdi İpekçi Caddesi in Teşvikiye. Some of the best designer clothes, jewellery, furniture and art shops in the city can be found here.

Mihrimah Sultan Mosque

Mihrimah Sultan Camii

E4 Hakimiyeti Milliye Cad, Üsküdar Üsküdar 9am-6pm daily (from 2:30pm Fri) Prayer times

One of Usküdar's most prominent landmarks, this massive structure sits on a raised platform; it was built by Sinan between 1547 and 1548 for Mihrimah Sultan, favourite daughter of Süleyman the Magnificent. Without space to build a courtyard, Sinan constructed a large protruding roof which extends to cover the *şadırvan* (ablutions fountain) in front of the mosque.

↓ Maiden's Tower, perched on a small islet off Üsküdar

28

Atik Valide Mosque

Atik Valide Camii

E4 Çinili Camii Sok, Üsküdar Üsküdar 6, 12A 9am-6pm daily (from 2:30pm Fri) Prayer times

The Atik Valide Mosque in Üsküdar is one of Istanbul's largest mosque complexes. Its name translates as "Old Mosque of the Sultan's Mother", as the mosque was built for Nur Banu, the mother of Murat III. She was the first of the sultans' mothers to rule the Ottoman Empire from the Harem *(p76)*. Completed by Sinan in 1583, it features a wide, shallow dome which rests on five semidomes, with a flat arch over the entrance portal.

The interior features three-sided galleries with richly stencilled undersides. The mihrab apse is covered with panels of fine İznik tiles *(p187)*, and both the mihrab and *minbar* are made of sculpted marble. Side aisles were added in the 17th century, while the iron grating and architectural trompe l'oeil paintings on the royal loge in the western gallery date from the 18th century.

The north courtyard has a flight of stairs leading to the *medrese*, where the *dershane* (classroom) extends over the street, with its structure supported below. The *şifahane* (hospital), built around a central courtyard east of the mosque, is also worth a visit.

Selimiye Barracks

Selimiye Kışlası

E5 Çeşmei Kebir Sok, Selimiye Harem 12, 12A Florence Nightingale Museum: 9am-5pm Sat (by appt only)

The Selimiye Barracks, originally made of wood, were completed in 1799 under Selim III (r 1789–1807). They were built to house the "New Army" that formed part of Selim's plan for reforming the Imperial command structure and replacing the powerful Janissaries. The plan backfired and Selim was deposed but the barracks were, nevertheless, a striking symbol of Constantinople's military might, perhaps becoming even more so when they were rebuilt in stone in 1829 by Mahmut II. The building still houses Istanbul's First Army Division and is off limits to the public.

The Florence Nightingale Museum is found within the Selimiye Barracks. It still contains some of the original furniture and the famous lamp which gave her the epitaph "Lady of the Lamp". Visits must be arranged in advance by calling the Army Headquarters on (0216) 343 73 10, four months in advance.

Nearby are two other sites worth seeing – the **Selimiye Mosque** and the **British War Cemetery** (also known as the Crimean Memorial Cemetery). The mosque was built in 1804 and is set in a lovely courtyard. The cemetery, south on Burhan Felek Caddesi, contains the graves of men who died in the Crimean War, World War I battles at Gallipoli *(p220)* and during World War II in the Middle East.

FLORENCE NIGHTINGALE

British nurse Florence Nightingale was a tireless campaigner for hospital, military and social reform. In 1854, during the Crimean War (1854-6), she led 38 British nurses to the Selimiye Barracks in Scutari (Üsküdar), successfully reducing the barracks' mortality rate from 20 to 2 per cent. Upon her return to Britain, she opened a training school for nurses.

Selimiye Mosque

Selimiye Mah, Selimiye Cami Cad 51/1, Üsküdar 9am-6pm daily (from 2:30pm Fri) Prayer times

British War Cemetery

Behind the Selimiye Barracks and Haydarpaşa pier Mon-Fri

Haydarpaşa Station

Haydarpaşa Garı

E5 Haydarpaşa İstasyon Cad (0216) 348 80 20 Haydarpaşa, Kadıköy For restoration

Haydarpaşa Station, featuring a tiled jetty, is still impressive, despite suffering from a fire in 2010. It's built on reclaimed land and surrounded by water on three sides.

→ Ortaköy Mosque, set beside the Bosphorus Bridge

The first Anatolian railway line, which was built in 1873, ran from here to İznik *(p186)*. The extension of this railway was a major part of Abdül Hamit II's drive to modernize the Ottoman Empire. Lacking sufficient funds, he applied for help to his German ally, Kaiser Wilhelm II. The Deutsche Bank agreed to invest in the construction and operation of the railway. In 1898 German engineers were contracted to build the railway lines running across Anatolia and beyond into the far reaches of the Ottoman Empire.

Construction on Haydarpaşa, the grandest of the stations, started in 1906. Its two German architects, Otto Ritter and Helmut Conu, chose to build on a grand scale, using a Neo-Classical German style. Work was completed in 1908.

The station ceased operations following the fire of 2010 but reopened in 2014 when a high-speed train service began operating between Istanbul and Ankara. However, it is currently closed (once again) due to ongoing excavations.

Ortaköy

E3 3 km (2 miles) from Beşiktaş Ortaköy 22RE, 40

At the foot of the Bosphorus Bridge, the suburb of Ortaköy has retained a village feel. Life centres on Ortaköy Meydanı, the quayside square, which was once busy with fishers unloading the day's catch. Nowadays, Ortaköy is better known for its *kumpir* (baked potatoes with various fillings) and a lively Sunday market, which crowds out the square and surrounding streets, and its shops selling the varied wares of local artisans. It is also the location for a thriving bar and café scene, which in the summer is the hub of Istanbul's nightlife.

Büyük Mecidiye Camii (better known as **Ortaköy Mosque**), Ortaköy's most impressive landmark, sits on the waterfront. It was built in 1853 by Nikoğos Balyan, who was also responsible for Dolmabahçe Palace *(p152)*.

Ortaköy Mosque
Mecidiye, İskele Sok 6

EAT

Dürümcü Enişte
A longtime neighbourhood stalwart, Dürümcü Enişte serves classic Turkish grilled-meat dishes and *dürüm* (kebab wraps).

E3 Teyyareci Fevzi Sok, Beşiktaş durumcueniste.com

Sefarad Meyhane
This traditional tavern offers a variety of seafood, meze and vegetarian dishes. Guests can also enjoy plenty of raki, Turkey's aniseed liqueur.

E3 Muvakkit Sok 33, Beşiktaş (0212) 261 29 83

Feriye
Tuck into Chef Birkan Erköylü's contemporary twists on traditional Anatolian dishes.

E3 Çırağan Cad 44, Ortaköy feriye.com

Bosphorus Bridge, with the cityscape in the background

Bosphorus Bridge

15 Temmuz Şehitler Köprüsü

E3 Ortaköy & Beylerbeyi 22, 22RE, 40T

Spanning the Bosphorus between the districts of Ortaköy and Beylerbeyi, this was the first bridge to be built across the straits that divide Istanbul. Construction began in 1970, and the bridge was inaugurated on 29 October 1973, to coincide with the 50th anniversary of the founding of the Turkish Republic *(p55)*. It is 1,074 m (3,524 ft) long, and is the world's ninth-longest suspension bridge, reaching 64 m (210 ft) above the water. In 2016, it was renamed as 15th of July Martyrs Bridge in memory of those who died during an attempted coup that took place on 15 July 2015.

The Bosphorus is especially popular in summer. This is when cool, refreshing breezes waft off the water, making boat tours and waterfront dining and strolls along the banks a highly sought-after experience.

PICTURE PERFECT
Bridging the Gap

Head to Nakkastepe National Garden *(Gümüsyolu Caddesi, Üsküdar)* on the Asian shore to capture spectacular hilltop views of the Bosphorus Bridge as it spans the strait.

Sakıp Sabancı Museum

Sakıp Sabancı Müzesi

F1 Sakıp Sabancı Cad 42, Emirgan Emirgan 40 from Taksim Sq; 22 from Kabataş 10am-6pm Tue-Sun sakipsabanci muzesi.org

With a superb view over the Bosphorus, the Sakıp Sabancı Museum is also known as the Horse Mansion (Atlı Köşk). Exhibitions comprise over 400 years of Ottoman calligraphy and other Koranic and secular art treasures. The collection of paintings is exquisite, with works by Ottoman court painters and European artists enthralled with Turkey. A Picasso exhibition in 2005 made this museum the first in Turkey to host a major solo exhibition of a Western artist. The museum continues to host must-see exhibitions.

Fortress of Europe

Rumeli Hisarı

F2 Yahya Kemal Cad 42, European side (0212) 263 53 05 Aşiyan 40, 40T from Taksim Sq; 22 from Kabataş 9am-5pm Tue-Sun (Apr-Sep: to 7:30pm Tue-Sun)

This fortress was built by Mehmet the Conqueror in 1452 as his first step in the conquest of Constantinople *(p53)*. Situated at the narrowest point of the Bosphorus, the fortress controlled a major Byzantine supply route. Across the straits is Anadolu Hisarı, which was built in the 14th century by Beyazıt I.

Beylerbeyi Palace's Blue Hall, designed in the German Baroque style

The layout of Rumeli Hisarı was planned by Mehmet himself. While his grand vizier and two other viziers were each responsible for the building of one of the three great towers, the sultan took charge of the walls. Local buildings were torn down to provide the stones and other building materials. One thousand masons laboured on the walls alone. It was completed in four months – a considerable feat, given the steep terrain.

The new fortress was garrisoned by a force of Janissaries, whose troops trained their cannons on the straits to prevent the passage of foreign ships. After they had sunk a Venetian vessel, this approach to Constantinople was cut off. Following the conquest of the city, the fortress lost its importance as a military base and was used as a prison, particularly for out-of-favour foreign envoys and prisoners of war. The structure was restored only in 1953.

The gardens, which are rich in Bosphorus flora such as redbud trees, display a piece of the chain once used to close the Golden Horn against attacks.

> **The Empress Eugénie of France (wife of Napoleon III) was a guest at the palace in 1869 on her way to the opening of the Suez Canal.**

35   

Beylerbeyi Palace

Beylerbeyi Sarayı

F3 Abdullah Ağa Cad 12, Asian side Beylerbeyi, Kuzguncuk Üsküdar 15, 15B from Üsküdar 9am-5pm Tue-Sun millisaraylar.gov.tr

Built in the Baroque style of the late Ottoman period, Beylerbeyi Palace was built between 1861 and 1865 to a design by Sarkis Balyan under the orders of Sultan Abdül Aziz. A previous palace had stood here, and the gardens were already laid out by Murat IV in 1639. As the Ottoman empire withered, palaces proliferated in a flourish of grandeur and showmanship. Abdül Aziz had Beylerbeyi built as a pleasure palace to entertain dignitaries and royalty. The Empress Eugénie of France (wife of Napoleon III) was a guest at the palace in 1869 on her way to the opening of the Suez Canal and had her face slapped by the sultan's mother for daring to enter the palace on the arm of Abdül Aziz. Other regal visitors to the palace included the Duke and Duchess of Windsor. The fountains, baths and colonnades were meant to impress, as were the lovely frescoes of Ottoman warships.

To keep himself distracted, Aziz also had a zoo built on the site and, apparently, delighted in the flocks of ostriches and several Bengal tigers. The zoo is no longer there, but the palace has been completely refurbished and restored to its former elegance.

Third-but-last of the line of sultans, the autocratic Abdül Hamit II spent six years as a prisoner in an anteroom of the palace and died there, virtually forgotten, after being deposed in 1909. There are superb views of the palace from the Bosphorus, from where the two prominent bathing pavilions – one for the Harem and the other for the *selamlık* (the men's quarters), can best be seen. The most impressive room is the reception hall, which has a pool and fountain.

BIRDS OF THE BOSPHORUS

In September and October, thousands of white storks and birds of prey fly over the Bosphorus on their way from their breeding grounds in Eastern Europe to wintering regions in Africa. Among birds of prey on this route you can see the lesser-spotted eagle and the honey buzzard. The birds also cross the straits in spring on their way to Europe but, before the breeding season, they are fewer in number.

A BOAT TOUR
UP THE BOSPHORUS

Distance 45 km (28 miles) **Duration** 2 hours minimum **Boarding point** Eminonü Pier **Stopping-off points** Anadolu Kavağı for lunch **Return** to Eminönü by bus, dolmuş or taxi

Up the Bosphorus
FURTHER AFIELD

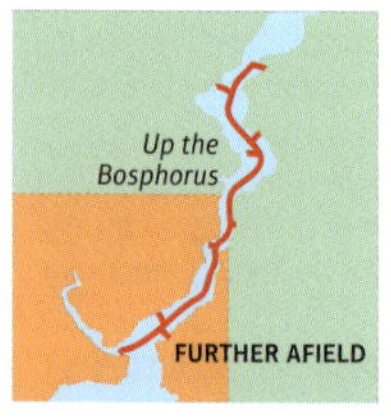

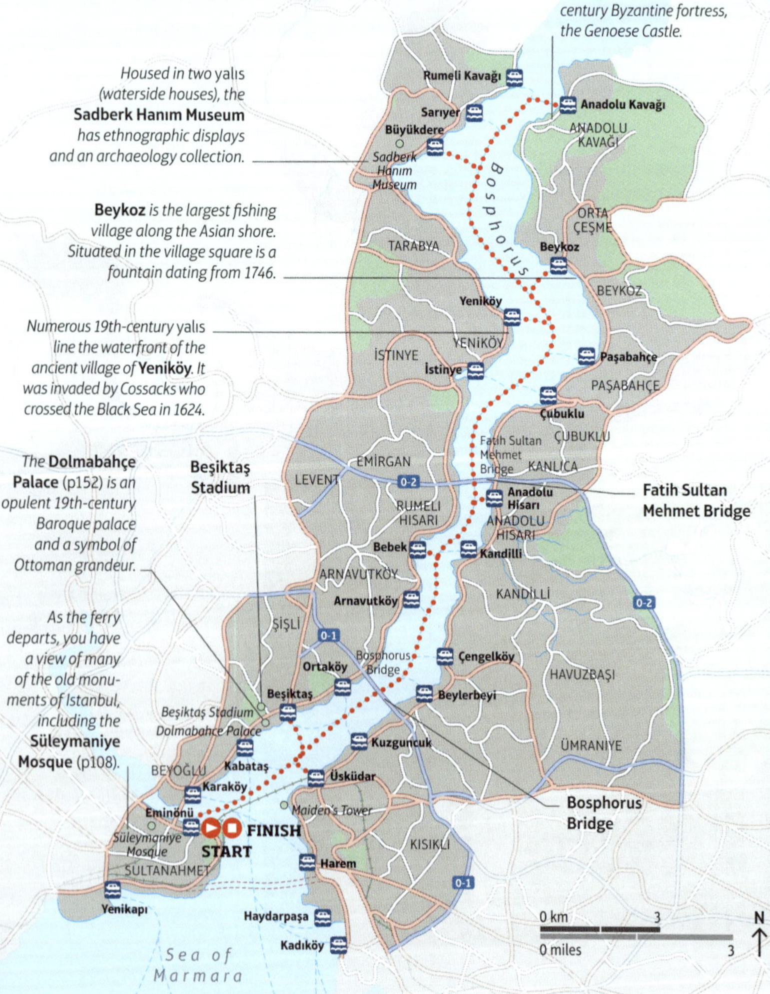

Locator Map
For more detail see p146

One of the great pleasures of a visit to Istanbul is a cruise up the Bosphorus. This relaxing cruise offers a great vantage point from which to view the city's famous landmarks. While you have the option of joining a pre-arranged guided tour or boarding one of the smaller boats that tout for passengers at Eminönü, the best way to travel is on the official trip run by Istanbul Şehir Hatları. The SH ferry offers a round-trip to the upper Bosphorus once or twice daily, stopping at six piers along the way, including a leisurely stop at Anadolu Kavağı for lunch. Passengers can either return to Eminönü on the same boat or make their way back to the city by bus, dolmuş or taxi. The route shown here covers the full Bosphorus Cruise.

Rumeli Kavağı
Anadolu Kavağı
Sarıyer
ANADOLU KAVAĞI
Büyükdere
Sadberk Hanım Museum
Bosphorus
ORTA ÇEŞME
TARABYA
Beykoz
BEYKOZ
Yeniköy
YENİKÖY
İSTINYE
İstinye
Paşabahçe
PAŞABAHÇE
Çubuklu
ÇUBUKLU
Fatih Sultan Mehmet Bridge
KANLICA
EMİRGAN
LEVENT
0-2
Anadolu Hisarı
RUMELI HISARI
ANADOLU HISARI
Bebek
Kandilli
ARNAVUTKÖY
KANDİLLİ
Arnavutköy
0-2
ŞİŞLİ
0-1
Bosphorus Bridge
Çengelköy
Ortaköy
HAVUZBAŞI
Beşiktaş
Beylerbeyi
Beşiktaş Stadium
Dolmabahçe Palace
Kuzguncuk
ÜMRANIYE
BEYOĞLU
Kabataş
Üsküdar
Karaköy
Maiden's Tower
Eminönü
FINISH
Süleymaniye Mosque
START
KISIKLI
SULTANAHMET
Harem
0-1
Yenikapı
Haydarpaşa
Kadıköy
Sea of Marmara
0 km 3
0 miles 3
N
The last stop on the trip brings you to the village of **Anadolu Kavağı** and a ruined 14th-century Byzantine fortress, the Genoese Castle.
Housed in two yalıs (waterside houses), the **Sadberk Hanım Museum** has ethnographic displays and an archaeology collection.
Beykoz is the largest fishing village along the Asian shore. Situated in the village square is a fountain dating from 1746.
Numerous 19th-century yalıs line the waterfront of the ancient village of **Yeniköy**. It was invaded by Cossacks who crossed the Black Sea in 1624.
The **Dolmabahçe Palace** (p152) is an opulent 19th-century Baroque palace and a symbol of Ottoman grandeur.
Beşiktaş Stadium
Fatih Sultan Mehmet Bridge
As the ferry departs, you have a view of many of the old monuments of Istanbul, including the **Süleymaniye Mosque** (p108).
Bosphorus Bridge

INSIDER TIP
Booking Tours

SH ferries run every 20-30 minutes between major terminals, with limited service on the upper Bosphorus. Book private tours (two to three hours) or arrange a luxury cruise through your hotel.

Picturesque setting of Ortaköy Mosque, located along the Bosphorus

EXPERIENCE TURKEY

Exploring the arid landscapes of Zelve

Houses in Burgazada, the Princes' Islands

THRACE AND THE SEA OF MARMARA

Stretching either side of Istanbul, this region has been strategically vital throughout history, providing trading routes from east to west and south to north. In 324 CE, Emperor Constantine chose Byzantium as the new capital, renaming it Constantinople. As the hinterland of the new imperial capital, the region remained crucial during the Byzantine era, with Nicaea (modern İznik) hosting the first Ecumenical Council of the Christian Church in 325 CE.

By the 14th century, the Ottoman Empire was steadily consolidating territory closer to Constantinople; Bursa was eventually captured and made Ottoman capital in 1326. Ottoman Bursa flourished as a commercial trade-route hub, while İznik became an important centre for artisans. In the mid-14th century, the Ottomans conquered Thrace, moving the capital to Edirne until 1453, when Constantinople was conquered and made the new capital, establishing the importance of the Sea of Marmara region.

The strategic importance of this region was again tested in the 19th and early 20th centuries, as Ottoman power waned. Edirne was occupied by Russia in 1877–8 and then by Bulgaria in 1913. During World War I, Allied forces tried – and failed – to seize control of the Ottoman waterways during Thrace's Gallipoli Campaign (1915–16). Today, the cities here remain centres of industry and agriculture.

BULGARIA
GREECE
Galabowo
Elhovo
Bolyarovo
Topolowgrad
Simeonowgrad
Harmanli
Lyubimets
Svilengrad
Malko Tarnovo
Kofçaz
Lalapaşa
Demirköy
Yıldız Dağları
Süloğlu
Kırklareli
Tundzha
Arda
EDİRNE
Hasköy
KIRKLARELİ
Madscharowo
Pınarhisar
Vize
Karacaoğlan
Havsa
Iwajlowgrad
Orestiada
Babaeski
Lüleburgaz
Mandra
Mikro Dereio
Büyükkarıştıran
Lissos
Uzunköprü
Ergene Irmağı
Megalo Dereio
Hayrabolu
Muratlı
Çorlu
Hamidiye
Küplü
Leptokarya
Banarlı
Aisymi
EDİRNE
TEKİRDAĞ
Paşayiğit
Tekirdağ
Ipsala
Alexandroupoli
Malkara
İnecik
Keşan
Kumbağ
Ballı
Karahisar
Tekir Dağı
Enez
Mecidiye
Şarköy
Marmara
Saros Körfezi
Bolayır
Marmara Adası
Gelibolu
Karabiga
Erdek
Lâpseki
Gallipoli Peninsula
Balikliçesme
Biga
Gökçeada
Kabatepe
Eceabat
Çanakkale
Gönen
İmbros
Serçiler
Çan
Etili
Yenice
ÇANAKKALE
Aesepus River
Balya
THRACE AND THE SEA OF MARMARA
Edremit
İvrindi
Burhaniye
BALIKESIR
Gömeç
Savaştepe

THRACE AND THE SEA OF MARMARA
Must Sees
1 Edirne
2 İznik
3 Bursa
Experience More
4 Princes' Islands
5 Polonezköy
6 Şile
7 Bird Paradise National Park
8 Uludağ National Park
BLACK SEA
Sea of Marmara
İğneada
Kıyıköy
Saray
Karacaköy
Durusu Gölü
Durusu
Çerkezköy
ISTANBUL
Istanbul Airport
Bahçeköy
Sarıyer
Beykoz
6 ŞILE
5 POLONEZKÖY
Sinekli
Çatalca
Seymen
Silivri
ISTANBUL p56
Büyük Çekmece
Küçük Çekmece
Istanbul Atatürk Airport
Sabiha Gökçen International Airport
Marmara Ereğlisi
THE BLACK SEA p300
PRINCES' ISLANDS 4
Gebze
Kocaeli (İzmit)
Gölcük
Degirmendere
KOCAELI
Dağları
Yalova
İmralı Adası
Armutlu
Gemlik
İznik Gölü
2 İZNİK
Sölöz
Avdan Dağı
Bandırma
Mudanya
BIRD PARADISE NATIONAL PARK
7
Nilüfer River
Bursa Yenişehir Airport
Yenişehir
Karacabey
3 BURSA
Kuş Gölü
Ulubat Gölü
BILECIK
Simav Çayı
8 ULUDAĞ NATIONAL PARK
İnegöl
Manyas
Mustafakemalpaşa
Susurluk
BURSA
Orhaneli
Keles
THE AEGEAN p196
ANKARA AND WESTERN ANATOLIA p272
Harmancık
Kepsut
Balıkesir
Dursunbey
KÜTAHYA
Tavşanlı
Bigadiç
0 kilometres 30
0 miles 30
N

EDIRNE

A2 Su Terazisi Sok 8 Karaağaç İskender Köyü Otogar İç Yolu, on the D100, 9 km (5.5 miles) SE of city centre edirne.com.tr/en

Edirne is a provincial university city that is home to one of Turkey's star attractions, the Selimiye Mosque. As this monument attests, Edirne was historically of great importance. It dates back to 125 CE, when the Emperor Hadrian joined two small towns to form Hadrianopolis, or Adrianople. For nearly a century, from the city's capture by Murat I in 1361 until Constantinople was conquered in 1453, Edirne served as the Ottoman capital. The city has one other claim to fame – its annual oil-wrestling championships held in late June or early July.

Beyazıt II Mosque

Beyazıt II Külliyesi

Yeni Maharet Cad
Daily

Beyazıt II Mosque stands in a peaceful location on the northern bank of the Tunca River, 1.5 km (1 mile) from the city centre. It was built in 1484–8, soon after Beyazıt II succeeded Mehmet the Conqueror (p53) as sultan.

The mosque and its courtyards are open to the public. Of the surrounding buildings, the old hospital, which incorporated an asylum, has been converted into the **Health Museum**. Patients were treated in this asylum – a model facility for its time – with water, music and flower therapies. The Turkish writer Evliya Çelebi (1611–84) reported that musicians used to perform at the facility three times a week. Its inner courtyard, unlike most later examples, covers three times the area of the mosque itself.

Did You Know?

The mosque's former madrasa is now home to the Museum for the Art of Calligraphy.

Health Museum

(0284) 224 09 22
9:30am-5:30pm daily

Mosque of the Three Balconies

Üç Şerefeli Camii

Hükümet Cad Daily

Until the fall of Constantinople, this was the grandest building of the early Ottoman state. It was finished in 1447 and takes its name from the three

↑ Selimiye Mosque, with its slender minarets dominating Edirne's skyline

balconies which adorn its southeastern minaret. Unlike its predecessors in Bursa *(p188)*, the mosque has an open courtyard, a feature that set a precedent for the imperial mosques of Istanbul. Both the mihrab and *minbar* can be seen from almost every corner of the prayer hall.

---

③

Old Mosque

Eski Ulu Cami

⌂ Muafakathane Sok
◷ Daily

The oldest of Edirne's major mosques, this is a smaller version of the Great Mosque in Bursa *(p192)*. The eldest son of Beyazıt I, Süleyman, began the mosque in 1403, but it was his youngest son, Mehmet I, who completed it in 1414.

A perfect square, the mosque is divided by four piers into nine domed sections. On either side of the prayer hall entrance there are Arabic inscriptions proclaiming "Allah" and "Mohammed".

↑ Early Ottoman-style interior of the 15th-century Old Mosque

STAY

Katre Taşodalar Otel

The restoration of this timber-and-stone Ottoman house, neighbouring the Selimiye Mosque, means you can bed-down in the birthplace of Sultan Mehmet II, who ruled during the 15th century.

⌂ Taş Odalar Sok 3, Meydan ☎ (0284) 212 35 29

Mihran Hanim Konağı Butik Hotel

This elegant late-Ottoman mansion features 19th-century-style rooms with beautiful carved-wood ceiling details.

⌂ Gazi Paşa Cad 30, Kaleiçi 🅦 mihranhanim.com

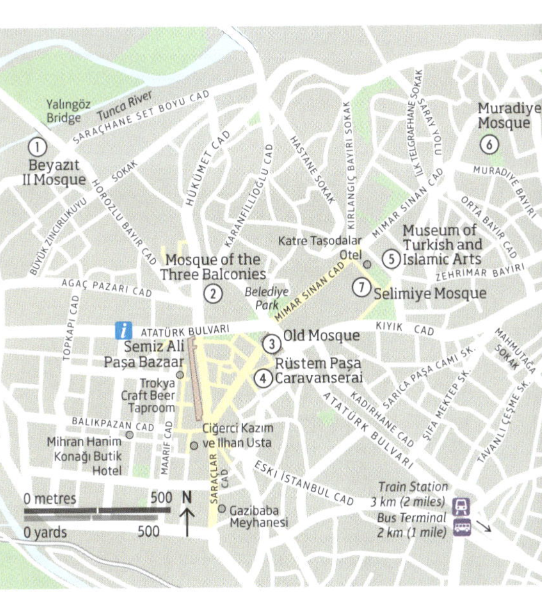

Rüstem Paşa Caravanserai

Rüstem Paşa Kervansarayı

Iki Kapılı Han Cad 57
(0284) 502 02 00

The renowned Ottoman architect Mimar Sinan *(p109)* designed this caravanserai for Süleyman's most powerful grand vizier, Rüstem Paşa, in 1560–61. The structure was constructed in two distinct parts. The larger courtyard, or *han (p119)*, was originally built for the merchants of Edirne. Today, this part of the structure makes up the large Rüstem Paşa Kervansaray Hotel, while the smaller courtyard, once an inn for other travellers, is now a student hostel.

A short walk away from the Rüstem Paşa Caravanserai, on the other side of Saraçlar Caddesi, is the Ali Paşa Çarşısı. This bazaar structure was also the work of Sinan, and dates back to 1589. It consists of a long, narrow street of vaulted shops.

The renowned Ottoman architect Mimar Sinan designed this caravanserai for Süleyman's most powerful grand vizier, Rüstem Paşa.

Museum of Turkish and Islamic Arts

Türk ve İslam Eserleri Müzesi

Taş Odalar Sok
(0284) 225 16 25
9am-7pm daily

Edirne's small collection of Turkish and Islamic works of art is located in a museum in the *medrese* of the Selimiye Mosque *(p184)*. Its first room is dedicated to the region's traditional sport of oil wrestling. Visitors are greeted by large-scale reproductions of historic miniature paintings that illustrate over 600 years of this athletic tradition. The images show the wrestling champions dressed in their traditional hand-stitched *kıspet* (leather shorts) and covered in olive oil. The displays have ceremonial importance, with roots in the local community.

Other objects on display include the original doors of the Beyazıt II Mosque, which are notable for their fine craftsmanship and historic value. There are also several military exhibits. Among these are some beautiful 18th-century Ottoman shields with woven silk exteriors, along with a selection of paintings depicting various military themes.

Muradiye Mosque

Muradiye Camii

Küçükpazar Cad
Daily

What is today a tranquil mosque was originally built

OIL WRESTLING

The Kırkpınar Oil-Wrestling Championships take place annually in late June or early July, on the island of Sarayiçi. The event is famed throughout Turkey and accompanied by a week-long carnival. The master of ceremonies, the *cazgır*, then invites the competitors to take part in a parade across the field, accompanied by music played on a drum *(davul)* and an oboe *(zurna)*. In the past, the bouts lasted up to two hours, but these days they are limited to no more than 40 minutes.

as a *zaviye* (dervish hospice) in 1421 by Sultan Murat II. According to legend, the sultan had a dream in which the great dervish leader Celaleddin Rumi *(p284)* appeared to him and requested that a hospice be constructed in Edirne. Taking this vision as divine guidance, Murat II commissioned the construction of the building, which initially served as a spiritual retreat and gathering place for dervishes. Only later was it converted into a mosque. The exterior stonework is characteristic of early Ottoman Edirne, with restrained decoration and clean, geometric lines. Its interior is notable for its massive calligraphic inscriptions, similar in scale and style to those found in Edirne's Old Mosque. Visitors will also notice several beautiful examples of15th-century İznik tiles *(p186)*. These blue-and-white tile panels are considered among the finest pre-Classical İznik works. Note that the mosque may be closed for visits outside regular prayer times.

Towering minarets and inner courtyard of Muradiye Mosque

EAT

Ciğerci Kazım ve Ilhan Usta

A local favourite, this family-run canteen, open since 1964, is the perfect spot to sample Edirne's local speciality of *tava ciğer* (fried calf's liver).

Osmaniye Cad 69, Merkez 9am-6pm Wed-Mon cigercikazimusta.com

Gazibaba Meyhanesi

Enjoy boisterous *meyhane* (traditional tavern) dining at this restaurant, with a menu of meze and grilled-meat mains, accompanied by plenty of raki and live *fasıl* (folk) music.

Zindan Altı Sok, Talatpaşa 11am-2am daily gazibabameyhanesi.com

DRINK

Trokya Craft Beer Taproom

One of Edirne's most popular nightlife spots, Trokya offers Turkish craft beers on tap, many of which are difficult to find elsewhere. The staff are friendly and the service is great. There's also live music from local, up-and-coming musicians.

Orhaniye Cad 4, Kaleiçi (0284) 212 86 87 4pm-2am daily

⑦

SELIMIYE MOSQUE

SELIMIYE CAMII

Mimar Sinan Cad, Edirne (0284) 225 16 25 Daily Prayer times

The apogee of mosque building and the culmination of a life's ambition for its architect, Mimar Sinan, Selimiye Mosque is the greatest of all the Ottoman mosque complexes.

Built on a slight hill, Selimiye Mosque is a prominent landmark. Its complex includes a *medrese*, housing a school, and the Selimiye Arasta, a covered bazaar. Commissioned by Selim II, construction started in 1569 and was completed in 1575, just one year after the sultan's death. The mosque marked the high point of Mimar Sinan's long career, and its dome was his proudest achievement. In his memoirs, he wrote: "With the help of Allah and the favour of Sultan Selim Khan, I have succeeded in building a cupola six cubits wider and four cubits deeper than that of Hagia Sophia." The dome of Selimiye, while comparable in diameter but actually slightly shallower than that of Hagia Sophia, achieves an elegance and balance that Sinan believed surpassed its grand predecessor.

INSIDER TIP
Müezzin Mahfili

Peek underneath the *müezzin mahfili* (elevated platform used by the muezzin to lead responses during prayer) to get a glimpse of its original 16th-century paintwork.

1

2

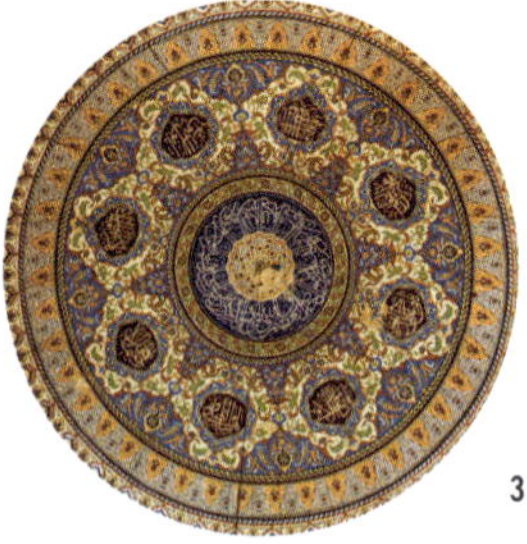

3

1 The interior is famous for its beautifully illuminated prayer hall.

2 Selimiye Mosque's distinctive dome and minarets, designed by imperial architect Mimar Sinan.

3 The intricately designed dome of the mosque, commissioned by the Ottoman Sultan Selim II.

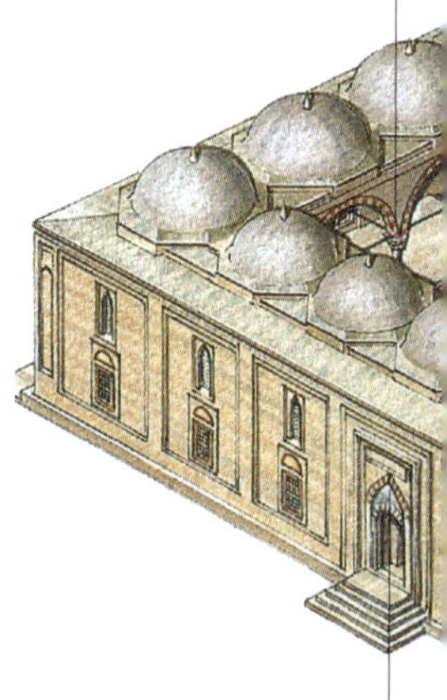

The columns supporting the arches of the courtyard are made of old marble, plundered from Byzantine architecture.

Above the courtyard portals are striking arches that were built using alternating red and honey-coloured slabs of stone.

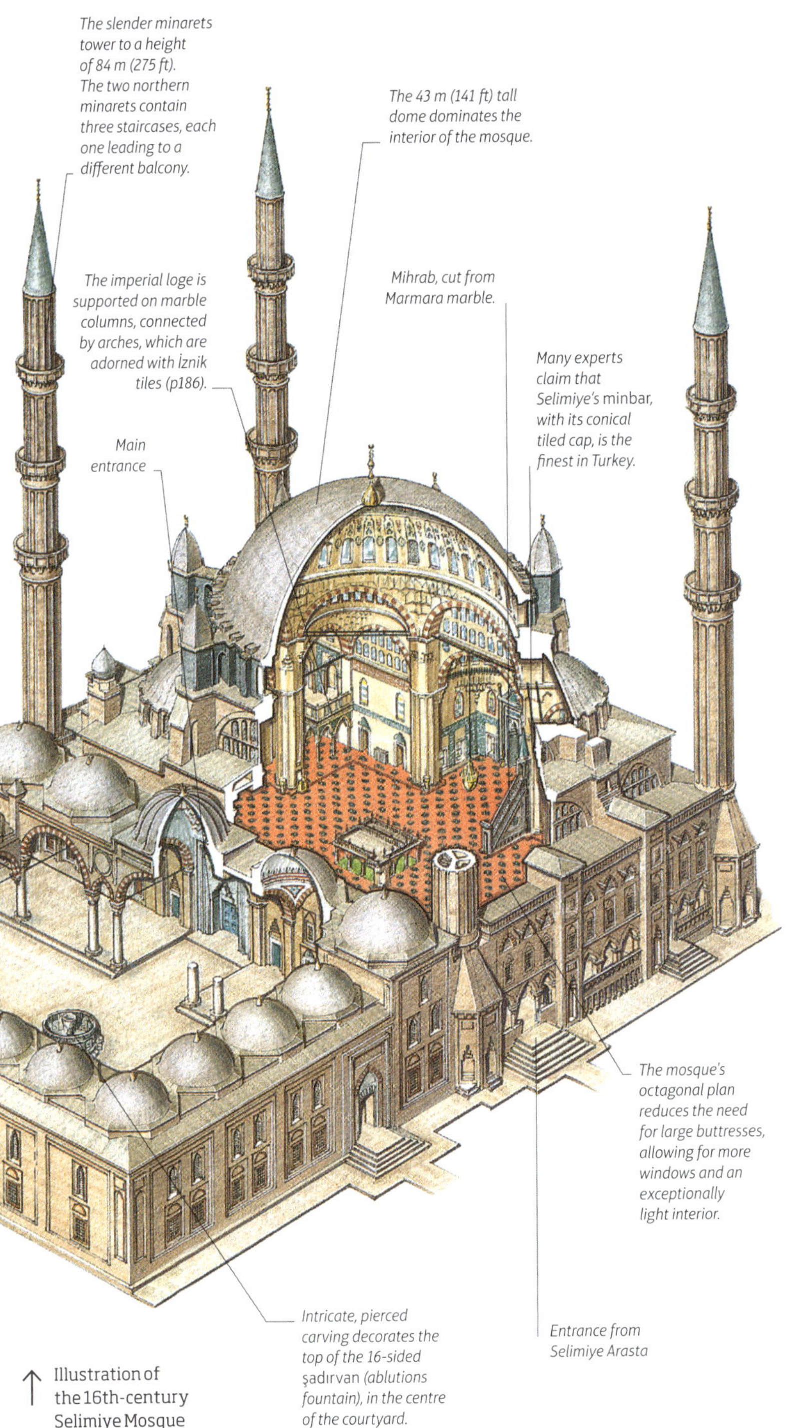

↑ Illustration of the 16th-century Selimiye Mosque

2

B3 Yeni Mahalle, Yakup Sok; (0224) 757 25 83
Sea bus from Istanbul to Yalova then dolmuş to İznik

İznik is a tranquil lakeside town that once held great importance as the Byzantine city of Nicaea. It was the site of major religious and political events, including the First Ecumenical Council in 325 CE, and later became famous for producing the finest Ottoman ceramics in the 16th century. Today, the town retains its ancient grid layout and is still enclosed by defensive walls and impressive gateways such as the Istanbul Gate.

Museum of İznik

İznik Müzesi

Mahmut Çelebi Mahallesi, Atatürk Cad 8am–5pm daily (summer: to 7pm) turkish museums.com

Housed in a modern, multistorey facility that opened in 2023, the Museum of İznik was earlier located in the Nilüfer Hatun Imareti. The museum's extensive collection is a chronological journey through the region's rich history, featuring thousands of artifacts from ancient Nicaea and the surrounding area, dating back as far as 6500 BCE.

The vast collection is spread over three floors. The ground floor focuses on the Roman and Byzantine periods, featuring impressive sarcophagi, including the Antigonus Sarcophagus, sculptures, grave steles and an extensive collection of ancient coins. A significant section of the upper floors is dedicated to the town's most famous export: İznik tiles *(Çini)*. Visitors can trace the development of world-renowned ceramics from the Seljuk and Ottoman periods through the exquisite examples on display. Larger stone artifacts are showcased in the garden outside.

İznik Turkish Islamic Arts Museum

İznik Türk İslam Eserleri Müzesi

Müze Sok (0224) 757 10 27 8am–5pm daily

Opposite the mosque, the Kitchen of Lady Nilüfer (Nilüfer Hatun İmareti), one of İznik's loveliest buildings, now houses the İznik Turkish Islamic Arts Museum. This *imaret* was set up in 1388 by Nilüfer Hatun, wife of Orhan Gazi, and served as a hospice for wandering dervishes. Its T-plan layout is a classic example of early Ottoman public architecture. Entered

The Clock Tower and Hagia Sophia Mosque in İznik

through a spacious five-domed portico, the central domed area is flanked by two more domed rooms. The museum has displays of Roman antiquities and glass, found during excavations of ancient Nicaea, as well as some examples of Seljuk and Ottoman tiles. Its garden courtyard also contains a collection of sarcophagi and column capitals, while the interior showcases the famous İznik ceramics.

Hagia Sophia

Ayasofya Camii

Atatürk Cad (0224) 757 10 27 Daily

One of the town's oldest surviving monuments, the church of Hagia Sophia stands at the intersection of the main streets, Atatürk Caddesi and Kılıçaslan Caddesi. It was in an earlier version of this church – a 6th-century basilica built by Justinian on the ruins of an older church – that the Second Council of Nicaea (the Seventh Ecumenical Council) was held in 787 CE, ending the first iconoclast period. The current building was erected after an earthquake in 1065. The remains of a fine mosaic floor, and also of a Deësis (a fresco depicting Christ, the Virgin and John the Baptist), are protected from damage behind glass screens. The church became a mosque after the Ottoman conquest in 1331, when Orhan Gazi added a mihrab and minaret, but was converted into a museum in the Republican era. Controversially, it was reconsecrated as a mosque in 2012. Today, carpets cover the mosaics, and the interior frescoes remain partially obscured. Visiting hours are restricted around daily prayers.

Green Mosque

Yeşil Camii

Müze Sok Daily (except prayer times)

Just off the eastern end of Kılıçaslan Caddesi, the 14th-century Green Mosque is named after the tiles covering its minaret. Commissioned between 1378 and 1391 by Çandarlı Kara Halil Hayreddin Pasha, the first Grand Vizier of the Ottoman Empire, it is a magnificent example of early Ottoman architecture. The building marks a transition from Seljuk to Ottoman style, featuring an elegant three-bay portico and a prayer hall covered by a single, high dome. Its minaret on the northwest corner was once adorned with turquoise and green tiles. Unfortunately, the original tiles have been replaced by modern copies of inferior quality.

İZNIK CERAMICS

İznik was one of two major centres (the other being Kütahya, *p290*) where fine, painted and glazed pottery was fashioned during the Ottoman period. The potteries reached their peak in the 16th century, when the famous "tomato red" colour was fully developed. Today visitors can see it sparkle on the superb tilework of the 1561 Rüstem Paşa Mosque *(p113)* in Istanbul.

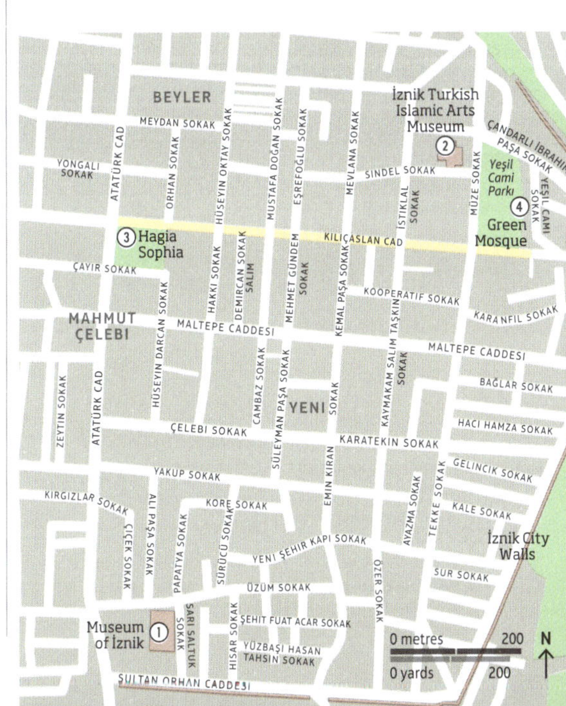

←
The city of Bursa, set against the slopes of Mount Uludağ

3

BURSA

B3 Ulucami Parkı, Orhangazı Altgeçidi Terminal Cad; (0224) 261 54 00 Atatürk Cad, near the State Theatre or behind Heykel; (0224) 220 18 48

Bursa, known as Yeşil Bursa ("Green Bursa"), lies on the lower slopes of Mount Uludağ and is famous for its parks and thermal springs. The city became the first Ottoman capital in 1326, and later prospered through the silk trade. Today, Bursa continues to thrive through its automotive, food and textile industries.

Yıldırım Beyazıt Mosque

Yıldırım Beyazıt Camii

Yıldırım Cad Daily (except prayer times)

This mosque is named after Beyazıt I, whose nickname was "Yıldırım", meaning "thunderbolt". This referred to the speed with which he reacted to his enemies. Built between 1390 and 1395, just after Beyazıt became sultan, the mosque at first doubled as a lodge for Sufi dervishes *(p288)*. It has a lovely portico with five domed bays.

Inside, the prayer hall and interior court (a covered "courtyard" in Bursa mosques, which prefigures the open ones preferred by later Ottoman architects) are divided by an impressive, gravity-defying arch. This rises from two mihrab-like niches. The walls of the prayer hall itself are adorned with several pieces of calligraphic design *(p116)*.

Green Tomb

Yeşil Türbe

Yeşil Cad Daily

The tomb of Mehmet I, built in 1421, stands elevated among tall cypress trees and is one of the city's most prominent landmarks. The tomb is much closer to the Seljuk style of architecture than classical Ottoman. Its exterior is covered in green tiles – mainly 19th-century replacements for the original faïence. The mihrab has intricate tile panels, including a representation of a mosque lamp hanging from a gold chain between two candles.

The sultan's sarcophagus is covered in exquisite tiles and adorned by a long Koranic inscription. Nearby sarcophagi contain the remains of his sons, daughters and nursemaid.

Green Mosque

Yeşil Camii

Yeşil Cad Daily (except prayer times)

Bursa's most famous monument was commissioned by Mehmet I in 1412, but it remained unfinished at his death in 1421 and still lacks a portico. Nevertheless, it is the finest Ottoman mosque built prior to the conquest of Constantinople *(p53)*.

The main portal is tall and elegant, with an intricately carved canopy, which opens into the entrance hall.

Beyond this is an interior court with a carved fountain at its centre. A flight of three steps leads up from here into the prayer hall. Above the entrance to the court is the sultan's loge *(p33)*. The tiling of the prayer hall was carried out by Ali Ibn İlyas Ali, who learned his art in Samarkand. This was the first time that tiles were used extensively in an Ottoman mosque, and it set a precedent for the widespread use of İznik tiles *(p187)*. The mosque's exterior was also once clad in tiles, but these have disappeared over time.

KARAGÖZ SHADOW PUPPETRY

A celebrated form of Turkish shadow theatre, Karagöz Shadow Puppetry features colourful leather puppets made from camel skin, which are projected onto a backlit screen. The shows blend satire and social commentary in an entertaining portrayal of everyday life in Turkish society. Bursa hosts an international Karagöz festival annually.

Museum of Turkish and Islamic Arts

Türk ve İslam Eserleri Müzesi

Yeşil Cad (0224) 327 76 79 Summer: 8am-7pm daily; winter: 8:30am-5:30pm daily

This museum is housed in a fine Ottoman-era building, once the *medrese (p33)* associated with the Green Mosque. A colonnade surrounds its courtyard on three sides and the cells leading off from this courtyard are now exhibition galleries. Exhibits date from the 12th to the 20th centuries, and include Seljuk and Ottoman ceramics, elaborately decorated Korans and costumes.

Bursa City Museum

Bursa Kent Müzesi

6 Kültür Sok (0224) 716 37 90 9:30am-5:30pm Tue-Sun

The former Justice courts have been restored as a lively museum that traces local life over many years. Displays show how culinary traditions, handicrafts, costumes, archaeological artifacts and city-planning concepts helped shape Bursa's urban identity. The museum also highlights key figures who influenced the city's cultural scene, including Bursa's civic leaders and Atatürk, as well as the local Karagöz shadow-puppet theatre, which is well represented through engaging exhibits.

EAT

İskender Tarihi Ahşap Dükkan

Savour Bursa's *İskender* kebab at the very restaurant where it was invented.

Ünlü Cad 7, Osmangazi
(0224) 221 46 15

Arap Şükrü Çetin

Established in 1930, this restaurant is known for its seafood dishes.

Sakarya Cad 6, Kuruçeşme, Osmangazi
arapsukrucetin.com

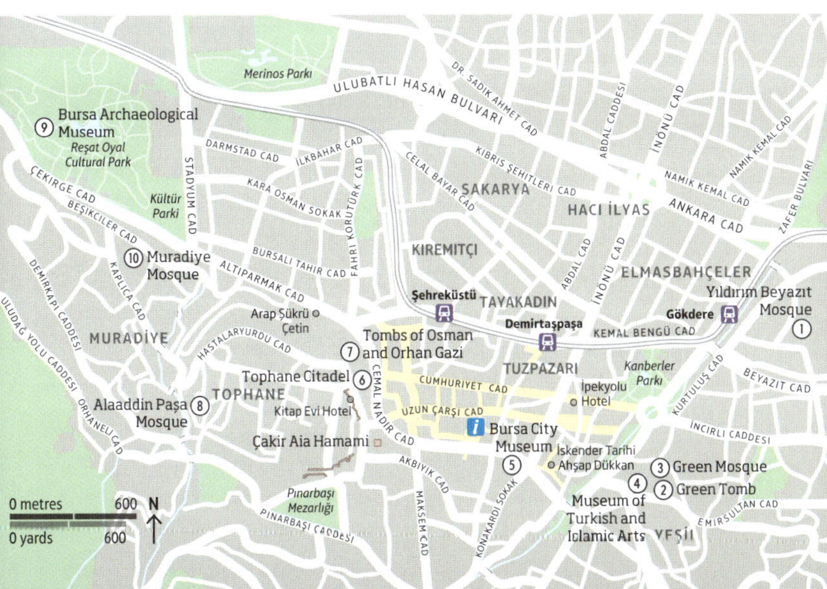

Façade of the Tophane Citadel, featuring its historic entrance, Saltanat Gate

Tophane Citadel

Hisar

Osmangazi Çıkmazı Sok
Daily

The citadel walls of Tophane, which mark Bursa's northern boundary, are the best-preserved section of the structure. The citadel fell into Ottoman hands when Orhan Gazi's troops broke through its walls. Later, he built a wooden palace inside the citadel and had the old Byzantine ramparts refortified. Until this era the walls had delineated the entire circumference of the ancient city. However, Orhan encouraged Bursa's expansion and developed the present-day commercial heart of the city further to the east.

Tombs of Osman and Orhan Gazi

Osman & Orhan Gazi Türbeleri

Yiğitler Cad **Daily**

Osman Gazi began the process of Ottoman expansion in the 13th century and tried to capture Bursa. But it was his son, Orhan, who took the city just before Osman Gazi died. Orhan brought his father's body to be buried in the baptistry of a converted church and he himself was later buried in the nave. The tombs that can be seen today date from 1868. A ceremonial changing of the guard takes place at Osman Gazi's tomb on the hour every day between 9am and 5pm.

Alaaddin Paşa Mosque

Alaaddin Paşa Camii

Alaeddin Mahallesi
Daily

Formerly known as the Alaeddin Mosque, the Alaaddin Paşa Mosque is considered the oldest surviving mosque in Bursa. It was built in 1335, just nine years after the city was captured in 1326. Commissioned by Alaeddin Bey, brother and vizier of Orhan Gazi, the mosque is notable despite its simple design. It consists of a simple domed square, fronted by a portico and supported by four Byzantine columns with capitals. The structure remains a key historical landmark that illustrates the earliest designs of Ottoman mosque architecture.

Bursa Archaeological Museum

Bursa Arkeoloji Müzesi

Reşat Oyal, Kültür Parkı
(0224) 234 49 18
8am-5pm daily

The Bursa Archaeological Museum displays a wide range of finds dating from the 3rd millennium BCE through to the Ottoman conquest of the city in 1326. The collection reflects the long and varied history of the region, which has seen Hittite, Roman, Byzantine and early Ottoman settlement.

Among the most notable exhibits are the ceremonial armour fittings, remarkable for their craftsmanship and decorative detail. The museum also holds an impressive selection of Roman glass, prized for its delicate forms and subtle iridescence. Other highlights include Roman

BURSA'S HOT SPRINGS

The thermal springs of Bursa's Çekirge neighbourhood have been famous since the 6th century CE, when Emperor Justinian's wife, Theodora, arrived with a retinue of 4,000 to take a dip. Today, this hilltop district, 5 km (3 miles) west of the centre, is known for its spa hotels. Both Çekirge's 14th-century Old Spa and the 16th-century New Spa in the central city draw on these waters for their thermal pools.

statues and bronze objects, alongside Byzantine religious artifacts and coins, all of which help illustrate the cultural and artistic traditions that shaped Bursa over the centuries.

Recent updates to the galleries, including improved labelling of exhibits, have made the displays more accessible and easier to follow for visitors.

Muradiye Mosque

Muradiye Külliyesi

2 Murat Cad (0224) 327 76 79 Daily

This mosque complex was built by Murat II, the father of Mehmet the Conqueror *(p53)*, in 1426. The mosque is notable for its graceful domed portico and a finely carved wooden door. Its interior is decorated with early İznik tiles *(p187)*. The *medrese (p33)*, next to the mosque, now serves as a medical centre. This square building has several cells surrounding a central garden courtyard. Its *dershane*, or main classroom, is adorned with an ornate brick façade.

The mosque garden, with its cypresses, flowerbeds and fountains, is one of Bursa's most tranquil retreats. Murat II was the last of the Ottoman sultans to be buried in Bursa and his mausoleum stands in the garden beside the mosque. The other 11 tombs in the garden are a reminder of the Ottoman code of succession, which recognized a future sultan as the strongest male relative. Competing male relatives could expect to be put to death or spend most of their lives in enforced solitary confinement, known as "the cage". This did not, however, prevent the ruling offspring from having a memorial built for a deposed brother. Selim II ("the Sot"), for example, had an elaborate octagonal mausoleum built in Bursa for his older brother, Mustafa.

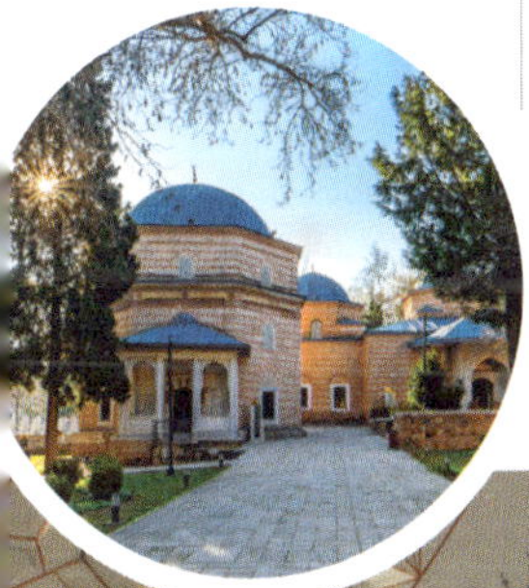

Painted dome of Muradiye Mosque, and *(inset)* its complex, set within a courtyard

STAY

Kitap Evi Hotel

Nestled in the citadel neighbourhood, this red mansion has artistically styled rooms, filled with antique details, plus a vine-draped courtyard restaurant with a trickling fountain.

Burçüstü Sok 21, Tophane, Osmangazi
kitapevi.com.tr

İpekyolu Hotel

This friendly, centrally located hotel was created by joining a cluster of Ottoman-era houses. Many of the rooms still feature the original decorative plasterwork.

Batpazarı Sok A-12, Osmangazi
ipekyolubutikhotel.com

A SHORT WALK
THE MARKET AREA

Distance 0.6 km (0.4 miles) **Time** 20 minutes
Nearest bus stop Ulu Cami

Bursa's central market area is a warren of streets and Ottoman *hans* (trading posts and overnight inns). The area emphasizes the more colourful and traditional aspects of this busy industrial city and is a good place to experience the bustle of inner-city life. Here, too, you can buy the local fabrics for which the city is famous, particularly handmade lace, towelling and silk. The silkworm was introduced to the Byzantine Empire in the 6th century, and for centuries there was a brisk trade in silk cocoons in Koza Han. Today, as well as silk products, you can also find handmade, camelskin Karagöz puppets *(p189)*.

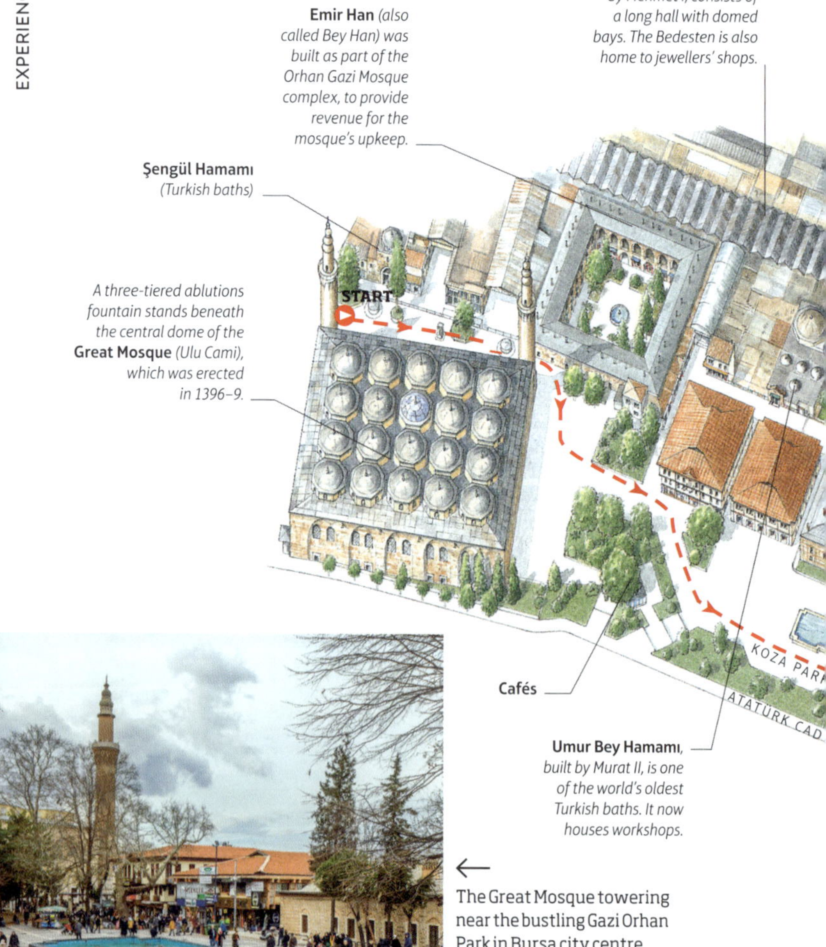

←
The Great Mosque towering near the bustling Gazi Orhan Park in Bursa city centre

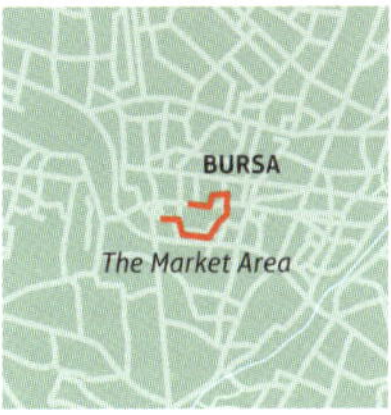

↑ Relaxing in the courtyard of the Koza Han, a historic centre of the silk trade

BURSA
The Market Area

Locator Map
For more detail see p189

0 metres 40
0 yards 40
N

BORSA SOK
FINISH
UZUN ÇARŞI CAD
ÇÖMEK SOK
BELEDIYE CAD

Geyve Han *is also known as Hacı İvaz Paşa Han.*

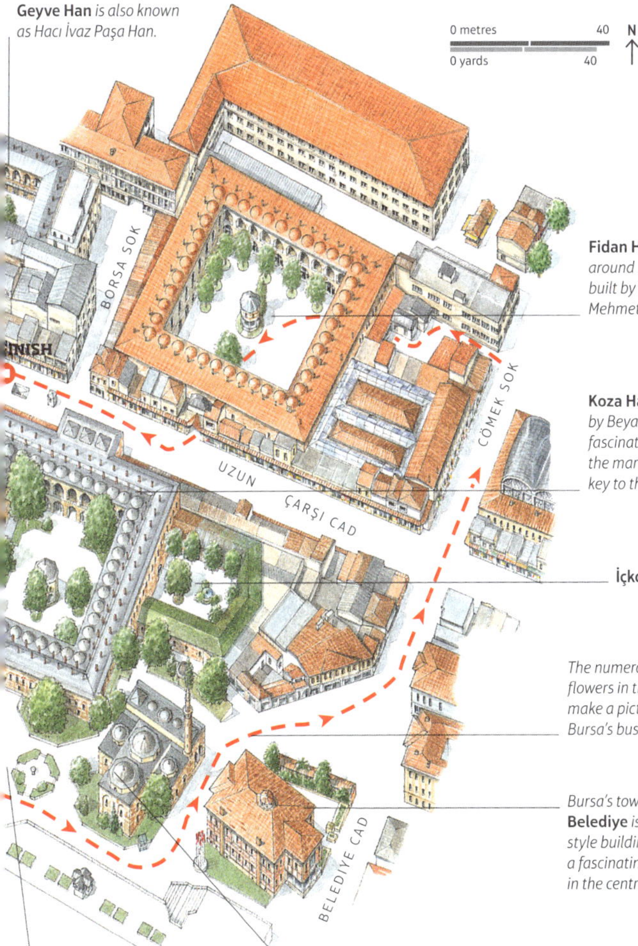

Fidan Han *dates from around 1470, when it was built by a grand vizier of Mehmet the Conqueror.*

Koza Han, *built in 1491 by Beyazıt II, is the most fascinating building in the market area and was key to the silk trade.*

İçkoza Han

The numerous bunches of flowers in the **Flower Market** *make a picturesque sight in Bursa's bustling market area.*

Bursa's town hall, the **Belediye** *is a Swiss-chalet-style building that forms a fascinating landmark in the centre of the city.*

Gazi Orhan Park, *in front of Koza Han, with fountains, benches and café tables, is a popular meeting place for locals.*

Built in 1339, 13 years after the Ottoman conquest of Bursa, **Orhan Gazi Mosque** *is the oldest of the city's imperial mosques.*

EXPERIENCE MORE

Princes' Islands

Kızıl Adalar

B3 12 km (7 miles) SE of Istanbul Kabataş, Kadıköy, Beşiktaş, Maltepe, Bostancı sehirhatlari.istanbul

The pine-forested Princes' Islands are just a short ferry ride from Istanbul. Most ferries call in turn at the four islands: Kınalıada, Burgazada, Heybeliada and Büyükada.

Easily visited on a day trip, the islands take their name from a palace built by Justin II on Büyükada, then known as Prinkipo (Island of the Prince) in 569. In Byzantine times the islands became infamous as a place of exile for royalty, and as the site of monasteries.

In the latter half of the 19th century, with the inauguration of a regular steamboat service from Istanbul, many wealthy foreigners settled on the islands. Zia Gökalp, a key figure in the rise of Turkish nationalism, lived here during the waning years of the Ottoman era.

Büyükada is the largest of the Princes' Islands, and it attracts visitors because of its beaches, outdoor summer culture and the Art Nouveau style of the wooden dwellings. Büyükada and Heybeliada shun any form of motorized transport except electric buses and scooters. At the top of Büyükada's wooded southern hill stands the Monastery of St George, built on Byzantine foundations.

Heybeliada, the second-largest island, houses the imposing former Naval High School (Deniz Harp Okulu), built in 1942. Less touristy than Büyükada, this island offers quieter pleasures such as lovely beaches and pine groves. The island's northern hill is the location of the Greek Orthodox School of Theology, which was built in 1841.

The smaller islands of Kınalıada and Burgazada are less developed and therefore more peaceful. Kınalıada is home to a fine Armenian church built in 1857. At Burgazada, visitors can see the Greek Orthodox Church of John the Baptist. It's possible to visit parts of the building, which is undergoing restoration with the aim of resuming educational operations in the near future.

Polonezköy

B3 38 km (23 miles) NE of Istanbul 15P to Mehmet Akif Ersoy Cad stop in Üsküdar, then 137 to Beykoz, then take a taxi

Polonezköy still reflects clear signs of the Polish roots of its founders, who came here in 1842 fleeing Russian oppression. United by politics, Poles fought in Abdül Mecit I's army against Russia in the Crimean War (1853–6). Exempted from taxes for their efforts in the war, they settled in their namesake village.

Polonezköy's old-world charm and culinary traditions are still there, but it has become popular for a day's outing or a weekend break.

There are excellent walks in the surrounding countryside and, even though villas and spas have sprung up, there are still several restaurants serving Polish specialities, including the wild boar for which the town was once well known.

The surrounding beech forest, which also offers pleasant walks, has become a conservation area.

← Picturesque street in Büyükada, one of the Princes' Islands

Şile has several fine, sandy beaches and a large, black-and-white striped lighthouse. In ancient times, the village, then known as Kalpe, was a port.

Şile

B3 46 km (28 miles) NE of Polonezköy Üsküdar

The quintessential Black Sea coastal town, Şile has several fine, sandy beaches and a large, black-and-white striped lighthouse. In ancient times, the town, then known as Kalpe, was a port. Şile's lighthouse, the largest in Turkey, was built by the French for Sultan Abdül Aziz in 1858–9. Apart from tourism, Şile is known for producing cotton, as well as a cool, loose-weave cloth, known as *şile bezi*, sold in local shops.

Bird Paradise National Park

Kuşcenneti Milli Parkı

A3 112 km (69 miles) W of Bursa (0266) 735 54 22 Bandırma Liman AVM, or take a taxi from Bandırma Sunrise-sunset daily

An estimated 266 species of birds visit Bird Paradise National Park at the edge of Kuş Gölü, the lake formerly known as Manyas Gölü. Located on the great migratory paths between Europe and Asia, the park is a combination of plant cover, reedbeds and a lake that supports at least 20 species of fish. The park will delight all bird-watchers. A good field guide and some mosquito repellent will enhance the experience.

At the entrance to the park, there is a small museum with displays about various birds. Visitors make their way to an observation tower.

Two main groups of birds visit the lake: those that come here to breed (March–July), and those that pass by during migration, either heading south (November) or north (April–May). Among the birds that breed around the lake are the endangered Dalmatian pelican, the great crested grebe, cormorants, herons, bitterns and spoonbills. Over three million birds fly across the area on their migratory routes – storks, cranes, pelicans and birds of prey like sparrowhawks and spotted eagles. April and May are the best months to enjoy this area.

Uludağ National Park

Uludağ Milli Parkı

B3 20 km (12 miles) S of Bursa (0224) 283 21 97 To Fatih Panaroma 1326 Museum, Bursa, then cable car to Sarıalan, followed by dolmuş to Uludağ Daily

One of a number of Turkish mountains to claim the title of Mount Olympus, Uludağ, at 2,540 m (8,340 ft), was believed by the Bithynians (of north-western Asia Minor) to be the abode of the gods. In the Byzantine era, it was home to several monastic orders. After the Ottoman conquest of Bursa, Muslim dervishes *(p288)* moved into the abandoned monasteries. Nowadays, no traces of Uludağ's former religious communities remain.

The main tourist season starts in November, when it becomes a ski resort, with a reliable cable-car service and good hotels. Spring and summer are the best times for visiting Uludağ National Park, as its alpine heights remain relatively cool. Visitors will find opportunities for peaceful walking and picnicking.

The park includes about 670 sq km (258 sq miles) of woodland. As you ascend, the deciduous beech, oak and hazel gradually give way to juniper and aspen, and finally to dwarf junipers. In springtime, the slopes are blanketed with hyacinths and crocuses.

Osman Gazi *(p190)* is supposed to have founded seven villages for his seven sons and their brides here. Cumalıkızık, on the lower slopes of Uludağ, is the most well preserved of the five surviving villages and it is a UNESCO World Heritage Site. Among its houses are many 750-year-old half-timbered buildings.

↑ Cable car crossing a snow-covered forest in Uludağ National Park

EAT

Uludağ Soğukpınar Alabalık Tesisi

Located just outside the park, this restaurant is a great place to enjoy traditional village dishes.

B3 Soğukpınar Uludağ Yolu 0542 599 1683 10am-9pm daily

The terraced travertine pools of Pamukkale

THE AEGEAN

The Aegean region, stretching along most of east Turkey, has deep roots in the country's classical past. It was first inhabited as early as the Palaeolithic period, and was home to the legendary ancient city of Troy in around 3000 BCE. Many of the remote classical sites in this region were also once part of ancient Caria, an independent district with boundaries that roughly corresponded to the present-day Turkish province of Muğla.

Caria's origins are disputed, but its resistance to Hellenic rule from the 7th century BCE onwards is well documented. By the 2nd century BCE, the Carians came under Roman rule, but they still retained some autonomy; the Carian symbol, a double-headed axe, can be found inscribed on remains from around this time.

Following the fall of the Western Roman Empire in the 5th century CE, the Aegean region came under the expanding Byzantine Empire, which ruled here intermittently over the next thousand years. After centuries of conquering efforts led by the Ottomans, the area eventually came under their rule in the 14th century and remained part of this empire until its decline in the 20th century.

Around this time, the Aegean's original tourist resorts, such as Kuşadası, Marmaris and Bodrum, thrived and were developed further. These resort towns remain popular visitor destinations in the 21st century.

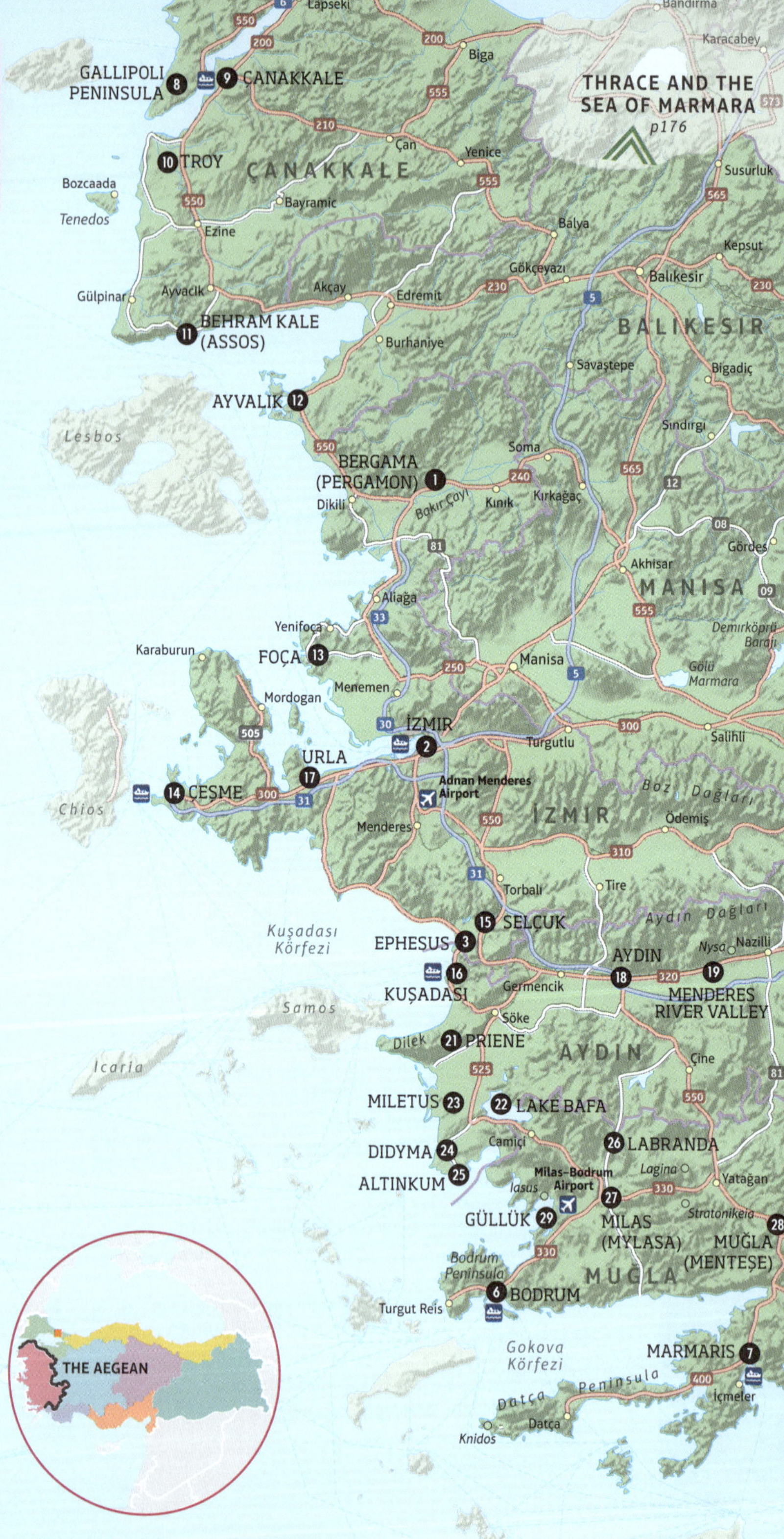
Lâpseki
Bandırma
Karacabey
Biga
GALLIPOLI PENINSULA 8
9 ÇANAKKALE
THRACE AND THE SEA OF MARMARA
p176
Çan
Yenice
10 TROY
ÇANAKKALE
Bozcaada
Tenedos
Bayramiç
Susurluk
Ezine
Balya
Kepsut
Gökçeyazı
Balıkesir
Gülpinar
Ayvacık
Akçay
Edremit
11 BEHRAM KALE (ASSOS)
BALIKESIR
Burhaniye
Savaştepe
Bigadiç
AYVALIK 12
Lesbos
Sındırgı
Soma
BERGAMA (PERGAMON) 1
Kınık
Kırkağaç
Dikili
Bakır Çayı
Gördes
Akhisar
MANISA
Aliağa
Yenifoça
Demirköprü Barajı
Karaburun
FOÇA 13
Manisa
Gölü Marmara
Mordogan
Menemen
İZMIR 2
Turgutlu
Salihli
URLA 17
Adnan Menderes Airport
14 ÇEŞME
Chios
Boz Dağları
İZMIR
Ödemiş
Menderes
Torbalı
Tire
Kuşadası Körfezi
15 SELÇUK
EPHESUS 3
Aydın Dağları
Nysa
Nazilli
AYDIN
16
18
19
KUŞADASI
Germencik
MENDERES RIVER VALLEY
Samos
Söke
Dilek
21 PRIENE
AYDIN
Icaria
Çine
MILETUS 23
22 LAKE BAFA
Camiçi
26 LABRANDA
DIDYMA 24
Lagina
ALTINKUM 25
Milas–Bodrum Airport
Yatağan
Iasus
27
Stratonikeia
GÜLLÜK 29
MILAS (MYLASA)
28
MUĞLA (MENTEŞE)
Bodrum Peninsula
MUGLA
6 BODRUM
Turgut Reis
THE AEGEAN
Gokova Körfezi
MARMARIS 7
Datça Peninsula
İçmeler
Datça
Knidos

THE AEGEAN
Must Sees
1 Bergama (Pergamon)
2 İzmir
3 Ephesus
4 Hierapolis
5 Aphrodisias
6 Bodrum
7 Marmaris
8 Gallipoli Peninsula
Experience More
9 Çanakkale
10 Troy
11 Behram Kale (Assos)
12 Ayvalık
13 Foça
14 Çeşme
15 Selçuk
16 Kuşadası
17 Urla
18 Aydın
19 Menderes River Valley
20 Denizli
21 Priene
22 Lake Bafa
23 Miletus
24 Didyma
25 Altınkum
26 Labranda
27 Milas (Mylasa)
28 Muğla (Menteşe)
29 Güllük
Nilüfer River
Yenişehir
Bursa
Ulubat Gölü
BURSA
İnegöl
Nilüfer River
Bozüyük
Orhaneli
Domaniç
Harmancık
Dursunbey
Tavşanli
Kütahya
Emet
KÜTAHYA
Simav
Demirci
Gediz
ANKARA AND WESTERN ANATOLIA
p272
Dumlupınar
Banaz
Selendi
Gediz Çayı
Uşak
UŞAK
Kula
Eşme
Alaşehir
Çivril
Sarıgöl
Adıgüzel Barajı
Buldan
Dazkırı
HIERAPOLIS
Sarayköy
Akçay
DENIZLI
Çardak
Denizli Çardak Airport
APHRODISIAS
Kemer Barajı
Tavas
Kale
DENIZLI
Acıpayam
ISPARTA
BURDUR
Bucak
Karamanlı
Kargı
Katrancık Dağı
Gölgeli Dağları
Çavdır
Gölhisar
Korkuteli
Döşemealtı
Çameli
Aksu
THE WESTERN MEDITERRANEAN
p238
Antalya
ANTALYA
Ortaca
Dalyan
Göcek
Dalaman
Elmalı
Ak Dağları
Bey Dağları
Fethiye
Seydikemer
Kemer
0 kilometres 40
0 miles 40
N

BERGAMA (PERGAMON)

A4 (0232) 631 28 84 (Bergama); (0232) 483 51 17 (Asclepieum) İzmir
Hours vary, call ahead

Perched on a hilltop above the modern town of Bergama, the ancient acropolis of Bergama (Pergamon) is one of the most dramatic sights in Turkey. Originally settled by the Aeolian Greeks in the 8th century BCE, it was revered for its power and wealth.

Ruled by one of Alexander the Great's generals (301–281 BCE), Bergama prospered under the Pergamene dynasty founded by Eumenes I (263–241 BCE), becoming one of the ancient world's main centres of learning. The last ruler of this dynasty, Attalus III, bequeathed the kingdom to Rome in 133 BCE, and Bergama became capital of the Roman province of Asia. The great physician Galen was born here in 129 CE, and established a famous medical centre, the Asclepieum, which is situated on a low hill around 8 km (5 miles) from the acropolis of Bergama.

Today, Bergama is recognized as a UNESCO World Heritage Site. Visitors can explore the remains of its library, theatre and gymnasium, and enjoy beautiful panoramic views across Bergama.

> **The great physician Galen was born here in 129 CE, and established a famous medical centre, the Asclepieum, 8 km (5 miles) from Bergama.**

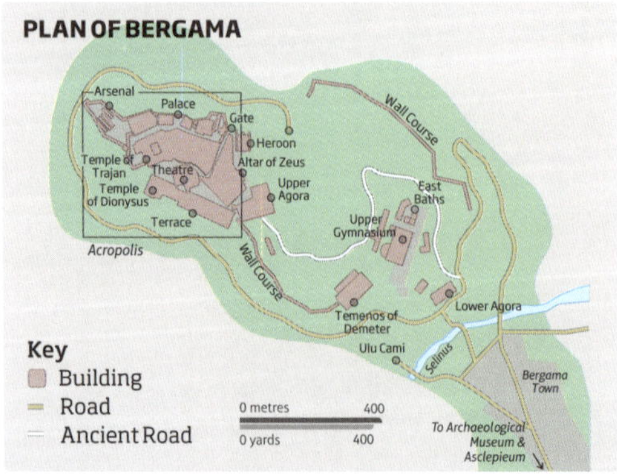

Arsenal

Eumenes II (197–159 BCE) extended the city walls until they reached a length of about 4 km (3 miles), enclosing the entire hilltop.

Illustration of the ancient city of Bergama's Acropolis

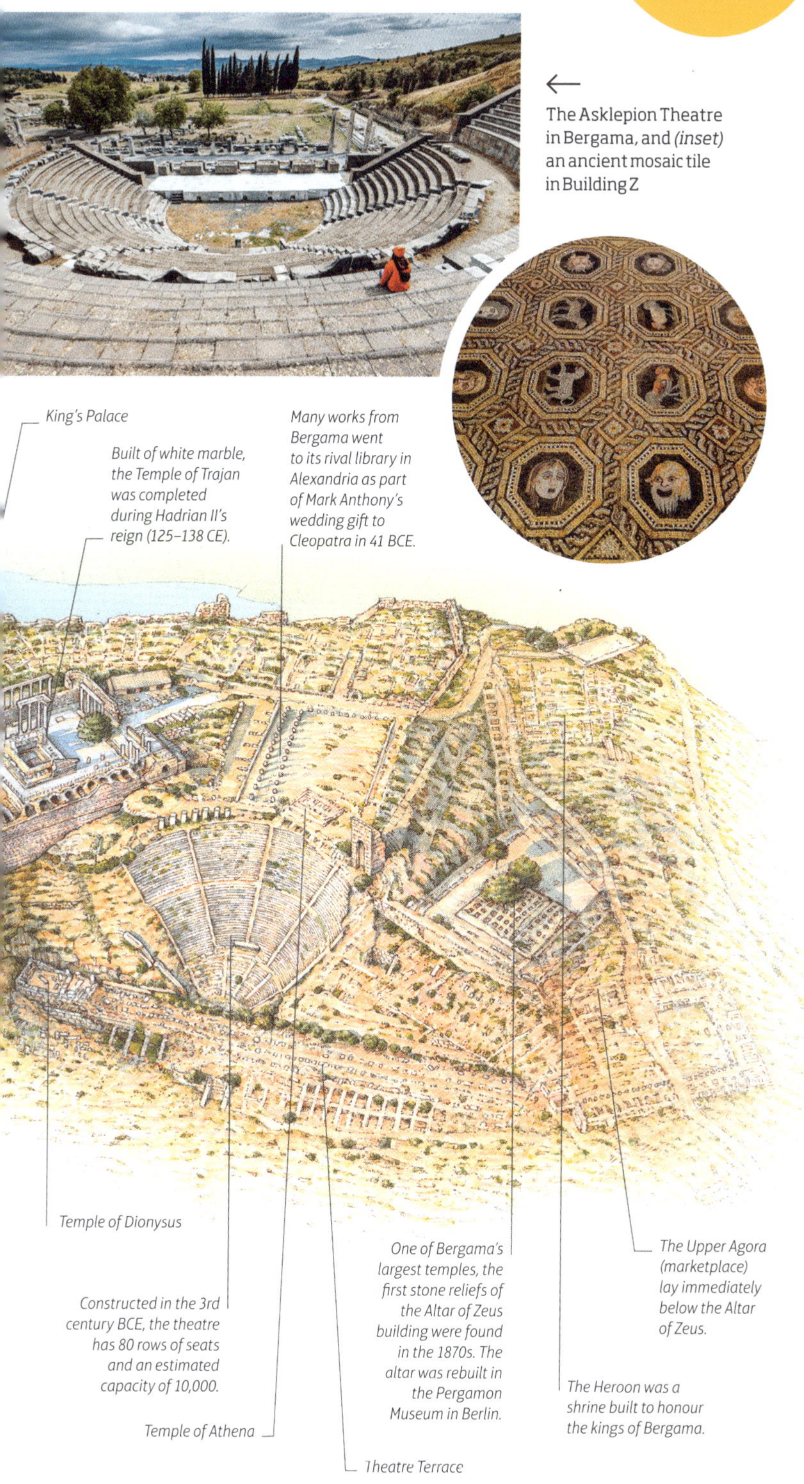

←

The Asklepion Theatre in Bergama, and *(inset)* an ancient mosaic tile in Building Z

2 İZMIR

A4 Adnan Menderes Alsancak Basmane, Alsancak 8 km (5 miles) NE of city centre Akdeniz Mah 1344 Sok No 2, Pasaport İzmir; (0232) 483 51 17

The most western-leaning of Turkish cities, İzmir has been a major trading hub since the 3rd century CE. Until 1922, it had a large Christian population, primarily Greek Orthodox, many of whom fled during the War of Independence. Today, İzmir serves as NATO's regional headquarters and enjoys a multicultural sophistication.

1 İzmir Culture and Arts Factory

İzmir Kültür Sanat Fabrikası

Atatürk Cad 129, Alsancak Alsancak Alsancak Gar 951, 930 9am-6:30pm & 7-9pm daily izmirkultursanatfabrikasi.gov.tr

This museum, located in a former cigarette factory, has displays of archaeological and ethnographic objects, as well as art from the İzmir Painting and Sculpture Museum.

The museum's focus is on the coast's history from Neolithic times to the present day. It has many excavated objects like ceramics, gold, glassware and textiles that illustrate the rise and fall of past civilizations.

The painting and sculpture collection has works by 19th- and 20th-century Turkish artists, including those from the early Republic era, such as Fahrelnissa Zeid and Bedri Rahmi Eyüboğlu.

2 Kemeraltı Bazaar

Kemeraltı Çarşısı

Kemeraltı Çarşısı Çankaya, Konak Konak İskele 72, 104

İzmir's historic shopping district, Kemeraltı Bazaar, is home to speciality food traders, cafés, craft workshops and produce stalls. It also features some of the city's *hans* (caravanserais), mosques and synagogues.

A notable attraction is the restored 1744 **Kızlarağası Han**. Its central courtyard has been converted into a café, while the surrounding rooms now house craft workshops that are perfect for buying copper and wood handicrafts.

In the southeast corner, the Havra Sokağı was once the centre of the Ottoman-era Sephardic Jewish community. There are several synagogues located on and near this street.

Kızlarağası Han

871 Sok, Kemeraltı Çarşısı
8am-9pm Mon-Sat
kizlaragasihani.com.tr

INSIDER TIP
İzmir's Synagogues

To book a visit or organize a tour of İzmir's synagogues, contact the İzmir Jewish Community Centre *(izmirjcc.org)* at least 24 hours in advance.

The city's iconic Konak Clock Tower in Konak Square

③ Kordon

⌂ Cumhuriyet Bul-Atatürk Cad Ⓜ Konak ⛴ Konak İskele

Central İzmir's 2-km (1-mile) *kordon* (seafront) runs from Konak Square, which is home to the symbolic Ottoman-era Konak Clock Tower that was built in 1901. This tower was one of 58 built throughout the empire to encourage the adoption of European timekeeping, and İzmir's is considered one of the finest examples.

A short stroll west is Konak Pier, Gustave Eiffel's 1890 customs house, which has now been transformed into a popular hub for shopping and dining. Continuing north from Pasaport Pier the waterfront becomes a large parkland with gardens, walking and cycling paths and swathes of grassy areas where families enjoy weekend picnics and students gather to watch the sunset. At the Kordon's northernmost point, a breakwater offers a perfect fishing spot and provides sweeping views across İzmir Bay.

EAT

Deniz Restaurant

A prime spot for meze and seafood dining.

⌂ Atatürk Cad 188/B, Konak Ⓦ denizrestaurant.com

Komposto

This is the best lunch stop while exploring Kemeraltı Bazaar.

⌂ 861 Sok 46, Konak ☎ (0232) 483 2183 ◻ D, Sat & Sun

Sevinç Pastanesi

This patisserie has been a local favourite since 1957.

⌂ Ali Çetinkaya Bul 27, Alsancak Ⓦ sevincpastanesi.com.tr

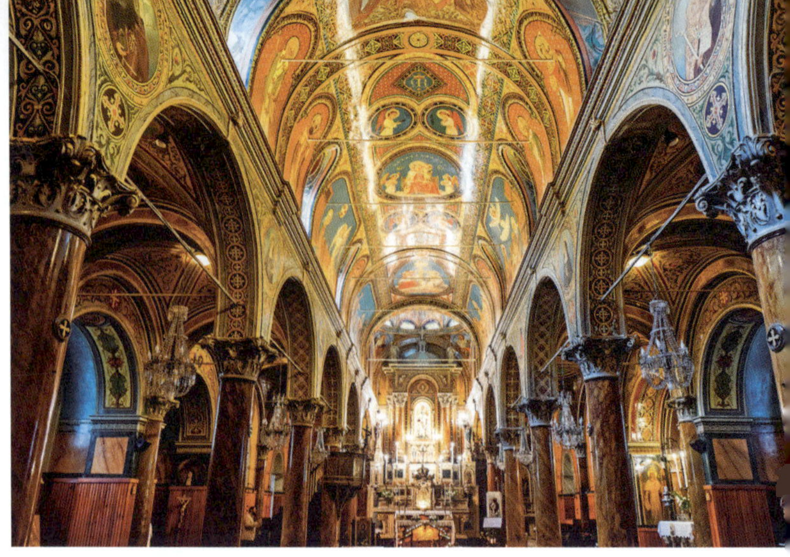

STAY

Key Hotel
Overlooking the waterfront, Key offers sleek, contemporary rooms with all mod-cons.

Atatürk Cad 1, Konak
keyhotel.com

Zeniva Hotel
This hotel is close to all the waterfront attractions.

Kızılay Cad 1, Konak
zenivahotel.com

Met Boutique Hotel
The Met offers comfortable and modern minimalist rooms.

Gazi Bul 124, Konak
(0232) 483 01 11

St Polycarp Church

Aziz Polikarp Kilisesi

Necatibey Sok 2 (0232) 484 84 36 For group visits by appt or prayer

The patron saint of İzmir, St Polycarp, was a Christian martyr and former bishop of Smyrna, who died in the 2nd century CE. His legacy is honoured in the city through the St Polycarp Church. This church is the oldest Roman Catholic church in İzmir and has served as the seat of the Catholic archbishop since 1929. Permission to build a chapel dedicated to the saint was granted in 1620 by Süleyman the Magnificent *(p54)*. To the right of the altarpiece is a self-portrait of Raymond Peré, who designed the Konak Clock Tower.

Asansör

Turgut Reis, Şht Nihatbey Cad 76/A 8am-midnight daily Restaurant: (0232) 293 47 77

Towering over the city, Asansör is a functioning 19th-century elevator in the Karataş district.

→ Asansör, an iconic landmark dominating İzmir's skyline

Magnificent nave leading to the altar at St Polycarp Church

Did You Know?

İzmir's earliest known settlement, dating back 8,500 years, is at Yeşilova mound, near Bornova.

Built in 1907 by wealthy Jewish banker Nesim Levi Bayrakłıoğlu, its original purpose was to connect the two districts and provide easier access between the narrow coastal lanes of Karataş and its hilly upper areas. The building features a rooftop restaurant that offers fine views over the city.

Nearby is the restored section of İzmir's old Jewish quarter, where you'll find the leafy Dario Moreno Street (Dario Moreno Sokaği), which is named after a 1960s singer who held a great fondness for the city.

Agora

Agora Ören Yeri, 816 Sok 29, Namazgah Mahallesi (0232) 483 46 96 8:30am-5:30pm daily (Apr-Oct: to 7pm)

The Agora, the original central market of the Roman city of Smyrna (now İzmir), functioned as the civic heart of the city until the Byzantine period.

The remains visible today date back to the 2nd century CE, when these structures were reconstructed under the rule of the Emperor Marcus Aurelius following an earthquake in 178 CE. There are several Corinthian columns with well-preserved capitols still standing, and enough arches, as well as part of a basilica (city hall), to give the flavour of a Roman town.

Velvet Castle

Kadifekale

From Konak Clock Tower, marked "Kale", then on foot

Kadifekale, which translates as "Velvet Castle" in Turkish, is a prominent landmark perched high above the city of İzmir. Also known by its ancient name Mount Pagos, the castle was built on Hellenistic foundations and originally, the castle's structure featured 40 impressive towers. Over the centuries, numerous additions were made to it by the Romans, Genoese and Ottomans. The castle is an ideal spot for an afternoon's outing, and offers unsurpassed, dramatic vistas that sweep across the modern city and over İzmir Bay.

Velvet Castle is an ideal spot for an afternoon's outing, and offers unsurpassed, dramatic vistas that sweep across the modern city and over İzmir Bay.

EPHESUS

A4 3 km (2 miles) W of Selçuk, on Efes Yolu
Selçuk tourist office; (0232) 892 69 45

An impressively preserved ancient Greek city, Ephesus was first established around 1000 BCE. It soon rose to fame as a centre for the worship of Cybele, the Anatolian Mother Goddess.

The city as it exists today was founded in the 4th century BCE by Alexander the Great's successor, Lysimachus. Later, under the Romans, Ephesus became the capital of the Roman province of Asia and the chief port on the Aegean; most surviving structures date from this prosperous period. As the harbour silted up the city declined, but played an important role in the spread of Christianity, notably through the missions of St Paul. Two great Councils of the early Church were held here in 431 CE and 449 CE. It is said that the Virgin Mary spent her last days nearby and that St John the Evangelist came from the island of Patmos to look after her.

HOUSE OF MARY

According to the Bible, the crucified Jesus asked St John the Evangelist to look after his mother, Mary. John brought Mary with him to Ephesus in 37 CE, and she spent the last years of her life here in a modest stone house. This house of the Blessed Virgin was rediscovered in the 19th century, based on a mystic's visions. Located at Meryemana, just 9 km (5 miles) from the centre of Ephesus, the original stone structure now serves as a small chapel and has been honoured with several papal blessings. The shrine, known as the Meryemana Kultur Parkı, is revered by both Christians and Muslims, with pilgrims of both faiths visiting, especially on 15 August every year for the Feast of the Assumption.

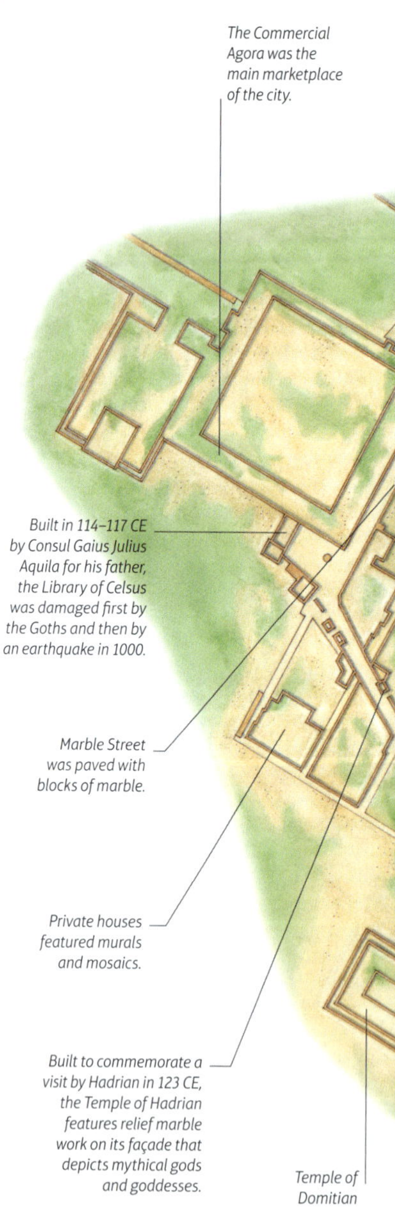

The Commercial Agora was the main marketplace of the city.

Built in 114–117 CE by Consul Gaius Julius Aquila for his father, the Library of Celsus was damaged first by the Goths and then by an earthquake in 1000.

Marble Street was paved with blocks of marble.

Private houses featured murals and mosaics.

Built to commemorate a visit by Hadrian in 123 CE, the Temple of Hadrian features relief marble work on its façade that depicts mythical gods and goddesses.

Temple of Domitian

1 The two-tiered Roman Library of Celsus framed by the surrounding ruins of the ancient city.

2 Well-preserved Corinthian columns supporting a curved arch of the Temple of Hadrian.

3 An ornate niche within the Library of Celsus featuring a marble statue of the goddess Episteme.

Carved into the flank of Mount Pion during the Hellenistic period, the theatre was later renovated by the Romans.

The skene (stage building) featured elaborate ornamentation.

Did You Know?

Water for Ephesus's fountains, including Trajan's, came from 42 km (26 miles) away via aqueducts.

The Gate of Hercules, at the entrance to Curetes Street, takes its name from two reliefs showing Hercules draped in a lion skin.

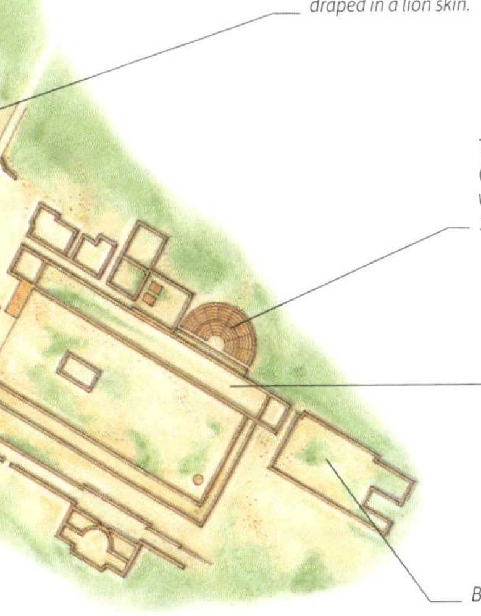

The Odeon (meeting hall) was built in 150 CE.

Key highlights of the ancient city of Ephesus

Lined with Ionic and Corinthian columns, the Colonnaded Street runs from the Baths of Varius to the Temple of Domitian.

Baths of Varius

4

HIERAPOLIS

B4 19 km (12 miles) N of Denizli İzmir-Denizli Denizli South gate: 6:30am-11pm daily; North gate: 8am-9pm daily (pedestrian access); ancient pool: 8am-7pm daily ktb.gov.tr

In Hellenistic times, the thermal springs at Hierapolis made the city a popular spa. Today, the ruins of the city still draw visitors, who come to swim in its mineral-rich pools and to see the bright white travertine terraces of nearby Pamukkale *(p210)*.

Founded by Eumenes II, king of Pergamon *(p200)*, Hierapolis was noted for its textiles, particularly wool. The city was ceded to Rome in 133 BCE along with the rest of the Pergamene kingdom. Later, in 60 CE, the whole place was destroyed by an earthquake, after which the city was rebuilt, eventually peaking in 196–215 CE. During the 6th century it finally fell into decline, becoming partially submerged by water and deposits of travertine. Note that there is an additional fee for visitors arriving by car.

Baths and church

The main thoroughfare was a colonnaded street called the Plateia, which ran from the Arch of Domitian to the south gate.

Site museum in Roman baths

Hierapolis's sprawling theatre, and *(inset)* exquisite marble reliefs adorning its walls

Swimming in Cleopatra's Pool at the ancient site of Hierapolis

The necropolis is the largest ancient graveyard in Anatolia, with more than 1,200 tombs.

Site of an early theatre

Agora

Church

The Martyrium of St Philip was built in the 5th century CE, on the site where the apostle was crucified and stoned in 80 CE.

Nymphaeum

The theatre, built in 200 BCE, could once seat 20,000 spectators.

The popular bathing pool may be the remains of a sacred pool associated with the Temple of Apollo.

Sixth-century basilica

Illustration of the Hellenistic city of Hierapolis

GATE TO HADES

The Temple of Apollo complex at Hierapolis contains a Plutonium, a sanctuary dedicated to Pluto, the god of the underworld. This spot was popularly regarded as the Gate to Hades because seismic activity resulted in deadly toxic fumes from the cave beneath. The Plutonium's oracle was consulted by animal sacrifice: birds and small animals were thrown into the cave, where they succumbed to the gas, thus proving the power of the oracle.

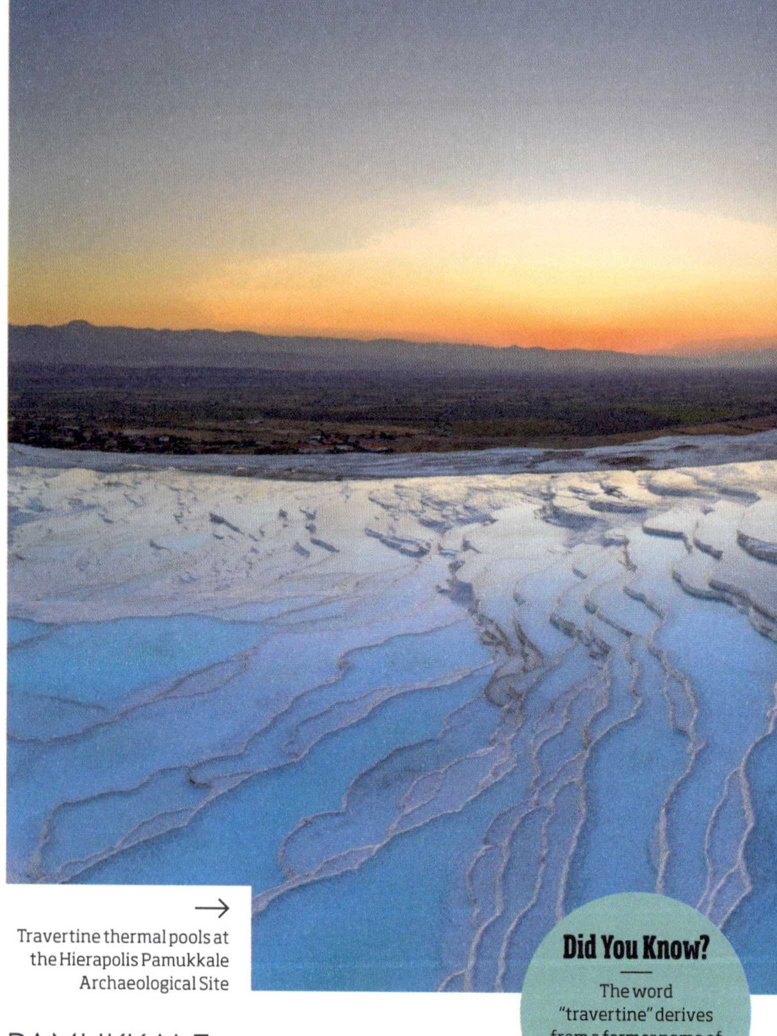

→

Travertine thermal pools at the Hierapolis Pamukkale Archaeological Site

Did You Know?

The word "travertine" derives from a former name of Tivoli, Italy, home to travertine quarries.

PAMUKKALE

Situated next to the ancient city of Hierapolis, Pamukkale's spectacular white travertine terraces are one of Turkey's most popular sights. The terraces are one of the most visited (and photographed) natural sites in the country, attracting more than two million visitors annually.

Pamukkale, the region's Turkish name, refers to the surface of the shimmering, snow-white limestone terraces, shaped over millennia by calcite-rich springs. The process involves mineral-rich waters dripping slowly down the mountain slope, collecting in pools and cascading over these terraces. When these waters, supersaturated with calcium carbonate, reach the surface, they lose carbon dioxide, depositing the calcium carbonate as a soft gel that eventually crystallizes into travertine, which then forms the white terraces that can be seen here.

Tourists can enjoy exploring the thermal pools today. However, in order to protect the delicate terraces, which were added as a UNESCO World Heritage Site in 1988, local authorities and UNESCO regulate the water flow and close certain sections periodically, allowing the formations at Pamukkale to regenerate naturally.

→ Breathtaking turquoise pools in travertine terraces

PICTURE PERFECT
Chasing Sunsets

The sunset at Pamukkale is the most picturesque time to photograph the iconic travertines; the wooden walkway southeast of the pools offers a good vantage point.

↑ Hot-air balloons floating over the travertine pools at Pamukkale

APHRODISIAS

B4 Between Aydın and Denizli, 30 km (18.5 miles) S of E87 highway to Geyre (0256) 448 80 86 Apr-Oct: 8:30am-6:30pm daily; Nov-Mar: hours vary, call ahead

The ancient site of Aphrodisias, located near the modern village of Geyre, was a shrine dating back to 5800 BCE. Neolithic farmers originally came here to worship Cybele, the Anatolian Mother Goddess of fertility and crops.

Turkey's ancient city Aphrodisias was dedicated to Aphrodite, the Greek goddess of love and beauty, and named in honour of the deity during the 2nd century BCE. For centuries it remained this way, but when the Romans defeated the Pontic ruler Mithridates in 74 BCE, Aphrodisias was rewarded for its loyalty with special privileges, including the status of a free city. It prospered as a cultural and artistic hub, home to a renowned school of sculptors who used high-quality marble from a nearby quarry and exported their works across the empire. During the Byzantine era, the city's Temple of Aphrodite became a Christian basilica. The city was eventually renamed Stauropolis, "City of the Cross", however a series of earthquakes and raids eventually led to its final abandonment by the 13th century.

Gable ends were surmounted by statues, called akroteria.

Fourteen columns of the Temple of Aphrodite have been re-erected. The lateral colonnades shown here became the nave of the Christian basilica.

The stepped platform was built on a stone foundation.

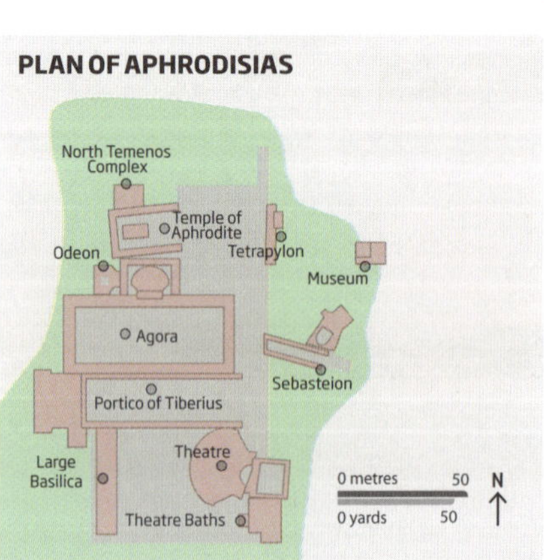

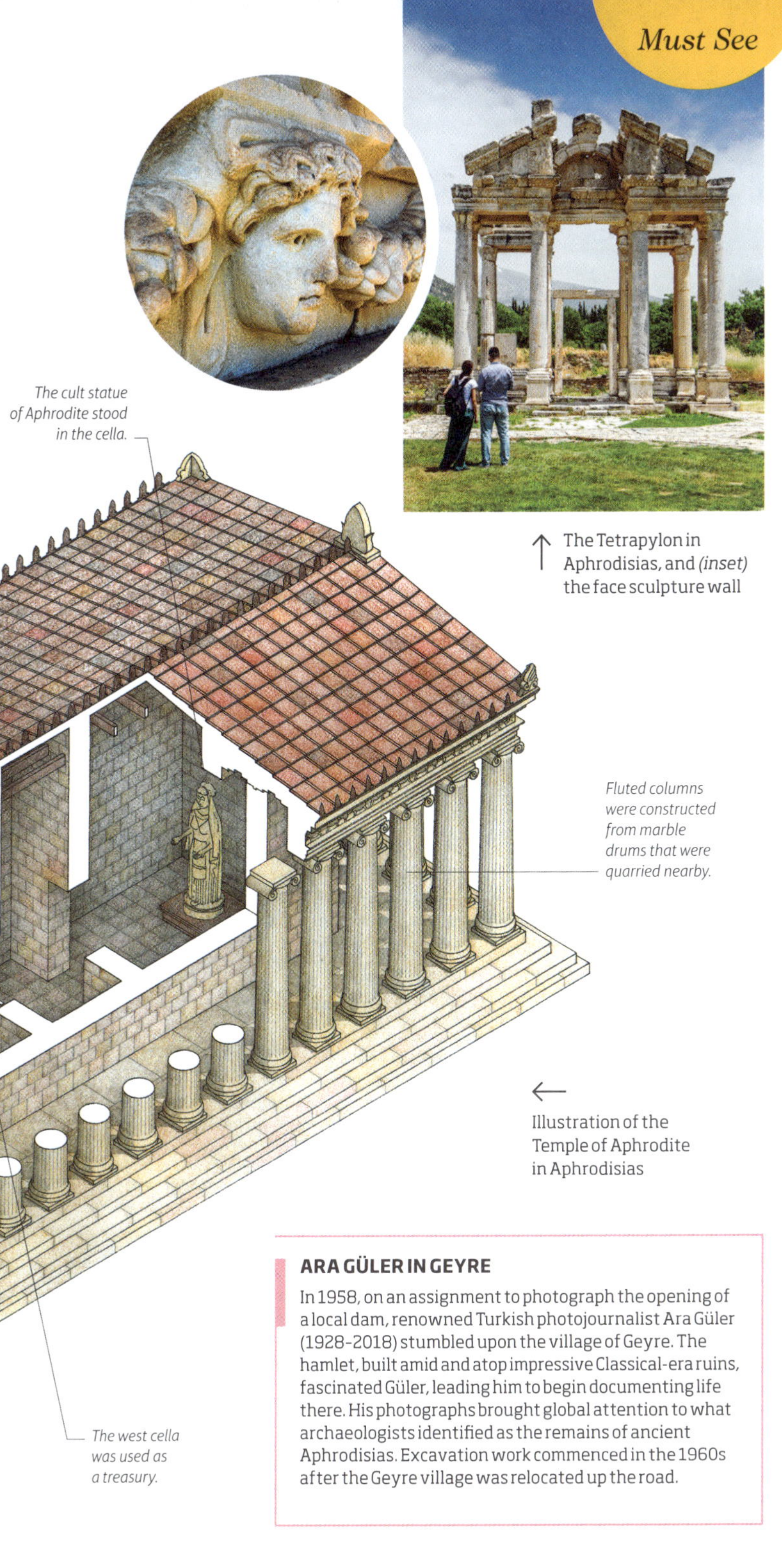

↑ The Tetrapylon in Aphrodisias, and *(inset)* the face sculpture wall

← Illustration of the Temple of Aphrodite in Aphrodisias

ARA GÜLER IN GEYRE

In 1958, on an assignment to photograph the opening of a local dam, renowned Turkish photojournalist Ara Güler (1928–2018) stumbled upon the village of Geyre. The hamlet, built amid and atop impressive Classical-era ruins, fascinated Güler, leading him to begin documenting life there. His photographs brought global attention to what archaeologists identified as the remains of ancient Aphrodisias. Excavation work commenced in the 1960s after the Geyre village was relocated up the road.

BODRUM

A5 Barış Meydanı; bodrum.goturkiye.com

Bodrum is the modern name for the ancient Dorian city of Halicarnassus, location of the famous mausoleum built by Mausolus, who made the city his capital. Modern Bodrum was the first Turkish town to experience a tourist boom, its major sight being the 15th-century Castle of St Peter, now a museum of nautical archaeology.

Harbour

Bodrum Limanı

Neyzen Tevfik Cad

Bodrum's ancient harbour today is a quieter spot than it was in the past. This was once the departure point for Halicarnassus's Carian queen, Artemisia I, who set out with her fleet to support Persian King Xerxes at the Battle of Salamis. Today, the Bodrum Yacht Marina occupies the harbour's western half. Here, a wide, palm-lined promenade runs along the waterfront, with restaurants and cafés lining the inland side of the road. Visitors can take a stroll along the harbour and enjoy views of the moored yachts across the water and the Castle of St Peter, which dominates the eastern tip of the harbour.

The marina pier is the ideal spot to arrange boat excursions on a gulet (traditional Turkish wooden yacht). From here, travellers can also catch the ferry for a day trip to the Datça Peninsula, or head further afield on the ferries to the nearby Greek Dodecanese islands of Kos, Symi and Rhodes.

ANCIENT BODRUM

Bodrum was the site of the Mausoleum of Halicarnassus, a magnificent tomb built for the Persian satrap Mausolus and his wife Artemisia II, which was once considered among the Seven Wonders of the Ancient World. Today, this architectural marvel has been reduced to ruins. To the west of the town stands the restored Myndos Gate, the sole surviving section of Halicarnassus's city walls. Bodrum is also home to a well-preserved theatre built in the 4th century BCE.

Bodrum Hammam

Cevat Şakir Cad, Fabrika Sok (opposite the bus station) 6am-midnight daily bodrum hamami.com.tr

Linked to the Çemberlitaş Baths in Istanbul *(p120)*, the Bodrum Hammam is housed in a lovely old stone building. Service is highly professional,

Bodrum Castle overlooking the marina and its anchored yachts

emphasizing cleanliness and an authentic Turkish bath experience. Masseurs are well trained and you are bound to feel like a "new penny" when you exit. The owners claim a 500-year lineage. If you wish to continue with further spa treatments after the standard hammam, or to add additional treatments, plan for a little extra time. The hammam runs a shuttle that will collect and return you, suitably pampered.

EAT

Marina Yacht Club

Soak up the stunning sunset views over the castle while tucking into classic European-style cuisine at the Marina Yacht Club.

Bodrum Marina, Neyzen Tevfik Cad 5
marinayachtclub.com

Zakka

Zakka offers traditional Turkish village staples, such as the home-style chicken *güveç* (stew).

Banka Sok 33/A Çarşı, Bodrum 0532 472 3942

La Pasion Bodrum

Enjoy tapas and paella in the charming, lantern-lit courtyard of this beautifully restored Greek-Ottoman house.

Uslu Sok 8, Bodrum
lapasionbodrum.com

Bodrum Bazaar

Bodrum Çarşısı

Off Cevat Şakır Cad
10am-late daily

Nestled in Bodrum's Old Town, among whitewashed buildings and narrow lanes, the Bodrum Bazaar offers a piece of Turkish culture that dates back to ancient times. It is widely considered one of the most beautiful markets in Bodrum. The bazaar's helter-skelter lanes spread out behind the impressive Castle of St Peter *(p216)*. However, visitors shouldn't expect an old-fashioned market; this district has been thoroughly modernized and redeveloped to cater to the summer influx of visitors to the town. As a result, much of the shopping here is also aimed squarely at the tourist trade. The area is dotted with chic, independent boutiques, showcasing artful displays of craftware, jewellery, textiles and fashion accessories, and there are dozens of cafés, patisseries, restaurants and cocktail bars. On warm evenings, the bazaar fills with walkers on a post-dinner stroll, or stopping by the shops, most of which are open until late.

This district also features historical landmarks such as the wall remnants of St Nicholas Church, built in 1780, which is on the eastern side of the bazaar, while near the western edge of the district is the small and charming Adliye Mosque.

Exploring the shops at the bustling Bodrum Bazaar

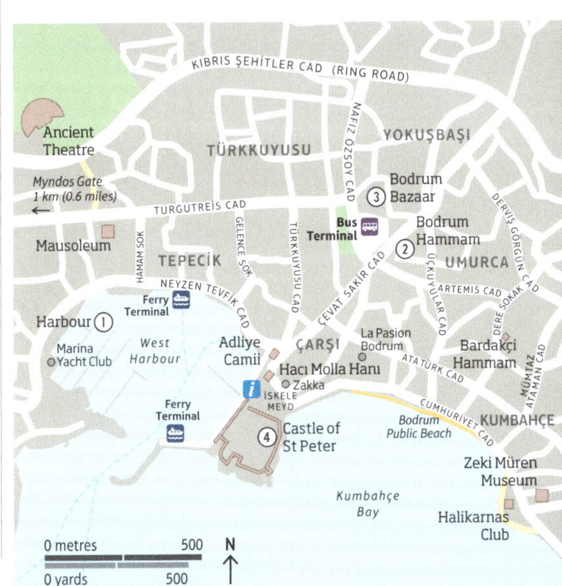

④

CASTLE OF ST PETER

BODRUM KALESI

Bodrum harbour 9am-4:30pm Tue-Sun
bodrum-museum.com

Bodrum's most distinctive landmark is its castle, founded in 1406 by the Knights of St John. In 2016, it was inscribed in the UNESCO Tentative List of World Heritage Sites in Turkey.

The Castle of St Peter in Bodrum has five distinctive towers, which each represented the languages of the city's formidable inhabitants. When Süleyman the Magnificent conquered Rhodes in 1523, both Bodrum and Rhodes came under Ottoman rule and the knights left for Malta. Neglected for centuries, the castle became a prison in 1895 and was damaged by shells from a French warship during World War I. In the early 1960s, it was used to store artifacts found by local sponge divers. This led to a fruitful Turkish-American partnership to restore the castle and put on display the spectacular undersea treasures found around Turkey. The innovative reconstructions of ancient shipwrecks and their cargoes have brought the museum international acclaim.

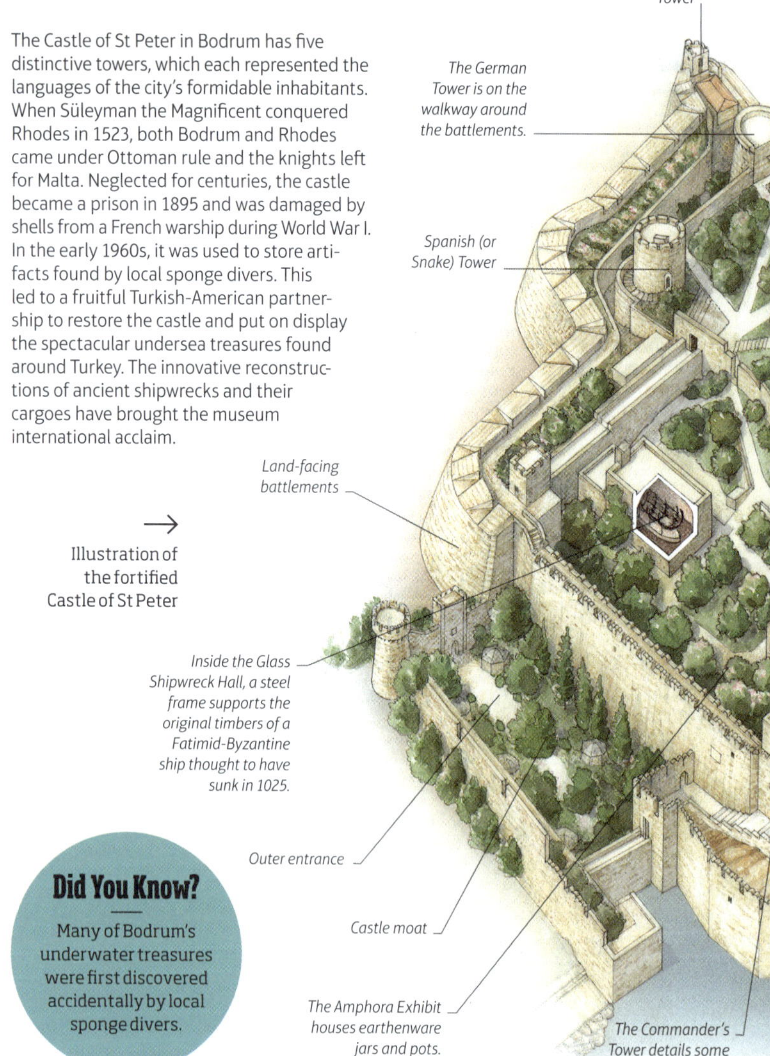

→ Illustration of the fortified Castle of St Peter

Did You Know?

Many of Bodrum's underwater treasures were first discovered accidentally by local sponge divers.

↑ Picturesque setting of the Castle of St Peter, with a view of the marina

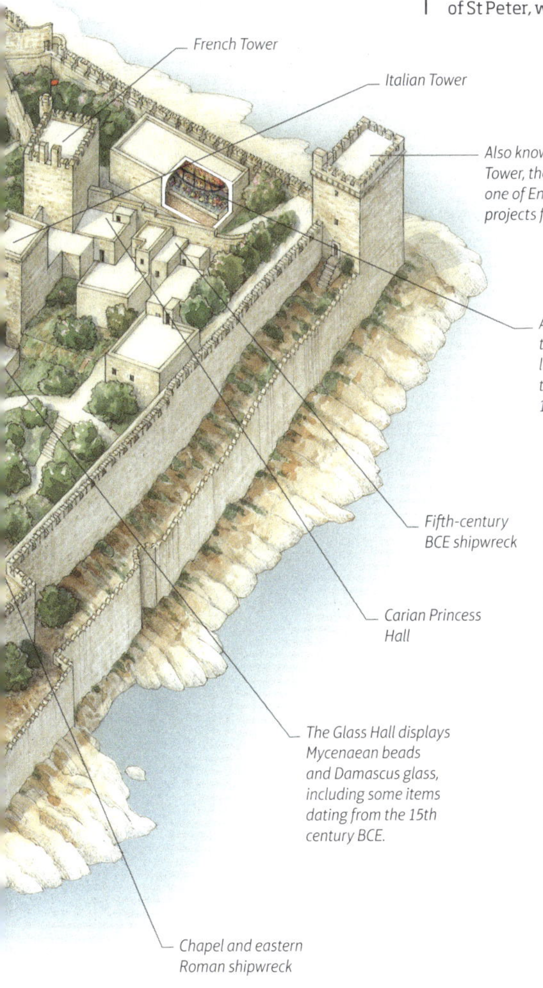

French Tower

Italian Tower

Also known as the Lion Tower, the English Tower was one of England's first foreign projects funded by taxpayers.

Ancient nautical life and trade are captured in this life-size replica of a ship that sank off Kaş in the 14th century BCE.

Fifth-century BCE shipwreck

Carian Princess Hall

The Glass Hall displays Mycenaean beads and Damascus glass, including some items dating from the 15th century BCE.

Chapel and eastern Roman shipwreck

↑ Interior of the English Tower at the Castle of St Peter

7

MARMARIS

A5 Iskele Meydanı (central harbour); (0252) 412 10

Like most of the resorts along the Aegean coast, it is difficult to envisage Marmaris as the quaint fishing village it used to be. It was extensively damaged by an earthquake in 1957, which destroyed most of the old town. Today, the rebuilt (and greatly expanded) town is a top holiday destination.

①

Netsel Marina

Netsel Yat Limanı

netselmarina.com

This luxurious marina has it all – parking, top-class restaurants, entertainment, bars, excellent shops and plenty of service facilities such as banks, ATMs and travel agents. All major currencies and credit cards are accepted for mooring, refuelling and other marina services.

Among several yacht brokerage firms here, **Gino Marine** will arrange luxury charter cruises for a view of Marmaris from the water. There is mooring capacity for just over 700 yachts up to 90 m (295 ft) long. The Netsel call sign on VHF channel 06 is "Port Marmaris". Marmaris is a safe anchorage, with no underwater currents, sandbanks or rocks, and can be approached night and day in most weather conditions.

Gino Marine
(0252) 316 21 66
ginogroup.com

②

Bar Street

39. Sok

Most tourist towns have their bars and pubs concentrated on a couple of streets. Those in Marmaris occupy much of 39 Sokak. Despite the noise, it is always worth strolling along the street and people watching. There are also a number of hotels and pensions in the area, but visitors in search of rest and relaxation would do better to look elsewhere.

③

The Old Quarter

Marmaris Kaleiçi

The Old Quarter around the castle is by far the

TOP 3 MARMARIS BEACHES

İçmeler Beach
İçmeler is a popular spot for swimmers due to its gently sloping shoreline.

Turunç Beach
A sandy beach, Turunç is famous for its boat excursions and water sports.

Kumlubük
This unspoiled beach offers deep, crystal-clear water in its bay.

↑ The small town of Marmaris backed by pine-forested mountains

most charming part of Marmaris. Many houses that were either abandoned or derelict have been restored to their former glory. Most belong to professional people who seem to be accustomed to strangers peeking into a shady courtyard or admiring a handsome brass knocker. Panorama Manzara Cafe, near the entrance to the castle, has a well-preserved interior. From the top terrace of the restaurant, you will get a wonderful view of the town and its numerous delightful "barbecue" chimneys. See if you can spot the one and only remaining original Greek chimney from here.

Castle and Museum

Marmaris Kalesi ve Arkeoloji Müzesi

(0252) 412 14 59
Apr-Oct: 8:30am-9:30pm daily; Nov-Mar: hours vary, call ahead

The original castle was rebuilt by Süleyman the Magnificent in 1522 after his successful campaign against Rhodes. Today, the restored structure is a museum housing a small collection of nautical items. There are also inscriptions and sculptures displayed in the courtyard. More engaging for most visitors, however, will be the panoramic view of the harbour and old renovated Greek houses.

Bazaar

Marmaris Çarşısı

The bazaar in Marmaris is the place to go for products such as leather goods, jewellery, herbs, spices and teas. A delicious local speciality is Marmaris honey, which is produced along the scenic Datça Peninsula *(p236)*. Both pine *(çam)* or flower *(çiçek)* honey are fragrant, thick and dark.

A number of large holiday villages are located in İçmeler, about 6 km (4 miles) around the bay from Marmaris. Transport to and from Marmaris is easy, as dolmuşes make the trip on a regular basis. İçmeler lacks the quaint atmosphere of an old Turkish town, but the area has more facilities and cleaner beaches, appealing to visitors (especially families).

EAT

Ali Usta Restaurant

This restaurant offers classic, hearty Turkish grill specialities.

207 Sok 16/1
(0533) 457 5928

Neighbours Restaurant

Located at the marina, this restaurant has a casual, welcoming ambience and a menu that features plenty of meze and salad options.

Yacht Marina, Barbaros Cad 259 (0252) 412 26 93

Kirtil Ev Yemekleri

Tucked away in the Old Quarter alleys of Marmaris, this spot is known for its home-style dishes.

36 Sok 69
(0252) 413 43 21

8

GALLIPOLI PENINSULA

A3 Çanakkale to Eceabat Bursa, Istanbul

The Gallipoli Peninsula was the scene of one of the bloodiest campaigns of World War I, in which more than 500,000 Allied and Turkish soldiers lost their lives. The region has three museums, and is dotted with cemeteries and monuments. Today, the peninsula is a largely unspoiled area of farmland and pine forest, scattered with small villages and stretches of sandy beach. In 1973, the Gallipoli Peninsula Historic Park was created in recognition of the area's great historical significance.

Çanakkale Destanı Tanıtım Merkezi

Kemalpaşa, 17900 Eceabat/Çanakkale (0286) 814 11 28 8:30am-6pm daily

This visitor centre also serves as a museum dedicated to the harrowing events of the Gallipoli campaign. It has a vast collection of exhibits designed to immerse visitors in the realities of this World War I conflict, including uniforms, weapons, letters, photographs, shrapnel and video simulations.

French Cemetery

Fransız Mezarlığı ve Anıtı

Also known as the Cape Helles Memorial, this cemetery stands as a solemn tribute to the French troops who died during the Anglo-French landing at Cape Helles on 25 April 1915. It features a sombre obelisk surrounded with rows of striking black crosses.

Mehmetcik Memorial

Mehmetçik'e Saygı Anıtı

Kemalpaşa, 17900 Kocadere/Eceabat/Çanakkale 9am-6pm daily

Officially unveiled in 1985, this memorial serves as a poignant reminder of the shared sacrifice of the Turkish and Allied armies in Gallipoli. The text engraved

→ The 57th Infantry Regiment Memorial and cemetery

Anzac Cove near Suvla Bay, overlooking the scenic Gallipoli Peninsula

on the memorial features a moving eulogy by Atatürk who was the commanding officer during the Gallipoli campaign. This famous eulogy unites the fallen sons of Turkey (Mehmetcik) with the Allied dead ("Johnnies").

④

Chunuk Bair

This was the battlefield where approximately 28,000 men lost their lives in an intense fight that took place between 6 and 9 August 1915, during World War I. Today, the historic site serves as a poignant memorial to this battle, with several monuments commemorating the lives lost.

INSIDER TIP
Underwater Park

The peninsula's 14 World War I shipwrecks are a wreck-diver's paradise *(diving gelibolu.com)*. The wrecks, including HMS *Triumph* and SS *Milo*, together form the Gallipoli Historical Underwater Park.

⑤

Suvla Bay

Suvla Koyu

Located on the Aegean coast of the Gallipoli Peninsula, Suvla Bay became the site of a major Allied landing on 7 August 1915. This operation was a desperate attempt by British forces to break the stalemate further south at the original April 1915 landing sites of Cape Helles and Anzac Cove. Although the operation failed to achieve its objectives, leading to heavy casualties, it played a significant role in the eventual decision to evacuate all Allied troops from the peninsula between December 1915 and January 1916.

STAY

Kirte Hotel

Located on the tranquil outskirts of Alçıtepe village, the Kirte Hotel offers a peaceful retreat for guests keen to experience rural peninsula life. It is conveniently situated near local historical sites and features contemporary, light-filled rooms.

Alçıtepe, Gelibolu
thekirtehotel.com

EXPERIENCE MORE

Çanakkale

A3 Eceabat, Kilitbahir Atatürk Cad İskele Meydanı 67; (0286) 217 11 87

Çanakkale occupies the narrowest point of the straits called the Dardanelles, which are 1,200 m (3,937 ft) wide at this point. In 450 BCE, the Persian King Xerxes built a bridge of boats here to land his troops in Thrace, and the final battles of the Peloponnesian War took place in these waters around 400 BCE.

During his campaign to take Constantinople in 1453, Mehmet II (the Conqueror) built two fortresses to secure the straits: Kilitbahir (on the European side) and Çimenlik (in Çanakkale harbour). Today, ferry services link Çanakkale with Kilitbahir and Eceabat on the other side. Çanakkale makes the most convenient base for tours of the Gallipoli battlefields *(p220)* across the straits.

The town has a harbour, a naval museum and a colossal wooden horse that stands on the town's waterfront. The name Çanakkale, meaning "pottery castle", reflects its past as a centre for producing high-quality kaolin for a flourishing ceramics industry. Today, this type of clay is imported, but the vitreous enamelware made in Çanakkale remains a top Turkish export.

A few kilometres south of the town is the **Archaeological Museum**, which is small but should not be missed.

Archaeological Museum

Barbaros Mahallesi, Yüzüncü Yıl Cad (0286) 217 23 71 8am-5pm Tue-Sun

SCHLIEMANN'S SEARCH FOR ANCIENT TROY

The German-born Heinrich Schliemann nurtured a lifelong ambition to discover Homer's Troy. In 1873, three years after starting excavations at Hisarlık, he stumbled upon what he claimed to be King Priam's hoard of gold and silver jewellery. The over-eager explorer damaged the site, but his finds demonstrated that Greek civilization started 1,000 years earlier than previously believed. Part of the hoard, which was on display in a Berlin museum, vanished after World War II. It reappeared in the Pushkin Museum in Russia in 1996.

Troy

A3 Tevfikiye Arkeo Köy İskele Meydanı 67, Çanakkale; (0286) 217 11 87

Few areas of Turkey have been as thoroughly excavated as Troy. Nine different strata have yielded pieces of a history that runs from around 4000 BCE until about 300 CE. Troy was the pivot of Homer's *Iliad* and was where the decade-long Trojan War (13th century BCE) was fought.

The site is located on the mound of Hisarlık, or "castle kingdom" in Turkish. The stonework and walls are impressive. Visible today are a defence wall, two sanctuaries (probably dating from the 8th century BCE), houses from various periods and a Roman theatre. The site called the Pillar House at the southern gate may have been the palace of King Priam.

The site is well marked with 12 information points and some ongoing excavations. The most visible attraction is a large wooden Trojan Horse, a reconstruction of the device

Trojan Horse statue overlooking the marina in Çanakkale

↑ Walking along the wooden footpath through the ancient ruins of Troy

used by the Greeks to deceive and ultimately vanquish the Trojans, and a universal symbol of treachery today. In August each year, Turkish schoolchildren release a white dove from the Trojan Horse to celebrate peace.

A short walk east of the site leads to the **Troy Museum**, which offers a curated exploration of Troy's history, mythology and excavations.

Troy Museum
5 km (3 miles) from main E87 road Çanakkale 8:30am–8pm daily muze.gov.tr

11 Behram Kale (Assos)

A3 To Ayvacık, 19 km (12 miles) N, then dolmuş

Nestled on the shores of the Gulf of Edremit and sheltered by the Greek island of Lesbos, 10 km (6 miles) offshore, it is easy to see why **Assos** enjoyed the reputation of being the most beautiful place in Asia Minor. Ancient Assos reached the pinnacle of its glory when Plato's protégé, Aristotle, founded a school of philosophy here in 340 BCE. In the 2nd century BCE, the town included not only the present citadel, with the remaining Doric columns of the Temple of Athena (built in the 6th century BCE), but also the village of Behram Kale, 238 m (781 ft) below.

St Paul is reputed to have passed through Assos on his third biblical journey, and the town is referred to in the Acts of the Apostles. After the fall of the Byzantine Empire, its commercial fortunes declined, but today this charming and cultured retreat attracts many artists and scholars, who leave the bustle of the city seeking to find a source of inspiration here.

As you come into the town, note the fine Ottoman bridge dating from the 14th century. There is also a mosque and a fort from this time, all built by Sultan Murat I. In the town, many of local homes often feature archways and overhanging balconies, vibrantly decorated with bright pink oleander and golden trumpet vine.

Assos
8.30am–9pm daily

INSIDER TIP
Thursday Market

Shop for local handicrafts along with village-made sauces and condiments every Thursday at Ayvalık's vast market, held in the central Market Square *(off Barbaros Caddesi)*.

12 Ayvalık

A4 1.5 km (1 mile) N of town centre Opposite the yacht harbour; (0266) 312 21 22

Ayvalık takes its name from *ayva*, the Turkish word for quince. Of the many villages along the Aegean coast peopled by Greeks until 1923, Ayvalık is the one that has most retained the flavour of a bygone age. There are many stone houses, and the town's mosques betray their Greek Orthodox origins.

Ayvalık's draws include its cobbled streets and leisurely lifestyle. The beach over at Sarımsaklı and the peninsula of Alibey are within reach by road and ferry.

Foça

A4 Foça Girişi No 1; (0232) 812 55 34

Phocaea, ancient Foça, was probably settled around 1000 BCE and was part of the Ionian League *(p227)*. Around 500 BCE the Phocaeans were famed as mariners, sending vessels powered by 50 oarsmen into the Aegean, Mediterranean and Black Sea. Near the centre of town, you will find a stone tomb known as Taş Küle.

About 23 km (14 miles) up the coast is the town of Yenifoça (New Foça), with good campsites and beaches. The military presence and proximity to Greek territory has restricted development so Foça has remained very green, with low-rise buildings. However its population dramatically increases in summer, drawing visitors from Istanbul and elsewhere to enjoy its temperate climate. Boat tours to the Siren Kayalıkları, the Siren Rocks, run during the summer months.

EAT

OD Urla

OD Urla's seasonal menu offers a modern twist on classic Turkish cuisine.

A4 9 Sok 28, Süt Pınarı Mevkii, Urla 1pm-midnight Tue-Sun odurla.com

Yengeç

Feast on seafood, with views of fishing boats bobbing in Urla's harbour.

A4 2121 Sok 6, İskele, Urla Noon-midnight daily yengec-restaurant.com.tr

Çeşme

A4 İskele Meydani 8; (0232) 712 66 53

The town's main feature is the 14th-century Genoese Castle of St Peter, a powerful symbol of Italian Renaissance mercantilism. Sultan Beyazıt II (1481–1512) fortified the castle to counter attacks by both pirates and the Knights of St John, who operated from bases on the island of Rhodes and at Bodrum *(p214)*. The castle contains a **museum** with nautical exhibits.

Unlike other more popular resorts, Çeşme is dedicated to promenading, yachting and the simpler pleasures of life. There are several fine restaurants, and the cosmopolitan, tolerant atmosphere attracts world-class performers, who come here for the month-long International İzmir Festival.

The long peninsula around Çeşme is serviced by a fast, six-lane highway from İzmir. However, you can still take the old road.

Museum

Castle of St Peter Apr-Sep: 8:30am-9pm daily; Oct-Mar: 8:30-5:30pm daily

15 Selçuk

A4 From İzmir or Denizli Atatürk Cad selcuk.gov.tr Agora Çarşısı 35; (0232) 892 63 28

The town of Selçuk is dominated by a 6th-century Byzantine citadel (Ayasoluk Hill) with 15 well-preserved towers. You enter the citadel through a Byzantine gate. At the foot of the hill is the Basilica of St John, built by the Emperor Justinian in the 6th century on the site of an earlier shrine. Restoration has brought back some of the basilica's former glory, and there are some fine frescoes in the chapel.

The **Ephesus Museum** is one of Turkey's best. Statues and frescoes from the site *(p206)* are displayed, and exhibits include a sculpture of Artemis, jewels and numerous artifacts thought to have come from the Artemision, the ancient Temple of Artemis.

The İsa Bey Mosque, an ornate 14th-century Seljuk mosque, is located near the museum. It is not always open to visitors but the exterior calligraphy and tilework are worth a visit.

Konak, traditional Ottoman houses, line

→ Çeşme Marina, as seen from Çeşme's Castle of St Peter

↑ An ancient marble bust from the Ephesus Museum

the streets of this small village famous for its fruit wines. Popular with Turkish tourists due to its picturesque setting, it can get very busy with coach tours.

At Çamlık is the **Open-Air Steam Train Exhibition**, a museum run by Turkish State Railways. There are more than 24 steam locomotives and other railway vehicles on display at the site.

Ephesus Museum
Behind the Tourism Information Office
8:30am-noon & 12:30-5pm daily ephesus.us

Open-Air Steam Train Exhibition
Çamlık, 12 km (7 miles) S of Selçuk on the E87

Kuşadası

A4 Liman Cad 13; (0256) 614 11 03

Kuşadası is a frequent port of call for luxury cruise liners. It has a lively restaurant and nightlife scene in the summer months.

The town's name, meaning "bird island", is taken from an islet, known as Pigeon Island, tacked onto the mainland by a causeway. A 14th-century Genoese fort reveals the town's commercial origins.

Dilek Peninsula National Park protects some of the last wild horses in Turkey and rare Anatolian lynx. The military presence has ensured that the area has been left undisturbed. Hike to the summit of Samsun Dağı (ancient Mount Mycale) for fine views of the peninsula.

Dilek Peninsula National Park
(0256) 646 10 79
Apr-Oct: 8am-7:30pm daily; Nov-Mar: 8am-5:30pm daily

HIDDEN GEM
Remains of the Kurşunlu Monastery

Within the Dilek Peninsula National Park lie the Byzantine ruins of Kurşunlu Monastery. This was built high in the mountains, making it a great spot to enjoy impressive views.

Urla

A4 40 km (25 miles) west of İzmir

Near the foot of the Çeşme Peninsula, Urla is a major foodie destination and a chic summer hangout popular among locals. Inland, its historic town centre is filled with Aegean cottages. Make the detour 4 km (2 miles) east to **Arkas Art Urla**, which displays an eclectic collection of European paintings, medieval armour and Renaissance tapestries.

Around 5 km (3 miles) north is Urla's seafront suburb with its beach and fishing harbour lined with seafood restaurants as well as a causeway. A short walk west from the harbour leads to the **Klazomenai Archaeological Site**, which displays the remains of the oldest olive-oil workshop in Turkey. To the east is the Bronze Age Limantepe archaeological site, one of the oldest ports in the Aegean. It's not open to the public due to ongoing excavations.

Arkas Art Urla
Arkas Sanat Urla Sefaköy Cad 23, Yenice, Urla
10am-6pm Tue, Thu-Sat
arkassanaturla.com

Klazomenai Archaeological Site
Klazomenai Antik Kent Işıklı Klaros Cad 8:30am-6pm daily muze.gov.tr

18

Aydın

A4 Adnan Menderes Mah-Denizli Bul 2; (0256) 211 28 42

Known in Roman times as Tralles, Aydın's tranquil appearance stems from long periods of prosperity. It was known variously as Caesarea and Güzelhisar before falling under Ottoman rule in the late 14th century. Frequent earthquakes have meant that there are few ruins to be seen, and the region is still subject to tremors.

The region is famous for its figs *(incir)*, black olives, cereals and cotton, and Aydın is a leading exporter of snails and salmon. In the 1920s, Atatürk *(p55)* targeted the region as the focus of a new state-owned cotton industry. Today, raw cotton and ready-to-wear clothing remain Turkey's biggest export commodities.

Suffering badly in the War of Independence, nowadays Aydın is more peaceful, with a **museum** and several distinctive mosques.

Museum

Next to the Forum shopping centre
(0256) 225 22 59
8:30am-5:30pm daily

A well-preserved theatre from the Roman period in Aydın

Menderes River Valley

Büyük Menderes Irmağı

A4

One of Turkey's main grain-growing regions, and a major producer of fruit and cotton, the Menderes Valley is made up of the Büyük Menderes (Great Meander) and Küçük Menderes (Lesser Meander) rivers, with a wide alluvial plain in between. The S-shaped bends formed by the slow-moving Büyük Menderes below Aydın have given us the word "meander".

Nysa, a Seleucid foundation dating from around 280 BCE, presents a lovely sight as you approach from Sultanhisar (just to the south). There is a theatre overlooking a tributary of the Büyük Menderes, and a gymnasium, library, agora and council house. The whole city is built in and over a ravine. Its claim to fame was as a sanctuary to Pluto, god of the underworld.

At Tire, north of Aydın, lie the remains of a number of caravanserais dating from the 14th and 15th centuries. In the wake of the capture of Constantinople in 1453, Mehmet II *(p53)* ordered the removal of the inhabitants of Tire, as part of the effort to repopulate the capital. There is a dramatic domed bazaar building located here and a lively bazaar is still held each week on Tuesdays.

PICTURE PERFECT
Capturing scenic Birgi

This delightful rural idyll is situated 115 km (72 miles) east of Izmir. The area is known for its cobblestone lanes and timber-framed Ottoman houses, many of which feature cantilevered overhangs.

Denizli

B4 554/1 Sok 5; (0258) 264 39 71

Denizli is often thought of as a tourist backwater, but the town has little need to pander to visitors. It is a thriving agricultural centre, a centre for carpet

Intricate stone carving at the Aydın Archaeological Museum

Denizli takes its name from the many springs that feed the River Lycus. Another city linked with water, Hydrela, was located here in pre-Roman times.

production and one of Turkey's major textile towns, continuing a prosperous trade begun as far back as Roman times. Today, Aegean cotton fibres fetch more on world markets than many other spun cottons.

Denizli, literally translated as "with sea", takes its name from the many springs that feed the River Lycus. Another city linked with water, Hydrela, was located here in pre-Roman times. Denizli is a good base for touring the ancient sites of Hierapolis *(p208)* and Pamukkale *(p210)*, the latter being about 22 km (16 miles) away.

The town was conquered by the Seljuks in the 11th century and came under Ottoman rule in 1428. At some point in between, when Denizli was known as Ladik, it seems that the inhabitants of nearby Laodiceia moved here after their own city was ravaged by one of the many earthquakes that have marked this region.

The Atatürk Ethnography Museum has some interesting local folk art and decorative artifacts on display. Denizli's Great Mosque (Ulu Cami) is also worth a visit.

Atatürk Ethnography Museum
Saraylar, Gazi Mustafa Kemal Blv 70
(0258) 262 00 66
8am-8pm Tue-Sun

---

21 

Priene

A4 8am-5pm daily

The ancient city of Priene has a breathtaking setting between the Büyük Menderes river and Mount Mycale. Like Miletus *(p228)* and Ephesus *(p206)*, it was a member of the Ionian League, a group of 12 city-states believed to have been settled by Greek colonists before 1000 BCE.

Laid out by the architect Hippodamos of Miletus in about 450 BCE, Priene is in a good state of preservation. The Temple of Athena, built in the 4th century BCE in honour of the city's patron goddess, is considered one of the great achievements of Ionian architecture. The work was supervised and financed by Alexander the Great *(p51)* when he occupied the city. Because of Priene's strong Greek ties, it was not viewed with favour by the Romans. Its importance declined and by Byzantine times it had been abandoned. This neglect has meant that Priene is one of the most intact Hellenistic settlements to be seen. The theatre, dating from the 3rd century BCE, could seat 5,000 people. The *bouleuterion* (council chamber) could hold 640 delegates. There is also a stadium, complete with starting blocks for athletes, and sanctuaries to Demeter and Kore. The lower gymnasium walls are adorned with school-boy graffiti from over 2,000 years ago.

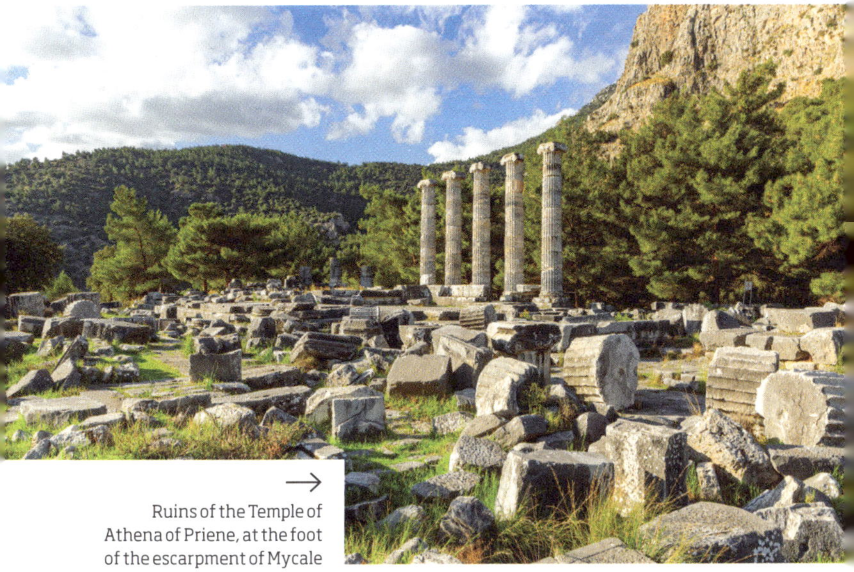

→ Ruins of the Temple of Athena of Priene, at the foot of the escarpment of Mycale

TOP 3
HIKES AROUND LAKE BAFA

Karahayıt Village to Yediler Monastery
This 8-km (5-mile) route to a Byzantine monastery is scattered with ruins from Latmos.

Kapıkırı Village to Bağarcık Village
Traverse 16 km (10 miles) from Lake Bafas' shore to Bağarcık using ancient paths across the hills.

Mount Latmos
Follow this 11-km (7-mile) trail to ascend the 1,300-m (4,490-ft) peak.

22

Lake Bafa

Bafa Gölü

A4 45 km (30 miles) S of Söke

Considered one of the most picturesque landscapes in Turkey, the Lake Bafa area is the setting for several classical gems, with the peaks of Mount Latmos as a backdrop. Rising to 1,300-m (4,490-ft), the mountain is aptly known as Beş Parmak (five fingers).

In ancient times, Lake Bafa was an arm of the sea. When silt eventually closed the gulf, the port of **Herakleia**, near the eastern shore of the lake, was left landlocked. The same process was responsible for the decline of Miletus and Priene *(p227)*. Lake Bafa, now a wetland and national park, is brackish and supports many species of fish.

Herakleia, also known as Herakleia-under-Latmos, occupies a dramatic setting at the lakeside. Its fortifications, towers and well-preserved Temple of Athena are tangible vestiges of its former status. Visitors can hire a local guide to show them the difficult-to-reach monasteries high up the mountain along the Carian Way and some of the prehistoric rock carvings in the area.

Euromos, located to the southeast of Lake Bafa, is one of the best-preserved temples in Turkey. Euromos was, in fact, an amalgamation of several cities, including Herakleia, owing allegiance to Milas *(p232)*. In time, rivalries emerged between them, and Euromos (meaning "strong" in Greek) turned out to be politically fickle. It opted to ally itself with Rome and Rhodes, not Greece.

Herakleia
10 km (6 miles) from Camiçi (by car on a track)

Euromos
12 km (7 miles) NW of Milas 8am-7pm daily (winter: to 5pm)

23 

Miletus

A4 8am-5pm daily

Although less impressive than Priene, Miletus was more renowned for its art, politics and trade than many other Greek cities. Known as Milet today, it was once the principal port of the Ionian League, and flourished as a centre for art and industry. In Roman times it supplied wool and textile dyes to the wool trade in Ankara *(p276)*. One of its sons, the scientist and mathematician Thales – known as one of the Seven Sages of Antiquity – correctly forecast a total eclipse of the sun in 580 BCE.

The Persians took control of the Ionian cities in the mid-6th century BCE. Miletus led a revolt against Persian rule in 500–494 BCE, but in 479 BCE succumbed to the tyrannical Persian king, Darius.

Of the surviving buildings, the finest is the 15,000-seat theatre, dating from 100 CE. Over the centuries, Greeks, Romans and Byzantines all made alterations to the structure. The *bouleuterion* (council chamber) was built in 175–164 BCE during the reign of the Seleucid king, Antiochus IV Ephiphanes. The well-preserved Baths of Faustina

date from 43 CE, and were named for the wife of Emperor Marcus Aurelius. The complex holds a *palaestra* (gymnasium), and there is a stadium nearby. The Baths of Faustina was a model for the development of the hammam *(p81)*.

Incongruously, a mosque reposes amid the ruins of ancient Miletus. The İlyas Bey (or Balat) Mosque was built in 1403 by İlyas Bey, emir (ruler) of the Beylik of Menteşe. It celebrated his return from exile at the court of the Mongol ruler Timur, also known as Tamerlane, after Timur's invasion of Anatolia in 1402. The mosque is built of brick and both white and coloured marble that was taken from Roman Miletus. There is splendidly detailed carving on the marble window grilles, screen and prayer niche (mihrab), and the use of coloured marble on the façade is impressive. The dome measures 14 m (45 ft) in diameter and was the largest built during the Beylik period. The mosque is a beautiful early forerunner of the Ottoman *külliye (p33)*, a building style that flourished during the 16th century. The *külliye* combined social welfare and residential functions with facilities for Islamic worship.

Didyma

A5 8:30am-7pm daily
Kaymakamlık Binası; (0256) 811 37 25

The prime reason to visit Didyma (modern Didim) is for the Temple of Apollo, built in the 7th century BCE to honour the god of prophecy and oracles. By 500 BCE, the shrine at Didyma was one of the leading oracles of the Greek world. It even had a sacred spring. Branchid priests, who were reputedly connected to the great oracle at Delphi, were in charge of the shrine. Marble from nearby Lake Bafa was used to build the temple. A carved relief of the head of Medusa, with its serpentine curls, has become almost synonymous with Didyma.

The well below the Medusa head was the place where arriving pilgrims would purify themselves before approaching the oracle.

In its heyday, the Temple of Apollo featured 108 Ionic columns. Only three are still intact. However, the surviving stumps are still impressive.

The Temple of Apollo was destroyed by Persians in the mid-6th century BCE, but was restored around 350 BCE by Alexander the Great. With the coming of Christianity, the temple was converted into a church and Didyma became a bishopric. In 1493, an earthquake destroyed the temple and Didyma was abandoned.

Did You Know?

In ancient times, the people of Miletus would mark the new year with a procession to the temple in Didyma.

Serene Lake Bafa with the peaks of Mount Latmos in the background

Sunloungers lining the shore at Didim's famous Altınkum Beach

Altınkum

A5 4 km (3 miles) S of Didyma

The protected sandy bay of Altınkum offers a relaxing spot to unwind, especially after a day spent tramping around classical ruins. Most day trips to Priene, Miletus and Didyma end up here. In fact, locals generally refer to the area as Didyma, or Didim. Like many idyllic retreats that have experienced rapid growth, Didyma's success has spilled over to nearby towns. Charter groups and tours flock to Altınkum and it can be very busy in summer. This was one of Turkey's original camping venues. As it grew, pensions opened, and Turkish families began to flock here for sun and sand. There are around half a dozen restaurants, one bar and a couple of supermarkets. For anything more than this by way of amenities, you will have to go to nearby Yenihisar (ancient Didyma).

Ruins of the Temple of Apollo in Didyma

Exploring some of the rocky remains of the archaeological site of Labranda ↑

Labranda

A5 15 km (9 miles) N of Milas (by car, taxi or on foot from Milas) 8:30am-5:30pm daily

Getting to Labranda is certainly worth the effort for those who persevere. This Carian sanctuary nestles high on the mountains above Milas, at an elevation of 610 m (2,000 ft). From early times, it fell under the jurisdiction of Milas (Mylasa). The remains of the sacred way leading there are one of the sights to note.

Despite being damaged by several fires and earthquakes, the remains of a stadium have been uncovered by Swedish archaeologists. Baths and a fountain house (which may have been a water storage depot) date from about the 1st century BCE and the area still boasts an abundant source of spring water. The most interesting buildings are three *androns* (banqueting halls), the second built by Mausolus *(p214)*, who ruled from nearby Milas.

The chamber tombs and sarcophagi, although pillaged, are unusual and reveal much about ancient burial practices.

Milas (Mylasa)

A5

The origins of Milas are uncertain and the many theories are largely unsubstantiated. What is clear is that its most noteworthy period was when it was capital of Caria and the administrative seat for the Persian satrap (subordinate ruler), Mausolus. Like most Carian cities, Milas was ruled in turn by the Persians, Alexander the Great, the Romans and the Byzantines before finally falling under Ottoman control in 1425.

The remains of the ancient city lie within the present town centre. The first thing you notice is the two-storey Gümüşkesen (silver money-bag) Monument, a structure of uncertain age. The lower floor is the actual tomb, with an aperture in the roof to provide sustenance to the deceased. The city's most intact monument is the handsome Baltılı (Axe) Gate.

As an administrative seat, Milas issued regulatory decrees, notably concerning money. Inscriptions dating from the 3rd century CE list detailed regulations that ban illegal conversions from imperial (Roman) to local money and black-market money dealings.

Yatağan, site of a thermal power station and known for its environmental pollution, has little to offer, but two interesting sights are located in the area. **Stratonikeia** was founded in 295 BCE. It was apparently named after the wife of Seleucas I, king of Syria. Work is currently underway at the ruins, which feature a large gymnasium, an agora (marketplace), a rather unkempt Hellenistic theatre with seating for 10,000 and the Temple of Sarapis, located in the village of Eskihisar on the 330 road, south of the city.

The town's small museum houses mainly Roman finds but includes a Mycenaean mug from about 1000 BCE.

Did You Know?

The town of Milas (Mylasa) is famous for its distinctive carpet-making traditions.

Lagina is located northwest of Yatağan and is best known for its association with the cult of Hecate, the Greek goddess of darkness and sorcery. The gate of the temple precinct dates from between 125 and 80 BCE. The Temple of Hecate would have stood here but the site has not yielded major finds.

Stratonikeia

 28 km (17 miles) E of Milas Summer: 8:30am-7:30pm daily; winter: 8:30am-5:30pm daily

Lagina

12 km (7.5 miles) NW of Yatağan Summer: 8:30am-7:30pm daily; winter: 8:30am-5:30pm daily

---

28

Muğla (Menteşe)

A5 110 km (68 miles) E of Bodrum

A bustling provincial centre located inland from the Bodrum Peninsula, Muğla attracts fewer tourists than the popular nearby beach resorts. However, this compact town offers several interesting sights from different eras, making it a worthwhile stop for history enthusiasts.

Most of the historic monuments speckle the streets north of the main square, Cumhuriyet Meydanı. The Kurşunlu Mosque, built in 1495, features a prayer hall with intricate fresco decorations added in the early 1900s, depicting illustrations of Mecca and seascapes. A short stroll north, the area around the clock tower is home to many well-preserved Ottoman buildings, including the wooden Yağcılar Han (an old caravanserai) and Muğla's timber and stone Grand Mosque (Ulu Cami) which dates from 1334 during the reign of the Seljuk *beyliks* (principalities). The higgledy-piggledy hillside Saberhane neighbourhood to the north-east of the centre is also worth exploring for its narrow lanes lined with preserved, traditional Ottoman houses.

EAT

Sultans & Kings Restaurant

Enjoy terrace dining featuring a diverse menu that ranges from European bistro-style favourites to Turkish grilled specialities.

A5 19 Sok 19/B, Altınkum sultansandkingshotel.com

Muğla Lokantası

This simple *lokanta* in central Muğla has local favourites, including hearty stews and plates of beans and rice.

A5 İsmet İnönü Cad 21A, Muğla (0252) 212 31 21

Güllük

A5

This is a lovely bay and harbour with a genuine nautical atmosphere. The real reason for coming to Güllük is to see the site of ancient **Iasus**, with its elaborate wall, 810 m (2,658 ft) long, built during the 5th century CE.

The fortunes of Iasus were tied to fishing. Bronze Age finds from here bear detailed inscriptions that have shed new light on the lifestyles of the ancients. Legends of boys frolicking with dolphins also originated here.

Iasus

18 km (11 miles) from main Milas road

The distinctive two-storey Gümüşkesen Monument in Milas

A DRIVING TOUR
THE BODRUM PENINSULA

Length 100-120 km (63-75 miles)
Stopping-off points Turgutreis is the only major town, with a number of petrol stations and amenities

The Bodrum Peninsula was originally peopled by the Lelegians, migrants from mainland Greece who maintained historic ties to the Carians. There were eight Lelegian cities, dating from as early as the 4th or 5th century BCE. Myndos was the most prominent, but Pedasa offers the most to see.

Today, the Bodrum Peninsula is renowned as a holiday paradise. Its secluded bays are ideal for yachting, water sports and getting away from it all.

Formerly an important sponge-fishing port, ***Yalıkavak*** *is an ideal spot for a meal. Local delicacies include sea beans and stuffed marrow flowers.*

Aegean Sea

Yalıkavak
Dirmil
Dağbele
48-55
Partipanas 361 m (1,184 ft)
Koyunbaba
Yakaköy
Çilekdağı 379 m (1,243 ft)
Gümüşlük
Peksimet
Yahşi
Kadıkalesi
İslamhaneleri
D330
Akçaalan
Turgutreis
Karabağ
Bağla

Gümüşlük *occupies the site of ancient Myndos, founded by King Mausolus (p214) in about 350 BCE. The remains of a sunken city lie offshore.*

Now a busy beach resort, the town of ***Kadıkalesi*** *takes its name from kadı (Arabic for "judge"), after a former resident. Visible on the hill are the remains of the castle and the old Greek church building, which has yet to be restored.*

The town of ***Turgutreis*** *is named after a famous Ottoman corsair and naval commander. Its rich alluvial soil is perfect for growing figs, which abound in this area.*

↑ Gümüşlük Bay on the peninsula's western coast

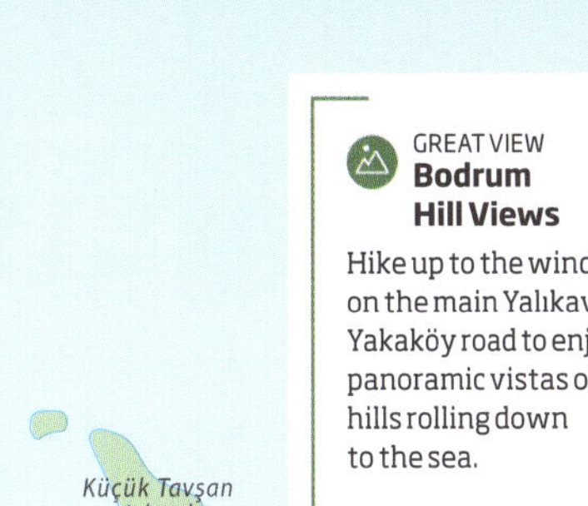

GREAT VIEW
Bodrum Hill Views

Hike up to the windmills on the main Yalıkavak-Yakaköy road to enjoy panoramic vistas of hills rolling down to the sea.

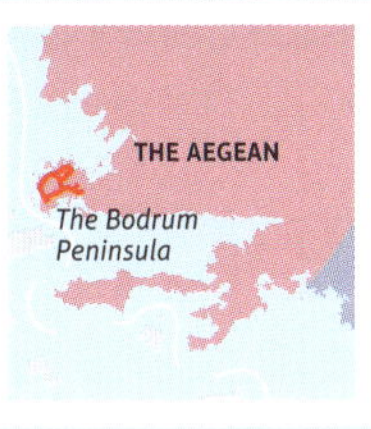

Locator Map

For more detail, see p198

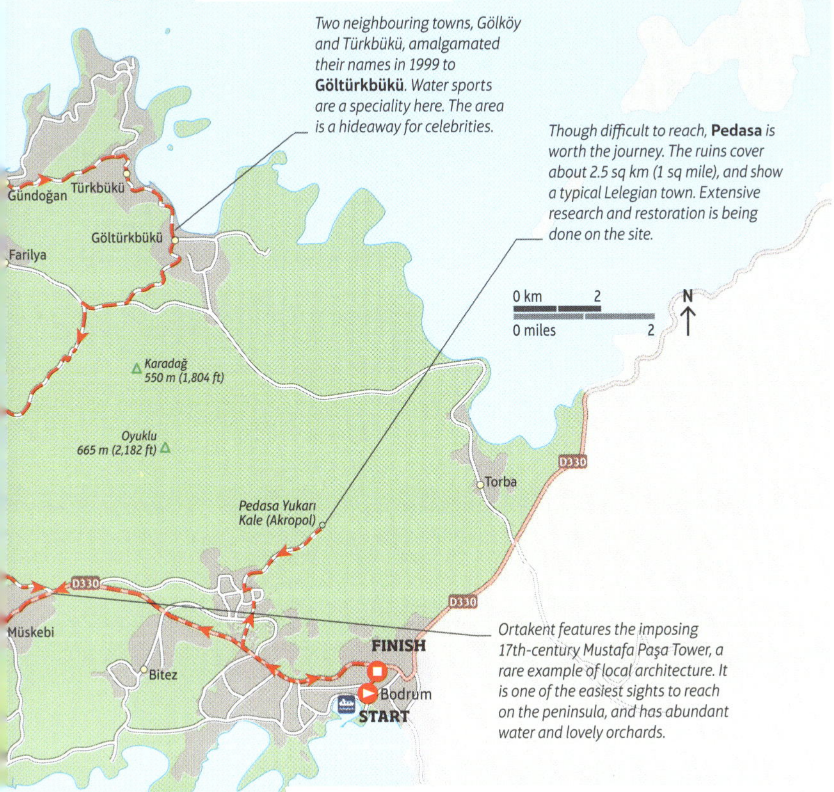

Küçük Tavşan Island

Two neighbouring towns, Gölköy and Türkbükü, amalgamated their names in 1999 to ***Göltürkbükü****. Water sports are a speciality here. The area is a hideaway for celebrities.*

Though difficult to reach, ***Pedasa*** *is worth the journey. The ruins cover about 2.5 sq km (1 sq mile), and show a typical Lelegian town. Extensive research and restoration is being done on the site.*

Gündoğan
Türkbükü
Göltürkbükü
Farilya
0 km 2
0 miles 2
N
Karadağ 550 m (1,804 ft)
Oyuklu 665 m (2,182 ft)
D330
Torba
Pedasa Yukarı Kale (Akropol)
D330
D330
Müskebi
FINISH
Bitez
Bodrum
START

Ortakent features the imposing 17th-century Mustafa Paşa Tower, a rare example of local architecture. It is one of the easiest sights to reach on the peninsula, and has abundant water and lovely orchards.

Çelebi Adası
Görecek Adası

Enjoying the sunshine along the coast of the Bodrum Peninsula

A DRIVING TOUR THE DATÇA PENINSULA

Length 107 km (67 miles) **Duration** 2 hours **Terrain** Mountainous **Stopping-off points** Datça, Palamut Bükü and Eski Datça.

The narrow finger of the Datça Peninsula, pointing westward from Marmaris, lies at the place where the Mediterranean and the Aegean meet. Locals claim that the air is rich in oxygen, thanks to the prevailing wind *(meltem)* and the mixing of salinity levels and current patterns in the sea. The route along the peninsula follows narrow and twisting roads, affording glimpses of the sea through pine-clad gullies. At the western tip, about 35 km (21 miles) west of Datça, lie the ruins of Knidos, one of the most prosperous port cities of antiquity. In its heyday it was home to an eminent medical school. The Carian Trail walking route circles the peninsula and continues eastwards towards Bozburun.

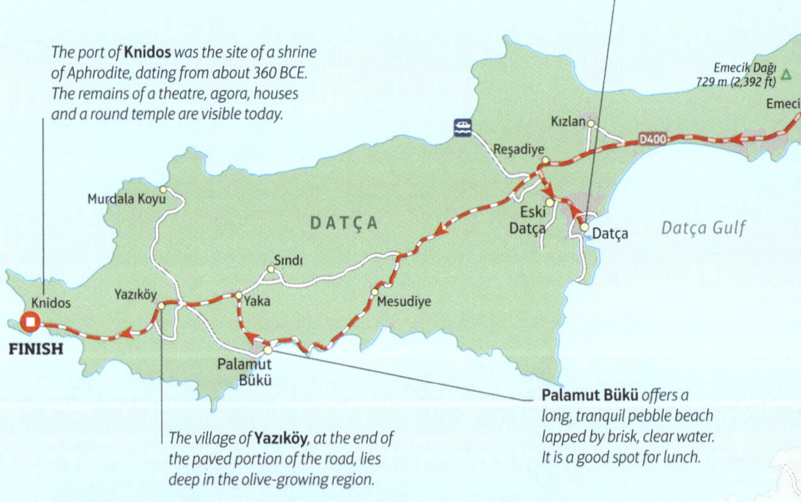

← The historic ruins of Knidos overlooking the sea

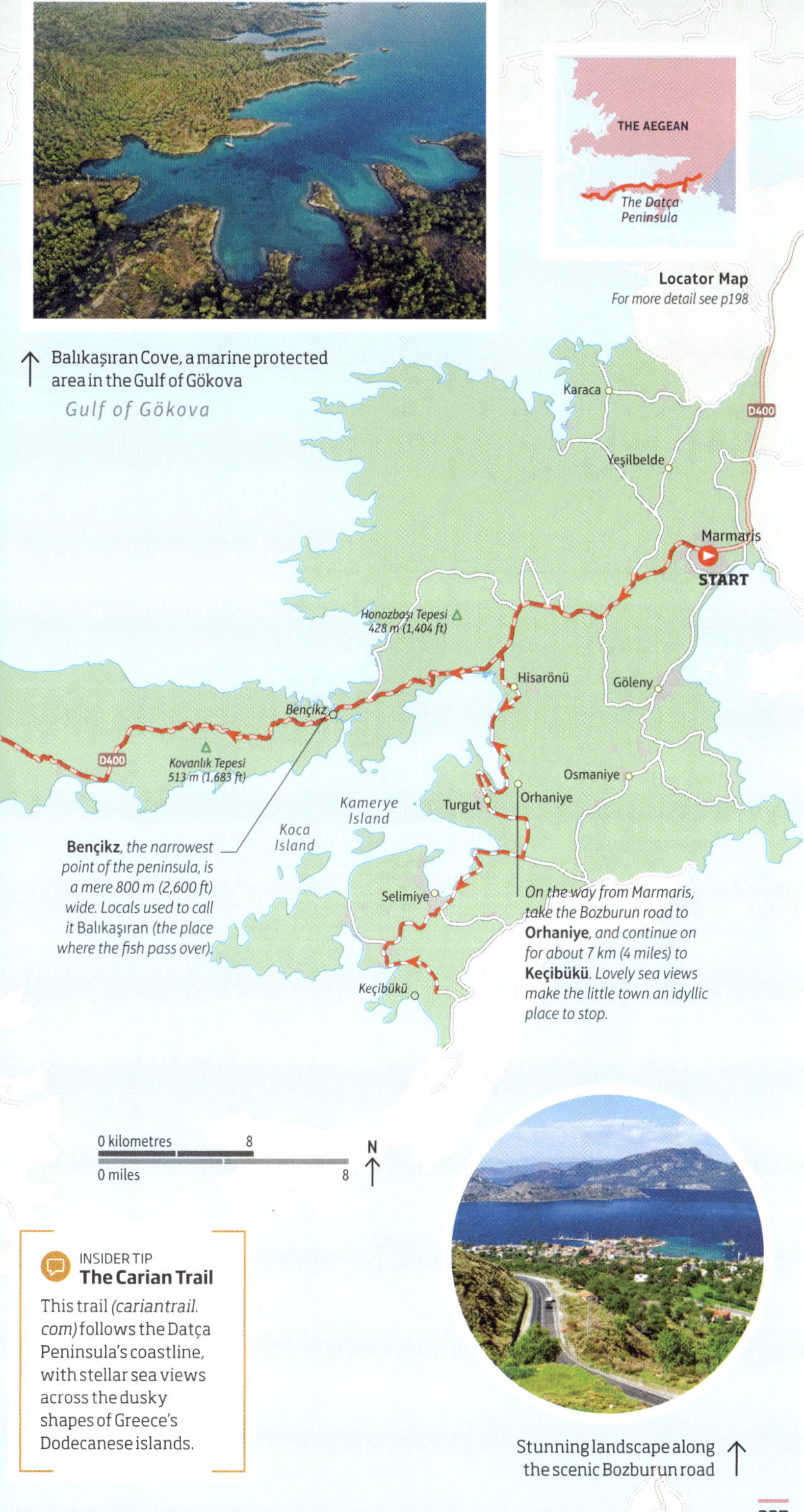

Balıkaşıran Cove, a marine protected area in the Gulf of Gökova

Bençikz, *the narrowest point of the peninsula, is a mere 800 m (2,600 ft) wide. Locals used to call it Balıkaşıran (the place where the fish pass over).*

On the way from Marmaris, take the Bozburun road to **Orhaniye***, and continue on for about 7 km (4 miles) to* **Keçibükü***. Lovely sea views make the little town an idyllic place to stop.*

INSIDER TIP
The Carian Trail

This trail *(cariantrail.com)* follows the Datça Peninsula's coastline, with stellar sea views across the dusky shapes of Greece's Dodecanese islands.

Stunning landscape along the scenic Bozburun road

diving
biking
canyoning

Cobbled streets of Kaş

THE WESTERN MEDITERRANEAN

Throughout antiquity, much of Turkey's western Mediterranean – from Fethiye to Antalya – was part of ancient Lycia. This Anatolian state dates back to the 15th century BCE, when it was called Lukka. In 546 BCE, the western Mediterranean was conquered by the Persian Achaemenid Empire, after which it fell to the Greeks before coming under Roman rule in 168 BCE as a Roman protectorate; in 43 CE, it was fully incorporated into the empire.

The region prospered during the Roman period. Cities such as Attaleia (modern Antalya), Telmessos (modern Fethiye), Patara, Perge and Side flourished as commercial trading hubs. By the Byzantine era, Antalya was a major naval port, as coastal towns were intermittently targeted by Arab raids. The Seljuk Turks encroached into the region by the 12th century, achieving complete rule over Turkey's western Mediterranean in the 13th century.

The harbour towns of this region, particularly Antalya, Fethiye and Side, remained important throughout the Seljuk era. Later, under Ottoman control, shifting trade routes meant the region lost its economic prominence. In the 20th century, the western Mediterranean was something of a backwater for the first fifty years of the Turkish Republic, until the region's fortunes changed dramatically during the 1970s, when tourism took off. Today, it remains a popular spot for tourists, and is home to a number of busy resorts.

THE WESTERN MEDITERRANEAN

Must Sees

1. Antalya
2. Side

Experience More

3. Dalyan
4. Köyceğiz
5. Kaunos
6. Göcek
7. Fethiye
8. Kayaköy
9. Saklıkent Gorge
10. Ölü Deniz
11. Pınara
12. Kalkan
13. Kaş
14. Patara
15. Üçağız, Simena and Kekova Island
16. Demre (Myra)
17. Olympos and Çıralı
18. Phaselis
19. Termessos
20. Perge
21. Selge
22. Aspendos

AFYONKARAHISAR
Eber Gölü
Çay
Şuhut
Sultandağ
Akşehir Gölü
Sandıklı
Akşehir
Yalvaç
Gelendost
Şarkikaraağaç
Dinar
Eğirdir Gölü
ISPARTA
Isparta
Burdur Gölü
Burdur
Beyşehir Gölü
Beyşehir
BURDUR
Katrançik Dağı
Sütçüler
ANKARA AND WESTERN ANATOLIA
p272
Kizilkaya
SELGE
Beşkonak
Köprü Çayı
Aksu Çayı
ANTALYA
Korkuteli
Akseki
TERMESSOS
PERGE
ASPENDOS
Aksu
ANTALYA
Antalya Airport
Serik
Gündoğmuş
SIDE
Manavgat
THE EASTERN MEDITERRANEAN
p260
Antalya Körfezi
Bey Dağları
Alakir Çayı
Kemer
Konaklı
Alanya
PHASELIS
Turunçova
OLYMPOS AND ÇIRALI
Kumluca
Finike
Mediterranean Sea
0 kilometres 30
0 miles 30
N

1

ANTALYA

B5 Cumhuriyet Cad; (0242) 280 23 00

Antalya's population has increased to over 2.5 million since Turkey's tourism boom began in the late 1980s. Mountains, beaches and a seaside setting have made the city one of Turkey's premier resort areas. Its most important remains are the Roman city walls and the imposing Hadrian's Gate.

1   

Antalya Necropolis Museum

Antalya Nekropol Müzesi

Ali Çetinkaya Cad 35/D (0242) 280 23 00 8:30am-5:30 daily

In 2008, during the redevelopment of this site, which originally housed a local bus terminal, construction workers began unearthing burial remains. Further archaeological excavations, carried out over the next two years, revealed the remnants of the eastern necropolis of ancient Attaleia, the original founding settlement of Antalya that was established in the 2nd century BCE by Attalus II of Pergamon. By 2010 archaeologists had unearthed over 800 graves, including ceramic vessels containing skeletons, chamber tombs and sarcophagi.

The museum, built to showcase this discovery, has been designed to sit atop a section of the necropolis, so that one area of grave-finds could be kept in situ. Raised walkways allow visitors to look down on the tombs below. There are also three halls displaying artifacts found during the excavations which cover the history of Attaleia, explain the settlement's funerary practices and burial rites, and cover the work and processes of the necropolis's systematic excavations.

Old Harbour

Kaleiçi Yat Limanı

İskele Cad, Kaleiçi

Antalya's Old Harbour is in the Kaleiçi (Old Town neighbourhood). It has been in use since the Roman era, when it would have been Antalya's main port. This only changed in the 20th century when a larger harbour was constructed west of Konyaaltı Beach. Today, the Old Harbour is a yacht marina with gulets (traditional wooden Turkish

> **Antalya's Old Harbour is in the Kaleiçi (the Old Town neighbourhood). It has been in us since the Roman era, when it would have been Antalya's main port.**

Antalya's Roman-era Old Harbour lined with yachts and boats

yachts) offering sightseeing excursions along the Gulf of Antalya's mountain-rimmed coastline. Visitors not keen to walk down the hillside lanes to get here can hop on the outdoor *asansör* (outdoor elevator), which zips between the harbour and Cumhuriyet Square on the clifftop above.

Fluted Minaret

Yivli Minare

A 13th-century minaret dating from the reign of Seljuk Sultan Alaeddin Keykubad *(p286)*, this has become the symbol of Antalya. This 38-m- (125-ft-) high minaret, composed of red brick and rising from a massive square stone base, is divided into eight fluted sections and was originally covered with turquoise and dark blue tiles, fragments of which are still visible today. The adjoining mosque is still used, and just above is the Fine Arts Gallery.

Clock Tower

Saat Kulesi

Kale Kapısı, Cumhuriyet Cad

Antalya's clock tower marks the Fortress Gate (Kale Kapısı) into the Kaleiçi neighbourhood. This gate was originally the main northern entrance into the walled Roman city. The clock tower is a much later addition, which was built by the Ottoman vizier in 1901 to honour the 25th year of Sultan Abdulhamid I's reign. Today, its distinctive silhouette is recognized as an iconic landmark of Antalya. Next to the tower is a statue of Attalus II, the city's founder.

Just to the south is the Tekeli Mehmet Paşa Mosque. This 17th-century mosque is noted for its beautiful stained-glass windows and intricate Arabic calligraphy decoration.

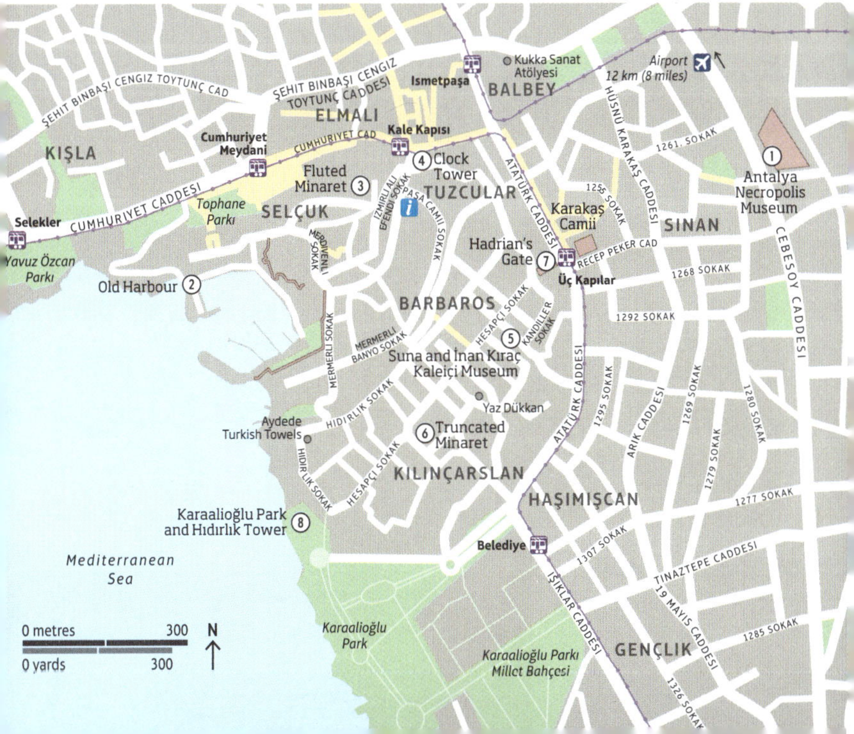

↑ The historic clock tower of Antalya, a landmark of the city

TOP 3 ANTALYA'S BEACHES

Konyaaltı Beach
Akdeniz Bul; 3 km (1 mile) W of the centre
Muze
A wide sweep of sand right in the city, this beach is known for its dramatic views of the Taurus Mountains.

Lara Beach
Lara Cad; 16 km (10 miles) E of the centre 511
East of Antalya's bustling centre, Lara is a long stretch of white sand, bordered by restaurants.

Kemer Beach
Kemer; 44 km (27 miles) S of Antalya Antalya
Kemer is one of Antalya's premier family-friendly resorts, largely due to its soft sandy beaches and calm seas.

Suna and İnan Kıraç Kaleiçi Museum

Suna ve İnan Kıraç Kaleiçi Müzesi

Kokatepe Sok 22, Kaleiçi (0242) 243 42 74
9am-6pm Tue-Sun

This charming museum is housed in two beautifully restored Ottoman mansions. One contains rooms re-created as they would have been in the 19th century, with lifelike mannequins. The other is a research library. A renovated Greek Orthodox church houses a collection of Çannakale pottery.

Truncated Minaret

Kesik Minare

Hesapçı Sok

The Truncated Minaret was badly damaged by a fire in 1851. Its various architectural styles, especially on the capitals, give clues to its past.

The Truncated Minaret overlooking a street in charming Kaleiçi

Although visitors are restricted from entering the site itself, its exterior is fascinating.

Hadrian's Gate

Üçkapılar

Atatürk Cad

Built to honour the visit of Emperor Hadrian in 130 CE,

Well-preserved ruins of Hadrian's Gate featuring Corinthian columns

The *Worker and Son* sculpture in front of the Beydağları Mountains

Hadrian's Gate consists of three arched gateways fronted by four Corinthian columns. For years, the structure was encased in the Seljuk city wall and was uncovered only in the 1950s. Restoration work has been carried out and the pavement between the arches stripped back to the Roman level, showing clearly the wheel ruts cut into the stone.

Karaalioğlu Park and Hıdırlık Tower

Karaalioğlu Parkı ve Hıdırlık Kulesi

Located on the southeastern side of the harbour, the park has a variety of mature exotic trees in which many wild ring-necked parakeets nest. It also has tea gardens with fabulous views over the Gulf of Antalya, Mount Tahtalı and the distant Beydağları Mountains.

The circular Hıdırlık tower dates from the 2nd century BCE, and was probably a lighthouse in Roman times. Locals linger here to watch the setting sun.

SHOP

Aydede Turkish Towels

This welcoming shop sells a wide variety of *peştamals* (Turkish hammam towels).

Hıdırlık Sok 27, Kaleiçi
0542 244 4466

Kukka Sanat Atölyesi

A tiny atelier in the metalworker market, this spot provides unique, hand-made leather goods.

Cengiz Toytunç Cad, Demirciler Çarşısı 13/5
0535 886 2045 Sun

Yaz Dükkan

Yaz Dükkan offers a high-quality collection of jewellery, craftwork and design pieces from independent Turkish creators.

Barbaros, Zafer Sok 11, Kaleiçi 0542 258 5800 Sun

SIDE

 C5 **i** Side Cad No 3, Manavgat; (0242) 753 12 65

In the 2nd century BCE, Side became a centre for pirates, who made large profits from slave trading. Today, the ancient breakwaters built in antiquity are visible offshore. From here, you can enjoy a pleasant boat trip up the Manavgat River, where you can see a waterfall and stop for lunch at a trout restaurant.

①

Theatre

Side Antik Tiyatro

Liman Cad 2 8am-5pm daily

Almost entirely freestanding, Side's large theatre was built on arches over Hellenistic foundations during the 2nd century CE. The lower seats are partially supported by the hillside, but the upper seats rest entirely on huge arches.

This was the largest theatre in Pamphylia, and could hold 17,000 spectators. There are 29 rows of seats above and 29 below the main lateral aisle. Changes to the structure of the building permitted the orchestra pit to be flooded in order to enact naval dramas. The stage building had two storeys, decorated, as at Perge *(p258)*, with friezes of the story of Dionysus. These are currently being displayed in the nearby agora or museum garden while restoration work is carried out on them.

Temples of Apollo and Athena

Apollon Tapınağı ve Athena Tapınağı

Cumhuriyet Blv 50

At sunset, the marble columns and re-erected pediments of the temples of Apollo and Athena frame superb views of the Gulf of Antalya. Around the temples is a basilica, built later in a contrasting rough aggregate stone. The Medusa heads of the friezes date from the 2nd century CE.

GREAT VIEW
Green Canyon

Take a relaxing boat trip on Green Canyon's reservoir, 25 km (16 miles) northwest of Side, to soak up stunning vistas of the surrounding lush green mountains and aquamarine water.

Side Museum

Side Müzesi

Liman Cad (0242) 753 10 06 Apr-Oct: 8:30am-8:30pm daily; Nov-Mar: 8:30am-5:30pm daily

The museum occupies a 5th-century bathhouse, the largest of Side's bath houses, and includes marble sarcophagi, a trio of statues known as the Three Graces and a statue showing Hercules holding the golden apples of the Hesperides. There are also portrait heads and tiny carvings that include a house complete with a dog peering

Ruins of a Roman-era theatre in the centre of the ancient city of Side ↑

around the door. The garden features a cupola with maze decoration and friezes.

---

④

Side Archaeological Site

Side Örenyeri

 **Liman Cad 2**

The arched gateway that marks the entrance to Side from its neighbouring town, Manavgat, blocks most vehicular traffic. Next to the arch is a fountain adorned with carved basins, dedicated to the Emperor Vespasian. From here runs a colonnaded street lined with plain granite columns and the remains of Roman shops leading to the main street. A local tractor pulls an open bus, saving visitors the walk over to the site from the bus station.

The site is also home to Side's ancient aqueduct, an impressive water-supply system installed in the city by the Romans. Outside the main gate was also a nymphaeum (ornamental fountain), which was fed by a two-storey aqueduct running on arches for 30 km (19 miles) from the Melas (now the Manavgat) River. In ancient times, sophisticated clay pipes were then used to distribute water to homes of the city's inhabitants from the city cisterns.

Outside the tall Roman city walls are necropoli, where visitors can see examples of temple tombs from the ancient period.

STAY

Kaktüs Boutique Hotel

This family-run hotel offers a home-away-from-home ambience.

Barbaros Cad 6
0543 716 9090

Acanthus Cennet Barut Collection

This five-star resort features chic contemporary rooms and a white-sand beach.

Özal Cad 35 **barut acanthuscennet.com**

Beach House Hotel

An Old Town favourite, this spot has modern rooms and a rooftop terrace with a plunge pool.

Barbaros Cad 78
0539 641 0452

EXPERIENCE MORE

Dalyan

A5 13 km (8 miles) from the main D400 road (0252) 284 42 35

This bustling resort takes its name from the Dalyan River (Dalyan Çayı), meaning "fishing weir", which flows through the town. Although the town is a fast-growing tourist centre, fishing has long been the mainstay of the local economy. Over the years, the town replaced ancient Kaunos as a fishery when the latter's harbour became choked by silt. A weir built on the river, together with a fish-processing plant, means that you can enjoy the delicious local red roe caviar. Local fish is available at waterside eateries.

The threatened loggerhead turtle has become a symbol of Dalyan, drawing increasing numbers of visitors to the area. This came about in 1986, when conservationists managed to persuade civic authorities to protect the turtles' breeding ground from development. Since then, local people have adopted the loggerhead turtle as a motif for the town. The Turtle Statue (Kaplumbağa Heykeli) on Cumhuriyet Meydanı is a tangible symbol of Dalyan's passion for conservation.

On the western bank of the Dalyan River is a row of six tombs cut into the cliffs. Constructed for wealthy citizens of Kaunos, the tombs *(p251)* are mainly of the house type and date from the 4th century BCE, with Ionic columns and triangular pediments. Most have a small chamber with three stone benches to accommodate the dead. The surviving inscriptions are mainly in Latin, for the tombs were reused during Roman times. They are fenced off and best viewed from some distance away. The rock tombs can be reached by riverboat tours, which depart from the Dalyan Sea Co-operative.

A short distance upriver from Dalyan (about 10 minutes by boat) lie the **mud baths** of Ilıca. With a constant temperature of 40°C (104°F), they are reputed to be beneficial for rheumatism and gynaecological disorders, and are certainly relaxing. Beyond Ilıca, at Sultaniye Kaplıcaları, on the shores of Lake Köyceğiz, a domed building lined with marble surrounds a natural pool where water wells up

LOGGERHEAD TURTLES

The loggerhead turtle *(Caretta caretta)* has become closely associated with Dalyan. Loggerhead turtles can mate several times in a season. Between May and September, the females arrive *en masse* to laboriously dig a pit and lay their eggs above the tide line. The sand keeps the eggs at an even temperature until they are ready to hatch.

→

Ruins of a theatre at the ancient Greek city of Kaunos

at 39–41°C (102–106°F). Locals report that, after the Adana earthquake of 1998, the water at the bathhouse gave off a plume of sulphur gas and that the water changed colour and appeared gassy.

Turtle Beach (İztuzu Plajı), which partly bars the mouth of the Dalyan River, has for centuries been a refuge for breeding loggerhead turtles and is now a protected area. The beach is closed to tourists at night so that the young turtles are not attracted by the bright lights, which would lead them away from the life-giving sea.

Mud Baths

 (0252) 266 00 77 Daily

Turtle Beach

12 km (7.5 miles) from the town centre

4

Köyceğiz

A5 30 km (19 miles) N of Dalyan (0252) 262 47 03

Independent Menteşe clans governed this area even after the beginning of Ottoman rule in 1424. By the late 1830s, when the English archaeologist Charles Fellows visited the area, the power of the family had declined, however. The family *konak* (manor house) has been restored. Another manor, once the centre of a cotton estate belonging to the *khedive* (viceroy) of Egypt, is now the Dalaman state farm. Many people in Köyceğiz village are distant descendants of enslaved Africans brought here to work on cotton plantations.

The Dalyan River meandering through the coastal town of Dalyan

5 

Kaunos

A5 6 km (4 miles) from Dalyan (0252) 614 11 50 Apr-Oct: 9am-8pm daily; Nov-Mar: 8:30am-5:30pm daily

The ancient city of Kaunos bordered the kingdoms of Lycia and Caria. Although a Carian foundation, its culture shared aspects of both states. The local tombs are Lycian *(p251)* in style, but were in fact carved by the Carians. Like Xanthos, capital of Lycia, Kaunos resisted the Persian general, Harpagus, during the 6th century BCE, for which many citizens of Kaunos were slaughtered in a final sally. The city was re-established and Hellenized, especially by the Carian ruler, Mausolus *(p214)*. Kaunos welcomed Alexander the Great, but after his death came under the rule of Rhodes. It won independence from Rome, but after supporting Mithridates against the Romans, the city was punished by return to Rhodian rule. Kaunos was known both for its figs and malarial mosquitoes. It was a major seaport until the harbour silted up.

At the site are walls built in the 4th century BCE for defence, a theatre dating from the 2nd century BCE, a temple to Apollo and a Roman bath. There is also a Doric temple and an agora (marketplace) with a nymphaeum (fountain).

Göcek

B5 15 km (9.3 miles) E of Dalaman Club Marina (private yacht club): (0252) 645 18 00; municipal yacht club: (0252) 645 19 38

Near the pass of the same name, and just south of the main D400 road, Göcek is now a major yachting centre. Popularized by King Charles and former Turkish president, Turgut Özal, the town has a remarkable concentration of upmarket facilities, including a luxury hotel and several waterside housing developments. Near the tip of the peninsula can be seen the ruins of the Roman town of Lydae.

INSIDER TIP

Köycegiz

A scenic 8-km (5-mile) shorefront trail runs between Köycegiz town and Eski Köycegiz. Winding through the surrounding sweetgum forests, this is an easy route for both hikers and cyclists.

↑ Exploring the ruins of an abandoned village near Kayaköy

EAT

Sezainin Yeri Balık Restaurantı
Sit on the shady bougainvillea-decked terrace and enjoy some of the best seafood meze and fish mains in town.

B5 Muammer Aksoy Bul 6/A, Fethiye (0252) 612 78 87

Çarıklı Et Restaurant
This popular stop on Fethiye's *kordon* (seafront) offers varied meals, from pasta to grilled-meat dishes.

B5 Cahit Gündüz Cad 11, Fethiye carikli.com.tr

Mozaik Bahçe Restaurant
Dine on speciality kebabs and spicy meze dishes at this leafy garden restaurant.

B5 91 Sok 2/A, Fethiye (0252) 614 46 53

Fethiye

B5 Fevzi Çakmak Cad 9/D; (0252) 614 15 27

A large market town and agricultural centre, Fethiye fringes a sheltered bay with a large harbour, making it a good place for water activities such as scuba diving and boating. In addition to having many upscale holiday resorts, Fethiye has a splendid farmers' market every Friday that attracts crowds of locals as well as visitors.

Modern Fethiye stands on the ruins of the Lycian city of Telmessus. Earthquakes in 1856 and 1957 levelled most of the ancient edifices, which included a temple of Apollo, but a Roman theatre near the harbour survives. Cut into the cliffs above the town's market are several Lycian temple tombs, some from the 4th century BCE. Charles Texier, a 19th-century French explorer, carved his initials on one of these tombs.

Fethiye Museum displays artifacts from the half-flooded ruins of Letoön *(p253)*, including stelae, which scholars used in their efforts to decode the Lycian language.

Kayaköy

B5 10 km (6 miles) SW of Fethiye Apr-Oct: 8:30am-7:30pm daily; Nov-Mar: 8:30am-5:30pm daily

Derelict Kayaköy, formerly known as Karmylassos, then Levissi, was a thriving Greek town until it was abandoned in the 1923 exchange of populations *(p55)*. About 400 roofless houses stand on the hillside overlooking a fertile plain. The Orthodox church of Panayia Pyrgiotissa has been restored and is the main focus of a movement for peace and international reconciliation.

Now a UNESCO World Heritage Site, Kayaköy and its ruins have been preserved as a historic settlement. Hundreds of rundown, yet mostly standing, Greek-style houses and churches cover a small mountainside. These ruins serve as a popular stopping place for tourists visiting Fethiye and nearby Ölüdeniz. Though the town is largely deserted, it receives tour groups and has roadside vendors selling handmade goods. A few houses have been restored and are currently occupied. The town was the inspiration for the novel *Birds Without Wings*, which focuses on the rise of Turkish patriotism after the Ottoman Empire.

THE LYCIAN TOMBS

Ancient Lycia, a federation of 19 independent cities, lay in the mountainous area between modern Fethiye and Antalya. Burials must have had an important role in the beliefs of the Lycians, for they cut hundreds of tombs into cliff faces and crags that can be seen throughout the area. Most have carved doors, beam ends, pitched roofs and prominent lintels – typical of construction in wood. During the 4th century BCE, the rulers of Xanthos (modern Kınık) produced some of the most remark able tombs, combining Greek and Persian styles. One of the most famous of these, the Nereid Monument, is now in the British Museum in London.

HOUSE TOMBS

House tombs usually had one to three storeys and were carved into solid rock. A sliding slab door opened into an inner chamber. Some tombs had exterior porticoes with carvings.

FREESTANDING TEMPLE TOMBS

These tombs had a temple façade and a portico, from which a door led to a grave chamber with benches for the dead.

PILLAR TOMBS

The pillar tombs are the oldest Lycian tombs. These are found only at Xanthos, the chief city of Lycia, and Apollonia.

SARCOPHAGUS TOMBS

These tombs had a stepped base, a lower grave chamber (called a hyposorion), a flat plate for the coffin and a lid. The pitched, rounded lid symbolized a house roof, and had a prominent ridge. From 500 BCE to 300 CE, elaborate "saddlebacked" sarcophagus tombs were produced.

↑ One of the pillar tombs in the city of Xanthos

↑ An ancient Lycian sarcophagus tomb

↑ Impressive Lycian tombs carved into the side of a cliff

Saklıkent Gorge

Saklıkent Kanyonu

B5 42 km (26 miles) SE of Fethiye

Saklıkent Gorge cuts into the rugged flank of the 3,016-m (9,895-ft) Gömbe Akdağı, and delivers a rushing stream of pure limestone-filtered water. From the restaurants at the base of the gorge, which specialize in local trout, you can walk for a few hundred metres into the gorge on platforms built over the torrent. To walk further up the canyon, you need to join a guided walk, led by one of the guides offering their services at the entrance.

If you enter by road and footpath, along the flank of Akdağı, there is quite a steep descent, but this brings you to the trout farms. At Saklıkent, 7 km (4.5 miles) from the main D400 road, consider a meal at one of the trout restaurants. Enjoy the cool air before you return to sea level – when the temperature is 40°C (104°F) at the coast, Saklıkent is refreshing. Also in the area is the ruined city of **Tlos**, one of the oldest and most important Lycian cities. Hittite records from the 14th century BCE refer to a settlement called Tlawa, which was probably Tlos. Built on a hill, with a commanding view over the valley of the Eşen River (Eşen Çayı) – known in ancient times as the Xanthos – the main Lycian/Roman remains consist of tombs hewn from rock, as well as a stadium, gymnasium and palaestra, and baths. In Byzantine times, Tlos was a bishopric, and the churches at the site were most probably former temples. The acropolis was used until the 19th century, when it was the stronghold of a pirate known as Kanlı Ali Ağa (Bloody Ali).

Agencies in Fethiye and Kaş offer tours of both Saklıkent Gorge and Tlos.

Tlos

Yakaköy, Saklıkent Yolu Apr-Oct: 8:30am-7:30pm daily; Nov-Mar: 8:30am-5:30pm daily

↑ Exploring the Saklıkent Gorge on a guided walk

Ölü Deniz

B5 20 km (12 miles) S of Fethiye Tourism Co-operative; (0252) 617 04 38

Made famous in the 1970s by visitors from Britain, the inviting beach and lagoon at Ölü Deniz (which means "Dead Sea" – because of the calm water) now adorn many posters promoting Turkish travel. The land behind the restaurant-fringed beach is lined with hotels, pensions and campsites. The lagoon itself is part of a national park, open dawn to dusk, with a small entry fee. The adjoining mountain, Baba Dağı, is the jump-off point for paragliders. Ölü Deniz also marks the start of the Lycian Way, Turkey's first long-distance walking route, which ends just short of Antalya.

THE LYCIAN WAY

The Lycian Way *(culture routesinturkey.com/the-lycianway)* is a well-marked trekking route covering 520 km (320 miles) along the craggy, forested coastal mountains between Fethiye and Antalya. This trail passes many of the region's most famous Ancient Lycian monuments and city sites. While completing the full route requires about 30 days, many hikers choose to cover individual shorter sections of the trail instead.

Pınara

B5 50 km (31 miles) SE of Fethiye Apr-Nov: 8:30am-7:30pm daily; Dec-Mar: 8:30am-5:30pm daily

One of the most important cities of ancient Lycia, Pınara, whose name means "round", is situated on and around a huge circular plug of rock above the village of Minare, some 5 km (3 miles) west of the main D400 road. Note, the turn-off is signposted and is passable by car.

The rock face is honeycombed with tombs, mainly square holes, which must have been sealed after use. The acropolis is approached by steps carved into the rock. A well-preserved theatre is cut into the hillside below, with baths nearby.

Kalkan

B5

The village of Kalkan has been permanently inhabited only since the eradication of malaria-bearing mosquitoes in the 1950s. In earlier times, the local people avoided the pests by migrating in summer

A street lined with boutique shops in the Old Town of Kaş

to the *yayla* (summer pasture) of Bezirgan, above the village. The core of stone, Greek-style houses built around the harbour is today surrounded by tiered ranks of modern villas on the hills. Good accommodation and restaurants make it an ideal base for visiting the ancient Lycian cities of Xanthos, Letoön and Patara.

Xanthos (now Kınık), the ancient capital of the Lycian League *(p251)*, is situated north-west of Kalkan. To reach it, travellers must take a 20-minute bus ride followed by a 20-minute walk to its location. The site is extensive and spectacular, and includes superb examples of Lycian tombs. A bilingual Greek-Lycian pillar found at the site helped researchers to decipher the Lycian language.

Letoön, site of the temples of Leto, Artemis and Apollo, was a cult centre favoured by Alexander the Great. Letoön and Xanthos are both UNESCO World Heritage Sites and reflect the way Hellenistic and Lycian cultures influenced each other.

Patara *(p256)* was once the major port of the Lycian League. Damaged by severe earthquakes in 141 and 240 CE, its harbour silted up.

Kaş

B5 7A Cumhuriyet Meydanı; (0242) 836 12 38

Kaş was built adjoining a long, narrow peninsula, over the ancient port city of Antiphellos (port of Phellos), and was noted for its cork oaks. In 1839, it was so tiny and impoverished that the English archaeologist Charles Fellows (who excavated the nearby Lycian site of Xanthos) had to cross to the island of Castellorizo to buy chickens to eat. Today, the situation is reversed: the islanders buy their chickens at Kaş market on Fridays. The harbours are filled with scuba-diving boats and yachts making trips to the Blue Cave and the sunken city at Kekova *(p256)*. Uzun Çarşı, the shopping street, has many original handicraft and antique shops. A 5th-century-BCE Lycian sarcophagus is at the top of the street.

The tourism information office in the main square can provide information on the annual Kaş/Lycia Festival, which makes good use of the tiny Hellenistic theatre located just west of the town.

EAT

Ala Restaurant

This restaurant serves traditional Turkish dishes like scallop carpaccio and walnut lamb.

B5 Hasan Altan Cad 41, Kalkan alakalkan.com

Blue Marlin

Blue Marlin specializes in seafood, prepared by the restaurant's chef-owner.

B5 İskele Sok, Yat Limani, Kalkan 0535 302 6410

Salonika 1881

Salonika 1881 serves up Turkish classics with a contemporary twist.

B5 Süleyman Yılmaz Cad 9, Kalkan salonika1881.com

Enjoying magnificent views from Patara's famous beach

Patara

B5 73 km (44 miles) S of Fethiye Kalkan

Accessible via the small agricultural village of Gelemış, Patara features an 18-km- (11-mile-) long beach – the longest in Turkey – backed by a coastal plain scattered with ruins. This Lycian port city is also home to the world's first "parliament" and is the birthplace of St Nicholas.

The main ruin complex includes a 5,000-seat theatre, a restored *bouleuterion* (council chamber), believed to have served as Ancient Lycia's parliament building, and a colonnaded street that once ran through the city centre.

Patara Beach, with its rolling sand dunes, is a crucial nesting site for turtles so remains wild with limited facilities. However, there is a café and loungers available for hire near the main entrance.

Üçağız, Simena and Kekova Island

B5 38 km (24 miles) E of Kaş Demre, Kaş

The picturesque waterfront village of Üçağız ("Three Mouths") is a 27-km (16-mile) drive south of the D400, just east of Kaş. Dolmuşes will drop you at the main road, but no scheduled transport leads directly to the village.

Built on the site of (and using stones from) the Lycian town of Teimiussa, houses, restaurants and pensions front a sheltered bay with three openings to the sea. There are some signs of subsidence, probably as a result of an earthquake that took place in about 530 CE. Submerged saddleback tombs *(p251)* can be seen at the Lycian site of Aperlae and the village of Kale (ancient Simena) nearby, where a castle built in around 1440 surrounds a tiny theatre cut into the rock. The marked Lycian Way *(p252)* nearby is great for a scenic stroll along the coast.

Above Demre, an asphalt road provides a shortcut to Üçağız. Daily boat tours call in to the pretty bay enclosed by Kekova Island (Kekova Adası).

GREAT VIEW
Simena Castle

Hike to the summit of Simena Castle for a sweeping vista across the bay, where half-submerged Lycian rock-tombs can be spotted.

Demre (Myra)

B5 100 m (100 yds) from main square

The small market town of Demre would have little appeal to visitors were it not for its claims to be home to the original Santa Claus, St Nicholas, and the proximity of the ancient site of Myra. St Nicholas legends originated in Mediterranean Patara (his birthplace), but the Church of St Nicholas is the most charming reason to linger in Demre. This petite Byzantine church is home to some long-concealed frescoes that have been brushed back into life.

The ancient city of Myra and the port of Andriake, 3 km (2 miles) southwest of Demre, date from around the 5th century BCE, and grew rich on coastal trade, supplying incense to Egypt and Constantinople.

The most popular parts of Myra are the theatre and two cliffs carved with spectacular house tombs. When British archaeologist Charles Fellows visited the site in 1840, the paint on the tombs was still visible and letters of the inscriptions were picked out in red and blue. The oldest part of Myra was on the acropolis hill, with a 5th-century-BCE defensive wall. Myra's water supply ran in channels cut into

THE REAL SANTA CLAUS

Nicholas, the 4th-century Bishop of Myra, was famed for his generosity and piety. There are two statues of St Nicholas (Noel Baba in Turkish) in Demre: one is a gift from the Russian Orthodox Church, and is mounted on a revolving pedestal. The saint's myrrh-impregnated bones were buried on his church's premises. Although this church was destroyed by the Arabs in 809, the bones survived and were moved to Bari, Italy, in 1087. The church at Demre was rebuilt by a Russian prince in the 19th century. Demre is also the headquarters of the St Nicholas Foundation.

the wall of the Demre gorge and the sulphur springs at Andriake provided therapeutic baths and healing drinking waters.

Olympos and Çıralı

B5 Off D400 highway (0242) 836 12 38

Finike is a market town set at the foot of the Gülmez Dağları, a long spur of the Taurus Mountains, and on the banks of the Karasu (Black Water) River.

In ancient times, Finike was known as Phoenicus. The original harbour, once noted for its export of the timber that was used in building the Ottoman fleet, is now buried under silt, and a modern yacht harbour has replaced it. In Byzantine times, the surrounding mountains were a source of cedar of Lebanon (used in shipbuilding), but the tree is rarely found in these parts today.

Finike has since prospered through the export of citrus fruit and other produce. Its fertile orchards brim with orange and lemon trees, and the town's logo is an orange. Not much is known about the early history of **Olympos**, although it was an influential member of the Lycian League. The site is reached by a narrow road through a gorge with a seasonally dry river bed. The ruined city occupies a charming setting adjoining a 4-km- (3-mile-) long beach. To the south is an extensive necropolis, including unique square tombs with sliding doors. A theatre, baths and landing stages also occupy the south bank. The northern side has an acropolis, more tombs, a temple dating from the time of Emperor Marcus Aurelius and a Byzantine bathhouse. The whole site is starred with anemones in spring; kingfishers whirr over the stream and ducks nest in the reeds.

Fronting the same beach as Olympos, but reached from the main road by a different valley, low-key Çıralı has more than 100 pensions and hotels nestling in the shade of citrus orchards. As well as a turtle-nesting beach, the main point of interest here is the Chimaera. Set at an altitude of 300 m (984 ft) are two outcrops of volcanic rock, where escaping natural gas is permanently alight. The flame is known as Yanartaş (burning stone). In ancient times, the fire was guided upwards to light a beacon to warn ships of danger. There is also a Byzantine church here, probably once a temple of Vulcan.

According to myth, this mountain is where the hero Bellerophon, mounted on the winged horse, Pegasus, killed the three-headed Chimaera by pouring molten lead into the monster's mouth.

Picturesque view of Simena as seen from the castle

Olympos

11 km (7 miles) E of D400 road From café on D400, or taxi Apr-Oct: 6:45am-7pm daily; Nov-Mar: 8am-6pm daily

18  

Phaselis

B5 40 km (24 miles) SW of Antalya 8am-6pm daily (Apr-Oct: to 7pm)

Decked with flowers in spring, the ruined city of Phaselis is a popular stopping place for cruise yachts.

The Lycian port city was sold to Greek settlers from Rhodes by a local shepherd in the 7th century BCE. They built an extensive town with three harbours around an acropolis on a headland. The canny Phaselians, noted for their skill in trade and commerce, invited Alexander the Great to winter here in 333 BCE, even presenting him with a golden crown in return for valuable protection. Phaselis became a pirate stronghold before it was absorbed into the Roman province of Lycia-Pamphylia in 43 CE. It survived Arab raiding, only to be eclipsed by Antalya in Seljuk times.

Most of the ruins date from the Roman era. They include a theatre, two sets of baths, an agora, an aqueduct leading from Mount Olympos and a marble gateway erected in honour of Emperor Hadrian.

> **Phaselis became a pirate stronghold before it was absorbed into the Roman province of Lycia-Pamphylia in 43 CE, and survived Arab raiding.**

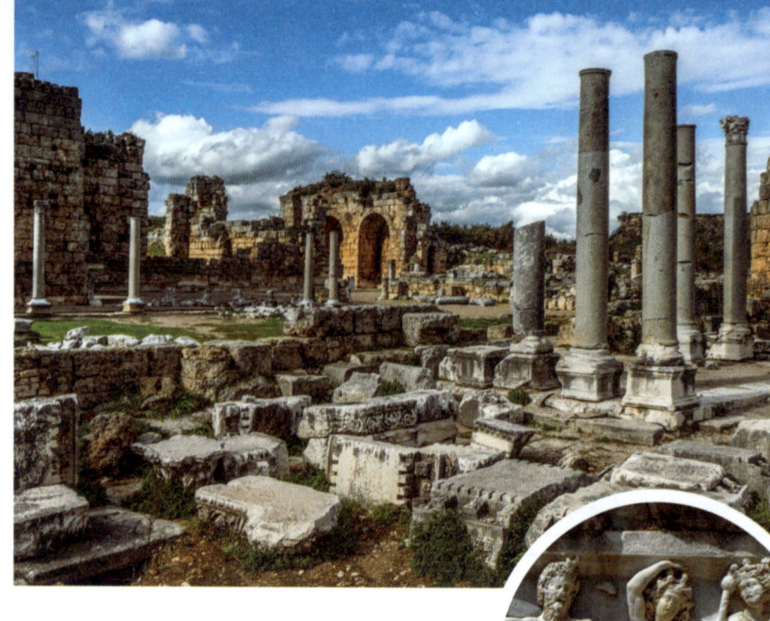

Ancient ruins of Perge, and *(inset)* its Roman reliefs

19 Termessos

B5 35 km (22 miles) NW of Antalya; 9 km (6 miles) off the main road 8am-7pm daily (last adm: 5pm)

Termessos was built by the Solymians in a strategic position on the shipping route to the Aegean. The Greek historian Arrian (around 95–180 CE) said of the location that "the two cliffs make a sort of natural gateway so that quite a small force can, by holding the high ground, prevent an enemy from getting through". The city's formidable natural defences convinced Alexander the Great not to attempt to take the city during the 4th century BCE.

The main buildings visible today are a theatre, the defensive walls below the gymnasium, the gymnasium itself, the temples of Hadrian and Zeus, an odeon (for musical performances), cisterns in the agora, the stoas (covered walkways) of Attalos and Osbaras, and the temple of Artemis. A large necropolis extends upwards as far as a modern fire-watch tower on the hill.

Termessos lies in Güllük Dağ National Park, which includes an area for breeding wild goats and deer, and may be the last refuge of the Anatolian lynx. The area is also known for its butterflies.

20 Perge

B5 18 km (11 miles) NE of Antalya 8am-8:30pm daily

Located on the Kestros River (modern-day Aksu), Perge was once a wealthy city. It declined in Byzantine times, and was abandoned in the 7th century CE. However, it still presents an impressive sight. The theatre is one of the most notable remnants: its frieze of Neptune can be seen in the Archaeological Museum in Antalya *(p242)*. The huge stadium is largely intact. Much excavation and reconstruction work has been done here, with explanatory panels near most major buildings.

A pair of Hellenistic towers marks the entry to the city. The towers front a courtyard with a fountain. On the left, baths with underfloor heating systems face a colonnaded agora. A water channel leads from a second fountain on the acropolis hill into a channel down the main street, which cooled the air in summer. Plancia Magna, the city's benefactress, was buried outside the walls; a marble statue of her is in Antalya Archaeological Museum.

21 Selge

B5 110 km (68 miles) NE of Antalya Daily

The village now occupying the site gives no idea of the former importance of Selge. Founded by Calchas of Argos

KÖPRÜLÜ CANYON NATIONAL PARK

Köprülü Canyon National Park is a very popular site for white water rafting. The Köprülü River slices through the mountains south of Antalya for 14 km (9 miles), with cliffs soaring up to 100 m (328 ft) high. Most rafting trips start from the canyon's Roman-era Oluk Bridge. North of this is a hiking trail along the original Roman road, which winds up to a viewpoint overlooking the canyon.

(who also founded Perge) in the 5th century BCE, it was the first Pisidian city to mint coins. Coins from Selge were used until the 5th century CE. The classical geographer Strabo cites olives, wine and medicinal plants as sources of revenue. Selge seldom features in classical histories, but we know from the Greek historian Polybius that, in 218 BCE, when Selge was at war with the city of Pednelissos, it was able to field an army of 20,000 men. Selge was defeated in this war and had to pay tribute to its enemy. However, it regained prosperity and independence and flourished, especially in the 2nd century CE.

Visible today are a theatre, a stadium, a large temple to Zeus, a smaller one to Artemis, and a cistern. The site, with its spectacular mountain surroundings and cool air, is now part of the Köprülü Canyon National Park.

Aspendos

C5 50 km (31 miles) E of Antalya 8am-8:50pm Early closing (4pm) for festival performances (on some days in Sep)

Aspendos, located on the Eurymedon River (now the Köprülü River), was once the easternmost city of the kingdom of Bergama *(p200)*. In Roman times it became an important trading centre. Today, its main attraction is a beautifully preserved Roman theatre, built around 162 CE by the architect Zeno. The structure is enclosed by a stage building that once had a timber canopy. The theatre hosts the annual Aspendos International Opera and Ballet Festival (usually held in the last two weeks of September). Aspendos also has a remarkable aqueduct, and numerous remains.

INSIDER TIP

Opera and Ballet Festival

This annual festival *(operabale.gov.tr)*, held in Aspendos in September, features major productions performed by Turkey's national ballet and opera companies.

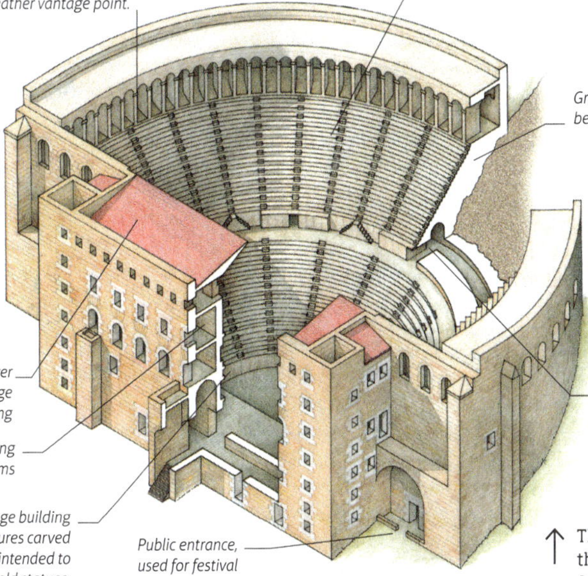

Running right round the top of the theatre, the restored arched gallery provided patrons with an all-weather vantage point.

Forty rows of marble seats divided into sections by staircases

Granite bedrock

The roof over the stage building

Covered passageway

Dressing rooms

The stage building features carved niches intended to hold statues.

Public entrance, used for festival performances today

↑ The Roman theatre in Aspendos

A train on a railway bridge in Adana

THE EASTERN MEDITERRANEAN

The origins of Turkey's eastern Mediterranean region stretch back to the Neolithic era. During antiquity, this region was known as Cilicia. The district of Tarsus was where Cleopatra and Mark Antony met in 41 BCE, and was later the birthplace of Saul of Tarsus (St Paul) in around 5 CE. The eastern Mediterranean area later became very connected to early Christian heritage – Antioch (Antakya) is thought to be the place where the term "Christian" was first used to describe the followers of the new religion.

From the 7th century onwards, Turkey's frontier position between the Byzantine and Arab empires resulted in it being passed between rulers: first from Byzantine to Arab, then to the Armenian Kingdom of Cilicia, back to the Byzantines, from Seljuk Turk to Crusaders, then to the Mamluk Egyptians, until the Ottomans took control in the 16th century.

When the Ottoman Empire disintegrated at the end of World War I, the southern part of the region, Sanjak of Alexandretta (incorporating İskenderun and Antakya), was occupied by France, making it part of French Mandate Syria; France handed the area to Turkey in 1939. Throughout the 20th century, the eastern Mediterranean transformed into one of Turkey's vital agricultural centres, known for its citrus and banana industries, with Adana and Mersin expanding to become the region's most important cities.

THE EASTERN MEDITERRANEAN

Must See

1 Adana

Experience More

2 Alanya
3 Anamur and Anemurium
4 Kızkalesi
5 Mersin (İçel)
6 Silifke
7 Hierapolis (Castabala)
8 Karatepe-Aslantaş Open-Air Museum
9 Payas
10 Samandağ
11 İskenderun
12 Antakya

NEVŞEHIR
Acıgöl
Aksaray
Derinkuyu
Yeşilhisar
Tomarza
Develi
Sarız
Tufanbeyli
KAYSERI
Çiftlik
Yahyalı
Göksun
Altunhisar
Niğde
Saimbeyli
CAPPADOCIA AND CENTRAL ANATOLIA
p318
NIĞDE
Feke
EASTERN ANATOLIA
p342
Ulukışla
Ereğli
Kale Daği
1,789 m (5,869 ft)
Seyhan Nehri
Kozan Barajı
Kesiksuyu Barajı
Kozan
Aydos Daği
3,480m (11,417 ft)
Pozantı
ADANA
Kadirli
KARATEPE-ASLANTAŞ OPEN-AIR MUSEUM
OSMANIYE
Karaisalı
Çatkit Suyu
İmamoğlu
Bolkar Dagları
Çamlıyayla
HIERAPOLIS (CASTABALA)
Seyhan Barajı
Sağkaya
Osmaniye
Meşelik
ADANA
Ceyhan
İslahiye
Arslanköy
Erzin
MERSIN
Adana Şakirpaşa Airport
Tarsus
Hanzali
Ceyhan Nehri
Dörtyol
Güzeloluk
MERSIN (İÇEL)
PAYAS
Nur Dağları
Aktepe
İskenderun Körfezi
Tuzla
Karataş
İSKENDERUN
Erdemli
Madenli
Kırıkhan
KIZKALESI
Hatay Airport
HATAY
Konacık
ANTAKYA
Mediterranean Sea
Harbiye
SAMANDAĞ
Yayladaği
Idlib
Jisr al-Shughur
Karsana
Dipkarpaz
Shathah
Lázikíja
SYRIA
Ein Keita
Tell Selhab
Mhardeh
Banjas
Tartus
Fahel
0 kilometres 40
0 miles 40
N

↑ Sabancı Central Mosque on the banks of the Seyhan River in Adana

1

ADANA

D5 Atatürk Cad 11; (0322) 363 14 48

Adana is an important manufacturing centre, with origins rooted in commerce and trade. The city lies on the Seyhan River, which is spanned by a Roman bridge. Adana was ruled by the Arabs, Seljuks, Armenians and Mamluks until it came under Ottoman sovereignty in 1516. Today it is a booming area of agriculture and industry, and features modern shopping malls alongside traditional bazaars and picturesque parks.

Ethnography Museum

Etnografya Müzesi

Adana Müze Kompleksi 42, Sok No 7 (0322) 454 38 55 8:30am-5pm Tue-Sun

The Ethnography Museum is housed in a former church situated to the west of the old town, and includes a reconstruction of an old Adana house. There is a collection of ceremonial weaponry and firearms, while the displays of copper kitchenware illustrate a prominent local trade. Visitors can explore a fascinating display on tents, carpets and textiles.

Archaeological Museum

Adana Müzesi

Adana Müze Kompleksi 42, Sok No 7 (0322) 454 38 55 8:30am-5pm Tue-Sun

Housed in the converted old National Textile Factory, now known as the Adana Museum Complex, this museum features eight halls. These halls display objects recovered from excavations of late Hittite sites, along with Hellenistic and Roman remains found both in and around the city. A highlight is the natural crystal figure of a Hittite god, Tarhunda, clad in a pointed hat, together with Urartian belts from around 600 BCE.

There is also a gold and silver ram-headed bracelet and a gold ring bearing the head of a woman. The fine Achilleus marble sarcophagus, from the 2nd century CE, has lively battle scenes; another sarcophagus is adorned with standing draped women.

Sarcophagus depicting the legend of Achilles, Archaeological Museum

PICTURE PERFECT
Varda Viaduct

Varda Viaduct, 60 km (37 miles) west of Adana, was built in 1907–1912 by German engineers working on the Baghdad Railway. Its photogenic arches appeared in the opening scene of James Bond film *Skyfall* (2012).

Sabancı Central Mosque

Merkez Camii

Fuzuli Cad
Daily (except during prayer times)

Completed in 1998, this is one of Turkey's largest mosques and rivals many in the Middle East in sheer size – it can accommodate up to 28,500 people and its principal dome is 54 m (177 ft) high. Its architectural style is inspired by Istanbul's Blue Mosque *(p92)* and the Selimiye Mosque *(p184)* in Edirne. Similar to the Blue Mosque *(p92)*, it features six minarets. All work on the mosque, down to state-of-the-art wireless acoustics, was carried out by Turkey's most prestigious artisans.

Roman Stone Bridge

Taş Köprü

The graceful, 14-arch Roman Stone Bridge over the Seyhan River is 319 m (1,056 ft) long. Built in the 2nd century CE, during the reign of Emperor Hadrian, the bridge may be one of the oldest still used by vehicular traffic. It originally had 21 arches, but only 14 of these are visible and in use today. The bridge has been restored several times, first by Emperor Justinian in the 6th century CE and later under the Ottomans.

Great Mosque

Ulu Cami

Abidinpaşa Cad
Daily (except during prayer times)

The Great Mosque was begun in 1507 by Halil Ramazanoğlu, scion of a powerful dynastic clan; however, it was not completed until 1541. The bands of black and white stone used for the mosque are a typical feature of Syrian religious architecture. The impressive tomb of the Ramazanoğlu family, located inside the mosque, is finished in beautiful tiles.

Covered Bazaar

Kazancılar Çarşısı

Near the clock tower on Ali Münif Cad
Dawn-dusk daily

Adana's clock tower overlooks the Covered Bazaar, where handicrafts, trinkets and food items are sold. Near the Covered Bazaar is the Çarşı Hamamı, a domed Turkish bath with a marble interior.

EAT

Ciğerci Edip Usta

A hidden gem, this restaurant is known for serving one of the best Adana kebabs.

Sarıyakup, Sok 16
7am-5pm Mon-Sat, 5am-1pm Sun

Adana Kadın Kooperatifleri Birliği

This spot operates as a cosy restaurant and a charming shop, selling crochet bags, soaps and jams.

Sarıyakup, Büyük Saat 8:30am-6pm daily

Kaya Kebap

Enjoy excellent Adana kebabs and other delicious items on offer at this popular restaurant.

Hurmalı, Sok 6
9am-9pm Mon-Sat

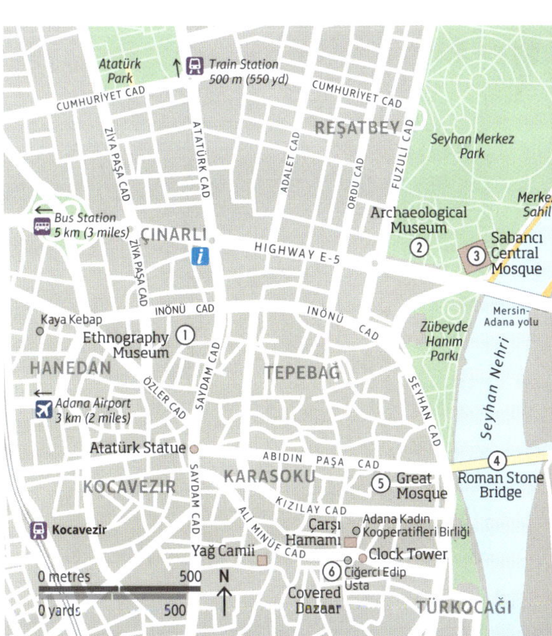

EXPERIENCE MORE

Alanya

C5 3 km (2 miles) W of city centre Damlataş Cad 1 (near the cave); (0242) 513 12 40

The promontory and castle of Alanya offer superb views of beaches and mountains. Now a large modern resort, in Roman times Alanya was called Coracesium, and was a stronghold of the pirates. After the defeat of the pirates in 65 BCE, Coracesium became a thriving city. The Seljuk ruler, Alaeddin Keykubad I, made Alanya his winter residence and fortified it heavily.

A double line of defensive walls mount the promontory to enclose the Citadel (Kale), inside which is a Byzantine church. It takes about an hour to walk to the top. Alternatively, you can take the cable car from Damlataş Beach, or use the hourly bus service.

The harbour is commanded by the 35-m (115-ft) Red Tower (Kızılkule), a restored hexagonal structure built by Alaeddin Keykubad I in 1226. The Red Tower protected Alanya's dockyard, or *tersane*.

Atatürk visited Alanya for a few days in 1935. The owner of the house where he stayed turned it into a **museum**. The ground floor has photographs and Atatürk memorabilia, and the upper floor displays the furniture of a typical Alanya house in Republican times.

There are several caves around the base of the cliffs. The best known is the **Damlataş Cave**, said to provide relief from asthma. Access is from the western beach, behind Damlataş restaurant.

Near the village of Ehmedek, once famous for its silk and lace handicrafts, is a *bedesten* (trading hall) converted into a hotel, with high-arched rooms around a courtyard. Nearby is the restored 16th-century Süleymaniye Mosque and a 13th-century *türbe* (tomb).

THE CRUSADES IN TURKEY

The history of Mediterranean Turkey is closely linked to the Crusades, military campaigns launched in the 11th century to reclaim the Holy Land. Crusader armies crossed Anatolia, capturing cities such as Edessa (Şanlıurfa) and Antioch (Antakya). The era peaked with the sack of Constantinople in 1204 *(p53)*. Military orders like the Knights Templar, Hospitallers and Teutonic Order were active along the coast, leaving their mark with structures like the Castle of St Peter at Bodrum *(p216)*.

Museum

Hilmi Balcı Cad, Damlataş Cad (0242) 513 12 28
8:30am–8:30pm daily

Damlataş Cave

Cave: Summer: 9am–9pm daily; winter: 9am–7:30pm daily

↑ Alanya Harbour with its iconic Red Tower, and (*inset*) stone arches in the city's shipyard

→ Preserved double row of columns at the ancient city of Pompeiopolis in Mersin

Anamur and Anemurium

C5 110 km (68 miles) SE of Alanya On the coast road Yeşilyurt Mah, Alparslan Türkeş Blv; Ersin Apt No 166/B; (0324) 814 40 58

The town of Anamur is bisected by the D400 coastal road, with the town centre to the north and the harbour to the south. There are several beaches and turtle nesting sites here.

Anemurim ("Place of the Winds"), first noted by the classical geographer Strabo (63 BCE–23 CE), was founded in the 1st century CE, and thrived under the Byzantines. It was battered by an earth-quake in around 580, and after the Arabs took Cyprus in 649, the city was abandoned.

On the coast road 2 km (1 mile) east of Anamur lies **Mamure Castle**. Today, the fortress is often used as a film set.

Anemurim
Apr-Oct: 9am-7pm daily; Nov-Mar: 8am-5pm daily

Mamure Castle
Mamure Kalesi
8am-7pm Tue-Sun

Kızkalesi

C5

Kızkalesi is situated where the narrow coastal strip opens out onto the Çukurova plain. Its chief landmarks are two **castles**, one on the shore, and its sister, 200 m (656 ft) out to sea. Regular boat services ferry people over to explore the ruins. The 12th-century castle on the shore was built on the ancient site of Korykos from the stones of Greek and Roman buildings preceding it.

Around 5 km (3 miles) northeast of Kızkalesi are the ruins of **Elaiussa Sebaste**. There is a Byzantine church and harbour buildings to the south of the road. Further along the coast, 4 km (3 miles) away, is Kanlıdivane ("Place of Blood"), a huge chasm 60 m (197 ft) deep, into which prisoners were thrown to their deaths. From this point onwards, the coast abounds in ancient ruins, although the population is sparse until you reach the holiday villages associated with Mersin.

Castles
8:30am-7pm daily

Elaiussa Sebaste
24 hours daily

Mersin (İçel)

D5 NE of city centre İstiklal Cad NE of city centre; (0324) 238 16 48 Near tourist office in the harbour area İsmet İnönü Bul 5; (0324) 280 22 00

Mersin is a harbour city with relatively few tourist attractions. The main reason to stay here is to catch a ferry to Northern Cyprus. Accommodation is plentiful and restaurants varied, with good fish and fast food. Mersin's **museum** contains local archaeological remains such as glass, earthenware and bronze items.

About 12 km (8 miles) west of Mersin lie the ruins of Pompeiopolis, with the remains of a harbour and a column-lined street that date from the 2nd century CE.

Mersin Museum
Adnan Mendedered Blv 54 (0324) 231 96 18
8:30am-7pm daily

STAY

Lemon Villa Hotel
Enjoy sweeping views of Alanya's harbour from this restored Ottoman villa with a courtyard and a plunge pool.

C5 Tophane Cad 20, Çarşı, Alanya (0242) 513 44 61

Villa Turka
Located in Alanya's hillside old quarter, this 200-year-old Ottoman mansion is the city's most stylish retreat, offering elegant rooms.

C5 Kargı Sok 7, Tophane, Alanya hotelvillaturka.com

BIRDS OF THE GÖKSU DELTA

South of the main coast road near Silifke, where the Göksu River reaches the sea, 145 sq km (56 sq miles) have been designated as a region of outstanding environmental importance. The two lagoons are home to migrating and permanently residing waterbirds, including Dalmatian pelicans, pygmy cormorants, marbled and white-headed ducks, ospreys and terns. The marshlands provide food for wagtails, egrets, spoonbills and squacco, grey and purple heron. The best times to see the birds are at dawn and dusk in spring and autumn. Bird-watchers need their own transport to tour the Delta, which is also an important nesting area for loggerhead and green turtles.

Silifke

C5 İnönü Blv Saray Mahallesi Gazi Osman Paşa Sok No 6; (0324) 714 11 51

Founded as Seleucia by one of Alexander the Great's generals, Silifke lies on an important route to Konya and the interior by way of the Göksu River valley. A temple of Jupiter, with its surviving columns topped by stork's nests, a Byzantine cistern and a Roman bridge can still be seen today. St Paul passed through here, and Thecla, his disciple, founded an underground church about 2 km (1 mile) east of Silifke. This is currently being restored. A Byzantine castle is accessible from the Konya road and, 9 km (6 miles) to the north, is a monument that points to where the Holy Roman Emperor Frederick Barbarossa drowned on 10 June 1190 while attempting to ford the deep Göksu River during the Third Crusade.

Silifke Museum, located 1 km (0.5 miles) west of the town, houses the Gülnür hoard, a superb collection of 5,200 silver and gold coins dating from the reign of Alexander the Great.

About 28 km (17 miles) north of Silifke lie the remains of an impressive Roman city at **Uzuncaburç**. Inhabited from Hittite times, the city was called Olba by the Greeks and Diocaesarea by the Romans.

Beside the road are several temple tombs, complete with sarcophagi. The centrepiece is the Temple of Zeus, with about 30 massive peristyle columns. However, the walls of the cella (which would have enclosed the statue of Zeus) were removed when the building was converted into a church. Other sights include a Greek theatre and two city gates. Also worth exploring are a Hellenistic tower, the necropolis and a pyramid-roofed mausoleum. Orchards surround the ruins today.

Silifke Museum

Taşucu Cad (0324) 714 1019 8am-6:45pm daily

Uzuncaburç

Apr-Oct: 8am-8pm daily; Nov-Mar: 8am-5pm daily

7 Hierapolis (Castabala)

D5 22 km (14 miles) N of Osmaniye 9am-7pm daily

On the road leading to the Hittite site of Karatepe, take some time to stop at the ancient Roman city of Hierapolis (Castabala) – not

Dramatic stone arches of the Olba aqueduct in Uzuncaburç, Silifke

A colonnaded street leading up to the acropolis at Hierapolis (Castabala)

to be confused with the more famous Hierapolis *(p208)*, near Denizli. Hierapolis (Castabala) was mentioned by the elder Pliny (23–79 CE) around 70 CE, indicating its significance in the Roman period. Today, visitors can walk along the remains of the city.

8 Karatepe-Aslantaş Open-Air Museum

Karatepe-Aslantaş Açık Hava Müzesi

D5 Cennetli Mah Kız Yusuflu Köyü 45 Winter: 8am-4pm daily; summer: 9am-7pm daily

Karatepe is a late Hittite fortress, built on a hill beside the Seyhan River, that dates back to the 9th century BCE. It is believed to have been the fortified residence of the Hittite king of Adana, Azatiwatas. The site was originally discovered in 1946 by German archaeologist H T Bossert and the famous Turkish archaeologist Halet Çambel, who dedicated decades to uncovering, documenting and preserving the site's remains.

Their excavation work uncovered two separate entrances, each lined with remarkable relief carvings and inscriptions written in both ancient Phoenician and Hieroglyphic Hittite. The site is notable for its *orthostats* (carved relief panels), which consist of carvings of sacrificial, hunting and feasting scenes. These carvings feature numerous figures of gods and sphinxes, interspersed with scenes of ordinary people, all completed in a cheerful cartoon style.

Today, this hilltop site offers views of the surrounding landscape. Situated about 70 km (44 miles) from Adana, it remains a rewarding and enjoyable excursion, valued both for its archaeological importance and its incredibly striking natural setting.

Did You Know?

Relief carvings at Karatepe show artistic influences from Assyria and ancient Egypt.

9 Payas

D5 22 km (14 miles) N of İskenderun In the town hall; 8am-5pm daily

Payas is the site of the Sokollu Mehmet Paşa complex. This is not a well-known site, but it is run with great enthusiasm by the local municipality. The complex has all the amenities that would have been required by Ottoman travellers, including a mosque, a bathhouse, a *kervansaray* and a theological college. The *kervansaray* was built in 1574 for Muslims making the *haj* (pilgrimage to Mecca).

The complex was designed by Sokollu Mehmet Paşa, one of the grandest viziers ever to serve the Ottoman state. A Serb who rose to power from humble beginnings, he served under three sultans between 1564 and 1579. It was under his initiative that Sultan Selim II (1524–74) seized Cyprus from the Venetians in 1571. However, Selim's fondness for wine earned him the nickname "the Sot". According to legend, he slipped in the bath while inebriated and never regained consciousness.

Samandağ

D5 25 km (15 miles) SW of Antakya Local dolmuş from Antakya

Samandağ is a modest, largely Arabic-speaking resort town near the border, where you will feel that you have already entered Syria. Along its long, windswept beach, you'll find a handful of small hotels and several seaside restaurants.

North of the town is the site of Seleucia ad Piera (modern-day Çevlik), founded as Antioch's port in around 300 BCE. This was the site of an important temple to Zeus, which still stands above the coast and affords sweeping views over the sea.

Ancient Antioch lay at the junction of important trading routes, and as a result Seleucia ad Piera developed into a major port serving the city. To protect the settlement and maintain access to the sea, Emperor Vespasian ordered the construction of a large diversion tunnel designed to channel floodwaters away from the port. Known as the **Titus Tunnel** (Titus ve Vespasianus Tüneli), it was completed by Vespasian's son, Titus, and remains an impressive example of Roman engineering. The tunnel runs for 1,380 m (4,527 ft) through solid rock and measures 7 m (23 ft) in height and 6 m (20 ft) in width, a remarkable accomplishment given the tools and methods available at the time. Its massive scale, achieved with basic hand tools and the labour of soldiers, engineers and locally conscripted workers, continues to impress visitors today.

Titus Tunnel

25 km (16 miles) SE of Antakya Summer: 8:30am-7pm daily; Winter: 8:30am-5pm daily

İskenderun

D5 312 Sok. No 7, off Sanayı Cad; (0326) 616 36 31 İstasyon Cad; (0326) 614 00 49 İskele Cad; (0326) 613 54 00

The city of İskenderun (formerly Alexandretta) was originally founded to

Along İskenderun's lovely waterfront, the wide seaside promenade is framed by elegant French colonial buildings.

commemorate Alexander the Great's victory over Persian emperor Darius at the Battle of Issus in 332 BCE. It was a major trading centre in Roman times due to its strategic position on the northeastern Mediterranean and it still remains an important port. İskenderun is known for its multicultural heritage, which is reflected in its remaining Christian and Jewish communities. The surviving Armenian, Catholic and Orthodox churches, currently undergoing restoration, are hidden away in the backstreets and alleys, along with mosques. While none of these religious buildings are particularly old, many are open to visitors on Sundays. Along its lovely waterfront, the wide seaside promenade is framed by elegant French colonial

↑ Stone entrance to the Titus Tunnel, carved through solid rock near Samandağ buildings. Locals and visitors alike gather here in the evenings to enjoy the cool sea breeze, watch the beautiful sunset over the bay, and take in the relaxed coastal ambiance.

Antakya

D5 Şehit Mustafa Sevgi Cas 8/A; (0326) 216 60 98 Abdürrahman Melek Cad, NE of town centre; (0326) 214 91 97

Antakya was founded by the Seleucids around 300 BCE on the banks of the Orontes (Asi) River and was known as Antioch. Over time it grew into one of the most significant cities of the Roman Empire, famed for its wealth, cultural diversity and intellectual life. It also became a major centre of early Christianity, attracting scholars, theologians and pilgrims from across the eastern Mediterranean region.

In the 7th century CE, Antakya was captured by the forces of Caliph Umar during the Arab–Byzantine wars. The city briefly returned to Byzantine rule in 969 CE, but in 1084 it fell to the Seljuk Turks. A little over a decade later, in 1097, the armies of the First Crusade laid siege to the city. Their capture of Antioch resulted in heavy casualties among both Christian and Muslim inhabitants, marking one of the most dramatic episodes of the Crusades.

In 2023, Antakya was devastated by a massive earthquake that reshaped the city and its surrounding region. Reconstruction remains a central priority, with large-scale restoration efforts aimed at preserving the city's cultural identity while ensuring its long-term resilience. Work is progressing across its historic centre, where nearly 300 registered heritage structures are undergoing emergency conservation and structural reinforcement.

Despite the challenges, several cultural landmarks have already begun to reopen. On the outskirts of the city, **St Peter's Grotto** – regarded as one of the earliest surviving Christian worship sites in the world – has welcomed visitors once again after undergoing essential safety and structural improvements. Its reopening has been seen as a powerful symbol of resilience, given the church's deep historical and spiritual significance.

Further progress can be seen at the Necmi Asfuroğlu Archaeology Museum, which houses the world's largest single-piece Roman-era mosaic. Following an extensive restoration and conservation programme, the museum reopened its doors in 2024. Visitors can now explore its impressive collection in a carefully reinforced and modernized facility. The reopening has restored one of Antakya's most remarkable archaeological attractions. Meanwhile, the nearby Hatay Archaeology Museum continues its own comprehensive strengthening and renewal programme, with reopening currently scheduled for late 2026.

St Peter's Grotto

Apr-Oct: 9am-7pm Tue-Sun; Nov-Mar: 8am-5pm Tue-Sun

↑ Roman mosaic on display in the Hatay Archaeology Museum, Antakya

TURKEY'S 2023 EARTHQUAKE

On 6 February 2023, a 7.8 magnitude earthquake struck southern Turkey, followed hours later by a second major shock measuring 7.7. More than 55,000 people lost their lives and around 1.5 million were left without homes. Antakya was among the worst affected cities, with entire neighbourhoods razed to the ground and much of the old city suffering severe destruction. Reconstruction efforts are now underway on a vast scale, with the total cost estimated at approximately US $103 billion. The city is working to restore housing, infrastructure and its cultural fabric while supporting those whose lives were greatly impacted by the disaster.

An intricate *muqarna* in a mosque in Beyşehir

ANKARA AND WESTERN ANATOLIA

The region of Ankara and Western Anatolia lies in the heart of Turkey. In its early history, it changed hands many times. During the Bronze Age, the Hittite Empire controlled the area before being overtaken by the Phrygian Kingdom and, later, the Lydian Kingdom and then the Persian Achaeminid Empire. In 333 BCE, Alexander the Great conquered western Anatolia – "solving" Phrygia's famed Gordian knot, thus prophesying that he would be ruler of Asia – and began the region's Hellenization.

Around this time, Celtic tribes of the Danube infiltrated western Anatolia, setting up the Kingdom of Galatia in 280 BCE, which they ruled from Ancyra (modern Ankara). Galatia became a Roman kingdom in the 1st century BCE, and then part of the Byzantine Empire in the 4th century CE, when towns like Ancyra, Iconium (modern Konya), Dorylaeum (modern Eskişehir) and Cotyaeum (modern Kütahya) flourished as Christian centres. In the 11th century, the entire region was captured by the Seljuk Turks, and Konya entered a golden age as capital of the Seljuk Sultanate of Rum.

After the Ottomans wrested control of western Anatolia, the area's prominence was maintained. Kütahya remained an important ceramics manufacturer, nearby Afyonkarahisar was a major opium producer and Ancyra's mohair industry continued to thrive. At the end of World War I, with Istanbul occupied by the Allied forces, Atatürk set up an alternative parliament in Ankara, paving the way for it to eventually become the new capital of the modern state of Turkey.

ANKARA AND WESTERN ANATOLIA
THE BLACK SEA
p300
THRACE AND THE SEA OF MARMARA
p176
THE AEGEAN
p196
THE WESTERN MEDITERRANEAN
p238
BOLU
ESKİŞEHİR
KÜTAHYA
ÇAVDARHİSAR (AİZANOİ)
PHRYGIAN VALLEY (FRIG VADISI)
SİVRİHİSAR
AFYONKARAHİSAR
EĞİRDİR
BEYŞEHİR
Zafer Airport
Isparta Süleyman Demirel Airport
ZONGULDAK
DÜZCE
KOCAELİ
BİLECİK
BURSA
BALIKESİR
MANİSA
UŞAK
DENİZLİ
ISPARTA
BURDUR
ANTALYA
MUĞLA
Sündiken Dağları
Sultan Dağları
Kuyucak Dağı
Ereğli
Devrek
Kandıra
Kaynarca
Akçakoca
Sakarya
Karapürçek
Geyve
Göynük
Yenişehir
Sakarya Nehri
Gölpazarı
Bursa
Bilecik
Nallıhan
Beypazarı
Sarıyar Barajı
Bozüyük
Mihalıççık
Porsuk Çayı
Harmancık
Tavşanlı
Porsuk Barajı
Şeyitgazi
Çifteler
Emet
Pessinus
Çat Deresi
Yazılıkaya
Simav
Altıntaş
Aslantaş
Bayat
Emirdağ
Banaz
Düzağaç
Yunak
Uşak
Bolvadin
Eber Gölü
Akşehir Gölü
Çay
Sandıklı
Selevir Barajı
Çavuşçu Gölü
Çivril
Akşehir
Ilgın
Yalvaç
Güney
Buldan
Çal
Senirkent
Dinar
Şarkikaraağaç
Eğirdir Gölü
Çiftliközü
Denizli
Burdur Gölü
Burdur
Isparta
Beyşehir Gölü
Serinhisar
Tavas
Yeşilova
Kovada Gölü
Çavdır
Çobanisa
Kale
Acıpayam
Karamanlı
Derebucak
Seydişehir
Suğla Gölü
Çameli
Çavdır
Cevizli
Akseki
Anatalya
Serik
Dalaman
Manavgat
Elmalı
Seydikemer

ANKARA AND WESTERN ANATOLIA
Must Sees
1 Ankara
2 Konya
3 Kütahya
Experience More
4 Soğuksu National Park
5 Bolu
6 Haymana Hot Springs
7 Polatlı and Gordion
8 Beyşehir
9 Çatalhöyük
10 Eğirdir
11 Afyonkarahisar
12 Sivrihisar
13 Phrygian Valley
14 Eskişehir
15 Çavdarhisar (Aizanoi)
CAPPADOCIA AND CENTRAL ANATOLIA p318
THE EASTERN MEDITERRANEAN p260
Safranbolu
Araç
KASTAMONU
KARABÜK
Gerede
Eskipazar
Ilgaz
Kurşunlu
Korgun
ÇANKIRI
Çankırı
Sabanözü
Kızılcahamam
SOĞUKSU NATIONAL PARK
Çubuk
Esenboğa International Airport
Ayaş
ANKARA
Elmadağ
Gölbaşı
POLATI AND GORDION
Balâ
Gavur Kalesi
Haymana
HAYMANA HOT SPRINGS
Yenice
Kulu
Samsam Gölü
KIRŞEHIR
Kırşehir
Himmetdede
Tuz Gölü
Cihanbeyli
Cihanbeyli Yaylası
Nevşehir
KONYA
AKSARAY
Aksaray
Derinkuyu
Sarayönü
Kadınhanı
Sultanhanı
Halıcı
Konya Airport
Niğde
Çamardı
NIĞDE
Karapınar
ÇATALHÖYÜK
İçeriçumra
Çumra
Bataklık Gölü
Ereğli Gölü
Ereğli
Ulukışla
May Barajı
Pozantı
ADANA
Kâzımkarabekir
Bozkır
Sarıoğlan
Karaman
KARAMAN
Adana
Hadim
Taşkent
MERSIN
Mersin
Sarıveliler
0 kilometres 50
0 miles 50
N

ANKARA

C4 Esenboğa Talatpaşa Bul East-west Ankaray line and north-south Metro line, with various stops; both operate from 6am-1am daily Mevlana Bulvarı 82 Anafartalar Cad 65; (0312) 485 48 00

Ankara, the modern capital of the Turkish Republic, is strategically located on the east–west route across the Anatolian steppe. A Phrygian settlement, initially called Ancyra, began here in 1200 BCE, according to archaeological evidence. The city was occupied by the Lydians and Persians before its absorption into the Roman Empire in 24 BCE. Annexed by the Seljuks in 1073, it served a military and commercial role until Byzantine times, when Angora (Ankara) goat wool became a major export. Atatürk chose Ankara as the new capital in 1923, which led to rapid development and caused land values to soar.

Atatürk Mausoleum

Anıtkabir

Anıt Cad, Anıttepe (0312) 231 79 75 Anıtkabır Anıttepe 9am-4pm daily (Apr-Oct: to 5pm)

Ankara's imposing mausoleum, built from 1944 to 1953, commands a hill to the west of the city. Twenty-four stone lions flank the pathway leading to the mausoleum. To one side of the central courtyard, bronze doors open into the marble-lined hall and cenotaph, where visiting heads of state and vast numbers of ordinary Turks still come to pay their respects to Turkey's supreme leader. İsmet İnönü, second President of the Republic, is entombed opposite. A hall nearby houses some splendid vintage cars used by Atatürk, and visitors can also admire a display of personal possessions and gifts presented to Atatürk by fellow heads of state over the years.

INSIDER TIP
Museum Access

Bags are not permitted inside the Painting and Sculpture Museum, but they can be stored in free lockers by the entrance. A combined ticket is available that covers the Ethnography Museum, too.

Painting and Sculpture Museum

Ankara Resim ve Heykel Müzesi

Türkocağı Sok, Altındağ, Ankara Ulus 9am-5pm Tue-Sun arhm.ktb.gov.tr

This art museum traces the evolution of Turkish painting and sculpture through the 19th and 20th centuries, featuring key Turkish artists. The collection spans from Ottoman portraiture of Abdülmecid Efendi and courtly scenes of Osman Hamdi Bey to Fahrelnissa Zeid's colourful expressionist and abstract works, and the Anatolian village scenes by Bedri Rahmi Eyüboğlu. Highlights include the Istanbul cityscapes and Anatolian landscapes by

The capital city with its historic castle displaying the Turkish flag

Impressionist painter Namık İsmail. The galleries demonstrate the shift in Turkish art from landscapes and portraiture towards abstract and experimental forms.

Often overshadowed by the adjacent Ethnography Museum, the large and comprehensive Painting and Sculpture Museum deserves ample time for art enthusiasts.

Ethnography Museum

Ethnografya Müzesi

Talat Paşa Bulvarı
(0312) 310 30 07 Ulus
9am-6pm daily

Set in a pretty, white marble kiosk (summerhouse), with beautiful Ottoman interiors, and carpets and mosque woodwork dating from Seljuk times onwards, the museum offers a charming record of Turkish costume and handicrafts through the years.

TOP 3 ETHNOGRAPHY MUSEUM HIGHLIGHTS

Taşkınpaşa Mosque Mihrab

This 14th-century, walnut-wood mihrab is covered in carved, interlacing geometric and floral designs.

Kırşehir Prayer Carpets

These 19th-century carpets, with a central mihrab motif, are prized for their palette of reds, yellows and blues.

Throne of Kaykhusraw III

The chaise-longue-like throne of Kaykhusraw III (Sultan of Rum; 1266-84) is decorated with Seljuk-era carvings.

Citadel

Hisar

Hisarparkı Cad
Hisar Daily

The Hisar, or Byzantine citadel, dominates the northern end of Ankara. The walls enclose a collection of wooden houses, with some restaurants, several car-pet shops and purveyors of antiques and collectables. Salman Sokak, or "Copper Alley", lives up to its nickname, with plenty of old and new copper pieces on offer. You will find bargains and bric-a-brac here, but few real treasures.

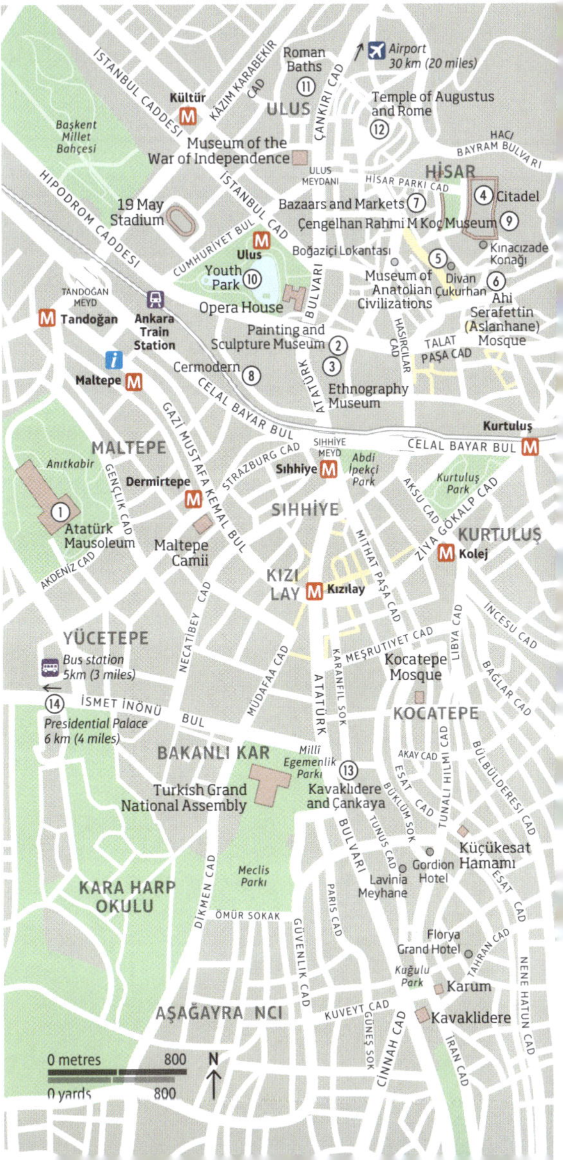

5

MUSEUM OF ANATOLIAN CIVILIZATIONS

ANADOLU MEDENIYETLERI MÜZESI

Saraçlar Sok (below the Citadel) M Ulus (0312) 324 31 60
Apr-Oct: 8:30am-7pm Tue-Sun (Nov-Mar: to 5:30pm)

Turkey's most distinguished museum showcases the rich history of Anatolia. Housed in two renovated Ottoman-era buildings, its chronological exhibits span millennia, from Paleolithic tools to Bronze Age treasures and superb Hellenistic and Roman art.

Located at the base of the ancient citadel, this museum displays the achievements of Anatolia's many diverse cultures. The collection, which is celebrated for its breadth and depth, systematically guides visitors through the chronological progression of human civilization. Exhibits range from simple Paleolithic stone tools to clay tablets inscribed in Assyrian cuneiform and exquisite Hellenistic and Roman sculptures. The displays include a statuette of the mother goddess from Çatalhöyük *(p294)*, Bronze Age treasures from the royal tombs at Alacahöyük *(p340)* and superb Hittite sculptures and orthostat reliefs.

Exhibits range from simple Paleolithic stone tools to clay tablets inscribed in Assyrian cuneiform and exquisite Hellenistic and Roman sculptures.

A Neo-Hittite lion sculpture from the gate of Aslantepe

TOP 4 MUSEUM HIGHLIGHTS

Çatalhöyük (8000-5500 BCE)
Clay mother-goddess statuettes and plaster wall paintings demonstrate the region's artistry.

Kültepe (1950-1750 BCE)
A set of the Assyrian trading colony's clay tablets and *rhytons* (drinking vessels).

Karkamış (1321-717 BCE)
Intricately carved basalt and limestone blocks depict procession scenes and gods.

Gordion Royal Tumulus (740 BCE)
An Iron Age Phrygian tomb with diverse burial items, including a lion-pawed table.

Archaeological finds on display, and *(inset)* the museum's Ottoman-style façade

Wooden columns inside the Ahi Şerafettin Mosque

EAT

Boğaziçi Lokantası
Try some of the best *lokanta* (ready made home-style dishes) in the city.

Denizciler Cad 1/A, Ulus, Ankara bogazicilokantasi.com.tr

Lavinia Meyhane
This modern *meyhane* (tavern) serves delicious Mediterranean meze, complemented with a great alcohol selection.

Bestekar Cad 74/1, Çankaya, Ankara laviniameyhane.com

Kınacızade Konağı
Lunch on *gözleme* (stuffed flatbreads) in the courtyard of this Ottoman mansion.

Kale Kapısı Sok 28, Kale, Ankara kinacizadekonagi.com

Ahi Şerafettin (Aslanhane) Mosque

Arslanhane Camii

Kale Sok, Kale, Ankara 402 9am-6pm daily (from 2:30pm Fri) Prayer times only

This is one of the five mosques included in Turkey's UNESCO World Heritage Site listing for wooden hypostyle mosques of medieval Anatolia. It's commonly referred to as the Aslanhane (lion house) Mosque. The name stems from a prominent lion statue that once stood in front of the structure. The mosque was built in 1290 and is also interesting for how the exterior has incorporated plenty of Roman and Byzantine blocks and decorative marble pieces into the building.

The mosque's interior is defined by a remarkable array of architectural features, such as the 24 wooden columns, topped by marble Roman capitals. These columns support an incredibly intricate *kündekari* (interlocking wooden patterns) timber roof. The mihrab is richly decorated with blue, black and white Seljuk tile-work set in a *muqarna* (stalactite vaulting) design.

Bazaars and Markets

Çarşılar ve Pazarlar

Ulus 9:30am-5:30pm daily

The most interesting shopping districts are in the Ulus/Hisar area. The streets to look for are Salman Sokak, Konya Sokak and Çıkrıkçılar Sokak. Markets cater to tourists and sell a wide range of jewellery, carpets, herbal remedies, spices, iron and copper trinkets, as well as

A carpet seller displaying colourful Turkish carpets in a bazaar in Ulus

HIDDEN GEM
Suluhan Caravanserai

This huge 16th-century caravanserai (*Şht Teğmen Kalmaz Posta Caddesi*) is a vibrant commercial hub today. Visitors can shop for trinkets, or stop for tea at one of the charming teahouses.

various textiles. Also look out for the Bakırçılar Çarşısı (Copperworkers' Bazaar) on Salman Sokak.

Local flea markets and produce markets are held in most districts at least once a week. One of the best takes place on Saturdays on Konya Sokak in the Ulus area.

Cermodern

Altınsoy Cad 3, Sıhhıye, Ankara Adliye
10am-7pm Tue-Sun
cermodern.org

Created from the industrial warehouses of a vast, disused railway depot, Cermodern is Ankara's most vibrant cultural hub. This is the capital's main location for holding world-class international art exhibitions and any large art show that's pegged to pass through the city.

The exhibition spaces within the museum maintain a consistently rich and varied calendar, ensuring that visitors will always find two to four temporary exhibitions on display at any given time. This programming spectrum ranges from prestigious, big-name retrospectives and solo events dedicated to focus on a single, internationally famed artist, to more contemporary and cutting-edge showcases. These latter displays showcase pioneering new work emerging from local as well as international artists. The museum also hosts a lively performing arts and theatre programme. The complex is home to a dedicated, modern theatre space that regularly stages a variety of performances, including modern and experimental plays. Complementing the drama are frequent music concerts spanning various genres, engaging talks and panel discussions featuring famed artists and writers, along with thoughtfully curated screenings of international and arthouse films.

In addition to these core offerings, Cermodern embraces the concept of well-being and community engagement by occasionally hosting hands-on activities such as art workshops for all skill levels and yoga lessons. To ensure visitors can maximize their experience, the institution maintains a comprehensive and fully up-to-date schedule on its official website, making it easy for visitors to check and confirm all current exhibitions, events, and timings before planning their arrival.

Çengelhan Rahmi M. Koç Museum

Çengelhan Rahmi M. Koç Müzesi

Sutepe Mah, Depo Sok 1, Altındağ, Ankara (0312) 309 68 00 10am-5pm Tue-Fri, 10am-7pm Sat & Sun

A sister museum to the Rahmi Koç Industrial Museum in Istanbul, the Ankara site is opposite the entrance to Ankara Castle in a restored 16th century kervansaray.

Eclectic exhibits range from toys, bicycles, prams and scientific instruments to air, rail and sea transport. Early motor cars include a 1918 Model T Ford. A replica of the Nile river boat from the film The African Queen is among the 1,200 items on display. There are two good on-site restaurants.

↑ Objects on display in the Çengelhan Rahmi M. Koç Museum

STAY

Divan Çukurhan

This restored 16th-century caravanserai offers rooms that blend the building's original features with a classic European style.

Depo Sok 3, Kale, Ankara **divan.com.tr**

Gordion Hotel

The popular Gordion consists of elegantly outfitted rooms, and houses a swimming pool and bar-restaurant.

Büklüm Cad 59, Çankaya, Ankara **gordionhotel.com**

Florya Grand Hotel

Just a short stroll from the Kavaklıdere district's restaurant, café and shops, this hotel offers minimalist Scandi-style rooms.

Bülten Sok 54, Çankaya, Ankara **floryagrand.com**

Youth Park

Gençlik Parkı

Atatürk Bulvarı **Ulus** **Opera, Ulus** **Dawn-dusk daily**

The Youth Park just south of Ulus is Ankara's liveliest and most popular area for urban recreation. Following extensive and careful renovation, the park has been transformed into a vibrant green space. A central feature is the large ornamental pool with fountains. Dotted around the park, are a number of pleasant cafés, where tea is traditionally served from a *samovar* (double-tiered metal pot) at tables overlooking the pool. There is also a funfair, often referred to locally as a Luna Park, featuring various rides and attractions. Furthermore, the park serves as a significant sports hub, encompassing a large sports stadium, tennis courts and a swimming pool.

The lovely Korean Garden, on the other side of Cumhuriyet Bulvarı, commemorates the oft-forgotten combat role played by Turkish soldiers during the Korean War (1950–54). The 45-m- (148-ft-) high Parachute Tower here was once popular with daredevils willing to pay to leap from its heights.

Roman Baths

Hamamları

Çankırı Cad, Ulus **(0312) 310 72 80** **Ulus** **8:30am-6pm**

Very little remains to be seen of the once-grand Roman baths that date back to the 3rd century CE. These baths were built to honour Asclepius, the Greek god of medicine. It inculded the typical sophisticated features that encompass three distinct rooms: the frigidarium (a cold room), a tepidarium (moderately heated room) and a caldarium (hot room).

Temple of Augustus and Rome

Augustus Tapınağı

Ulus **Daily**

This temple was commissioned and built in around 20 BCE by King Pylamenes of Galatia to honour a visit by the great Roman emperor, Augustus. The inscription on the outer walls, which reads as *Res Gestae Divi Augusti* ("The Deeds of the Divine Augustus") is one of the few surviving testaments to authenticate Augustus's accomplishments.

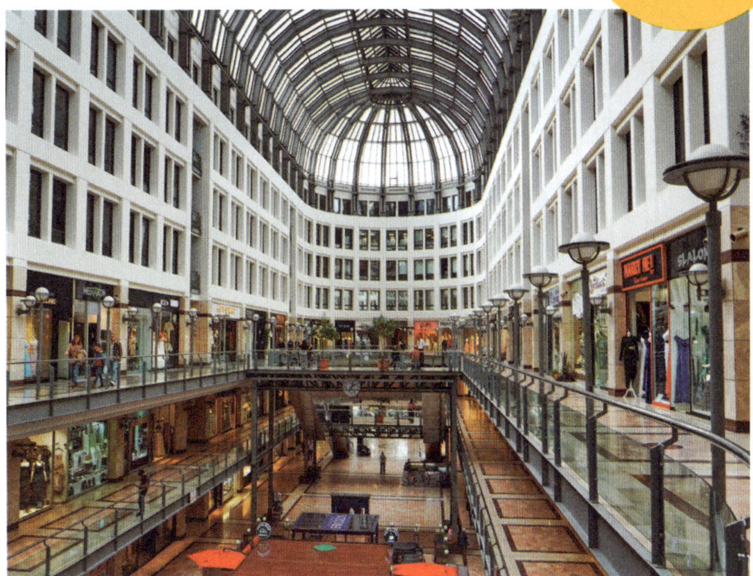

In the 4th century CE, as Christianity became more established, the temple was transformed into a Byzantine church.

Adjoining the temple are the mosque (dating from 1425) and tomb of **Hacı Bayram Veli** (1352–1429), founder of the Bayrami religious sect. The fine Seljuk wooden interior, in particular, is worth seeing. Some renovation work was done in the 17th century by the famous architect Mimar Sinan *(p109)*.

Nearby is the **Column of Julian**, reaching 15 m (49 ft) and dating from 362 CE. The column commemorates a visit by this Roman emperor.

Hacı Bayram Veli
Ulus Daily (except during prayer times)

Column of Julian
Jülyanüs Direği Ulus

Ruins of the 3rd-century CE Roman Baths of Ankara

13 

Kavaklıdere and Çankaya

Ankara's up-market shopping areas cater for the diplomatic corps and government elite. The most exculsive and fashionable shops can be found south of Kızılay in the suburbs of Kavaklıdere and Çankaya, where many foreign embassies are located. Going south on Tunalı Hilmi Caddesi, parallel to Atatürk Bulvarı, you reach Kuğulu Park and Cinnah Caddesi. Both streets are studded with designer boutiques showcasing high-end fashion, accessories and luxury items. Karum, opposite the park, is an exclusive shopping centre. Do not expect bargains here.

Did You Know?

"Karum" denotes the ancient Assyrian *"karu"* trade posts, essential to early Anatolian history.

↑ Karum shopping centre in Çankaya, lined with high-end stores

14 

Presidential Palace

Cumhurbaşkanlığı Köşkü

Çankaya Cad (0312) 427 43 30 Çankaya 1-5pm Sat & Sun

Set in a beautiful formal garden, the presidential palace is not open to the public. However, visitors can view Atatürk's well-preserved house within the grounds, which is now a museum.

The father of the Turkish republic, Mustafa Kemal Atatürk, moved here in 1921 and this is where he planned the direction his country would take in years to come. The house has a slightly sombre or contemplative atmosphere. The ground floor is decorated in a traditional, classic Ottoman fashion, while upstairs provides visitors with a glimpse of Atatürk's lifestyle and personal tastes. Advance booking is essential, so call ahead before visiting.

Cityscape of Konya with the magnificent Mevlâna Museum and mosque ↑

2

KONYA

C4 20 km (12 miles) N of city centre Ferit Paşa Cad 11 km (7 miles) NW of city centre Mevlâna Cad 65, (0332) 353 40 20 (ext 147/148)

Set on the high Anatolian steppe, Konya has been inhabited since Hittite times. The city's heyday was in the 12th century as the capital of the Seljuk Sultanate of Rum. Today, Konya has transformed into a modern city that maintains its rich Islamic heritage. At its heart lies the Alaeddin Park (Alaeddin Tepesi), a low hill dominated by the Alaeddin Mosque, Konya's largest.

Mevlâna Museum

Mevlâna Müzesi

Aslanlı Kışla Cad Mevlâna 9am–7pm daily muze.gov.tr

The city of Konya has close links with the life and work of Rumi, or Mevlâna, the 13th-century founder of the Mevlevi Dervish sect – better known as the "whirling" dervishes *(p288)*. Rumi developed a philosophy of spiritual union and universal love, and is regarded as one of the Islamic world's greatest mystics. He settled in Seljuk-ruled Konya and is believed to have died here in 1273.

The museum is an enlargement of the original *tekke* (dervish lodge). Here, life-like mannequins, clad in traditional dress, illustrate the spiritual aspects of the daily life of an initiate in the lodge. It also contains the tomb of Rumi and the *semahane* (ceremonial hall), once the setting for the whirling ceremony. The *semahane* now has displays of memorabilia, manuscripts and musical instruments.

Alaeddin Mosque

Alaeddin Camii

Alaeddin Tepesi, Adliye Bul Alaeddin 9am–6pm daily (from 2:30pm Fri) Prayer times

This early-13th-century mosque on Alaeddin Hill is one of the most important Seljuk monuments in Konya. It was originally part of a larger Seljuk palace complex.

Inside the prayer hall, the ornately carved wooden *minbar* (prayer pulpit) is notable for an inscription that dates it to 1155, making it the earliest piece of Seljuk artistry in Turkey. Both the marble mihrab and central dome are bordered by aqua blue and

INSIDER TIP

Sema Performances

From June to September, there is a free outdoors *sema* (whirling dervish performance) held every Thursday, at 8:45pm in the Mevlâna Museum's rose-garden.

black Seljuk tile-work that is decorated with geometric designs and Kufic script. Note the entrance in the mosque's northern wall incorporates stonework from earlier Roman and Byzantine buildings.

Several Seljuk sultans are buried in the mosque's courtyard. Alaeddin Hill itself is a manicured park, with tea-gardens and cafés, and is a great spot for taking a break.

> **Alaeddin Hill itself is a manicured park, with tea-gardens and cafés, and is a great spot for taking a break.**

Karatay Museum

Karatay Medresesi

Ankara Cad **Kültürpark**
9am-7pm daily
muze.gov.tr

In a city with a glut of beautiful architecture, the Karatay Museum still stands out as one of Konya's finest buildings. Its 13th-century domed *medrese* has a grand gateway, decorated with *alaq* (striped) stonework and *muqarna* (stalactite vaulting) detailing that showcases the influence of Syrian and Egyptian architecture.

Inside, the geometric patterned blue-and-black tile-work of the central dome and walls has been preserved. Exhibits in the *medrese*'s halls display the exuberant artistry and intricate detail of Seljuk ceramics. Much of the collection hails from the archaeological excavation of Lake Beyşehir's Kubad Abad Palace. Many pieces are decorated with figurative representations of humans and animals despite Islam's aniconism, which demonstrates the Seljuk Turks' fusion of their shamanistic roots with Islam two centuries on from their conversion. The *medrese* was built by Emir Celaleddin Karatay, whose tomb is on site.

↑ Vaulted ceilings adorned with motifs at the Karatay Museum

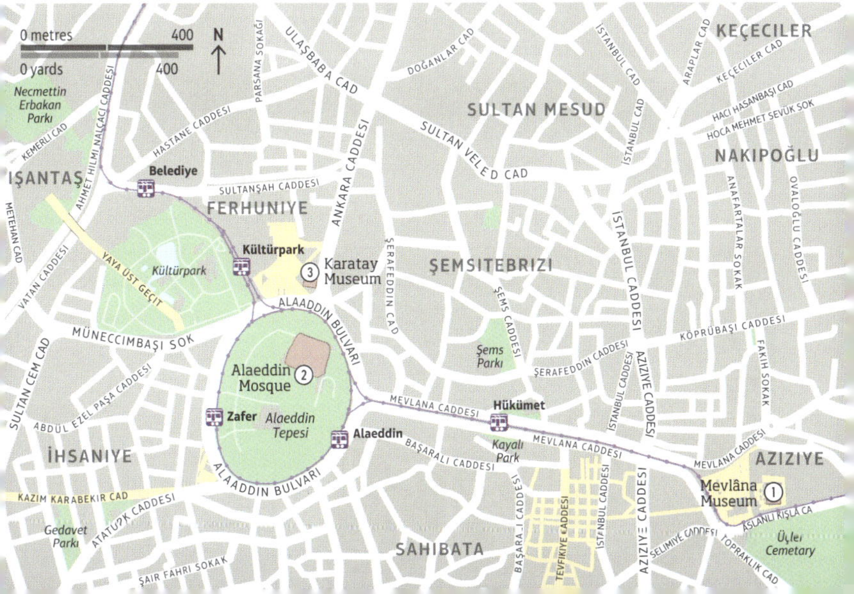

0 metres 400
0 yards 400
N
Necmettin Erbakan Parkı
IŞANTAŞ
Belediye
FERHUNIYE
Kültürpark
Kültürpark
③ Karatay Museum
SULTAN MESUD
ŞEMSITEBRIZI
KEÇECILER
NAKIPOĞLU
Alaeddin Mosque ②
Zafer
Alaeddin Tepesi
Alaeddin
Hükümet
Şems Parkı
Kayalı Park
İHSANIYE
AZIZIYE
Mevlâna Museum ①
Gedavet Parkı
SAHIBATA
Üçler Cemetary

A SHORT WALK AROUND ALAEDDIN PARK

Distance 1 km (half a mile) **Time** 20 minutes
Nearest bus stop Alaeddin Bulvarı

Konya is set on a high, bleak plain in the middle of the Anatolian steppe. Known for its rich heritage and Islamic traditions, this ancient city has a modern and prosperous appearance. It was known as Iconium to the Romans and Byzantines.

At the heart of the city lies the circular Alaeddin Park (Alaeddin Tepesi). It was finished in 1220 by Alaeddin Keykubad I, the greatest and most prolific builder of the Seljuk sultans. As you wander, take in the tranquil surroundings full of history and nature.

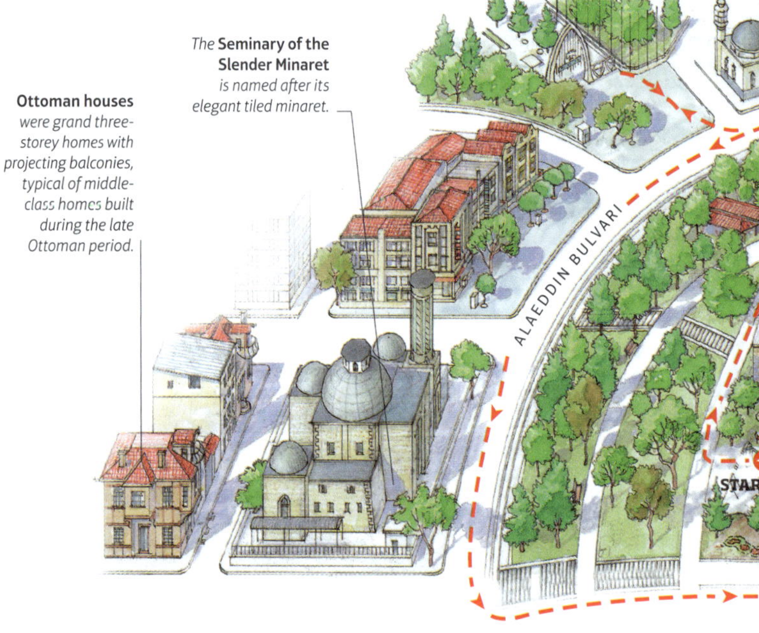

Fairs are now held elsewhere, so the shady gardens of the ***Konya Fairground*** *are a cool, restful retreat.*

The ***Seminary of the Slender Minaret*** *is named after its elegant tiled minaret.*

Ottoman houses *were grand three-storey homes with projecting balconies, typical of middle-class homes built during the late Ottoman period.*

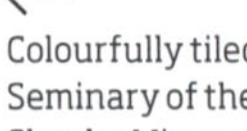

Colourfully tiled Seminary of the Slender Minaret

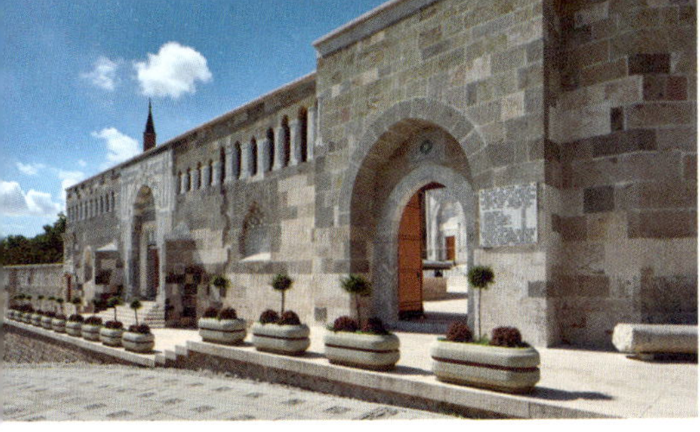

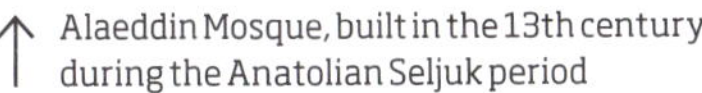

↑ Alaeddin Mosque, built in the 13th century during the Anatolian Seljuk period

KONYA
Around Alaeddin Park

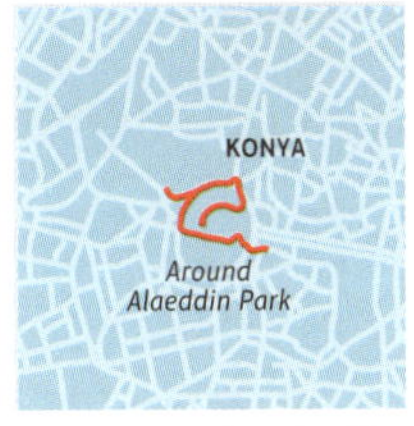

Locator Map

For more detail see p285

A concrete arch covers the remains of the **Villa of Sultan Kılıç Arslan**, *a Seljuk landmark. Nearby are tea gardens.*

Located in the Great Karatay Madrasa, a 13th-century Seljuk theological school, the **Karatay Museum** (p285) *houses a collection of ceramics and tiles.*

The **Alaeddin Mosque** (p284) *is set in wooded surroundings on a site that has been used since prehistoric times.*

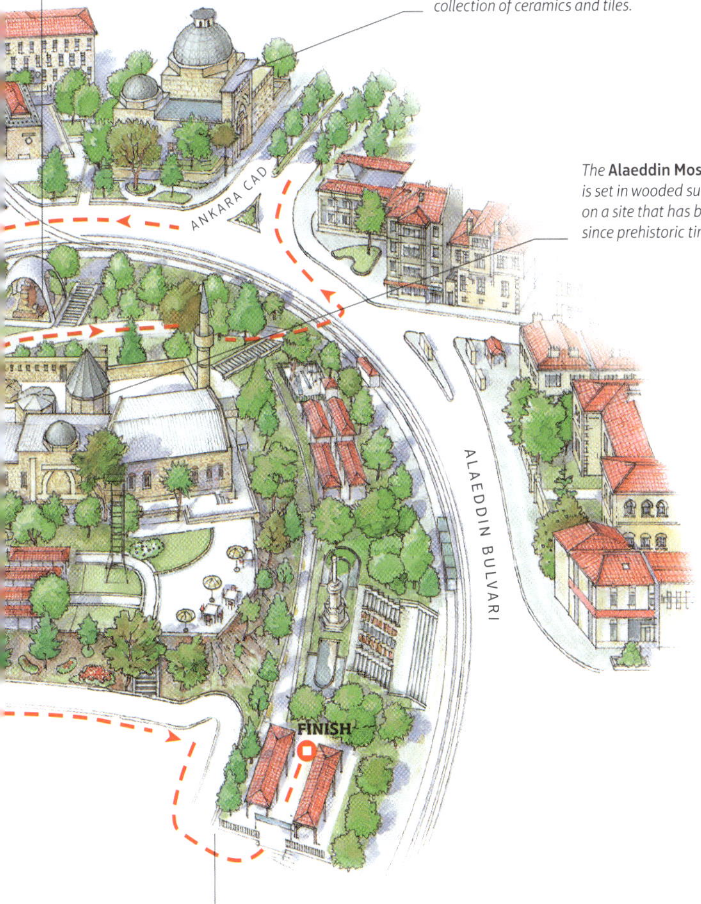

ANKARA CAD
ALAEDDIN BULVARI
FINISH

Car park

0 metres 80
0 yards 80
N

THE WHIRLING DERVISHES

The Mevlevi order, better known as the whirling dervishes, was founded by the Sufi mystic Rumi, also called Mevlâna. He believed that music and dance represented a means to induce an ecstatic state of universal love and offered a way to liberate the individual from the anxiety and pain of daily life.

Did You Know?

Musical accompaniment is symbolic: the *ney* (reed flute) represents longing for God's love.

THE SEMA RITUAL

Rumi's greatest work, the six-volume *Masnevi*, consists of 25,000 poems that were read in the *tekkes* (lodges) of the Mevlevi order he inspired. This profound spiritual practice has been recognized by UNESCO as an Intangible Cultural Heritage of Humanity. Central to the practice of the dervishes is the *sema*, or whirling ceremony, which comprises several parts, each with its own meaning. Love is the central theme of the mystical cycle of the *sema*, which symbolizes the sharing of God's love among earthly beings. For man, the dance is a spiritual ascent to divine love. The *sema* combines both spiritual and intellectual elements, emphasizing self-realization and the ultimate goal, which is perfect union with God.

The *sema* consists of five parts, the first three of which are prayers, greetings and musical improvisations. This music, particularly the lament of the *ney* (reed flute), is crucial, representing the soul's yearning for God's love. The ritual then moves into four *selams* (salutes): truth through knowledge; the splendour of creation; total submission before God; and coming to terms with destiny.

The whirling dervishes usually wear a wide white skirt, symbolizing the ego's

shroud, and a tall, conical felt hat, the *sikke*, which represents the ego's tombstone. At the start of the *sema* ritual, the dervishes greet one another and salute the soul, which is "enslaved" by shapes and bodies. Next, they extend their arms, to allow divine energy to enter the right palm, move through the body and pass out through the left palm into the earth before whirling, the climax of the *sema*. The movement concludes with a bow, signifying the return to a state of subservience. After the ritual, verses from the Koran are read, including a prayer for the peace of all souls.

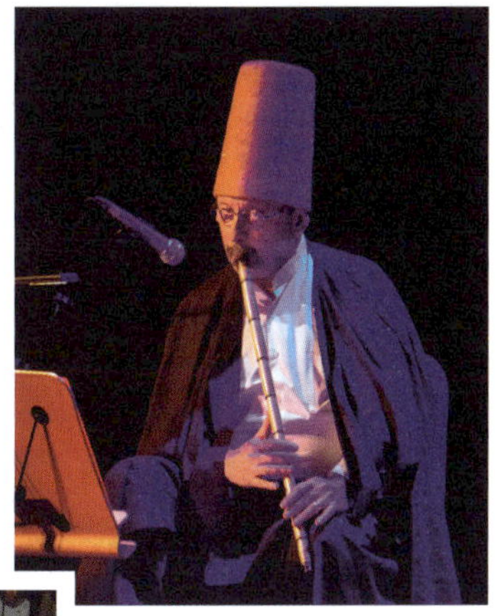

↑ A musical performance at Rumi's commemoration ceremony

← A Mevlevi ceremony in Kasımpaşa

↑ Whirling dervishes at the Galata Mevlevi Lodge Museum

↑ Great Mosque of Kütahya, with the cityscape in the background

3

KÜTAHYA

B4 İstasyon Cad Atatürk Bulvarı Hükümet; (0274) 223 62 13

Kütahya's earliest inhabitants were the Phrygians in the 7th century BCE. In the 16th century, the city rose to prosperity under Sultan Selim I, when ceramic artisans from Persia settled here. Over 300 years later, in 1833, Paşa Muhammad Ali occupied Kütahya. Today, this is a peaceful and devout town and most shops shut during prayer times on Fridays.

Kossuth House Museum

Kossuth Evi Müzesi

Macar Sokak (off Gediz Cad) (0274) 223 62 14 8:45am-5pm Tue-Sun

This house/museum complex was the home of Hungarian freedom fighter Lajos Kossuth, who sought refuge in Turkey after leading an unsuccessful revolt to free his homeland from the rule of the Habsburgs in 1848. Kossuth and his family stayed here as the guests of the Ottoman government in 1850–51, and the 19th-century stone-and-wood house where they lived has changed remarkably little since that time.

The statue of Kossuth in the rose garden was erected in 1982, and Hungarians renew friendship ties here annually on 5 April. The house is also referred to as "the House of the Hungarian Patriot".

Fortress

Kale

Up Gediz Cad from the Kossuth House Museum

The ruined fortress resembles many other Ottoman-period citadels. Not much is known about its history, but the Kütahya-born historian and traveller Evliya Çelebi (1811–82) wrote that it had 70 towers.

One of the few remaining ones has been extensively restored with other restoration ongoing. Most people come here for the delightful revolving restaurant, Döner Gazino, at the top.

Döner Gazino
8:30am-11:30pm daily

Kütahya Tile Museum

Kütahya Çini Müzesi

Gediz Cad (0274) 223 69 90 8:30am-5:30pm Tue-Sun

Since 1999, the Tile Museum has been housed in a restored 15th-century soup kitchen *(imaret)* located behind the Great Mosque (Ulu Cami). This is one of Turkey's best small museums. The displays focus on tiles, vases, ewers and decorative porcelainware produced in the town from the 14th century to the present, and are arranged around a typical ornamental pool *(şadırvan)*.

HISTORIC KÜTAHYA MANOR HOUSES

The town's spacious period houses date mainly from the 18th and 19th centuries. These historic *konaks* are classic examples of Ottoman domestic architecture, often built with a half-timbered frame. Their current state of disrepair offers only a hint of their former grandeur. They usually have three storeys, projecting balconies, and front and back entrances. Look near the Ulu Cami on Ahi Erbasan Sokak (in Gazi Kemal Mahallesi) and Germiyan Sokak for typical examples.

Great Mosque

Ulu Cami

End of Cumhuriyet Cad, Börekciler Mahallesi
Daily

This is the biggest mosque in Kütahya, but not the oldest. Building started under Sultan Yıldırım Beyazıt early in the 15th century, but it was not finished until the time of Mehmet II (1451–81). Many of the marble columns come from Aizonoi *(p299)*. In 1889, during the reign of Kütahya Governor Veysel Pasha, the old structure was demolished down to its foundations, and construction of the mosque, now with its dome and marble columns, began. The wooden pulpit is a beautiful work, built without using any nails.

The Sakahanesi (water-sellers' square) near the mosque is a popular local gathering place.

Bazaars

Çarşılar

9am-7pm daily

Kütahya's bazaars occupy two buildings. The Grand Market (Büyük Bedesten) was built in the 14th century and stands on Çemberciler Caddesi. The 15th-century Small Market (Küçük Bedesten) is just next to it on Kavafiye Sokak (Shoemaker's Street). Don't miss the vaulted ceilings. Today, the bazaars sell chiefly vegetables and second-hand goods. More specialized traders overflow into the surrounding streets.

EAT

Kütahya Lalezar Konağı

This Ottoman house serves dishes such as *sini mantı* (baked dumplings in tomato sauce).

Germiyan Cad 78
0507 708 1937

Tarihi Ulucami Köftecisi

This place serves some of Kütahya's best *Köfte* (meatballs), grilled or smothered in yoghurt.

Dönenler Camii Meydanı, Osmanlı Cad 9
(0274) 212 44 46

Hayat Lokantasi

A local *lokanta* where you can fill up on hearty soups and dishes of *guveç* (stews).

Poyraz Sok 1
(0274) 223 80 49

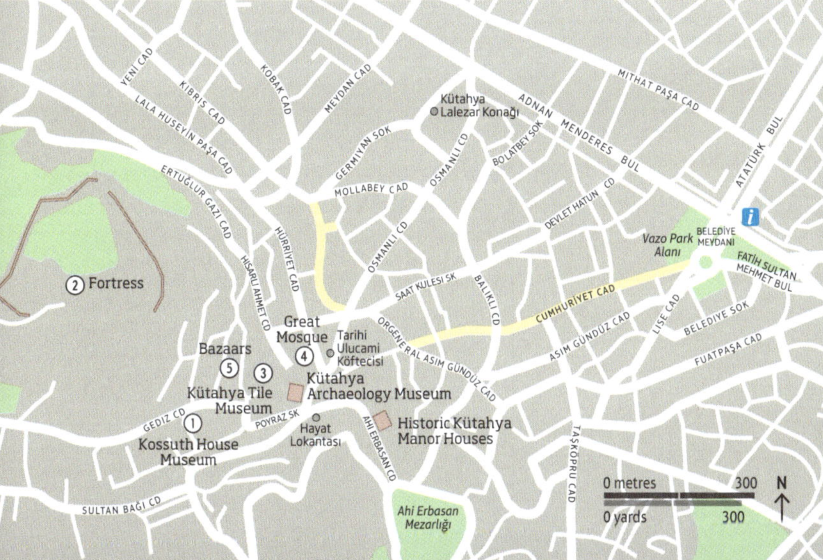

EXPERIENCE MORE

Soğuksu National Park

Soğuksu Milli Parkı

C3 Soğuksu Milli Parkı, 82 km (51 miles) N of Ankara (0312) 736 11 15 (national park office)

This beautiful, safe forest area, situated at an altitude of 975 m (3,200 ft), is an ideal retreat from the city. It features well-marked hiking trails and picnic spots, perfect for walking and trekking.

The region's many natural hot mineral springs have been developed to create spa resorts. One of the best of these is Kızılcahamam. Of all the thermal spas scattered around Ankara, it is also the most suited to tourists. There are comfortable hotels and other facilities for visitors who want to stay for a few days. Some treatments involve not only bathing in, but also drinking, the mineral-rich waters, which contain bicarbonate, chloride, sodium and carbon dioxide.

Bolu

C3 137 km (85 miles) NE of Ankara: take toll motorway (E89) from Ankara towards Istanbul, or highway (no toll) E80 (0374) 212 22 54

The Bolu area is known for its deciduous forests and a steep mountain pass, which affords great views. It also produces a tasty ewe's milk cheese. At Kartalkaya, 42 km (26 miles) east of the city of Bolu, one of Turkey's best ski centres is open from December to March.

Haymana Hot Springs

Haymana Kaplıcaları

C4 Haymana Kaplıca, 60 km (38 miles) S of Ankara

Haymana is one of six thermal spas within easy reach of Ankara, and its history extends as far back as Roman times. It is worth coming here for the relaxing atmosphere and to experience the feeling of physical wellbeing after a good soak. At Haymana, the waters emerge at 45°C (113°F) and you can smell the calcium, magnesium, sodium and

LAKE ABANT NATIONAL PARK

Around 34 km (21 miles) south of the city of Bolu, this vast crater-lake is a jewel of Turkish nature, renowned throughout the country for its unspoiled, wild beauty. Its expansive shoreline, approximately 7 km (4 miles) in length, is rimmed by a dense and thriving forest. The area was officially proclaimed a national park in 2022. The best time to visit is in October when Lake Abant is surrounded by vast tracts of russet-red and yellow leaves, or between December and February when the entire area is blanketed in a winter wonderland of snow.

Kartalkaya Ski Resort, near Bolu, backed by snowcapped mountains

HIDDEN GEM
Infidel's Castle

A sight worth visiting near Haymana is the Hittite-era Infidel's Castle (Gavur Kalesi). Strategically perched on a cliff, it holds of an underground cult tomb with two adjoining tomb chambers, and was discovered in 1930.

bicarbonate. There are several good hotels here; note, all visitors need to contact the hotels directly for bookings.

Polatlı and Gordion

C4 94 km (58 miles) W of Ankara Ankara to Polatı, then taxi

The village of Yassıhöyük stands on the site of Gordion, the capital of ancient Phrygia, dating from around the 8th century BCE. There are several sights worth seeing here, and you can easily tour the site in the course of a day trip from Ankara. If you wish to stay over, however, the nearby town of Polatlı, some 18 km (11 miles) to the southeast, is well supplied with hotels and some good restaurants.

Gordion was famous as the seat of the legendary King Midas, whose touch was said to have turned everything to gold. Legend has it that this power turned on Midas when he touched his daughter, as well as his food and drink. The problem was solved only when the god Dionysus took pity on him and granted him a cure. It is thought that Midas took his own life in 695 BCE after a crushing military defeat.

Phrygia reached its zenith in the middle of the 8th century BCE, but Gordion was made famous again by Alexander the Great *(p51)*. In 333 BCE, after wintering in Lycia, Alexander led his army northwards from Sagalassos to Gordion. Here, he came upon and cut the Gordian knot, fulfilling a prophecy that whoever loosed the bond would become the ruler of the known world.

Today, about 80 burial mounds of Phrygian kings have been excavated in the Gordion area over the past 40 years. The most interesting of these is the **Midas Tomb** (Midas Tümülusü), which lies within the grounds of the **Gordion Museum** (Gordion Müzesi). The large mound is thought to cover the chamber in which the king was buried, and is 50 m (164 ft) in height. When archaeologists opened the tomb they found the skeleton of a man of around 60 years of age, who is now believed to be another king from the same dynasty.

The acropolis has also been excavated, and shows layers of civilization from the Bronze Age to Greek and Roman times. Although the acropolis gives an idea of the size and extent of the historic settlements in the region, most of the mosaics found there have been moved and are now kept in the museum. In other places, simple roof structures have been erected to protect excavated mosaics from the elements.

The Gordion Museum was established in 1963, and has been nominated for several awards over the years. It displays Bronze Age, Hittite, Hellenistic, Greek and Roman finds, but its displays concentrate on the Phrygian period, and feature many superbly crafted artifacts. The exhibits include ceramics, woodwork and several bronze vessels found in the Midas Tomb, as well as musical instruments and more.

Midas Tomb

9am-6pm daily

Gordion Museum

9 km (5 miles) N of the town (0312) 638 21 88
9am-6pm daily

Admiring the archaeological displays at the Gordion Museum

Interior of the Eşrefoğlu Wooden Mosque, located in Beyşehir

HIDDEN GEM

Eflatun Pınar Hitit Anıtı

Head 22 km (13 miles) north of Beyşehir to seek out this ornamental Hittite pond, with its wall of carved stone-block reliefs depicting gods and lions.

8 Beyşehir

C5 90 km (56 miles) W of Konya Konya

Beyşehir is the largest of the freshwater lakes in what is known as Turkey's Lake District, and holds the distinction of being the third-largest lake in the country. Its expansive, yet relatively shallow waters are a thriving habitat for several fish species, such as carp, perch and pike. The town of the same name, at the southeastern corner of the lake, features an unusual combined weir and bridge.

One of the main reasons for coming to Beyşehir is to see the **Eşrefoğlu Mosque** (Eşrefoğlu Camii), dating from 1297. The wooden interior, with its 48 wooden columns and mihrab (prayer niche) decorated with cut tiles, is among the finest examples of this type of architecture remaining from the Beylik period.

Eşrefoğlu Mosque

 Next to the Bedesten, NW after crossing the weir bridge Daily

9 Çatalhöyük

C5 52 km (32 miles) S of Konya To Çumra, then minibus or taxi catalhoyuk.com

Dating from as early as 7400 BCE, Çatalhöyük is one of the world's earliest urban settlements. It was originally discovered and excavated by James Mellaart in 1958. Research under the leadership of Ian Hodder resumed in 1993. The site is on the UNESCO World Heritage List.

It is thought that roughly 10,000 people lived here in flat-roofed square houses with rooftop entrances and high windows. The city was the focus of a culture that produced an array of mural decoration, decorative textiles and pottery.

Visitors can enter the site only when accompanied by an official museum guide. The **Çatalhöyük Museum** displays replicas of the latest finds, and there are "virtual reality" exhibits in houses and shrines. Artifacts displayed here are reproductions because the originals are in museums in Konya or the superb Museum of Anatolian Civilizations *(p278)* in Ankara.

Çatalhöyük Museum

 (0332) 351 32 07 9am-6pm Tue-Sun

10 Eğirdir

B4 204 km (127 miles) W of Konya (0246) 311 42 18 2 Sahil Yolu; (0246) 311 43 88

Ringed by mountains rising to 3,000 m (9,842 ft), the town of Eğirdir makes a good base for walkers, birders and flower enthusiasts. In May, the hills display a variety of blooms and become a stop-over for migrating birds. Eğirdir makes an ideal base for exploring the northern sections of the St Paul trail, which is the country's second-longest long-distance walk.

On Lake Eğirdir's northwest shore, Antiocheia-in-Pisidia is famous as the place where St Paul first preached to the Gentiles. The ruins include the basilica of St Paul, a Roman theatre and a synagogue.

Davraz Ski Centre is operational from December to late April. There are three hotels at the centre itself, and more accommodation in Çobanisa village, some 7 km (4 miles) below.

Davraz Ski Centre

Hours vary, check website davrazkayak merkezi.com

SAGALASSOS

Sprawling across a high slope, in the Taurus Mountains, the ancient city of Sagalassos is one of Turkey's most spectacular sights. Around 81 km (50 miles) south from Eğirdir, these Roman-era ruins of what was once Psidia's main centre include the Antonine Nymphaeum - a massive, ornate fountain complex that archaeologists have incredibly restored to working order - and a 9,000-seat Roman theatre.

Afyonkarahisar

B4 227 km (140 miles) NW of Konya (0272) 213 00 22 Nedim Helvacıoğlu Cad; (0272) 229 90 10 Anıt Parki, Hükümet Konaği Yanı; (0272) 213 54 47

Afyonkarahisar, meaning "opium", is known for its white and dark purple opium poppies in May. Opiates are extracted for medicinal purposes at a factory in nearby Bolvadın. The town museum has exhibits detailing various methods of opiate extraction. Local products include soft, white marble, which is found in huge slabs along the roadsides and is used for everything from gravestones to kitchen basins. Afyonkarahisar Kaymağı, a rich clotted cream, is usually served on small metal trays and eaten with honey for breakfast. A 225-m (738-ft) crag, possibly used as a fortress by the Hittites and Byzantines, towers over the town and can be reached by climbing 650 steps.

The Seljuks left the greatest mark on Afyonkarahisar's history, highlighted by the 1272 **Great Mosque** (Ulu Cami), which features a geometric wooden ceiling and 40 wooden columns with intricately carved capitals.

The **Afyonkarahisar Archaeological Museum** contains Roman artifacts, excavated from around Isparta, Uşak, Burdur and Kütahya.

Afyonkarahisar was Atatürk's headquarters for the final stages of Turkey's War of Independence, which reached a climax with the victory over the advancing Greek army at Dumlupınar on 26 August 1922. The **Victory Museum** (Zafer Müzesi), known more for its classical Anatolian architecture than for its contents, recalls the heady days of national liberation. Most of the top Republican commanders stayed in this building during the campaign. There is also a war memorial at nearby Dumlupınar.

Great Mosque (Ulu Cami)

Daily

Afyonkarahisar Archaeological Museum

Kurtuluş Cad 96
(0272) 215 11 91
8:30am-5:30pm daily

Victory Museum (Zafer Müzesi)

Opposite the Governor's Building 8:30am-12:30pm & 1:30-5:30pm Tue-Fri (from 9am & to 5pm Sat & Sun)

↑ White and purple poppies blossoming in a field in Afyonkarahisar

Scenic Lake Eğirdir and its connected town

Sivrihisar

C4

Sivrihisar is the ancient town of Justinianopolis, built by Emperor Justinian *(p52)* to guard the western route to Ancyra (ancient Ankara). The modern town is spread out at the foot of a crag, on which lie the remains of the original Byzantine fortress. The Great Mosque (Ulu Cami), built in 1247, is an excellent example of a Seljuk mosque. Some of its 67 wooden pillars have intricately carved and painted capitals. A warren of pretty Ottoman houses surrounds the mosque, and the Sivrihisar area is famous for fine hand-woven kilims.

14 km (9 miles) to the south of Sivrihisar lie the ancient ruins of Pessinus, near the modern village of Ballıhisar (honey castle). During the 3rd century BCE, Pessinus was an important Phrygian cult centre but was abandoned in around 500 or 600 CE. Sights include the scant remains of a temple of Cybele, the Anatolian mother goddess. However, nothing is left of the stadium and theatre. At one time, it is believed that there were over 360 springs here, and the remains of hydraulic works can still be seen. The site is open to the public and access is free, if not easy.

THE PHRYGIAN WAY

Turkey's long-distance Phrygian Way *(culturerouteslinturkey.com)* is a 506-km- (314-mile-) long, waymarked route that runs through the former heartland of the Ancient Phrygians. The main trailhead is at the Phrygian capital of Gordion *(p293)*. From here, the route traverses west, following the path of the Porsuk river (ancient Tembris river) into the Phrygian Valley area, where rock-spire-studded canyons are scattered with Phrygian ruins.

Phrygian Valley

Frig Vadisi

B4 65 km (40 miles) S from Eskişehir

The countryside between Eskişehir and Afyonkarahisar is speckled with the monuments of the Iron Age Phrygians, set amid valleys of wind- and water-whittled rock like a mini-Cappadocia *(p324)*. Altogether, this region is known as Phrygian Valley though it comprises several different areas. It's best explored by car as transport options are thin.

The main site is **Midas City**, in Yazılıkaya village, 65 km (40 miles) south of Eskişehir. This collection of temple façades, cisterns, tombs, altars and chambers, all hewn out of the rugged rock, is the remnants of a Phrygian cult-centre. It's centred round the monumental Midas Tomb, which despite the name, as with the name of the site itself, has no known connection with King Midas and isn't a tomb. The monument is a temple, dedicated to the Anatolian goddess Cybele, and its façade is covered in reliefs.

↑ Admiring a view of the pretty Ottoman houses in the city of Sivrihisar

↑ Enjoying a gondola ride along the Porsuk river in Eskişehir

Heading south, Phrygian Valley's other major site is the Phrygian necropolis home to the Aslantaş ('Lion Rock') Tomb with its carved lions. The site is 35 km (22 miles) north of Afyonkarahisar, near Lake Emre.

Midas City
Midas Şehir Yazılıkaya
8am–5pm daily
muze.gov.tr

Eskişehir

B4 Valilik Binası, ground floor; (0222) 230 17 52

Dominating the main road from Istanbul to Ankara, Eskişehir (ancient Dorylaeum) has prospered from trade for centuries, but has also been ravaged by passing armies. It was badly damaged during the War of Independence and has few historical monuments. Today, it is a major railway junction, as well as the home base of the Turkish air force.

Eskişehir has a large student population and is also a mining centre, with supplies of borax, chrome and manganese, as well as meerschaum (or "sea foam"), a soft, porous, heat-resistant, light white clay used to make elaborate carved tobacco pipes, which are popular among visitors to Turkey. The **Meerschaum Museum** (Lületaşı Müzesi) has displays of historic pipes and old photos of the mines. You can watch carvers at work on Sakarya Caddesi, and purchase pipes and other items made from meerschaum. Additionally, you can also jump on a gondola ride along the Porsuk river, which will take you around the city.

Meerschaum Museum
İki Eylül Cad
(0222) 233 05 82
9am–5pm Tue–Sun

Çavdarhisar (Aizanoi)

B4 (0274) 223 62 13
Apr–Oct: 9am–7pm daily; Nov–Mar: 9am–5pm daily

The Phrygian site at Aizanoi (today's Çavdarhisar) does not feature on most tourists' itineraries, but a visit here will be highly rewarding. Aizanoi reached its zenith in the 2nd century CE, when it was transformed from a minor set-tlement into a large, thriving city and sanctuary of Zeus, ruler of the gods. Today, the nearby cave at Steunos can be reached only with a four-wheel-drive vehicle.

The most impressive remains are of the Temple of Zeus, built during the reign of Emperor Hadrian (117–138 CE). There is a crypt underneath the temple that is believed to have been the seat of the cult of Cybele, the mother goddess of Anatolia.

The scattered remains of a theatre, municipal gymnasium and stadium are visible today. These were envisaged on a scale that would rival cities like Ephesus or Pergamon. In 1970, an earthquake demolished much of the site. Some fine mosaics of Phrygian gods can be seen in the ruins of the bathhouse and gymnasium.

STAY

La Vie Konak

This Ottoman mansion, within easy strolling distance of all the Odunparazı district sights, is known for its helpful staff and comfortable rooms.

B4 Mücellit Sok 5, Eskişehir
0544 128 2626

Yuva Otel

The rooms inside this Ottoman house are all about contemporary minimalist style.

B4 Vehbi Cem Aşkun Sok 2, Eskişehir
0532 282 9756

Tea leaves being sorted in Rize

THE BLACK SEA

Ancient Greeks founded colonies along the Black Sea coastline from the 8th century BCE onwards. Known in antiquity as the Kingdom of Pontus, the region was annexed by Rome in 63 BCE and later absorbed into the Byzantine Empire. As the Byzantines lost their Anatolian heartland to the Seljuk Turk advance in the 11th century, the Black Sea's Kingdom of Trebizond (1204–1461) rose as a smaller Christian state.

By the 15th century, the Black Sea coastline became part of the Ottoman Empire. Ports like Sinop were vital for the Ottoman navy, while agricultural towns like Giresun remained key for their exports. Throughout the Ottoman era, the coast continued to be home to a large community of Orthodox Christian Pontic Greeks, while people originally from Armenia and Georgia who converted to Islam became part of the Black Sea's distinctive Laz and Hemşin cultures.

In the 20th and 21st centuries, the importance of industry in the area has continued. The city of Rize's tea plantations began producing large-scale crops in the 1940s, and today the city is closely associated with Turkey's tea-growing industry. Meanwhile, ongoing hazelnut exports are a major economic force in Giresun today.

ISTANBUL
p56

THRACE AND THE SEA OF MARMARA
p176

ANKARA AND WESTERN ANATOLIA
p272

CAPPADOCIA AND CENTRAL ANATOLIA
p318

4 AMASRA
5 KÜRE MOUNTAINS NATIONAL PARK
1 SAFRANBOLU
6 KASTAMONU

İnebolu
Abana
Ayancık
Sinop
Cide
Gerze
Bartın
BARTIN
KASTAMONU
SINOP
Zonguldak
Zonguldak Airport
Boyabat
Taşköprü
Durağan
Ereğli
İstanbul
Kandıra
Akçakoca
ZONGULDAK
Karabük
Araç
Altınkaya Barajı
Ilgaz Dağı Milli Parkı
Tosya
Vezirköprü
Kocaeli
Sakarya
Düzce
Çerkeş
Osmancık
Havza
Geyve
Kızılcahamam
Bilecik
Nallıhan
Bozüyük
AMASYA
Ankara
Delice
Eskişehir
ESKİŞEHİR
Polatlı
Karakeçili
Sorgun
Kütahya
KÜTAHYA
Çifteler
YOZGAT
KIRŞEHİR
Gediz
Kırşehir
Boğazlıyan
Uşak
Afyonkarahisar
UŞAK
AFYONKARAHİSAR
Cihanbeyli
Nevşehir
Kayseri
AKSARAY
Akşehir
Aksaray
DENİZLİ
Kaklık
Konya
Isparta
ISPARTA
Beyşehir
KONYA
Çeltikçi
Ereğli
ANTALYA
Karaman
Korkuteli
Antalya
Mersin
Mut
MERSİN
Alanya
Finike
Gazipaşa
Silifke
Aydıncık

0 kilometres 100
0 miles 100
N

THE BLACK SEA
Must Sees
1 Safranbolu
2 Trabzon
3 Sumela Monastery
Experience More
4 Amasra
5 Küre Mountains National Park
6 Kastamonu
7 Samsun
8 Zigana
9 Gümüşhane
10 Bayburt
11 Uzungöl
12 Rize
13 Fırtına Valley
14 Hopa
15 Artvin
16 Yusufeli
RUSSIA
GEORGIA
Black Sea
SYRIA
Anapa
Novorossiysk
Adygeysk
Belorechensk
Nevinnomyssk
Goryachy Klyuch
Cherkessk
Dzhubga
Tuapse
Solenoe
Karachayevsk
Sochi
Adler
Gantiadi
Terskol
Lakhamula
Pitsunda
Sokhumi
Ochamchire
Tsageri
Zugdidi
Samtredia
Poti
Khulo
Batumi
Bafra
SAMSUN
Terme
Samsun–Çarşamba Airport
Ünye
Ordu
Bulancak
Giresun
ORDU
Taşova
Gölköy
SUMELA MONASTERY
Dereli
GIRESUN
ZIGANA
GÜMÜŞHANE
Şebinkarahisar
TRABZON
Trabzon Airport
RIZE
UZUNGÖL
BAYBURT
HOPA
Borçka
ARDAHAN
ARTVIN
Ardeşen
FIRTINA VALLEY
YUSUFELI
Göle
Oltu
İspir
Narman
Horasan
ERZURUM
Erzurum
Turhal
Reşadiye
Tokat
İmranlı
Yıldızeli
Sivas
EASTERN ANATOLIA p342
Erzincan
ERZINCAN
SIVAS
Kangal
Gürün
Pınarbaşı
MALATYA
Elâzığ
ELAZIĞ
Malatya
KAHRAMANMARAŞ
Saimbeyli
Gölbaşı
ADIYAMAN
Adiyaman
Siverek
ŞANLIURFA
Şanlıurfa
Gaziantep
KILIS
HATAY
Gouvernement Aleppo
Raqqa Governorate
10
850
855
865
40
100
50
915
950
200
877
260
300
815
825
360
52
885

SAFRANBOLU

C3 Kayadibi Sok 1; safranbolu.gov.tr

Safranbolu's character unfolds across three distinct historic districts. Kıranköy, a former non-Muslim quarter with European-style stone houses, is where artisans lived above their shops. Over in Çukur lie half-timbered workshops, while the Bağlar summer resort is where spacious garden homes can be found.

Cinci Hanı

Çeşme Mah, Cinci Han Sok
cincihanotel.com

The 350-year-old Cinci Hanı, a refuge for travelling merchants and now a hotel, gives a good idea of the scale of commerce centuries ago. This imposing stone caravanserai was commissioned in 1645 by the influential Cinci Hoca. Its massive, fortress-like walls enclose a vast central courtyard, which is surrounded by two storeys of arched arcades. The *han* was originally built with 63 rooms to accommodate merchants, their goods, and their animals, serving as a vital and secure stop on the Silk Road. Today, non-guests are welcome to admire the architecture from the courtyard or visit the restaurant.

Köprülü Mehmet Paşa Mosque

Köprülü Mehmet Paşa Camii

Çeşme, Celal Bayar Cad 19 Daily

The mosque, located near the massive Cinci Hanı, opened for worship in 1661. It was commissioned by the Grand Vizier Köprülü Mehmet Paşa and is the largest mosque in Safranbolu. A fine example of 17th-century Ottoman architecture, its helmet-shaped dome is a key feature. The complex includes a library, a central ablution fountain and a rare 19th-century sundial.

Kazdağlı Mosque

Kazdağlıoğlu Camii

Çeşme Mah, Çarşı Meydanı Daily

Located in the main square, the mosque was built in 1779. It was constructed on the site of an older mosque at the entrance to the historic bazaar. The building is a classic square-plan Ottoman design, constructed from stone and brick and covered by a large brick dome.

Did You Know?

Saffron fields made Safranbolu a prominent 17th-century trade-route stop.

↑ Safranbolu's historic Ottoman houses terraced on the surrounding hills

It features a three-part portico for latecomers and a single-balcony brick minaret.

Market Area

Safranbolu Eski Çarşı

Eski Çarşı (Old Bazaar)
safranbolu.bel.tr

Restored *konaks* line the narrow Arasta Sokak (Market Street). Some of these old houses have been turned into guesthouses, complete with historic décor and furniture.

Kaymakamlar House

Kaymakamlar Konağı

Hıdırlık Yokuşu Sok, Eski Çarşı **9am-5:30pm daily**
safranbolu.bel.tr

Safranbolu's historic merchant-mansions have been saved from falling into dilapidation by being turned into boutique hotels, cafés and shops. As a result, much of their maze-like original layout has been sacrificed for modern comforts. This house, preserved as a museum, is a time capsule of traditional Safranbolu style. Inside, it's all polished dark-wood floors, skinny staircases, painted timber ceilings, and rooms that are stacked to the brim with traditional furniture and fittings as they would have been in the 19th century.

STAY

Leyla Hanım Konağı

This hotel's rooms feature Safranbolu's signature panelled walls of wood cupboards. The garden area comes with a plungepool, resident tortoises and sweeping views.

Hükümet Sok 25
leylahanimkonak.com

Gülevi

These three traditional houses, hemming a sprawling garden, have been updated to create a boutique with rooms that effortlessly merge contemporary luxury with heritage design.

Mescit Sok 24
canbulat.com.tr

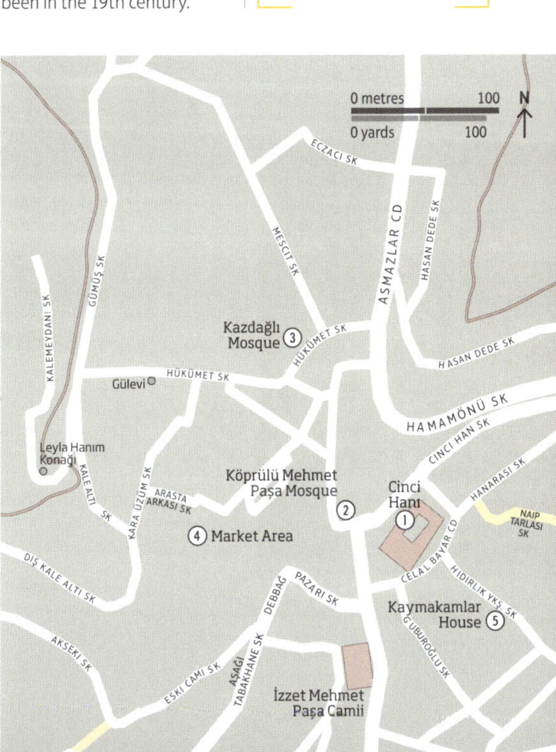

A SHORT WALK
SAFRANBOLU

Distance 0.6 km (0.4 miles) **Time** 20 minutes
Nearest bus stop Safranbolu Otogar

Due to its important architectural heritage, Safranbolu has been declared a World Heritage Site. In Ottoman times, the town lay on a major trade route. Safranbolu's market area, a warren of narrow streets and merchant shops, has many restored Ottoman dwellings. Its many handsome three-storey, stone-and-timber *konaks* (mansions) were erected by wealthy merchants and artisans.

Today, the market maintains its historical charm with shops selling crafts, textiles and spices along with delicious double-roasted Turkish delight.

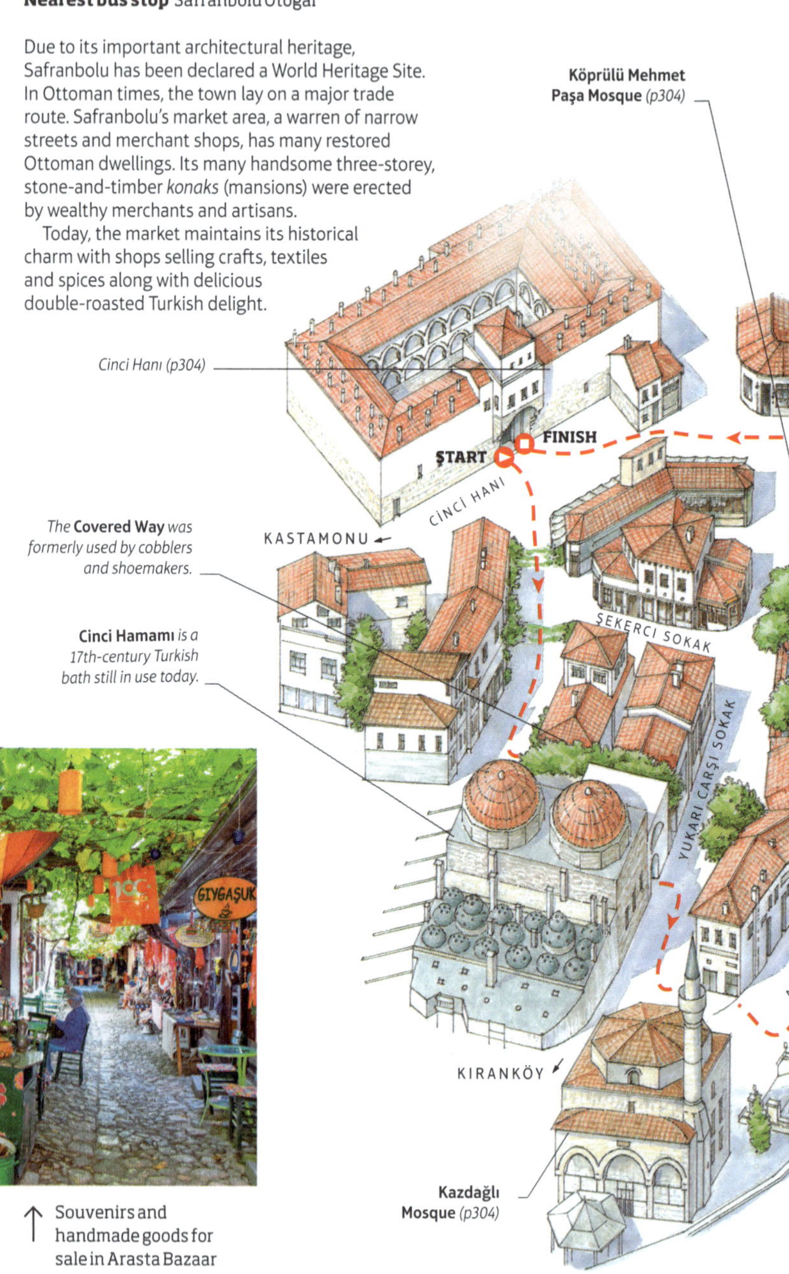

↑ Souvenirs and handmade goods for sale in Arasta Bazaar

Locator Map

For more detail see p305

↑ Cobbled street lined with souvenir shops and historical buildings, Safranbolu

GRAIN MARKET

KUNDURACILAR SOKAK

ESKI HAMAM SOKAK

CEBICI SOKAK

ARASTA SOKAK

MÜTEÜSO SOKAK

SOKAK

An interesting **sundial** *occupies the shady courtyard of the Köprülü Mehmet Paşa Mosque.*

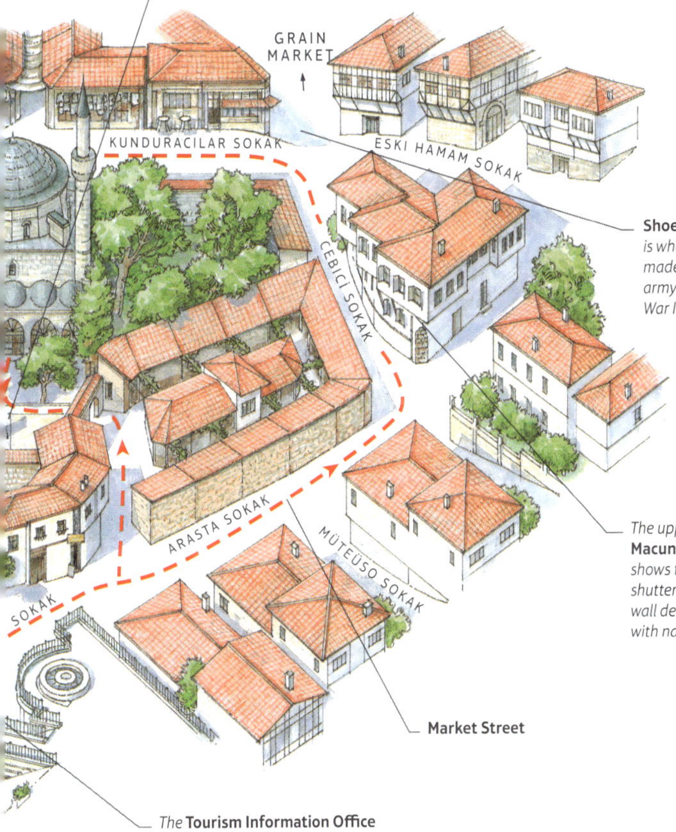

Shoemakers' Street *is where boots were made for the Ottoman army during World War I.*

The upper storey of **Macunlar Mansion** *shows typical wooden shutters and stencilled wall decorations made with natural dyes.*

Market Street

The **Tourism Information Office** *is located in the Arasta (market) area. It is based within a restored original Ottoman house, built in the distinctive style for which Safranbolu is famous.*

0 metres 25

0 yards 25

N

TRABZON

F3 İskenderpaşa Mah, Belediye Cad; (0462) 326 47 60

The earliest evidence of civilization in Trabzon dates from 7000 BCE. At the beginning of the 13th century, the Comnene dynasty established a Byzantine state with its capital at Trabzon. In 1461, Trabzon fell under Ottoman rule.

GREAT VIEW
Boztepe Summit

For panoramic vistas across Trabzon's coast, take the staircase behind the 14th-century ruin of Kızlar Monastery (a nunnery) to this summit's observation deck and café.

①   

Hagia Sophia

Aya Sofya

Ayasofya Müzesi
Dawn-dusk daily

This restored 13th-century Byzantine church, situated just a kilometre from the city centre, is by far the most impressive sight in Trabzon. It was originally built by the Comnene emperor, Manuel VII Palaeologus. In 1577, it was converted to a mosque and, after serving as an ammunition depot and also as a hospital, became a museum in 1957. In 2013, the museum was controversially reconsecrated as a mosque.

The patterned mosaics here date from Byzantine times, and you can still see the original coloured marble covering of the floor. Restoration work on the old frescoes is intermittent. The best frescoes, in the narthex, are perfectly visible, while the faded ones in the nave are hidden behind a screen.

St Anne's Church

Küçük Ayvasıl Kilisesi

Kahraman Maraş Cad

An Armenian church built in the 9th century, St Anne's has a beautiful exterior and the entrance is adorned with crucifixes and angels. With advance notice to the tourism office, groups are allowed inside to view the interior. Another Armenian church, St Basil's (Büyük Ayvasil), is also located nearby.

Gülbahar Mosque and Tomb

Gülbahar Hatun Camii

Şenol Güneş Cad

Built in 1514 by Sultan Selim the Grim in memory of his mother, Gülbahar, this is one of the few mosques in the city that was not originally

a church. Gülbahar was noted for her charity work, and the mosque was built as part of an *imaret*, an Ottoman social welfare institution consisting of a soup kitchen and hostel for students and the poor. The main place of worship was the black-and-white stone section, with its five cupolas. The mosque is all that remains of the complex. Just to the east is Gülbahar's octagonal tomb.

The Byzantine Hagia Sophia Mosque overlooking the Black Sea

New Juma Mosque

Yeni Cuma Camii

Follow signs from Fatih Hamamı on Kasım Sok
Dawn-dusk daily

In the 14th century, this was the Church of St Eugenius, named for the martyred 5th-century archbishop of Carthage. In Ottoman times, the church became a mosque.

Trabzon Museum

Trabzon Müzesi

Uzun Sok, Zeytinlik Cad 10 (0462) 322 38 22 9am-5:30pm daily

Trabzon Museum occupies the Kostaki Mansion, built between 1898 and 1913 for a wealthy Greek banker. The finely restored house is a stunning example of Italian Baroque and Rococo style, with most materials imported from Italy. Its opulent interiors feature lavish ceiling paintings and murals. The ground floor displays the mansion's original reception rooms, while other floors contain displays of local archaeology, including Roman and Byzantine artifacts, and ethnography, such as traditional clothing and weaponry.

EAT

Şehir Klubü Restoran

This tavern is where locals head to eat *hamsi* (Black Sea anchovies) and meze.

Nemlioğlu Cemal Sok 1 trabzon sehirkulubu.com

Cemilusta

Cemilusta's menu ranges from specialities such as *kuymak* (cheese fondue) and *turşu kavurma* (sautéed pickled vegetables) to classic grilled-meat dishes.

Meydan, İskele Cad cemilusta.com.tr

İskele Meyhanesi

A contemporary *meyhane* (Turkish tavern) featuring lots of meze dishes and fresh seafood.

Şht İbrahim Karaoğlanoğlu Cad 40 0532 408 0272

SUMELA MONASTERY

SÜMELA MANASTIRI

F3 55 km (34 miles) S of Trabzon, in Altındere National Park
Lower entrance: (0462) 230 19 66; Upper Entrance: (0462) 531 10 64
Apr-Oct: 9am-6pm daily; Nov-Mar: 8am-4pm daily

Sumela Monastery sits high up on the cliffs of Mount Mela, south of Trabzon. It was founded in the 4th century by two Greek monks, Barnabas and Sophronius, who were guided to the site by an icon of the Virgin, allegedly painted by St Luke.

After the deaths of Barnabas and Sophronius, Sumela became a place of pilgrimage. Dramatically clinging to a sheer rock face 1,200 m (3,900 ft) above the Altındere Valley, it was decorated with frescoes depicting biblical scenes from the life of Christ and the Virgin Mary. Its treasures once included priceless manuscripts and silver plates. Though rebuilt several times, the ruins visible today date largely from the 19th century.

In the Ottoman era, Sumela enjoyed the protection of the sultans, but it was abandoned following the 1923 population exchange between Greece and Turkey and suffered severe damage during the War of Independence. Extensive restoration work has since been carried out to preserve the monastery.

INSIDER TIP
Forest Path

A 1-km (0.5-mile) path winds through pine forest to the often mist-shrouded monastery. It takes 30 minutes to make the steep ascent, offering dramatic views along the way.

← Exploring the inner courtyard of the Sumela Monastery, and *(inset)* dramatic setting of the monastery within a steep cliff

Though badly damaged by vandals, lovely fresco panels cover the walls of the church.

The cells used by the Greek Orthodox monks as living quarters are ranged along the five-storey outside building overlooking the Altındere valley.

Illustration of the Sumela Monastery on Mount Mela ↑

↑ Aerial view of Ilıca waterfall in Küre Mountains National Park

EXPERIENCE MORE

Amasra

C3 Mehmet Paşa Cad 1 D2A

The picturesque and tranquil town of Amasra is located about 15 km (9 miles) from Bartın. In the 6th century BCE, Amasra was called Sesamus, and its inhabitants were known as Megara. By the 9th century CE, Amasra was of sufficient importance to be designated a bishopric. It was destroyed by Arab raiders, and then rebuilt in the 12th century by the Genoese.

They recognized the trading advantages that Amasra could give them and rented the castle and harbour from the Byzantines. The two fortresses built by the Genoese during the 14th century can still be seen today. One overlooks the main harbour and the other sits at the harbour mouth. Amasra came under Ottoman rule in 1460.

Interesting places to see in the town include the **Fatih Mosque**, a former Byzantine church, and the 19th-century **İskele Mosque**. Some portions of the city walls are still standing.

PICTURE PERFECT
Güzelcehisar Lava Columns

From Amasra, head 36 km (22 miles) south-west to Güzelcehisar's coastal boardwalk. The Late Cretaceous period basalt lava columns line this 5-km- (3-mile-) long stretch of cliffs.

Fatih Mosque
Town centre Daily (except during prayer times)

İskele Mosque
On the harbour Daily (except during prayer times)

Küre Mountains National Park

Küre Dağları Milli Parkı

C3 95 km W of Kastamonu

The thick fir- and beech-forested Küre Mountains stretch for over 300 km (186 miles), scattered with canyons, waterfalls and cave systems. It is one of Turkey's most richly biodiverse areas, home to 157 endemic flora species, 32 of which are rare.

The park's most famous sight is steep Horma Canyon where a 3-km-(1.9-mile-) long wooden boardwalk snakes above the canyon's turquoise stream, ending at gushing Ilıca waterfall. Near Muratbaşı village, an observation deck offers panoramic views over Valla Canyon's deep, 16-km- (10-mile-) long slash. There is a hiking trail network through the mountains, but, unfortunately, the routes are overgrown and not way-marked, so hiking should only be attempted by very experienced walkers with a local guide.

Kastamonu

C3 Cumhuriyet Meydanı

Kastamonu is well known for outdoor activities as

well as for crafts. The pastures of nearby Daday offer some of the very finest trail riding in all of Turkey. The local women are famed for hand-printed tablecloths and upholstery fabrics made from cotton and flax. Other specialities of the area include colourful knitted wool socks and fruit jams.

During the 11th century, Kastamonu was controlled by the powerful Comnene family, rulers of Trabzon *(p308)*. Indeed, the town's name probably comes from Castra Comneni (Latin for "camp of the Comnenes").

The town fell under Ottoman rule in 1459. During this era, the region around Kastamonu produced rice, iron, cotton fabrics and mohair, mostly for export. Kastamonu Castle was built by the Byzantines in the 12th century and was kept in good repair by the Seljuks and Ottomans. Today, its remains serve as a fire tower and lookout point.

The **Kastamonu Museum** displays finds from Byzantine and Ottoman times, and has a room that commemorates Atatürk's 1925 visit to the town.

The town's main mosques are the Atabey Mosque (uphill, behind the Aşir Efendi Han shopping centre), with its 40 wooden pillars and stone door, and the İbni Meccar Mosque, built in 1353 by the Çandaroğulları family. This lovely mosque in stone and wood is also known as *Eli güzel* ("beautiful hand").

About 63 km (39 miles) south of Kastamonu is **Ilgaz Mountain National Park**, reachable by dolmuş or your own transport. Visitors to the park can see bears, foxes and deer. There is also a deer breeding and research station. This area offers excellent skiing from November until March. A culinary speciality here is whole lamb, cooked *tandır* style (in a wood-fired clay oven) for four to five hours until the meat falls off the bone. The dish is traditionally eaten with the fingers.

Kastamonu Museum
İsfendiyarbey Mahallesi, Cumhuriyet Cad 6 (0366) 214 10 70
8:30am-5:30pm daily

Ilgaz Mountain National Park
(0336) 212 58 71

Samsun

D3 Atatürk Kültür Merkezi, Atatürk Blv 167; (0362) 431 12 28

Apart from producing a popular cigarette brand, Samsun also holds a proud place in Turkish hearts as the place where Atatürk came after his escape from Istanbul on 19 May 1919, to draw up plans for a Turkish republic. Today, this anniversary is celebrated as a national holiday and a Youth and Sports Day.

Samsun has two museums devoted to the revered memory of Atatürk and his legacy. The **Gazi Museum** occupies a former hotel where he stayed in 1919 and has displays of his clothing, various personal items and a collection of photographs.

The **Archaeological and Ethnographic Museum** is a treasure-trove of antiquities from the surrounding villages. It has Bronze Age artifacts as well as ceramics, bronze and brass implements, glass and mosaics dating from the Hittite, Hellenic, Roman and Byzantine eras. There is also some beautiful gold and silver jewellery, as well as several fine handwritten books and artistic, hand-woven kilims.

About 80 km (50 miles) southwest of Samsun in the **Havza** district are a number of thermal springs *(kaplıca)* that are popular.

Gazi Museum
(0362) 435 75 35
8:30am-6:45pm daily

Archaeological and Ethnographic Museum
Cumhuriyet Meydanı (0362) 431 68 28 Apr-Oct: 9am-7pm daily; Nov-Mar: 8am-5pm daily

STAY

Uğurlu Konakları
This welcoming mansion offers personalized service and comfortable rooms with Turkish carpets and dark-wood detailing.

C3 Şeyh Şaban-ı Veli Cad 47, Kastamonu ugurlukonaklari.com

Atatürk Monument in Samsun

A ruined Byzantine church in the old part of Gümüşhane

8 Zigana

 E3

After visiting the Sumela Monastery, travellers can return to Trabzon or continue further southwest to reach the spectacular alpine area known as Zigana and situated in the Kalkanlı Mountains. With only one resort and limited skiing available, most visitors prefer to come for day trips here.

Fog and snow cover the Zigana area for about seven months of the year, and it is usually damp here. Heavy winter snowfalls make access difficult and even dangerous.

To get to Zigana, you can drive through the 1,500-m (4,291-ft) mountain tunnel, the longest in Turkey.

A more scenic route runs parallel to the main 885 road through Hamsiköy village. It is worth stopping here to sample the excellent local cuisine. The speciality is a nourishing, creamy rice pudding.

9 Gümüşhane

 E3 **Valilik Binası; (0456) 213 10 07**

Gümüşhane (silver works) takes its name from the rich deposits of silver ore found here. In the late 16th century, silver was more valuable than gold. However, by the late 19th century, the silver industry had declined.

Before World War I, the area was a focus of conflict between the Russians and the Ottomans, for Gümüşhane occupied a strategic position on the trade route between Anatolia and Persia (Iran).

Here, visitors can explore the surrounding castles, and several mosques. The most interesting of these is the Süleymaniye (or Küçük) Camii. There is one hammam (Turkish bath), offering separate facilities for men and women.

10 Bayburt

 F3

Situated on the Çoruh River, Bayburt is the capital of the smallest of Turkey's 81 provinces. Bayburt Castle was probably built in Byzantine times, but there is evidence of an older fortress on the site.

The castle has a violent history. It had to be rebuilt by the Byzantine Emperor Justinian and was repaired by both Seljuks and Ottomans following various attacks. At its peak, there were 300 houses within the complex. Provision for daily needs included a bakery and flour mill. The community even produced its own paint.

Today, visitors can see a theological school, a mosque, hammams and kitchens, as well as a

Sweeping view of Bayburt city from Bayburt Castle

Did You Know?

Gümüşhane is renowned for its rosehip *(kuşburun)* syrup and sweet cherry jam *(kiraz reçeli)*.

INSIDER TIP
Baksı Museum

This art museum *(baksi.org)* in Bayraktar village, Bayburt, offers a unique setting, where a modern, industrial dome houses cutting-edge contemporary art displayed alongside traditional artisan work.

dervish lodge. The eastern corner contains the remains of a church built between the 8th and 14th centuries.

About 20 km (12 miles) northwest of Bayburt are the remains of underground cities dating from Byzantine times. These are usually open to visitors. For details, enquire at the tea garden entrance or at the tourism office in the city centre.

Outside Bayburt, on the way to Aşkale and Erzurum, travellers must negotiate a spectacular mountain pass that rises to the dizzying height of 2,302 m (7,552 ft). Around 45 km (28 miles) from Bayburt is the startlingly modern Baksi Museum, which displays a selection of contemporary art exhibitions and ethnographic displays.

Uzungöl

F3

For mountain scenery, only a few places in Turkey can compare with this alpine lake, which was carved out during the Ice Ages. At an altitude of over 1,000 m (3,280 ft), Uzungöl (Long Lake) is a hidden gem surrounded by lush greenery and remote meadows. Located in a high mountain valley, the lake and village at first appear inaccessible. The surrounding mountain forests and fog, occasionally enveloping the lake at night, also add to the scenery.

Today, Uzungöl is a popular destination, with dozens of hotels ringing the lake. However, visitors can still escape the crowds by hiking and camping in the surrounding hills, fishing or simply relaxing. The local lake trout is excellent.

Outside Bayburt, on the way to Aşkale and Erzurum, travellers must negotiate a spectacular mountain pass that rises to the dizzying height of 2,302 m (7,552 ft).

STAY

Dudi Konak
Perched on the Fırtına Valley slope, this traditional Hemşin timber mansion is Çamlıhemşin's classiest stay.

F3 Konaklar 60, Çamlıhemşin
dudikonagi.com

Çamlıhemşin Taşmektep Otel
Stay in a restored 1937 schoolhouse, now converted into a small hotel with modern rooms.

F3 Halil Şişman Cad, Çamlıhemşin
camlihemsin tasmektep.com

Elevit Tatil Köyü
Located 12 km (7 miles) south of Çamlıhemşin, this hotel offers wooden bungalows and suites.

F3 Zilkale Mevkii, Çamlıhemşin
elevittatilkoyu.com

12 Rize

F3 0.8 km (0.5 miles) west of the city Valilik Binası, A Blok, Kat 5; (0464) 280 17 00

In ancient times, Rize was ruled by the Pontic kings *(p330)* and was known as Rhizus. The name means "rice", although the city is now better known for its tea.

Rize was strongly fortified by the Byzantines in the 6th century and later became part of the Comnene empire. Like Trabzon, it came under Ottoman control in 1461.

In Ottoman times, many people left Rize to seek work in Russia. There they learned the art of bread- and pastry-making, which they brought back with them when they returned. Today, many of Turkey's master pastry chefs and bakers come from Rize.

Visitors will notice many locals clad in the versatile *Rize bezi*, a light cloth made of silk, cotton or wool, in black and purple. It is mainly used as a head covering for women, but also doubles as a useful rain bonnet.

The small **Rize Museum** has some lovely displays of local life and lore.

Rize Museum
Piri Çelebi Mah, PTT Arkası (0464) 214 02 35
9am-5pm Tue-Sun

13 Fırtına Valley

Fırtına Vadisi

F3 42 km (26 miles) E of Rize

East of Rize, the road turns off to the Fırtına Valley. About 20 km (12 miles) further east a second turning goes to Çamlıhemşin. The road rises steeply and the air is filled with the smell of boxwood trees. This area lies deep within the Kaçkar Mountains (Kaçkar Dağları), which reach a peak altitude of 3,932 m (12,900 ft).

The local inhabitants, the Hemşin, were once Christian Armenians who converted to Islam. They delight in their seasonal festivals, folklore traditions and distinctive costumes.

A staple food of the valley is *mıhlama* (gooey dip made from cornflour mixed with cheese), that is served hot from the baking pan. Sometimes, *lor* (white, unsalted cheese) is served alongside *mıhlama* as a breakfast dish.

There are two castles near Çamlıhemşin. One is Kale-i Bala, above the village of Hisarcık Köyü, dating from 200 BCE. Further up the valley is the Zilkalesi (Bell Castle), with eight ramparts overlooking the valley of the Storm River (Fırtına Çayı).

Road conditions can be challenging outside the

↑ Dramatic Zilkalesi rising above trees in the Fırtına Valley

short summer season. A four-wheel-drive is recommended, as local dolmuş services run less frequently in winter.

Locals have devised an ingenious solution for navigating the steep valleys: the *vargel*, a cable car on a pulley system. It is powered by electricity or can be operated manually when needed. This simple yet effective transport offers a striking bird's-eye view of the remote mountain gorges.

Hopa

F3 On W bank of river

Hopa is the last main town before the frontier with Georgia. It is a garrison town, and there is a strong military presence. Hopa was a major port in ancient times, and is still the main seaport (after Trabzon) on the eastern Black Sea coast. Today, the town is dominated by the boat-building industry and a large thermal power station.

Artvin

F3 Katliotopark Binası, Kat 3; (0466) 212 30 71 artvin.gov.tr

Artvin receives more rain than any other place in Turkey, so everything grows wonderfully here. The people of Artvin are known for their many festivals, which feature traditional dancing, games, music, food and costumes.

Around Artvin are a number of beautiful villages. Şavşat, about 55 km (34 miles) to the east on the road to Ardahan, is a lovely alpine hamlet. The road goes on to Veliköy and, 19 km (11 miles) further on, reaches the **Karagöl-Sahara National Park**, which has extensive forests and lakes.

Five dams have been built in the mountains around Artvin and Yusufeli as part of the Çoruh River Development Plan. These dams generate power for the region, but many have drawn criticism as their construction has destroyed parts of the local environment and threatened the survival of native species.

Karagöl-Sahara National Park

(0466) 531 20 29

May-Oct: daily

Yusufeli

F3 68 km (42 miles) S of Artvin or 150 km (93 miles) NE of Bayburt

The area north of Yusufeli is a nature lover's paradise, with some of the most rugged scenery in Turkey. The original town was completely submerged after the completion of the Yusufeli Dam on the Çoruh River in 2023, and residents were relocated to a newly built town above the dam. West of the town, a new tunnel-exit on the highway provides access to the non-submerged section of Tekke village, and the Dört Kilise (Four Churches), a 10th-century Georgian monastery complex.

The twisting road heading north from Yusufeli is the access point to the village of Altıparmak in the Kaçkar Mountains, 31 km (19 miles) north, and Olgunlar, another 25 km (15 miles) southwest on the same road. Both are excellent bases for hiking and climbing in the Kaçkars.

TURKISH TEA

Turkey's first tea plants were brought from Japan in 1878, but the industry did not take off until the 1930s. The moist climate of the Black Sea coast provides superb growing conditions. Rize is the centre of the Turkish tea industry, and the home of the country's Tea Institute (Çay Enstitüsü).

To sample the best tea, look for *tomurcuk* (the flowering bud of the tea bush). Leaves from other parts of the plant are not as flavourful. Turks prefer the black tea sold in local markets; green tea is exported. Specialized fragrant teas are also produced, again mostly for export.

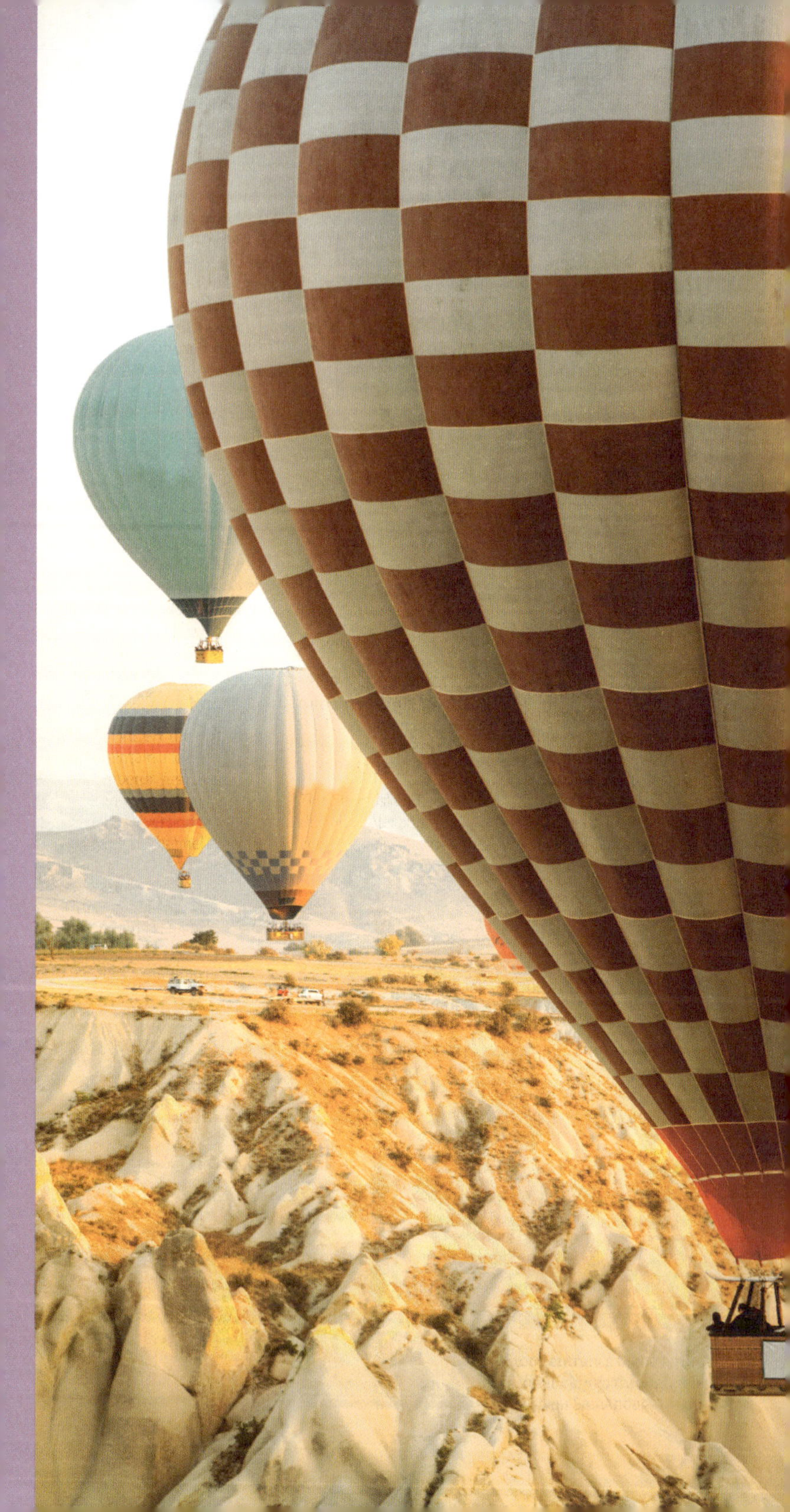

Hot-air balloons rising over Cappadocia

CAPPADOCIA AND CENTRAL ANATOLIA

This central region saw the Bronze Age rise of Anatolia's Hittite civilization. From their capital Hattuşaş (modern Boğazkale) here, the Hittites controlled a territory that encompassed much of modern Turkey. Many of the cities in the region have their roots in Hittite settlements; the Hittites are also thought to have been the first to carve underground defensive structures out of Cappadocia's volcanic tuff landscape.

By the end of the Iron Age, Cappadocia was a kingdom that covered a large stretch of central Anatolia. The Battle of Zele (Zile), near Amasya, was where Julius Caesar famously "Came, Saw, and Conquered" in 47 BCE, though full Roman rule over the region was only secured in 17 CE.

Christianity arrived in Cappadocia by the 3rd century CE, and the early Byzantine period saw the 4th-century Cappadocian Fathers play a key role in developing Christian theology. During the Arab–Byzantine wars from the 7th to 11th centuries, locals utilized and extended the underground structures carved out by the Hittites.

By the 11th century, Seljuk Turks captured much of this region, and Sivas, Tokat and Kayseri became major centres, which continued into the Ottoman era. Today, the region is a key tourist destination, especially the historic cave towns at Göreme.

ANKARA AND WESTERN ANATOLIA
p272
THE EASTERN MEDITERRANEAN
p260
SINOP
KASTAMONU
KARABÜK
ÇANKIRI
ANKARA
KIRIKKALE
ÇORUM
YOZGAT
KIRŞEHIR
AKSARAY
NIĞDE
KONYA
KARAMAN
MERSIN
ADANA
HATTUŞAŞ 3
ALACAHÖYÜK 19
ÇORUM 20
GÖREME OPEN-AIR MUSEUM 1
KAYSERI 2
NEVŞEHIR 5
ZELVE 6
DERINKUYU 7
Ürgüp 8
AVANOS 9
KAYMAKLI 10
MUSTAFAPAŞA 11
MOUNT ERCIYES 13
SOĞANLI 14
NIĞDE 15
GÜZELYURT 16
IHLARA VALLEY 17
AKSARAY 18
Kapadokya Airport
Erkilet International Airport
Hasan Dağı 3,268 m (10,721 ft)
Pozantı Dağı 2,689 m (8,822 ft)
Tuz Gölü
Hirfanlı Barajı
Kızıl Irmak
Delice Çayı
Kırklar Dağı
Ala Dağları
Yay Gölü
Obruk Yaylası
Çamlık Milli Parkı
Sultansazlığı Milli Parkı
Kültepe
Kastamonu
Safranbolu
Karabük
Eskipazar
Çerkeş
Atkaracalar
Ilgaz
Tosya
Saraydüzü
Vezirköprü
Osmancık
Merzifon
İskilip
Mecitözü
Orta
Çankırı
Kızılcahamam
Şabanözü
Kahramankazan
Akyurt
Kalecik
Ankara
Sungurlu
Alaca
Bazlamaç
Boğazkale
Çekerek
Büyükyağli
Kırıkkale
Keskin
Yozgat
Sorgun
Yerköy
Çiçekdağı
Şefaatli
Sarıkaya
Kaman
Çayıralan
Boğazlıyan
Kozaklı
Kırşehir
Mucur
Kulu
Şereflikoçhisar
Haci Bektaş
Ortaköy
Cihanbeyli
Yeşilhisar
Develi
Sultanhanı
Yahyalı
Bor
Kemerhisar
Karapınar
Çumra
Ereğli
Ulukışla
Aladağ
Pozantı
Kazımkarabekir
Karaman
İmamoğlu
100
795
180
190
77
805
200
765
260
25
33
38
021
750
300
815

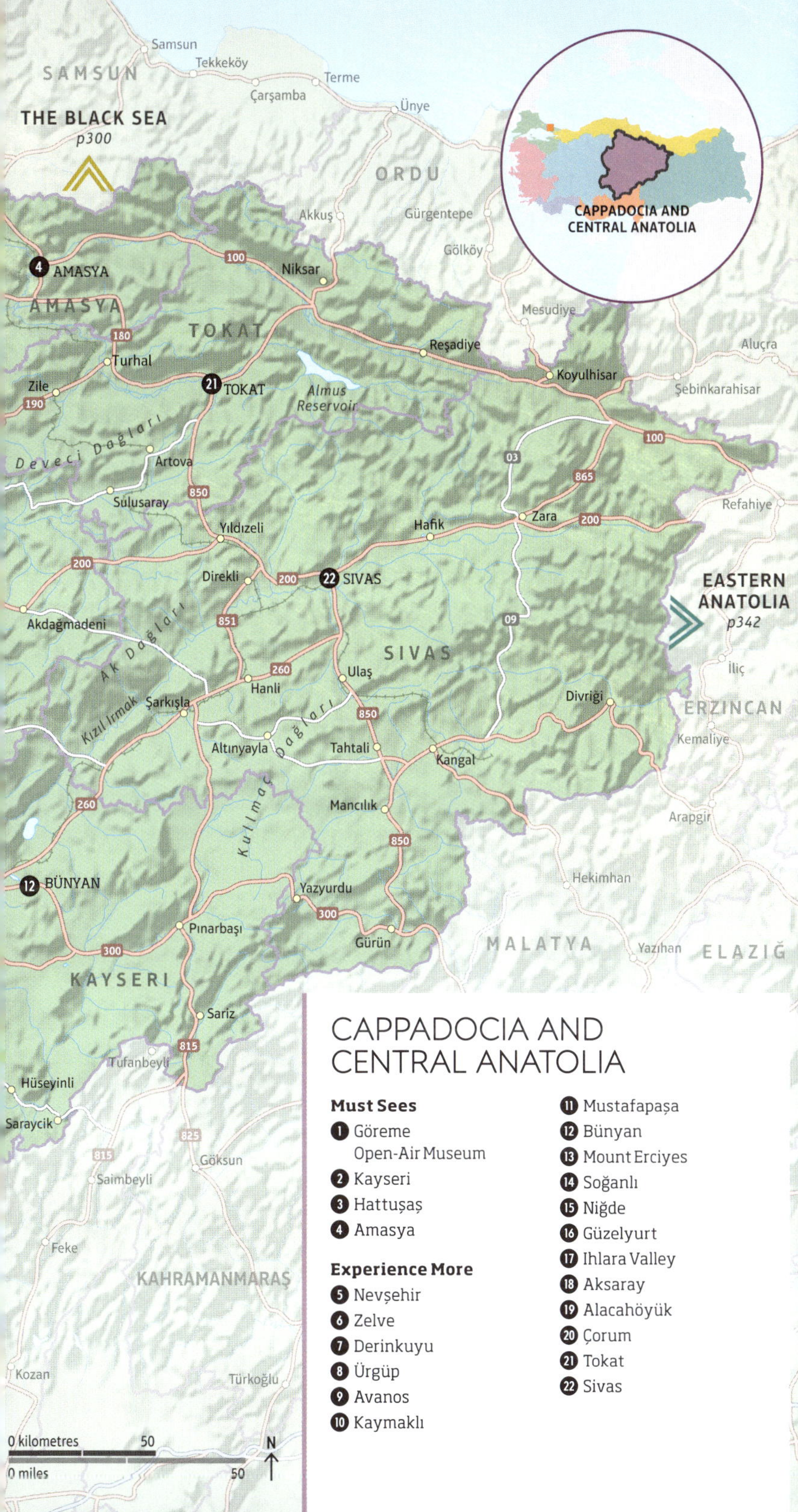

CAPPADOCIA AND CENTRAL ANATOLIA

Must Sees

1. Göreme Open-Air Museum
2. Kayseri
3. Hattuşaş
4. Amasya

Experience More

5. Nevşehir
6. Zelve
7. Derinkuyu
8. Ürgüp
9. Avanos
10. Kaymaklı
11. Mustafapaşa
12. Bünyan
13. Mount Erciyes
14. Soğanlı
15. Niğde
16. Güzelyurt
17. Ihlara Valley
18. Aksaray
19. Alacahöyük
20. Çorum
21. Tokat
22. Sivas

1

GÖREME OPEN-AIR MUSEUM

GÖREME AÇIK HAVA MÜZESI

D4 15 km (9 miles) E of Nevşehir (0384) 271 21 67
Apr-Oct: 8am-7pm daily; Nov-Mar: 8am-5pm daily

The Göreme Valley holds the greatest concentration of rock-cut chapels and monasteries in Cappadocia. Many of the churches feature Byzantine frescoes depicting scenes from the Old and New testaments.

Göreme Open-Air Museum, made up of a number of historic religious structures, is located within the impressive Göreme Valley. The cultural importance of the valley has been recognized by the Turkish government and they have restored and preserved the many caves to create the Göreme Open-Air Museum. The area's significance was such that, in 1985, UNESCO declared the Göreme Valley a World Heritage Site.

At the heart of northern Cappadocia's fairy-tale landscape, the small village of Göreme is extremely popular with tourists. There are dozens of pensions and hotels here (many with cave rooms), as well as restaurants. It is also a good place from which to arrange tours of the region and to take part in outdoor activities ranging from walking the valleys to hot-air ballooning. The main attraction is the village's open-air museum.

INSIDER TIP
Balloon Tour Operators

Keep in mind not all balloon tour operators are reputable. It is wise to check their websites for details on insurance and the number of passengers accommodated in the basket.

STAY

Melek Cave Hotel
The atmospheric cave rooms at this friendly hotel are complemented by the great views over town from its breakfast terrace.
Ünlü Sok 23
melekcave.com

Taşkonak Hotel
This cave hotel offers impeccably decorated rooms, all carved from the rock. The hotel can also help book activities such as balloon flights.
Güngör Sok 23
taskonak.com

The walking route starts at the car park near the entrance.

Monks lived and worked in the Kızlar Monastery, a hollowed-out formation.

→ Rock-cut caves at the Göreme Open-Air Museum, and *(inset)* ceiling frescoes inside Karanlık Church

↓ Key highlights of the Göreme Open-Air Museum

Noted for the sophistication of its frescoes, the Elmalı Church dates from the 11th century.

Barbara Church takes its name from a fresco, which is thought to depict St Barbara.

ROCK FORMATIONS OF CAPPADOCIA

One of Turkey's most popular sights, Cappadocia covers a relatively small area - around 300 sq km (116 sq miles). The area around Nevşehir *(p334)*, together with nearby Ürgüp *(p334)* and Göreme *(p322)*, offers the best opportunities to see the bewitching natural formations for which the region is celebrated.

Cappadocia's distinctive landscape was created around 30 million years ago, when erupting volcanoes blanketed the region with ash. The ash solidified into an easily eroded material called tuff, overlain in places by layers of hard volcanic rock.

Over time, the tuff was worn away, creating distinctive formations, including the capped-cone "fairy chimneys" near Ürgüp. In winter, temperature changes cause the rocks to expand and contract and eventually to disintegrate. In the triangle defined by Nevşehir, Ürgüp and Avanos *(p335)*, the tuff layer was originally up to 100 m (328 ft) thick. As the older tuff continues to erode, younger cones are formed, in a process that has been taking place for around 10 million years.

The softness of the tuff made it easy to excavate in order to create dwellings. In some places, as at Derinkuyu *(p334)*, whole complexes were constructed underground.

↑ Hot-air balloons over rock formations at Göreme Historical National Park

Did You Know?

Volcanic activity in Anatolia is a result of the region's location along the boundaries of two tectonic plates.

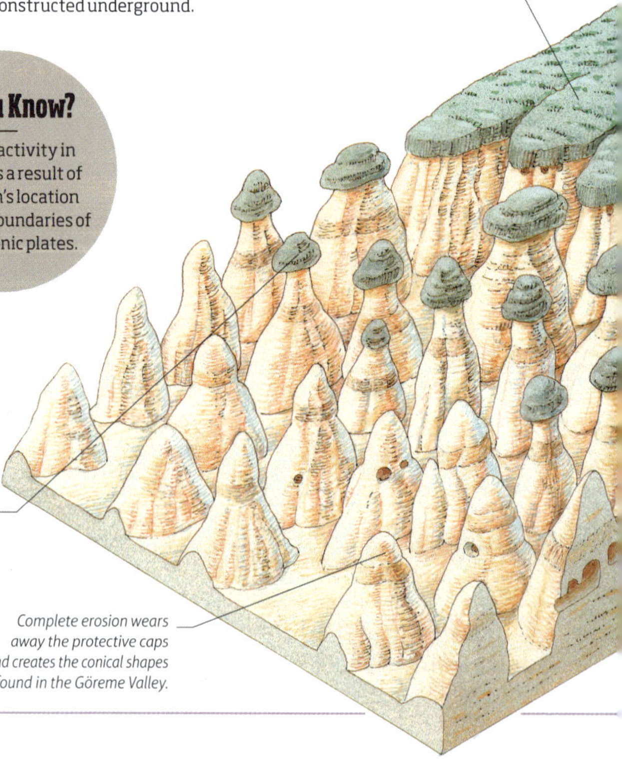

Lava flows harden into a protective layer over the tuff.

Protective caps give a tubular shape to the eroded formation.

Complete erosion wears away the protective caps and creates the conical shapes found in the Göreme Valley.

FAIRY CHIMNEYS

These extraordinary formations are called "fairy chimneys" because early inhabitants of Cappadocia believed that they were the chimneys of fairies, who lived under the ground. Some of them reach heights of up to 40 m (130 ft).

Elongated Shape

These columns are capped with layers of slightly harder material.

Pedestal Shape

Created when a lump of basalt rests atop a tuff column.

Cone Shape

Erosion thins tuff beneath the basalt cap, which then falls off.

1 Towering fairy chimneys capped with hard layers, at Pasabag Valley, Cappadocia.

2 An ancient cave in Nevşehir, topped with basalt, rests upon a tuff column shaped like a pedestal.

3 Distinctive cone-shaped rock formations where erosion has caused the basalt caps to fall off.

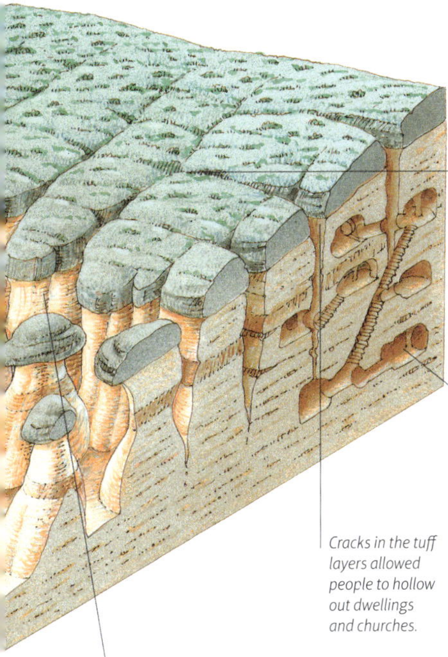

Erosion widens cracks and fissures, separating sections from the main body and allowing for the development of strange shapes.

←

Illustration showing various rock formations and their uses

Underground complexes

Cracks in the tuff layers allowed people to hollow out dwellings and churches.

Cavities below the hard layer are turned into dwellings.

KAYSERI

D4 Osman Kavuncu Blv Selimiye Hoca Ahmet Yesevi Blv 42; (0352) 222 03 63

Dominated by Mount Erciyes, Kayseri has been contested by Persians, Arabs, Mongols and Ottomans. Located at the junction of five major routes, it was an important hub in the Roman road network and the site of an imperial munitions factory.

Gevher Nesibe Medical History Museum

Gevher Nesibe Tıp Tarihi Müzesi

Sinan Park (0352) 222 4777 8:30am-5:30pm daily

The complex also known as the Çifte Medrese consists of two adjoining theological centres, the Gıyasiye Medresesi and the Şifahiye Medresesi. The Seljuks placed great emphasis on learning – this extended to anatomy and medicine. This was the first Seljuk academy of medicine and is also home to the Seljuk Civilization Museum. There was also an operating theatre and accommodation for psychiatric patients here. The architectural scheme incorporates arches, vaulted antechambers *(eyvan)* and an open courtyard.

Three Bazaars and Citadel

Kapalıçarşı ve Kalesi

Behind the Ulu Cami

Kayseri's historic bazaars surround the city's Citadel, creating a lively hub of trade. The Covered Bazaar *(Kapılı Çarşı)* dates back to 1859, while the Bedesten and Vizir Han go back to the 15th and 16th centuries respectively.

Rising next to the bazaars is the Citadel, whose north wall and ramparts were first constructed under Emperor Justinian in the 6th century. However, little of the outer fortifications can be seen today. The black basalt structure originally featured 195 bastions and remains an impressive landmark.

Güpgüpoğlu Stately Home

Güpgüpoğlu Konağı

Tennuri Sok, Cumhuriyet Mah (0352) 222 95 16 8am-5pm Tue-Sun

A family home built between 1417 and 1419, the house has

The Covered Bazaar *(Kapılı Çarşı)* dates back to 1859, while the Bedesten and Vizir Han go back to the 15th and 16th centuries respectively.

←

Kayseri's skyline set against the dramatic slopes of Mount Erciyes

Did You Know?

Kayseri's name comes from Caesarea, a title given in 14 CE to honour Caesar Augustus.

been carefully preserved and restored to its former glory, with each room highlighting specific aspects of Ottoman life. There are guest rooms, a bridal chamber, meeting areas and men's and women's quarters. Notable features are the built-in cupboards *(yüklük)*, and the kitchen area, which consists of a pantry and a large main kitchen *(tokana)*.

Hunat Hatun Mosque Complex

Hunat Hatun Camii ve Medresesi

Seyyid Burhanettin Blv 1
Prayer times

This *külliye* (religious and educational institution adjoining a mosque) was one of the first mosque precincts the Seljuks built in Anatolia, although the minaret was erected in 1726. The complex has a mosque, training centre and hammam (Turkish bath) for men and women, and also includes the mausoleum of Mahperi Hunat Hatun, wife of Alaeddin I Keykubad *(p286)*. Her inscription on the east door dates back to 1238.

Archaeology Museum

Arkeoloji Müzesi

Cumhuriyet Mah, Kazancılar Cad 2 (0352) 222 21 49 and 232 48 12
8am-5pm daily

The museum is located within the Kayseri Castle and has 14 exhibition halls. The displays run in chronological sequence from the Bronze Age to the Byzantine period. The most valuable and interesting items on display at the museum are the series of cuneiform tablets documenting the commercial transactions of the Assyrian trading colony which flourished here during the late Hittite era *(p329)*.

EAT

Kemal Koçak Et Lokantası

An elegant restaurant south of the city centre, famous for its steaks.

Erciyes Blv 38
kemalkocak.com

Chef Remzi Restaurant

Sample local cuisine, served with a twist.

Farabi Cad 50A
chefremzi restaurant.com

Elmacıoğlu İskender Kebap

This kebab restaurant is located in a great spot, just outside the castle.

Millet Cad 5
3522 226 965

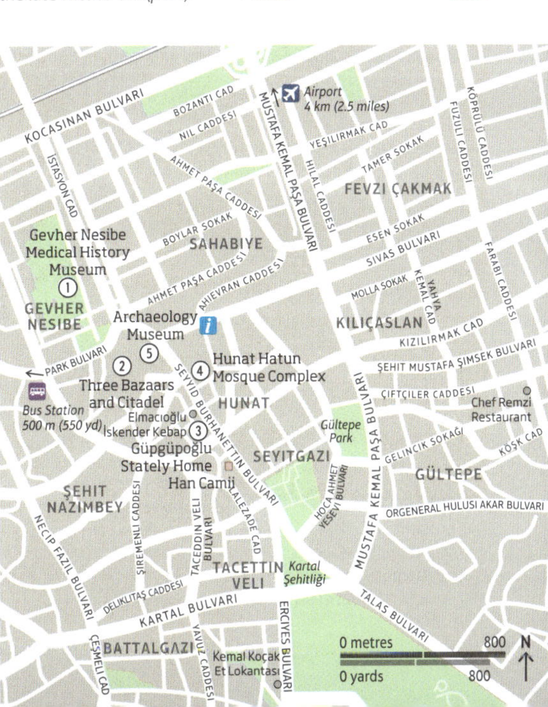

3

HATTUŞAŞ

D3 Part of Çorum Museum, within Hattuşaş National Park
(0364) 452 20 06 8am-5pm daily (Apr-Sep: to 7pm)

Hattuşaş, the ancient Hittite capital city, was built around 1600 BCE in a strategic location. This spot, which has been occupied since the 3rd millennium BCE, is bordered on three sides by steep ravines. A UNESCO World Heritage Site, it is one of the most important ancient sites to be found in Anatolia. Thousands of clay and bronze tablets have been discovered, providing crucial insight into the ancient Hittite civilization.

Lion's Gate

Aslanlıkapı

The Lion's Gate takes its name from the two lion statues that guarded the city over 3,000 years ago. The lions here are only replicas – the originals are now in the Museum of Anatolian Civilizations in Ankara *(p278)*.

Great Temple

Büyük Mabet

One of the best-preserved Hittite temples, the Great Temple was built around 1400 BCE, and was dedicated to the storm god, Teshub. The temple complex here houses ritual chambers, administrative areas and storage rooms.

The Citadel

Büyükkale

The walled citadel was the seat of government at Hattuşaş. A monumental staircase within this structure led up to three courts, one of which also contained the living quarters of the royal household.

Reconstruction of the King's Gate

Kral Kapısı

The monumental King's Gate (Kral Kapı) derives its name from the regal-looking Hittite war god on the stone relief guarding the entrance. The city wall is built with huge, roughly worked stone blocks, and extends for an impressive length of about 7 km (4 miles), circling the Upper and Lower cities. The height of the stone portion was about 6 m (20 ft). Like the other structures in the city, this would have been overlaid with sun-dried brick.

←

The formidable Lion's Gate of the ancient capital city of Hattuşaş, and *(inset)* the sprawling complex of the citadel

HITTITE CIVILIZATION

The Hittites, a major Indo-European civilization, arrived in Anatolia from the Caucasus region around 2000 BCE. Over the next few centuries, they built up a powerful state, with a capital at Hattuşaş (now known as Boğazkale). At its height, the Hittite kingdom controlled much of Anatolia and was a formidable force on the Near Eastern stage, rivalling both Egypt and Babylon. Hittite art reached its peak between 1450 BCE and 1200 BCE, and Hittite artisans were renowned as superb carvers and metalworkers.

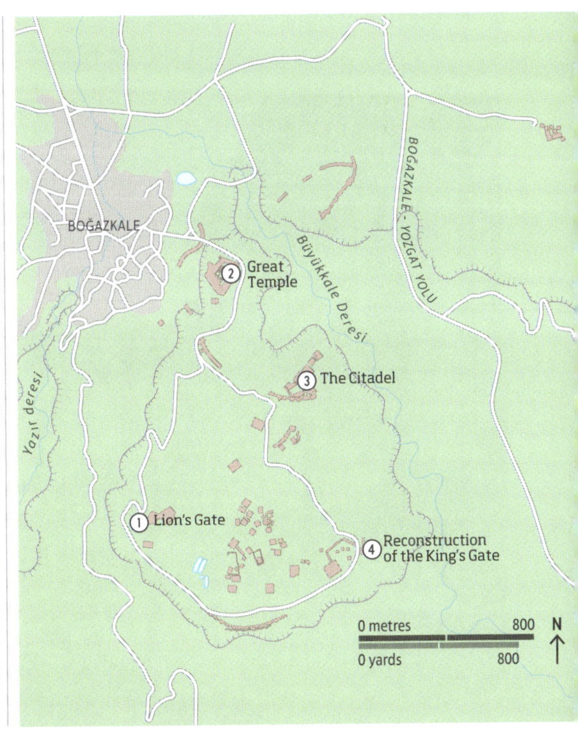

4

AMASYA

D3 2 km (1 mile) W of city centre; (0358) 218 12 39
2 km (1 mile) NE of city centre; (0358) 218 80 12
Atatürk Cad, near Bimarhane; (0358) 218 50 02

Lying in a secluded valley of the Yeşilırmak River, Amasya has seen the passage of nine civilizations, from the Hittites to the Ottomans. In the 15th century, Amasya was second only to Bursa *(p188)* in cultural and trading importance. By the 1800s, the city excelled as the empire's leading centre for Islamic education.

Citadel

Kale

The original Hittite fortress was reinforced by the Pontic king, Mithridates. He built eight layers of walls, with 41 towers, to protect a self-sustaining complex with a palace, cisterns, storage areas and a cemetery. Accessible by car or an hour's walk on paved roads, the fortress offers splendid views of the Rock Tombs.

Rock Tombs

Kral Kaya Mezarları

Entrance under the railway line off Hazeranlar Sok 8am-5pm daily (to 6pm in summer)

The Rock Tombs of the Pontic kings are among Amasya's most striking landmarks, carved high into the limestone cliffs. Dating from around 333 BCE to 44 BCE, these monumental tombs span both the Hellenistic and Roman periods. About 1 km (0.5 miles) from the main tombs lies the Mirror Cave (Aynalı Mağrası). It is famous for a vivid wall painting depicting the Virgin Mary and the Apostles, a later addition from the Byzantine era.

Teaching Hospital Complex

Daruşşifa/Bimarhane Medresesi

Atatürk Cad 9am-5pm daily (to 6pm in summer)

The outer walls of the original asylum date back to 1308. The complex served not

Did You Know?

Many Ottoman princes served as governors in Amasya before becoming sultan of the empire.

only as a hospital but also as a medical research centre, a school for interns and a hospice for those suffering from mental illness. Physicians here also used music and speech therapy to soothe and heal disturbed patients. The intricately carved front portal, adorned with fine stonework, represents a rare architectural remnant of the Ilhanid Persian empire of the 13th century. Today, this beautifully restored building houses a café and the offices of the local Music and Fine Arts Directorate.

④   

Hazeranlar Mansion

Hazeranlar Konağı

Hattuniye Mah
(0358) 280 17 00
For restoration until 2027

This historic mansion, one of Amasya's most elegant examples of 19th-century Ottoman architecture, dates back to 1865. It was commissioned by a local treasury officer, Hasan Talat Efendi, in memory of his sister, Hazeran Hanım (Lady Hazeran). The layout, typical of the time, features separate areas for men and women. The carpets, from the late Ottoman period, are particularly fine.

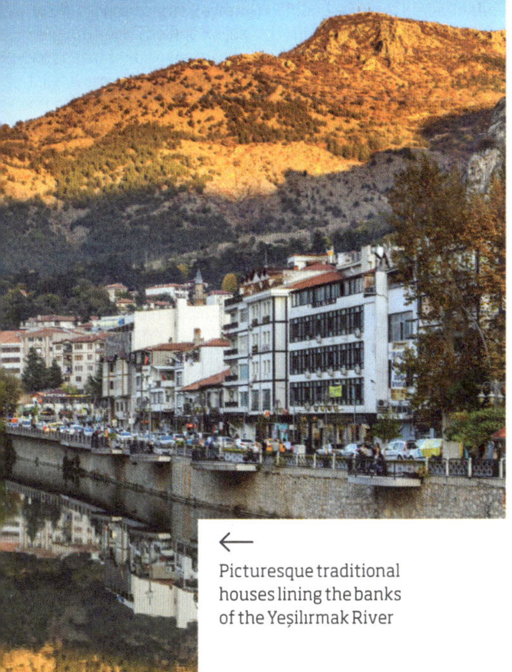

←
Picturesque traditional houses lining the banks of the Yeşilırmak River

STAY

Lalehan Hotel

A stylish riverfront hotel, Lalehan offers comfortable rooms with contemporary décor, and a rooftop terrace.

Mehmet Paşa Cad 31
lalehanotel.com

Bayezid Han Konak

This 19th-century mansion has now been converted into a boutique hotel.

Ziya Paşa Blv 4A
bayezidhan.com

Çifte Konak Butik Otel

Conveniently situated in the city centre, this impressive Ottoman mansion features period furnishings.

Habibi Sok 44
0544 924 3666

⑤ 

Sultan Beyazıt Mosque and Theological College

Sultan Beyazıt II Kullıyesı

Mustafa Kemal Paşa Cad
During prayer times

This was Amasya's primary theological complex, surpassing all other centres of religious learning in the region. Built during the prosperous and stable reign of Sultan Beyazıt II (1481–1512), the college educated young students in both religious principles and loyalty to the state, ensuring the continuity of Ottoman values. The wonderful domes and finely decorated portals are inspirational in themselves, and the lovely oak trees in the courtyard are said to date back to the mosque's foundation itself.

⑥ 

Archaeology and Ethnography Museum

Arkeoloji ve Etnografik Müzesi

Mustafa Kemal Paşa Cad 91 (0358) 218 45 13
Apr–Oct: 8am–7pm daily; Nov–Mar: 8am–5pm daily
Noon–1pm daily

The museum has been recently renovated and modernized, creating a more spacious and engaging environment for visitors. Among its most notable exhibits is a finely crafted bronze statue of the Hittite storm god, along with an impressive collection of Roman coins that were minted locally.

However, the museum is best known for its impressive collection of mummies, dating from the Ilhanid period (around the 14th century), when Amasya was an important administrative and cultural centre under Mongol rule. These well-preserved mummies, discovered in Anatolia, were once kept in a dim and

→ Chandelier on display at the Archaeology and Ethnography Museum

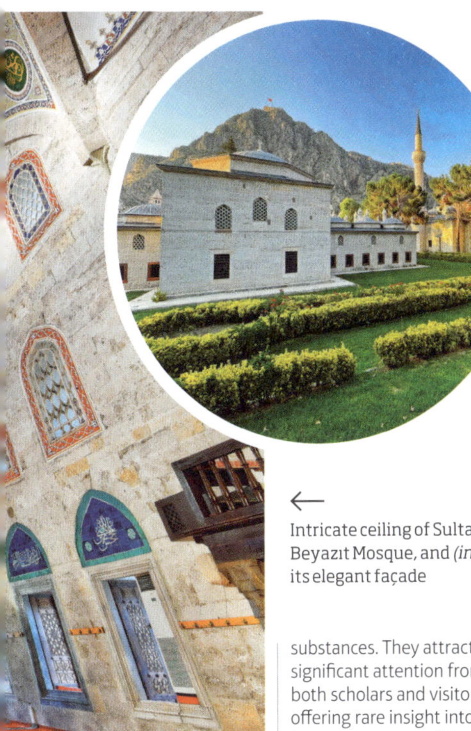

Intricate ceiling of Sultan Beyazıt Mosque, and *(inset)* its elegant façade

HIDDEN GEM
Partridges in an Apple Tree

One of the highlights of The Archaeology Museum in Amasya is a Roman mosaic depicting three partridges in an apple tree, found in the mosaic hall on the first floor.

confined tomb adjacent to the museum but are now displayed with proper lighting and, in temperature-controlled glass cases, with informative panels explaining their origins.

Unlike the mummification practices of ancient Egypt, the process in Anatolia was simpler and natural, where the bodies were not embalmed with resins or oils, but desiccated through environmental conditions and the use of herbal substances. They attract significant attention from both scholars and visitors, offering rare insight into funerary customs of the time.

The museum also displays various ethnographic artifacts from daily life in Ottoman rule, including textiles, calligraphy, metalwork and woodcarving.

Blue Seminary

Gök Medresesi

Mustafa Kemal Paşa Cad (Torumtay Sok)
During prayer times

A theological complex dating from 1267, the Blue Seminary in Amasya is a remarkable example of 13th-century Seljuk architecture. The entrance features a monumental, deeply recessed portal (or crowned gate) typical of Seljuk structures. Originally serving as both a mosque and a Koranic school, the complex reflects the Seljuks' commitment to education. Its name derives from the striking turquoise and blue tiles and the glazed bricks used in its construction. Its ornate wooden doors, intricately carved with geometric and floral motifs, form a striking contrast to its otherwise simple stone interior. These original doors are now housed in the Archaeology and Ethnography Museum.

Adjoining the seminary is the Torumtay Türbe, a finely built square tomb completed in 1279 to honour Emir Torumtay, the Seljuk governor of the province and founder of the seminary. The tomb is renowned for its elaborate stone carvings and the distinctive pyramidal roof crowning its cylindrical drum base.

EAT

Amaseia Mutfağı

The restaurant offers local fare such as *manti* (meat dumplings) and *dolma* (stuffed vine leaves).

Hazeranlar Sok 3
(0358) 218 22 23

Küçükağa Restaurant

Located in the city centre, it has a great menu of Turkish options.

Zübeyde Hanım Cad 25 **(0358) 212 91 90**

Amasya Anadolu Mantı Evi

Courtyard restaurant specializing in *manti* dumplings.

Hazeranlar Sok 57
(0358) 212 30 30

EXPERIENCE MORE

Nevşehir

D4 Kapadokya; (0384) 421 44 50 Gülşehir Cad, Nevtur: (0384) 213 11 71 and 213 12 29; Göreme Tur: (0384) 213 55 37 and (0348) 213 47 09 In front of the State Hospital; (0384) 212 95 73

As the capital of Cappadocia, Nevşehir serves as an excellent starting point for touring the region. Known as Nyssa in antiquity, the town houses the Kurşunlu Mosque and *medrese (p33)*, dating from 1725, as well as a historic castle and an impressive museum. The surrounding valleys, filled with striking tuff rock formations and troglodyte (underground) cities, are the most popular attractions, but visitors are likely to leave the Nevşehir area with strong memories of fields of sunflowers, chickpeas, donkeys and sugar beets, as well as apricots drying on rooftops. Christianity has a long history in the Nevşehir region, with monks and hermits inhabiting Cappadocia as early as the 4th century.

Zelve

D4 20 km (12 miles) NE of Nevşehir Apr-Oct: 8am-7pm daily; Nov-Mar: 8am-5pm daily

A secluded monastic retreat, Zelve lies in a series of deep valleys and is dotted with several rooms and caves on many levels. Metal walkways and stairs lead to less accessible chapels and hideaways which hold a few frescoes. In 1950 an earthquake shook the Çavuşın/Zelve area, and the cave dwellings remain somewhat unkempt today. The nature of the site will appeal to the fit and adventurous. Many of the caves and rooms are only accessed by clambering through dark holes and tunnels, so bring a torch and spare batteries.

Two small churches lie on the valley floor: the Üzümlü Kilise (Grape Church) and the Balık Kilise (Fish Church), both featuring ornate carvings. The latter is now an Ottoman mosque, but with a stone steeple.

Derinkuyu

C4 30 km (18.5 miles) S of Nevşehir Apr-Oct: 8am-7pm daily (Jun-Sep: to 9pm); Nov-Mar: 8am-5pm daily

There are believed to be about 200 underground complexes in this region, but only a few have been excavated. Of these, Derinkuyu (deep well) is the biggest. It is thought to have been a temporary refuge to around 20,000 people. The eight-level complex is 60 m (197 ft) deep. A long "transit" tunnel was supposed to have linked Derinkuyu with a similar "ant hill" settlement at Kaymaklı, about 10 km (6 miles) away. At peak times (11am–3pm) the tunnels can get uncomfortably crowded.

Ürgüp

D4 12 km (7 miles) E of Nevşehir Parkı İçi; (0384) 341 40 59

Ürgüp is now so synonymous with the troglodyte cities built

Exploring the rock formations and ancient caves of the Zelve Valley

EAT

Ziggy Cafe

This restored cave restaurant serves delicious meze. There's a jewellery shop on the ground floor.

D4 Tevfik Fikret Cad 24, Ürgüp ziggycafe.com

Solem Restaurant

Solem serves up a tasty menu full of local and international flavours.

D4 Ahmet Refik Cad 25, Ürgüp cappadociaqr.com/solem

Apetito Restaurant

This family-run spot offers a small menu of local dishes. The kebabs are a must-try.

D4 Ahmet Refik Cad 4, Ürgüp (0533) 133 40 28

during Byzantine times that it is easy to overlook the town's Roman and Seljuk history. Ürgüp's ancient name was Assiana, and it was known as Başhisar under the Seljuks. Seljuk influence can be seen in the 13th-century remains of the Kadıkalesi (castle) and the Altıkapı Tomb. Near the Nükrettin Mausoleum is a library named after Tasinağa, a 19th-century town squire. Until 1923, when Turkey became a republic, the town had a large Greek population.

Ürgüp is a convenient base to tour Cappadocia. There are plenty of pensions and hotels, yet the town has retained its village charm. This area has always been well known for its farm produce, particularly for grapes. Ürgüp-labelled wine is refreshing and light. In general, the white wines are more authentic and interesting than the reds.

Ceramics for sale in Avanos, and *(inset)* a potter shaping clay ↑

9 Avanos

D4 16 km (10 miles) NE of Nevşehir Atatürk Cad; (0384) 511 43 60

Watered by the Kızılırmak (Red River), Avanos is a pretty, leafy town noted for its pottery and ceramics. Carpet-weaving and tapestry-making are equally important local skills.

In Roman times, Avanos was called Venessa. It fell under Ottoman suzerainty in 1466 along with Nevşehir. Today, it is a typical country town, albeit without grand mosques or *medreses*. In the town centre is the Yeraltı (Ulu) Mosque, dating from the 15th century, and the Alaeddin Mosque, built by the Seljuks.

Ceramics and wine are the town's lifeblood. Visitors can purchase many serviceable pottery items, while exquisite porcelain designs are the stock in trade of places like Güray Seramik. These pieces are thrown by hand, then painted and glazed. The intricate designs are painstakingly reproduced from the İznik originals *(p187)*.

About 5 km (3 miles) east of Avanos is Sarıhan, a Seljuk *han* or caravanserai built in 1238 on the classic square plan. The repaired *han* gives a good idea of the accommodation facilities, as well as stables and a small mosque, available to traders making the long trek along the Silk Route. It also hosts atmospheric whirling dervish shows.

HIDDEN GEM
Güray Museum

Avanos' remarkable underground Güray Museum *(guraymuze.com/en)* straddles the line between contemporary and traditional cave architecture. It's home to a beautiful collection of ancient and modern ceramics.

↑ Exploring the narrow corridors and low, carved chambers at Kaymaklı

10  Kaymaklı

D4 20 km (12 miles) S of Nevşehir Apr-Oct: 8am-7pm daily (Jun-Sep: to 9pm); Nov-Mar: 8am-5pm daily

Discovered in 1964, Kaymaklı is the second most important underground city in the region. It is believed to have housed thousands of people from the 6th to 9th centuries. Although five levels are open to visitors, experts believe Kaymaklı has eight levels. The underground area is thought to cover an area of about 2.5 sq km (1 sq mile).

Being smaller and less crowded than many of the region's other underground cities, the rooms and their various functions are easy to see. It is still advisable, however, to arrive there early.

 11 Mustafapaşa

D4 6 km (4 miles) S of Ürgüp

Formerly known as Sinasos, Mustafapaşa is a perfectly preserved Greek village, whose inhabitants left during the exchange of populations between Greece and Turkey in 1923. The houses have a wealth of carved stonework, wall paintings and reminders of the former inhabitants' lifestyles. Although some houses are neglected, the balconies and sculptured windows are sure to delight. The large, 18th-century Church of Constantine and Helen draws pilgrims from Greece. Of note are the monastery of St Nicholas and the Church of St Basil, the latter located outside the village.

A large number of these houses have been restored to their former Greek appearance and are now boutique hotels.

Did You Know?

Some Cappadocian Greeks, known as the Karamanlides, spoke Turkish but wrote it in the Greek alphabet.

→ Skiing on the breathtaking snowy peaks of Mount Erciyes

 12 Bünyan

D4 35 km (22 miles) E of Kayseri

Bünyan lies east of Kayseri, just off the main highway to Sivas. This peaceful town offers an inviting rural charm and is a great destination for a relaxed half-day

excursion. The town is often included in sightseeing tours of the region.

The economic mainstay of the town is handicrafts, most notably the exquisite carpets hand-woven by local women. Visitors can observe the weavers at work on their looms and learn about the intricate designs and the amount of work involved. Bünyan carpets are renowned for their fine quality and distinctive technique. The local weavers use thin, high-tensile mercerized cotton to make bedspreads, floor rugs and prayer mats. This meticulous weaving method ensures that each finished carpet lies perfectly flat.

Mount Erciyes

Erciyes Dağı

D4 25 km (16 miles) S of Kayseri

Mount Erciyes, at a height of 3,917 m (12,851 ft), is Cappadocia's dominant natural landmark. Locals

INSIDER TIP

Skiing at Mount Erciyes

Turkey's sixth-highest peak, Mount Erciyes is a popular destination for skiers. Visitors will find excellent facilities, including resorts and ski schools, and 150 km (93 miles) of slopes.

regard this extinct volcano with respect because of its role in shaping the landscape when it buried the area in volcanic dust and ash millions of years ago. The residual tuff – fine-grained, compressed volcanic ash – is the area's major geological feature *(p324)*. The calcium in the tuff enriches the soil, encouraging the growth of trees and vines.

Between the two peaks (Greater and Lesser Erciyes) are two lovely moraine lakes, Cora and Sarı. Mount Erciyes is also a ski centre with a chairlift and a lodge. The skiing season usually runs from December to April. Hiking is possible in summer, but you will need experience and proper equipment.

Soğanlı

D4 38 km (24 miles) S of Ürgüp Sunrise–sunset

The main attraction of the Soğanlı Valley is that it is quiet and undisturbed. It is possible, even, to think of this valley as a microcosm of the whole Göreme Valley. There are six interesting churches to visit here, though it is thought that more than 100 flourished at one time. All six are in good condition and can be seen on foot during a day trip.

The delicate, pastel tones of Soğanlı's frescoes differ from the harsher hues to be seen in the churches at Göreme, where ongoing restoration has produced stronger colours.

The distinctive, colourful cloth dolls sold throughout Cappadocia are produced by Soğanlı's handicraft industry.

Niğde

D5 End of İstasyon Cad Adana Yolu Belediye Sarayı; (0388) 232 33 93

Known in Hittite times as Nahita, Niğde survived 10th-century Arab raids better than its neighbours. Its position on a major Mediterranean trade route attracted the Seljuks, allowing the town to thrive as a regional capital until the Mongol invasions *(p53)*.

The Seljuks enriched the town with fine architecture: the Alaeddin Mosque (1223), recognized for its superb stonework, ornate portal and typical squat minaret, and the Great Mosque (Ulu Cami), which was built around 1335. There is also a Seljuk tomb, the Hüdavend Hatun Türbe, featuring characteristic octagonal forms.

Niğde's *bedesten* (bazaar), with its fine clock tower, is a vestige of the town's heyday. The museum has sections on ethnography and Asian civilizations, and displays the mummified remains of a nun from the Ihlara Valley. A popular item is Niğde's deliciously creamy ewe's milk cheese, which is "packaged" in a woolly sheepskin. Such local cheeses are called *tulum peynırı*.

There are several interesting places near Niğde. The Byzantine monastery church at **Eski Gümüş** was restored in the early 1990s and is one of the best-kept secrets in Turkey. The frescoes here are outstanding.

For mountaineers, the Aladağlar Mountains offer great climbing. The best starting point is the village of Demirkazık, 65 km (40 miles) east of Niğde. Northeast of Niğde is **Sultansazlığı Bird Sanctuary**, Turkey's most important bird sanctuary after Bird Paradise National Park *(p195)*. Covering 172 sq km (66 sq miles), these marshes are vital wetlands in Europe and the Middle East, protected by the Ramsar Convention of 1971. The reserve is a haven for around 300 bird species, including ducks, flamingos, terns, cranes, egrets and plovers. Partridges, swordbeaks, whimbrels and pelicans all come here to breed. The best birdwatching spot is the lookout at Ovaçiftlik.

CLIMBING IN THE ALADAĞLAR MOUNTAINS

The Aladağlar Mountains are the place to go for top tier climbing opportunities. From the village of Demirkazık, 65 km (40 miles) east of Niğde, you could tackle the highest peak in the region, also called Demirkazık, or enjoy the five-day route across the starkly beautiful plateau to the deep blue Yedigöller lakes. It's best to go with a guide: travel agencies in Göreme *(p322)* can help to arrange trips.

Eski Gümüş

9 km (6 miles) NE of Niğde (0388) 232 33 90 Apr-Oct: 8am-7pm daily; Nov-Mar: 8am-5pm daily

Sultansazlığı Bird Sanctuary

70 km (44 miles) SW of Kayseri (0352) 658 55 49 8am-6pm daily

16

Güzelyurt

D4 37 km (22 miles) SE of Aksaray Aksaray, Ihlara Valley (infrequent)

Güzelyurt, meaning "beautiful homeland", is a charming, friendly town surrounded by

←

Eski Gümüş monastery, and *(inset)* frescoes decorating its interior

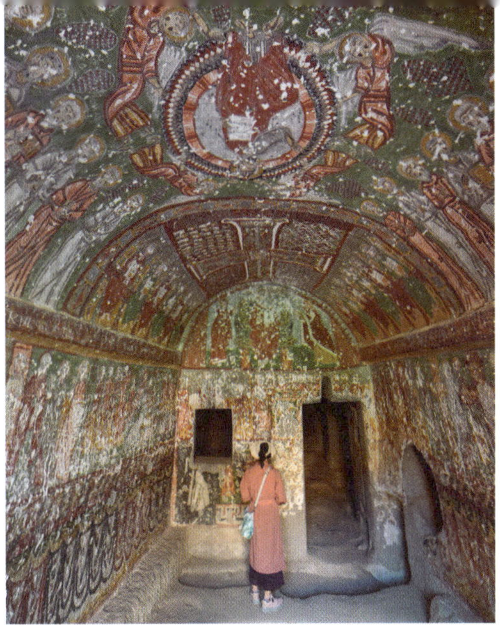

→ Interior frescoes of one of the rock churches in the Ihlara Valley

citrus groves and is popular for both horse riding and mountain biking.

Although it was originally home to over 50 Greek Orthodox churches, few remain today. The church of St Gregory of Nazianzus, one of the four founders of the Greek Orthodox Church, first built in 385 CE and rebuilt in 1896, is now a mosque.

A government protection order is in force in Güzelyurt, so all restoration and construction work must conform to official guidelines. Local stone must be used and the buildings must be appropriate to the town.

The valley 4 km (2.5 miles) to the northeast of the town, also known as the Monastery Valley, has an abundance of rock-carved churches.

Ihlara Valley

Ihlara Vadisi

C4

Many find the Ihlara Valley more captivating than the rock churches and dwellings in the region. The setting is dramatic, with the Melendiz River winding along the canyon floor.

The valley's main 5-km (8-mile) section lies between the village of Selime (north) and the town of Ihlara (south).

INSIDER TIP
Natural Wines of Gelveri

Cappadocia's high-mineral volcanic soil yields intensely flavoured wines. Try some at Gelveri in Güzelyurt, which produces natural wines in clay amphorae.

Of the 60 or so original churches in the valley, which was known as Peristrema in Greek times, only about 10 can be seen and some of the interior frescoes are in less than pristine condition.

Most of the churches in the valley date from the 11th century. Their names signify their use or a peculiar feature: Hyacinth, Black Deer, Crooked Stone and Dovecote. The frescoes inside depict scenes from the lives of the saints and ascetic monks or punishments.

It was once believed that a medical school, where the art of mummification was taught, existed between the villages of Belisırma and Yaprakhisar.

Aksaray

C4 4 km (2.5 miles) W of town centre Taşpazar Mahallesi, Sok 1; (0382) 213 24 74; 212 46 88

Aksaray was known as Archelais in Roman times, named after Archelaus II, the last king of Cappadocia. By 20 BCE, the kingdom was a virtual protectorate of Rome and the king's status was merely symbolic.

From the south, Aksaray is overlooked by the twin peaks of Mount Hasan (Hasan Dağı), an extinct volcano known as "little sister" to Mount Erciyes. Aksaray is close to the eastern end of the Tuz Gölü (Salt Lake). In Ottoman times, the lake brought prosperity to Aksaray as it was the main source of salt for almost all of Anatolia.

Though seemingly quiet, Aksaray features fine Seljuk architecture, with vestiges of the original ochre-coloured sandstone. Worth seeing are the Great Mosque (1314), with its beautifully carved *minbar* (pulpit), and the **Zinciriye Medresesi**, a 14th-century Koranic school that now serves as the museum.

Aksaray has its own leaning tower, the Eğri (Leaning) Minaret, on Nevşehir Caddesi. The minaret is part of the Kızıl (Red) Minare Mosque, which was built in 1236 during the reign of the great Seljuk Sultan Alaeddin Keykubat I *(p286)*. The mosque was built on sand, which has shifted over time, causing the minaret to lean.

Zinciriye Medresesi

Belediye Cad 28
9am–5pm daily

19

Alacahöyük

D3 50 km (30 miles) SW of Çorum

Located between Sungurlu and Çorum, Alacahöyük is the third most important site (after Hattuşaş and Yazılıkaya) among the Hittite sites in this region. Most of the artifacts found at the site are displayed in museums in Ankara *(p278)* and Çorum.

Excavations at Alacahöyük have yielded items ranging from the Chalcolithic period (5500 BCE–3000 BCE) up to the Phrygian period (750 BCE–300 BCE) – a staggering time span that makes the site one of Turkey's most important archaeological centres.

At the site itself, the Sphinx Gate is a reminder of Egyptian influences. The royal tombs can also be seen. The **Alacahöyük Museum** displays earthenware pots used for burial rites.

Alacahöyük Museum
(0364) 422 70 11
Summer: 8:30am-6:30pm daily; winter: 8am-5pm daily

Çorum

D3 Osmancık Cad 4 Sok No 17; (0364) 212 05 10

The town of Çorum dates from Roman times, when it was known as Niconia. The surrounding area is rich in Hittite history, making it likely that the site was inhabited as early as 1400 BCE. Throughout Turkey, the name of Çorum is associated with roasted chickpeas *(leblebi)*, one of the many snacks that Turks munch compulsively. A particularly delicious local cheese is Kargi, made from cow's milk. Çorum makes a good base from which to tour two major Hittite sights, Hattuşaş *(p328)* and Alacahöyük. Both are located to the southwest of the town.

The **Çorum Museum** sprawls over several buildings. It is a serious and informative place with many artifacts and ethnographic displays, among them very good Hittite objects, as well as local *kilims* (rugs).

Çorum Museum
Town centre (0364) 213 15 68 Apr-Oct: 8am-7pm daily; Nov-Mar: 8am-5pm daily

Tokat

D3 1.2 km (0.75 miles) NE of town centre; (0356) 214 22 20 Hükümet Binasi; (0356) 214 37 53

Tokat deserves a place on the itineraries because there is a lot more to see here than ruins. The Seljuks left the most to see, but the town is also known for resisting Ottoman rule. In protest at Ottoman authority, Turcoman tribesmen took to wearing distinctive red headgear, thus earning the name of Kızılbaşı (redheads), which became a term for "rebels".

← Bronze burial finding at Alacahöyük

STAY

Yazmacılar Han Otel
This hotel is housed in a beautifully restored caravanserai. There's a good restaurant onsite.

D3 Halit Sok 3 (3562) 121 211

Osman Paşa Konağı Butik Oteli
Set in a historic mansion, this boutique hotel retains fine period details, including elegant wooden ceilings.

D3 Behzat Blv 29, Sokak 23 tokatosman pasabutikotel.com

The town flourished after Sultan Beyazıt I won control of trade routes to Erzincan. Trade caravans then began to use the Amasya–Tokat route, skirting Trabzon (Trebizond), to reach Bursa *(p188)*, the commercial jewel of the 15th and 16th centuries.

The Seljuks and Ottomans endowed Tokat with many fine buildings, especially the Blue Seminary (Gök Medrese) and two restored 19th-century Ottoman *konaks* (mansions): the Madımağın Celal'ın House and the Latifoğlu House. If time is limited, Tokat's interesting **Archaeological Museum** is the place to go.

Tokat has a proud 300-year tradition of hand-printed textiles *(yazmacılık)*. The craft still thrives in the Gazi Emir Han near the busy commercial hub of Sulu Sokak. The town is also renowned for copper-working, with finely hammered trays and vessels, as well as ceramics in bold primary colours.

→ Entrance to Sivas's Heavenly Seminary, and *(inset)* its interior

Specialities include *pekmez*, a delicious drink made from concentrated grape juice, and the full-bodied, fruity Karaman red wine.

The city of Sebastopolis is located 68 km (42 miles) southwest of Tokat. The modern name, Sulusaray (Watery Palace), comes from the thermal springs, which bubble water at 50°C (122°F). Interesting finds here include a city wall, bath chambers and a temple.

Archaeological Museum
Sulu Sok (0356) 214 15 09 8am-4:45pm Tue-Sun

Sivas

E4 İstasyon Cad; (0346) 221 10 91 2.5 km (1.5 miles) SE of city centre Atatürk Kültür Merkezi; www.sivas.gov.tr

Situated at an altitude of 1,275 m (4,183 ft), Sivas is the highest city in Central Anatolia. Known as Sebasteia in Roman times, its position on a caravan route made it an important trade centre.

Sivas boasts the cream of Seljuk architecture, with tiles, intricately etched stonework, star mosaics, honeycombed decorative motifs and bold blue hues all in evidence. The Heavenly Seminary (Gök Medresesi), built in the 1200s, and Twin Minaret Seminary (Çifte Minareli Medresesi), with its outstanding carved details, should not be missed. The Darüşşifası (Medical Hospice) housed a hospital. The Bürüciye Medresesi (1271) has a quiet courtyard and some excellent tilework.

The Sivas Congress (to consolidate Atatürk's plans to free Turkey from foreign domination) was held in a schoolroom here in 1919. The room is preserved in the **Sivas Atatürk and Congress Museum**. Local artisans are known for producing long-stemmed wooden pipes, penknives and bone-handled knives.

Sivas Atatürk and Congress Museum
Mehmetpaşa, Taşlı Sok (0346) 221 04 46 8am-5pm daily

TURKISH KANGAL

For centuries, shepherds tending their flocks in the high mountains of Anatolia have required reliable protection for their sheep against predators such as wolves. This led to the development of the Kangal, a large and powerful guardian dog named after the town of Kangal, 85 km (52 miles) south of Sivas. Calm by nature but fearless when defending livestock, Kangals have long been valued as working companions. Their thick coats range in colour from white or grey to light brown, and they are recognizable by their distinctive black muzzle. Today, Kangal is regarded as one of the world's finest livestock guardian breeds.

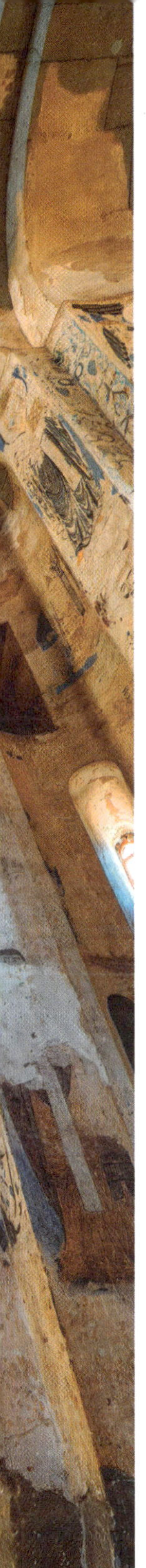
Interior of the Armenian Church of the Holy Cross near Lake Van

EASTERN ANATOLIA

Turkey's vast eastern flank has played a key role in history since the early glimmers of civilization. Neolithic Göbeklitepe is known as the world's earliest temple; near Malatya, Arslantepe is often described as the first organized state; and, during the Iron Age, the Urartu Kingdom ruled over a swathe of eastern Anatolia, with their capital at Van.

From the Classical era onwards, this area became an important land bridge and home to a number of groups, including followers of the Syriac Christian faith who were based around Mardin during the early Byzantine period. Later, in around the 10th century, the Bagratuni Armenian Kingdom formed a buffer state between the Byzantine and Abbasid empires. By the 12th century, much of the region had fragmented into independently ruled Kurdish and Seljuk Turk principalities.

It was only during the Ottoman era that this region – with its population of Kurdish, Turkish, Armenian, Syriac Christian, and Jewish people – was first ruled by one central power. However, the region's multi-religious identity changed after World War I, and throughout the 20th century the area suffered from a lack of economic development and armed conflict between the Turkish state and Kurdish separatists. In recent years, however, investment projects and ceasefire agreements have begun to turn around the region's fortunes.

EASTERN ANATOLIA

Must Sees

1. Mount Nemrut
2. Göbeklitepe
3. Diyarbakır
4. Ani
5. Erzurum

Experience More

6. Gaziantep
7. Şanlıurfa
8. Doğubayazıt
9. Mardin
10. Lake Van
11. Kars

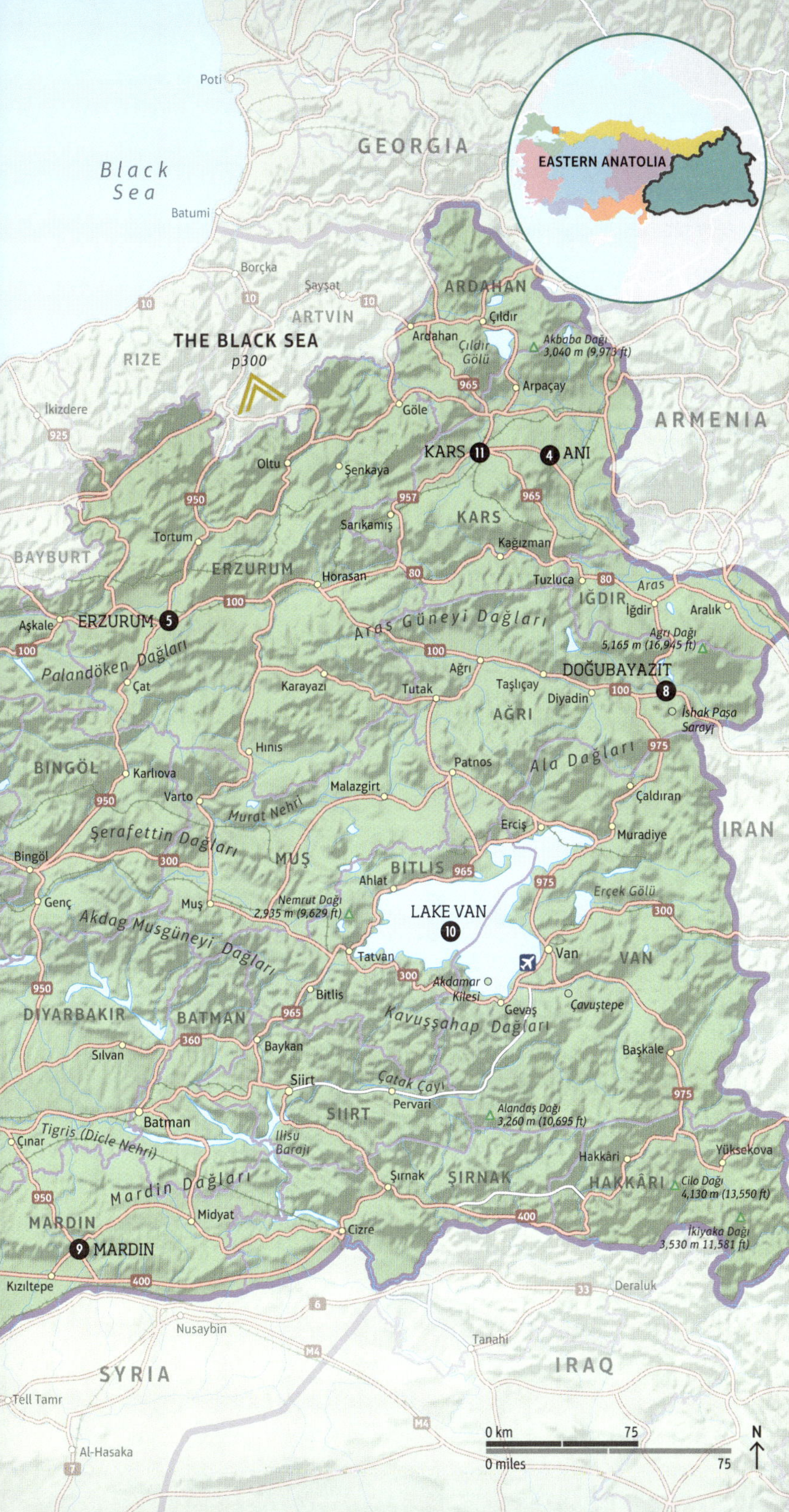
EASTERN ANATOLIA
GEORGIA
Black Sea
THE BLACK SEA
p300
ARMENIA
IRAN
IRAQ
SYRIA
LAKE VAN
ERZURUM
KARS
ANI
DOĞUBAYAZIT
MARDIN
Poti
Batumi
Borçka
Şavşat
ARTVIN
RIZE
İkizdere
ARDAHAN
Çıldır
Ardahan
Çıldır Gölü
Akbaba Dağı 3,040 m (9,973 ft)
Arpaçay
Göle
Oltu
Şenkaya
Sarıkamış
Kağızman
Tuzluca
Aras
IĞDIR
Iğdir
Aralık
Ağrı Dağı 5,165 m (16,945 ft)
BAYBURT
Tortum
Horasan
Aşkale
Aras Güneyi Dağları
Palandöken Dağları
Çat
Karayazi
Ağrı
Taşlıçay
Diyadin
Tutak
AĞRI
İshak Paşa Sarayı
Hınıs
BINGÖL
Karlıova
Varto
Patnos
Ala Dağları
Malazgirt
Çaldıran
Murat Nehri
Şerafettin Dağları
Erciş
Muradiye
Bingöl
MUŞ
BITLIS
Ahlat
Genç
Muş
Nemrut Dağı 2,935 m (9,629 ft)
Erçek Gölü
Akdag Musgüneyi Dağları
Tatvan
Van
VAN
Akdamar Kilesi
Gevaş
Çavuştepe
Bitlis
Kavuşşahap Dağları
DIYARBAKIR
BATMAN
Baykan
Sılvan
Başkale
Siirt
Çatak Çayı
Pervari
Alandaş Dağı 3,260 m (10,695 ft)
SIIRT
Batman
Ilısu Barajı
Tigris (Dicle Nehri)
Çınar
Yüksekova
Şırnak
ŞIRNAK
HAKKÂRI
Hakkâri
Cilo Dağı 4,130 m (13,550 ft)
Mardin Dağları
MARDIN
Midyat
Cizre
İkiyaka Dağı 3,530 m 11,581 ft)
Kızıltepe
Deraluk
Nusaybin
Tanahi
Tell Tamr
Al-Hasaka
0 km 75
0 miles 75
N

MOUNT NEMRUT

NEMRUT DAĞI

E5 58 km (36 miles) from Kâhta, 90 km (55 miles) from Adıyaman in Nemrut Dagi National Park (0416) 725 50 07 May-Oct: 8am-sunset daily Winter months (dates vary)

The huge stone heads on the summit of Mount Nemrut (Nemrut Dağı) were built by King Antiochus I Epiphanes, who ruled the Commagene Kingdom between 64 and 38 BCE.

To glorify his rule, King Antiochus had three enormous terraces (east, west and north) cut into the mountaintop. Colossal statues of himself and the major gods (both Greek and Persian) of the kingdom were placed on the terraces, ranging from 8 m to 10 m in height (26 ft to 33 ft), and the summit became a sanctuary where the king was worshipped. Today's visitors can still see the remains of the east and west terraces (not much is left of the north terrace), which also feature large, detailed stone reliefs. The enigmatic site was discovered in 1881 by a German engineer, Karl Sester, but was not fully documented until the 1990s.

Did You Know?

Antiochus set aside funds for celebrations for his birthday and coronation here, even after his death.

↑ Miniature reconstruction of huge statues of gods on Mount Nemrut

→ Stone relief depicting Apollon Mithras near Mount Nemrut

TOP 3 HISTORIC SITES NEAR MOUNT NEMRUT

Karakuş Tumulus
Burial mound for King Mithridates II's family, located around 30 km (18 miles) southwest.

Cendere Bridge
Ancient Roman bridge over the Cendere river, approximately 21 km (13 miles) southwest.

Yenikale Ruins
Yenikale, meaning "new castle", dates back to the 13th century; the site is found 17 km (10 miles) southwest.

↑ West terrace of Mount Nemrut scattered with detailed stone reliefs

The excavation site of Göbeklitepe, considered to be the world's oldest temple

2 GÖBEKLITEPE

E5 19km (12 miles) east of Şanlıurfa
8:30am-7pm daily muze.gov.tr

The gentle hills northeast of Şanlıurfa hide Göbeklitepe, one of the world's greatest archaeological treasures. Now a UNESCO World Heritage Site, this staggeringly ancient circular temple offers fascinating insights into humanity's earliest days.

It's almost impossible to visualize quite how old Göbeklitepe is: with an estimated age of nearly 12,000 years, it predates the pyramids of Egypt by 7,000 years. Thought to be the world's oldest temple, archaeologists believe that it was built before humanity embraced agriculture and still lived as hunter-gatherers. Lost to history until archaeological digs in the 1960s, Göbeklitepe is now covered by a large protective roof and surrounded by well-designed walkways, allowing visitors to see it from above without damaging the remains. Divided into separate buildings, the ruins contain many pillars with impressive carvings on them, depicting animal and human figures with symbolic importance: Building D's image of a vulture god, for example, may hint towards burial rituals. Make sure to use the audio-guide, included with your ticket – it will guide you around the site and make sure you don't miss any of the fascinating details.

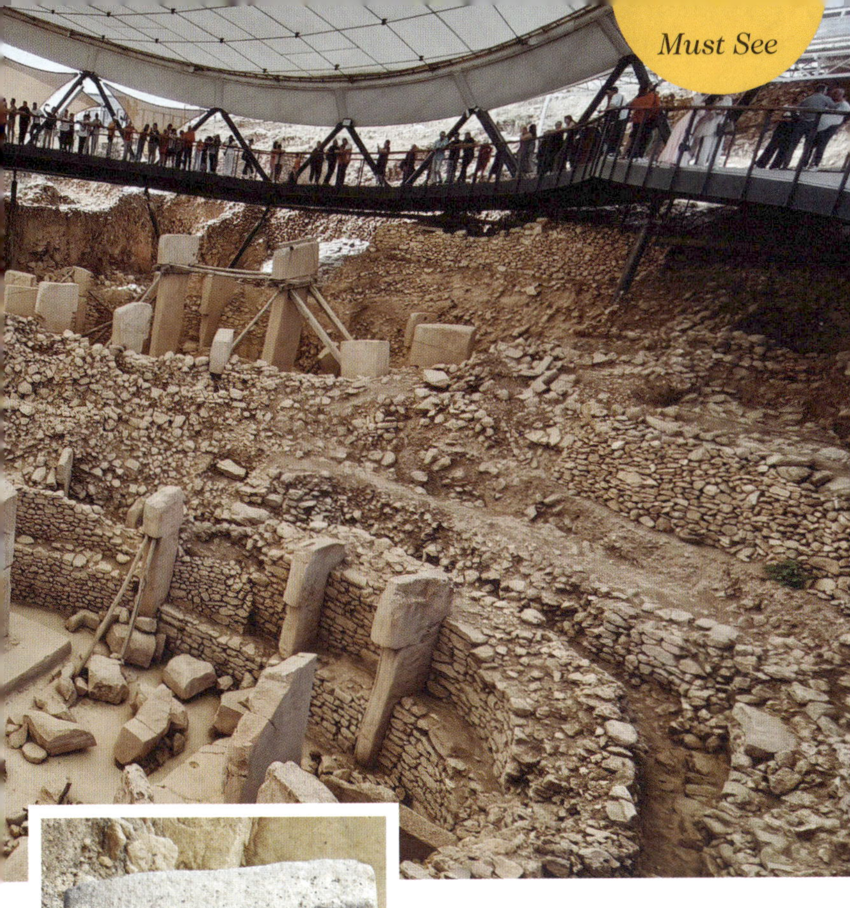

↑ T-shaped stone relief column of animal figures at Göbeklitepe

Lost to history until archaeological digs in the 1960s, Göbeklitepe is now covered by a large protective roof and surrounded by well-designed walkways, allowing visitors to see it from above without damaging the remains.

ONGOING EXCAVATIONS

Göbeklitepe may be remarkable, but it's not necessarily unique: in the same region around Şanlıurfa, excavations are underway at numerous similar sites. The most impressive is Karahan Tepe, 46 km (29 miles) east, where more than 200 pillars like those of Göbeklitepe have been discovered, along with several remarkable carved stone sculptures. These are now on display at Şanlıurfa's Archaeological Museum. Additionally, some archaeologists believe that the site may be the earliest known human village, predating even the construction of Göbeklitepe by several centuries, dating to somewhere between 10,000 and 9500 BCE.

In September 2023, Turkish and German experts discovered further sculptures from the so-called Tepeler cultures: a statue of a vulture and a 2.3-m- (8-ft-) high anthropomorphic statue were found.

DIYARBAKIR

F5 Dağ Kapısı Burçu Giriş Bölümü; (0412) 228 22 00

Southeastern Turkey's liveliest city, Diyarbakır is situated on the edge of a high bank dropping down to the Tigris River. It is also the unofficial capital of Turkey's Kurdish-dominated southeast. The city is renowned for the gigantic watermelons sold in its markets. Watered by the Tigris River, the melons can reach weights of up to 50 kg (112 lb).

Diyarbakir's Churches

Diyarbakır'ın Kilise

Meryaman Kilise: Uçak Sok 10; St Giargos Kilesesi: Savaş, Göçmen Sok 17

Diyarbakır is home to two historically important churches. Its oldest church is the Syrian Orthodox Church of the Virgin Mary (Meryaman Kilise), possibly dating back to the 4th century. Its historic complex includes a courtyard and an interior known for its iconostasis and ornate altar. The Armenian Apostolic Church of St George (St Giargos Kilesesi), currently undergoing restoration work, is thought to be one of the largest churches in the Middle East.

Hasan Paşa Hanı

Gazi Cad Mon-Sat

Located opposite the Great Mosque (Ulu Cami), and built by governor Verizade Hasan Paşa, this 16th-century *han* *(p119)* is still used by traders, and has some decent jewellery, carpets and antiques on the upper floor, while the courtyard is packed with cafés serving Turkish breakfasts, Kurdish style. Its black basalt façade is dignified by a bold white limestone frieze.

THE STONE HOUSES OF DIYARBAKIR

Visitors will quickly spot that the city has a distinctive style of architecture, with the houses and buildings of its old town mostly constructed from large blocks of black basalt. Often, a contrast to the black is offered by interspersing yellow blocks, especially around archways. Building façades are beautifully decorated with geometric patterns, and sometimes, images of mythical creatures.

↑ Hazreti Süleyman Mosque, below the historic citadel

Great Mosque

Ulu Cami

Gazi Cad **Daily**

A fairly plain building with a basilica-plan style, the Great Mosque is the most significant building in Diyarbakır, and is regarded as one of the holiest places in the Islamic world. It was built on the site of a church around 639 CE after the Arabs captured the city. In 1091–2, the Seljuk ruler Malik Şah remodelled the building, using the revered Great Ummayad Mosque in Damascus as a model.

The interior is quite spacious. Notably, the central section's ceiling is adorned with hand-drawn calligraphy from the Ottoman period. Elsewhere in the mosque there are inscriptions and decrees by different Seljuk, Akkoyunlu, Artuqids and Ottoman rulers.

Meanwhile, the courtyard buildings are built from black basalt with bands of white limestone, faced with blind arches; these are in turn supported by impressive Roman columns interspersed with a number of Seljuk friezes.

EAT

Cigerci Hüsnü Usta

This no-frills spot just south of the Great Mosque is renowned for its liver kebabs, cooked on a charcoal barbecue.

Kazancılar Sok
(0531) 397 50 75

Mustafa'nın Kahvaltı Dünyası

On the upper floor of the gorgeous medieval Hasan Paşa Hanı, this restaurant serves Diyarbakır's best Turkish breakfasts. The *sigari borek* may very well be the best you'll ever taste.

Gazi Cad
mustafaninkahvalti dunyasi.com

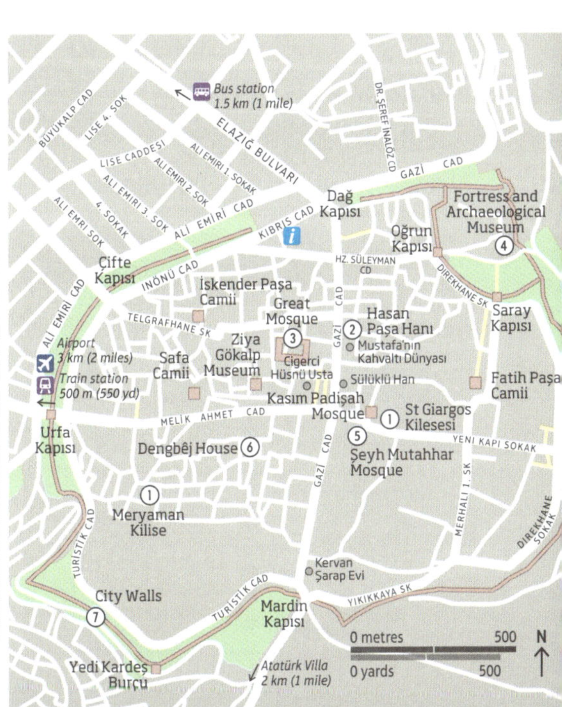

Dört Ayaklı Minare, the four-legged minaret at Şeyh Mutahhar Mosque

Fortress and Archaeological Museum

Diyarbakır Kalesi ve Arkeoloji Müzesi

Hazrat Suleiman Cad 9am-5pm Tue-Sun muze.gov.tr

The immense black basalt walls of Diyarbakır's castle are an imposing sight, but they contain a lively interior, criss-crossed with paths over the grassy courtyard which is a popular gathering spot for the city's inhabitants. The walls can be climbed, and the battlements afford splendid views over the city and the river valley below, but take care – there are no safety rails and precipitous drops. Alongside the picturesque Hazreti Süleyman Mosque, the fortress courtyard contains the city's Archaeological Museum, housed in a handsome late Ottoman building, which contains a well-presented collection of finds from local sites. Perhaps the most impressive pieces are those found at the ancient site of Körtiktepe: dating back more than 10,000 years, the intricate decoration on the artifacts is incredible. Next to the museum, the semi-ruined Church of St George is beautiful and well worth a quick explore, and the courtyard café is also a tempting place to linger.

Şeyh Mutahhar Mosque

Şeyh Matar Camii

Yeni Kapı Cad Daily

This was the last of the great mosques built under the reign of the Akkoyunlu (White Sheep) Turkomans. It is unusual for its free-standing minaret supported by four 2-m- (6.5-ft-) high basalt pillars carved from a single block of stone, known as the Dört Ayaklı Minare (four-legged minaret). It is said that your wish will be granted if you walk seven times around its pillars.

Dengbêj House

Dengbêj Evi

Kılıçı Sok (0412) 229 20 34 9:30am-4:30pm Tue-Sun

Dating back to the pre-Islamic period, *dengbêj* is a Kurdish tradition in which epic stories – ranging from tales of heroic deeds to stories of doomed love – are sung by musical storytellers, passing down oral histories from generation to generation. In the 1980s, when use of the Kurdish language was criminalized, singing *dengbêj* songs was illegal and those doing so – or even owning cassette tapes of *dengbêj* – risked persecution by the authorities. The laws against the use of Kurdish were repealed in 1991, and gradually the *dengbêj* tradition was revived, with Diyarbakır's authorities opening the Dengbêj House in 2007 in a sign that the cultural importance of this almost lost

art was now appreciated. Here in a beautiful 18th-century building, locals and tourists alike gather and listen to the mesmerizing songs and experience oral traditions that have survived for centuries, despite many attempts to stamp them out.

City Walls

Diyarbakır Surları

The black walls encircling the city – said to be visible from space – were originally built by the Romans (who captured Diyarbakır from the Sassanids in the 3rd century CE), since the city lacked natural defences. The Byzantines added to the structure, but what can be seen today is mainly the work of Seljuks, who captured the city in 1088.

Constructed from blocks of black basalt, the walls are pierced by four major gates (Harput, Yenikapı, Mardin and Urfa) and studded with 72 towers. The walls are 12 m (39 ft) high and more than 5 km (3 miles) in length.

The **Atatürk Villa** was given to the founder of the Turkish Republic in 1937 by the citizens of Diyarbakır. On display are period photographs and personal effects. It is situated a few kilometres south of the city, off the road to Mardin, and has expansive views of the Tigris and the Dicle Köprüsü (Tigris Bridge).

Atatürk Villa

8:30am-noon & 1:30-5pm daily

GREAT VIEW
City Walls

The Tower of the Seven Brothers (Yedi Kardeş Burçu), located between the Mardin and Urfa gates and built in 1208, provides a particularly good vantage point.

DRINK

Sülüklü Han

This medieval building with a gorgeous courtyard in the centre is now home to one of Diyarbakır's most atmospheric cafés, often filled with Kurdish music and lively chatter.

Değer Sok
(0530) 934 01 05

Kervan Şarap Evi

One of the very few places in Diyarbakır serving wine, this little bar also offers small plates of cheese, olives and the like.

Gazi Cad
(0530) 151 27 21

↑ Fortified city walls and cityscape of Diyarbakır

ANI

G3 · 44 km (27 miles) E of Kars · Apr-Oct: 8am-6:30pm daily; Nov-Mar: 8am-5pm daily (heavy snow in winter may restrict access)

The ruins of Ani, located on the border with Armenia, are one of the most evocative historical sites in Turkey. Once a thriving medieval city, Ani's significant remains are today a key tourism draw.

Set on a windswept, grassy plateau along the Barley River, the site contains important remnants of Armenian architecture, including the city walls protecting its northern border, parts of which are still intact. In 961 CE, Ani became the capital of the Bagratid kings of Armenia. It reached its apogee under King Gagik I (990–1020), when it was known as "the city of a thousand and one churches". Sacked by the Turks in 1064, Ani eventually recovered, only to be razed by an earthquake in 1319. Located on the sensitive Turkish-Armenian border, parts of the site are off-limits to visitors – stick to the marked trail. Photography is also restricted, so avoid pointing your camera across the border.

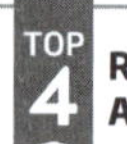

RUINS AT ANI

Seljuk Palace
Well-preserved palace, with a decorated portal.

Fire Temple
These ruins are thought to be the oldest surviving structure in Ani.

St Gregory of Tigran Honents Church
Armenian-style church, with intricate exterior carvings and colourful frescoes inside.

St Gregory of Gagik Church
Remains of a clearly once-substantial circular church.

Church of St Gregory of Gagik

The Church of St Gregory of Abugramentz, a 12-sided rotunda, is one of three churches dedicated to the saint.

The Citadel is the oldest part of Ani and housed most of its residents until 961, when the Bagratids moved their capital here from Kars.

City Walls

Maiden's Castle

Illustration of the historical site of Ani

Did You Know?

The south entrance of Ani Cathedral was once reserved for the king.

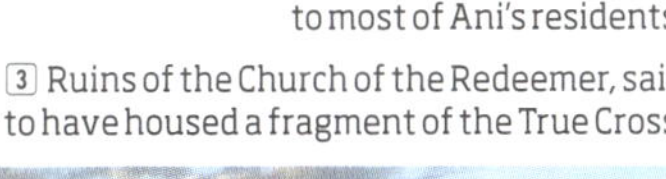

1 Richly decorated ceiling frescoes inside the St Gregory of Tigran Honents Church.

2 The 7th-century Citadel ruins, once home to most of Ani's residents.

3 Ruins of the Church of the Redeemer, said to have housed a fragment of the True Cross.

ERZURUM

F4 Cemal Gürsel Caddesi 9; (0442) 235 09 25

Sprawling across a vast plain at an altitude of almost 2,000 m (6,560 ft) and ringed by mountains, Erzurum is Turkey's coldest city. Because it was located astride the main caravan route from India to Europe, and controlled the passage between the Caucasus and Anatolia, Erzurum was fought over and ruled by many peoples – Byzantines, Sassanids, Arabs, Armenians, Seljuk Turks, Mongols and Ottomans. Its most famous sights date from Seljuk times. Like Kars, the city was in Russian hands for over 40 years and as a result has an organized grid-pattern street layout. In 1919, Atatürk's Nationalists met here to map out the frontiers of modern Turkey. Today, Erzurum has a university and a large garrison population. It hosts tournaments of the fast-paced horseback game, *cirit*.

Erzurum Museum

Erzurum Müzesi

Rabia Ana, Şahinbey Sok 2 (0442) 233 04 14 Apr-Oct: 8am-9pm Tue-Sun; Nov-Mar: 8am-5pm Tue-Sun

Exhibits here range from Urartian metalwork and pottery to the jewellery of the Hellenistic and Roman eras.

Lala Mustafa Paşa Mosque

Lala Mustafa Paşa Camii

Cumhuriyet Caddesi

This charming Ottoman mosque, built in 1562, conforms to a typical square-plan design, with columns and cupolas around a courtyard with a fountain. Original tilework adorns the interior.

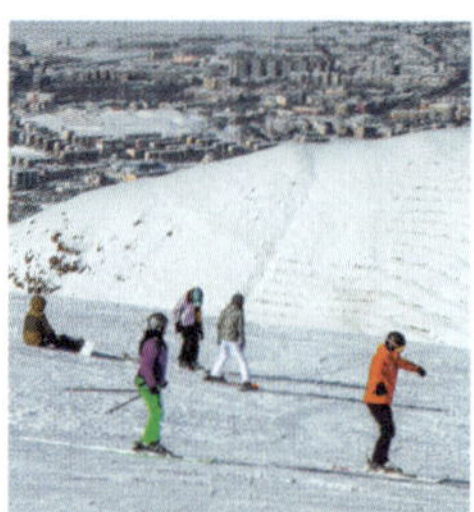

SKIING IN THE ERZURUM AREA

Just south of Erzurum is Palandöken Dağı, a 3,271-m (10,732-ft) mountain which is home to one of Turkey's best ski resorts. With 43 km (27 miles) of runs, there's an excellent mix of easy, medium and difficult slopes to explore, and a good network of gondolas to transfer you between them.

Yakutiye Seminary

Yakutiye Medresesi

Cumhuriyet Cad Apr-Oct: 8am-7pm Tue-Sun; Nov-Mar: 8am-5pm Tue-Sun

Built in 1310 by Hoca Yakut, governor of the İlhan Mongols,

this ornate Koranic school is regarded as the city's most beautiful building. The carved stonework is very appealing and the short minaret features an elaborate lattice of brick and turquoise tiles.

Citadel

Erzurum Kalesi

N of Çifte Minareli Medresesi (0442) 213 7357 Apr-Oct: 8am-6:30pm daily; Nov-Mar: 8am-5pm daily

The citadel was built in the 5th century, during the reign of Byzantine Emperor Theoosius. It was restored in 1555 by Sultan Süleyman I (the Magnificent) and served as the eastern base of the Janissaries. Inside are a ruined clock tower and a mosque.

Twin Minaret Seminary

Çifte Minareli Medrese

Cumhuriyet Cad
9am-7:30pm daily

The two minarets that flank the portal of the Çifte Minareli Medresesi have become the symbols of Erzurum. They are thought to have been built in 1253 on the authority of Hunat Hatun, daughter of Seljuk Sultan Alaeddin Keykubad II. At the rear of the complex is the 12-sided tomb that contains her remains.

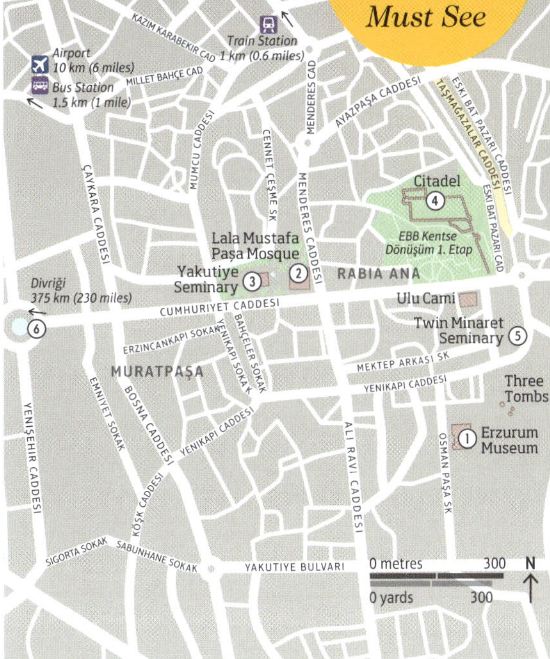

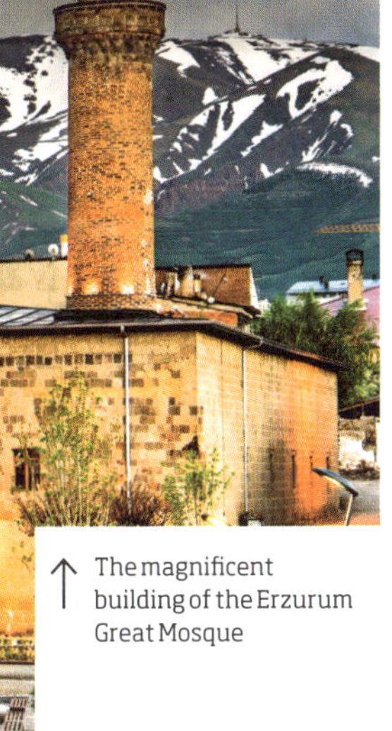

↑ The magnificent building of the Erzurum Great Mosque

Divriği

After the Seljuk victory at Manzikert (Malazgirt) in 1071 *(p52)*, Divriği became the seat of the Mengüçek state and was ruled by the Mengüç family from 1142 to 1252. Among many fine buildings they left behind is the *külliye* (mosque-hospital complex). The ornate portals of the **Ulu Cami**, or Great Mosque, and the adjoining *daruşşifa* (hospital) display especially rich decoration.

Ulu Cami
Daily

PICTURE PERFECT
Three Tombs

Just south of Erzurum's centre stand three splendid 13th-century tombs. Built of attractive yellow and red stone, and topped with elegant domes, they make a gorgeous photo.

EXPERIENCE MORE

Gaziantep

E5 Yüzyıl Parkı; (0342) 230 59 69

Named Ayntap, or pure spring, by the Byzantines, Gaziantep's modern prefix of *gazi* (war hero) derives from heroic resistance to French and English invaders in 1920. The site has been occupied for 8,000 years and was a strategic defence hub in Hittite times (1200–700 BCE).

Just below the citadel is a bazaar, where artisans produce and sell copperware and furniture inlaid with mother-of-pearl, a craft for which the city is famous.

The central **Gaziantep Archaeological Museum** is worth a visit to see Hittite and Roman statuary. The museum was repaired after it sustained damage during an earthquake in 2023.

The jewel of the city's museums is the state-of-the-art **Gaziantep Zeugma Mosaic Museum**. It is the world's largest mosaic museum, housing more than 3,500 sq m (37,660 sq ft) of largely 2nd- and 3rd-century CE mosaics rescued from the floodwaters of a dam on the nearby Euphrates. Its most famous exhibit is the Zeugma Girl mosaic, which is a regional idol and symbol of the Zeugma excavations. Also housed in the museum is a splendid statue of Mars, and superb reconstructions of courtyard villas.

Gaziantep is an important agricultural and industrial centre, and olives, grapes and pistachio nuts are grown around the city. The city's distinctive cuisine is famed throughout the country, particularly sweet pastries such as pistachio-filled baklava. To find out more about the city's cuisine, it is worth visiting **Emine Göğüş Culinary Museum** in the bazaar quarter below the castle.

The jewel of the city's museums is the state-of-the-art Gaziantep Zeugma Mosaic Museum, the world's largest mosaic museum of largely 2nd- and 3rd-century CE mosaics.

Gaziantep Archaeological Museum

Istasyon Cad
(0342) 324 88 09
Hours vary, call ahead

Gaziantep Zeugma Mosaic Museum

Konukoğlu Blv
(0342) 325 27 27
Summer: 8:30am-7pm daily; winter: 8:30am-5pm daily

Emine Göğüş Culinary Museum

Hasırcı Sok
(0342) 220 08 88
9am-6pm daily

Şanlıurfa

E5 Atatürk Blv, Vilayet Binası, Kat 3; (0414) 312 53 32

The city of Şanlıurfa is one of the most interesting in the region. First settled by the Hurri peoples around 5,500 years ago, it was occupied by a succession of peoples, such as the Hittites, Assyrians, Greeks and Romans. Alexander the Great named it Edessa, and the Ottomans renamed it Urfa.

Enjoying a boat ride in the turquoise waters at Balikligol in Sanlıurfa

The city acquired the prefix *şanlı* (glorious) through the role it played in resistance to the French in 1920.

Most visitors come here to see the Gölbaşı (lakeside) area at the foot of the citadel. This pleasantly landscaped garden contains Balikligol, the Pool of Abraham, said to be the site where he was saved from the vengeful Assyrian king, Nimrod (Nemrut). A small cave nearby is said to be the birthplace of Abraham.

The stone covered bazaar, or Kapalı Çarşı, is an Ottoman structure, with designated rows of streets devoted to particular trades. Traditional crafts and skills predominate, and it is a good place to shop for locally produced cloth. Don't miss the Gümrük Hanı in the bazaar. This beautifully shady Ottoman-era court-yard building is full of locals drinking tea and coffee, and playing endless games of backgammon.

The Şanlıurfa Mosaic Museum situated west of the Gölbaşı area, contains superb 3rd- to 5th-century-CE late Roman and Byzantine mosaics, which were discovered in situ in 2007 during excavations for an urban infrastructure project.

Doğubayazıt İshak Paşa Sarayı, and *(inset)* the palace's elegant interior ↑

Doğubayazıt

G4

Situated on the main road between Turkey and Iran, Doğubayazıt is a half-hour drive from the border. Mount Ağrı (Ararat), Turkey's highest mountain, rises 5,165 m (16,945 ft) above the landscape. Although said to be the resting place of Noah's Ark, no definitive evidence has ever been found to support this claim. Access is difficult and prospective climbers need to obtain permission from the Ministry of Culture and Tourism in Ankara *(p276)* or through the local Turkish Embassy.

The impressive **İshak Paşa Sarayı** lies 8 km (5 miles) southeast of Doğubayazıt. The fortress-like palace has been occupied by Ottoman and Russian troops at various times.

The lavish arrangement of 366 rooms includes a harem with 14 bedrooms, *selamlık* (men's quarters) and a small but beautiful mosque.

Nearby attractions include the sulphur springs at Diyadin, and the Meteor Çukuru (meteor crater), just before the Iranian border.

HIDDEN GEM
Harran Beehive Houses

It is worth making the 45-km (28-mile) trip southeast of Şanlıurfa to see the unique beehive houses of Harran, once an important city, which was destroyed by the Mongols in the 13th century.

İshak Paşa Sarayı

İshak Paşa Sok, 8 km (5 miles) SE of town centre
Summer: 9am-7pm Tue-Sun; winter: 9am-5pm Tue-Sun

Mardin

F5 (0482) 212 18 52

Superbly situated atop a limestone crag overlooking the Mesopotamian plain, Mardin is justly famed for its beautiful vernacular architecture. Many of its superb stone houses have been converted into boutique hotels and, after Gaziantep, it is arguably the most popular tourist city in southeast Turkey. The city was captured by Muslims in about 640 CE and ruled by various Arab and Kurdish states until the 11th century. Some exceptional theological buildings, such as the Zinciriye Medresesi and the Kasımiye Medresesi, date from the 14th and 15th centuries respectively.

The unusual terrace-style dwellings and many narrow, labyrinth-like streets invoke the style and form of their Arab heritage. A city landmark is the **Mardin Museum**, whose archaeological section displays works from 4000 BCE until the 7th century BCE.

The Ulu Cami, a 12th-century Syrian-style mosque, built by an Artukid chieftain, is another city symbol. It is noted for its huge minaret, which soars above the city and is decorated with teardrop-shaped relief carvings and has inscriptions in Kufic Arabic script. There is a fascinating bazaar surrounding the mosque.

A state-of-the-art ethnography museum housed in a beautifully restored period stone building, **Sakip Sabancı City Museum** is the place to find out about the traditional way of life in Mardin. Exhibits range from audiovisual presentations on metalworking and fabric printing to superb photographs of the city's myriad mosques and churches. Temporary exhibitions are also held at the museum.

Beautifully set in a peaceful valley below dramatic bluffs some 6 km (4 miles) southeast of Mardin is **Deyr-az-Zaferan**. It is known as the Saffron Monastery due to the colour of the yellowish stones it is built with. A guide accompanies visitors around the picturesque monastery dating back to the 5th century and still in operation. There is also a café, and one guestroom is available for overnight stays.

PICTURE PERFECT

Deyr-az-Zaferan

Located southeast of Mardin is Deyr-az-Zaferan. Its golden-hued stone façade makes for a magnificent sight, especially during sunrise and sunset, contrasting beautifully against the backdrop of the Mesopotamian plain.

Mardin Museum

Cumhuriyet Meydani, Latifiye Mah, Mardin (0482) 212 16 64 Summer: 8:30am-5:30pm Tue-Sun; winter: 8am-5pm Tue-Sun Mon

Sakip Sabancı City Museum

Gül Mahallesi Eski Hükümet Cad, Mardin (0482) 212 93 96 8am-5pm Tue-Sun

Deyr-az-Zaferan

6 km (4 miles) SE of Mardin Apr-Oct: 8:30am-noon & 1-5pm daily; Nov-Mar: 8:30am-noon & 1-4:30pm daily

Lake Van

G4 Cumhuriyet Cad 105; (0432) 216 20 18

The startlingly blue waters of Lake Van (Van Gölü) mirror the surrounding peaks, the highest of which soars to a dizzying 4,058 m (13,313 ft). The lake is seven times larger than Lake Geneva and may be up to 400 m (1,312 ft) deep.

The Van basin was once the centre of the Urartian civilization. The remnants of their fortified capital straddle the imposing **Rock of Van**, located close to the eastern

→ Picturesque Mardin, overlooking the Mesopotamian plain

shore of the lake. This rock outcrop, sheer on its southern side, was once the premier settlement of the Kingdom of Urartu. The most obvious remains left by this remarkable civilization are their cuneiform inscriptions, seen on the entrance to the Tomb of Argishti, which is reached by steps from near the top of the rock. The remains of an Ottoman mosque now crown the rock, while at its feet spread the remnants of old Van, a walled settlement destroyed in World War I. A few kilometres away is the modern city of Van. Although the centre lacks historical interest, it has plenty of decent restaurants. Try the famed Van breakfast, which includes clotted cream and honey, plus fried eggs and strips of lamb.

The high point of a visit to the Lake Van area is the exquisite 10th-century Armenian **Church of the Holy Cross** (Akdamar Kilise), on a small island a few kilometres from the southern shore of the lake. Beautifully restored, the exterior boasts a remarkable series of bas-relief carvings and friezes showing biblical scenes. Its classical beauty makes this church one of the most photographed buildings in eastern Anatolia. The frescoes that adorn the interior walls and cupola are unique in their artistic merit. Following the restoration of the church, services have been held, attracting many worshippers from both the Armenian community in Istanbul and from Armenia itself.

On the lake's northwestern shore is the crescent-shaped crater lake on Nemrut Dağı (not the mountain with the statues near Kâhta) and the Seljuk cemetery and *kümbet* (domed tombs) at Ahlat. Both are worth a visit and can be accessed from Tatvan.

Rock of Van

Van Kalesi Apr-Oct: 8:30am-7pm daily; Nov-Mar: 8:30am-5pm daily

Church of the Holy Cross

40 km (25 miles) SW of Van Apr-Oct: 9am-6pm daily; Nov-Mar: 8am-4pm daily

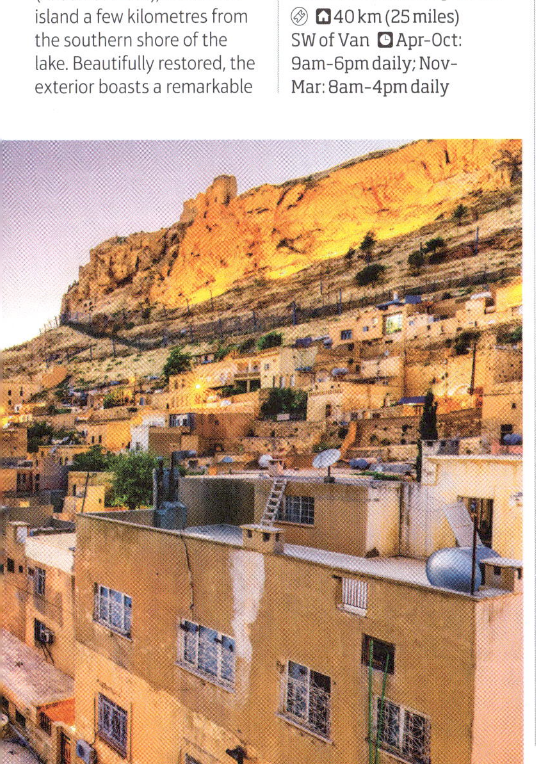

STAY

Kar's Otel

Housed in a Russian-era building constructed of black granite, this hotel features a central courtyard.

G3 Halitpaşa Cad 33, Kars
karsotel.com

Kars

G3 Cumhuriyet Hakim Ali Rıza Aslan Sok 15; (0474) 212 68 17

Remote but strategically very important, Kars is set on a grassy plain that is backed by distant peaks. The word *kar* means "snow" in Turkish and winters here are long and cold, while the spring and autumn rains turn streets to mud. The brief summer season is hot, dry and dusty.

Founded in the 10th century by the Armenian King Abas I, Kars was once a metropolis of around 100,000 inhabitants. It was held by the Russians from 1878 to 1919, and the grid plan and numerous run-down Neo-Classical houses are significant reminders of their presence here.

The small **Archaeological Museum**, just east of the town centre, is surprisingly good, particularly its displays of *kilims* (rugs) and carpets.

Most visitors come to Kars to see Ani *(p354)*, a visually dramatic, ruined 10th-century Armenian city 43 km (27 miles) to the east, on the border with Armenia.

Archaeological Museum

Cumhuriyet Cad 365
(0474) 212 38 17 8am-5pm Tue-Sun

NEED TO KNOW

A boat cruising along the Dalyan River

BEFORE YOU GO

Things change, so plan ahead to make the most of your trip. Be prepared for all eventualities by considering the following points before you travel.

ELECTRICITY SUPPLY

Power sockets are type C and F, fitting two-pronged plugs. Standard voltage is 230 volts.

Passports and Visas

For entry requirements, including visas, consult your nearest Turkish embassy, or check the official **Turkish e-visa** website. Citizens of many countries, including the UK, EU nations, Canada, the USA, New Zealand and Japan, do not need a visa and are granted a stamp upon entry, allowing a multiple-entry, 90-day stay. Tourist visas – purchased online, at least 48 hours before travel, from Turkey's official e-visa website – are necessary for Australian and South African visitors. These are normally issued for 90-day stays with multiple entry.

Turkish e-visa
W evisa.gov.tr

Government Advice

Now more than ever, it is important to consult both your and the Turkish government's advice before travelling. The **UK Foreign, Commonwealth and Development Office (FCDO)**, the **US Department of State**, the **Australian Department of Foreign Affairs and Trade** and the **Turkish Ministry of Foreign Affairs** offer the latest information on security, health and local regulations.

Australian Department of Foreign Affairs and Trade
W smartraveller.gov.au

Turkish Ministry of Foreign Affairs
W mfa.gov.tr

UK Foreign, Commonwealth and Development Office (FCDO)
W gov.uk/foreign-travel-advice

US Department of State
W travel.state.gov

Customs Information

You can find information about laws relating to goods and currency taken in or out of Turkey on Turkey's **Ministry of Trade** website.

Turkish Ministry of Trade
W trade.gov.tr

Insurance

We recommend taking out a comprehensive insurance policy covering medical care, theft, loss of belongings, cancellations and delays, and reading the small print carefully. All visitors should, at least, take out travel medical insurance, as the cost of emergency treatment in Turkey's private healthcare system can be exorbitant.

Vaccinations

No inoculations are required to visit Turkey, but it's recommended for travellers to make sure their vaccinations for Hepatitis A and Tetanus are up-to-date.

Booking Accommodation

Turkey offers a range of accommodation, from boutique hotels set in restored Ottoman mansions to family-run *pansiyons* (pensions) and the cave-hotels of Cappadocia.

During summer, prices peak along the coast and in the main tourism centres. Hotels at this time can fill up fast, so it's worth booking ahead.

Money

Turkey's currency is the Turkish lira. Due to high inflation, hotels, tour companies and main tourist attractions quote prices in euros and then calculate the exchange rate into lira on the day – consequently, we have used euros for the price categories in Stay and Eat listings throughout the guide. It's a good idea to carry cash for smaller purchases and when in more rural regions. It is customary to tip waiting staff 10 per cent, and to round up taxi fares.

Travellers with Specific Requirements

Turkey remains a challenging destination for travellers with specific requirements. However, newer museums and public buildings are equipped with facilities for wheelchair users, and some historic sites have features such as ramps. Visitors with accessibility requirements have free admission to many sights. Turkey's high-speed train network and the public transport in big cities have improved accessibility features. The rest of the public transport system, though, remains difficult to navigate for people with accessibility requirements. The Turkish accessibility rights organization Tourism for All *(Herkes İçin Turizm)* has more information on accessibility across Turkey.

Language

Turkey's official language is Turkish. Kurdish is the first language of approximately 20 per cent of the population. In areas popular with tourists, English is widely understood.

Opening Hours

Situations can change quickly and unexpectedly. Always check before visiting attractions and hospitality venues for up-to-date opening hours and booking requirements.

Opening hours vary from day to day and season to season. Although the opening times have been checked at the time of going to print, it is advisable to use these as a rough guideline only.

Mondays Some museums are closed.

Fridays Mosques are closed to non-worshippers until after midday prayer.

Sundays Post offices, banks and shops are closed.

Public holidays Islam uses the lunar calendar, so dates for major festivals change annually.

PUBLIC HOLIDAYS

1 Jan	New Year's Day
Mar	Şeker Bayramı (Eid al-Fitr; dates vary)
23 Apr	National Sovereignty and Children's Day
May	Kurban Bayramı (Eid al-Adha; dates vary)
1 May	Labour and Solidarity Day
19 May	Youth and Sports Day
15 Jul	Democracy and National Solidarity Day
30 Aug	Victory Day
29 Oct	Republic Day

GETTING AROUND

Whether you're visiting for a trip along the coast or venturing inland to Anatolia's heart, discover how best to reach Turkey and travel like a pro.

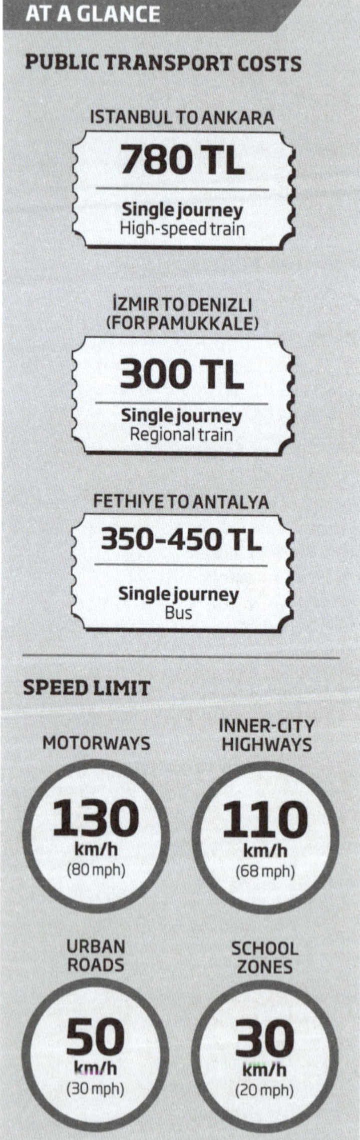

Arriving by Air

Turkey's main international airports are Istanbul Airport and Sabiha Gökçen, both in Istanbul, and Ankara Esenboğa. Nearly all airports are served by regular airport buses run by **Havaş**, or a similar service, and public transport connects city airports to their centres.

Turkey's main domestic airlines are **Turkish Airlines**, **Pegasus Airlines** and **AJet**. Most domestic flights connect through one of Istanbul's airports.

AJet
W ajet.com
Havaş
W havas.net/en
Pegasus Airlines
W flypgs.com
Turkish Airlines
W turkishairlines.com

Train Travel

International Train Travel

Istanbul's Halkalı Train Station is the eastern terminal for the daily *Istanbul–Sofia Express* from Sofia, Bulgaria, and the daily (Jun–Oct) *Bosphorus Express* from Bucharest, Romania. Both are sleeper services. Istanbul's Marmaray trainline also stops at Halkalı Train Station, providing a connection to the neighbourhood of Sirkeci; neither of these routes can be booked in advance online.

Domestic Train Travel

Ankara Train Station is the main hub for domestic rail travel in Turkey. From here, high-speed train (YHT) routes head west to Istanbul via Eskişehir, south to Konya, and east to Sivas. In Istanbul, the most central YHT station is Söğütlüçeşme Train Station. As well as the high-speed services, there are multiple sleeper services running across Anatolia. Trains can be booked at stations, on the **Turkish Railways (TCDD)** website, or via their official app. A passport is required to purchase tickets.

Turkish Railways (TCDD)
W ebilet.tcddtasimacilik.gov.tr

GETTING TO AND FROM THE AIRPORT

Airport	Distance to City	Airport Bus	Public Transport	Journey Time
Istanbul	44 km (27 miles)	Havaist 275 TL	Istanbul Metro	80 mins
Sabiha Gökçen (Istanbul)	48 km (30 miles)	Havabus 283 TL	Istanbul Metro	85 mins
Antalya	15 km (9 miles)	Havaş 180 TL	Antalya AntRay Tram	30 mins
Adnan Menderes (İzmir)	18 km (11 miles)	Havaş 180 TL	İzmir İzban City-Rail	30 mins
Milas-Bodrum	35 km (22 miles)	Havaş 170 TL	None	35 mins
Ankara Esenboğa	26 km (16 miles)	Ankara Air 180 TL	City bus	60 mins

JOURNEY PLANNER

Plotting Turkey's major train routes, this map is a handy reference for inter-city rail travel. Journey times are for the fastest available service.

••• Direct train routes

Samsun
Istanbul
Amasya
Kars
Bandırma
Ankara
Eskişehir
Sivas
Kayseri
Tatvan
İzmir
Selçuk
Konya
Denizli
İsparta
Diyarbakir
Adana

Istanbul to Eskişehir	3 hrs
Eskişehir to Ankara	1.5 hrs
Ankara to Konya	1.5 hrs
Ankara to Sivas	3 hrs
Eskişehir to Denizli	8.5 hrs
Denizli to İsparta	3.5 hrs
İzmir to Eskişehir	10 hrs
İzmir to Denizli	5 hrs
İzmir to Selçuk	1.5 hrs

İzmir to Bandırma	6 hrs
İzmir to Konya	13 hrs
Kayseri to Adana	6 hrs
Ankara to Kars	26 hrs
Ankara to Tatvan	25 hrs
Ankara to Diyarbakır	3 hrs
Sivas to Amasya	5 hrs
Amasya to Samsun	3 hrs

Long-Distance Bus Travel

The Turkish long-distance bus network is efficient, comfortable and covers the entire country. Bus stations are called *otogars* and are usually located outside the city centre. There are frequent daily services in and out of major cities.

Turkish bus booking websites **Nereden Nereye** and **Obilet** list a comprehensive schedule of most – but not all – services. Companies with an extensive route network include **Flixbus** (operated by Kamilkoç buses in Turkey), **Metro Turizm**, **Pamukkale Turizm** and **Istanbul Seyahat**. A passport is required to purchase tickets. On popular routes, there are so many services that it's usually possible to turn up at the *otogar* an hour before departure and purchase a seat.

Istanbul's Esenler Bus Station (*Esenler Otogarı*) is the western terminal for buses to and from other countries including Bulgaria, Germany and Greece.

Flixbus
W kamilkoc.com.tr
Istanbul Seyahat
W istanbulseyahat.com.tr
Metro Turizm
W metroturizm.com.tr
Nereden Nereye
W neredennereye.com
Obilet
W obilet.com/
Pamukkale Turizm
W pamukkale.com.tr

Dolmuş

A dolmuş is a minibus that runs a defined route on a scheduled timetable. They are the most efficient form of transport between smaller towns, and in many rural areas, they are the only form of public transport. In most areas, they can be flagged down, and they drop passengers off anywhere along the route. Fares are paid on-board, in cash, direct to the driver. One major exception to this rule is within the province of Muğla – the region that incorporates the major tourist destinations of Fethiye, Dalyan, Marmaris, the Datça Peninsula and the Bodrum Peninsula – where all dolmuş transport is paid for by Muğla Card or by contactless credit or debit card.

Boats and Ferries

International Ferries

Turkey has several international ferry routes. The main ferry companies are **Bodrum Express Lines**, **Bodrum Feribot**, **Erturk**, **Marmaris Ferry**, **Meis Express** and **Turyol**. Major routes between Turkey and Greece include Ayvalık to Lesvos, Bodrum to Kalymnos and Marmaris to Rhodes. Return day trips are available on many routes.

Bodrum Express Lines
W www.bodrumexpresslines.com
Bodrum Feribot
W bodrumferibot.com
Erturk
W erturk.com.tr
Marmaris Ferry
W marmarisferry.com
Meis Express
W meisexpress.com
Turyol
W turyolonline.com

Domestic Ferries

IDO sea-buses have several daily services crossing the Sea of Marmara between Istanbul and the southern shore towns of Mudanya, Bandırma and Yalova. In Istanbul, ferries depart from terminals at Yenikapı, Kabataş and Kadıköy. Regular ferries, run by **Gestaş**, zip across the Dardanelles between Çanakkale and the Gallipoli Peninsula, and to various nearby islands. Gestaş also operates ferries between Tenedos and Geyikli. **Bodrum Feribot** runs a daily ferry service between Bodrum and the Datça Peninsula. The Lake Van ferry between Tatvan and Van is predominantly a cargo ferry that sometimes takes foot passengers if asked. Crossings are daily in both directions, and bookings can be made with the operator **Van Gölü Feribot İşletme Müdürlüğü** directly by phone or at the ferry pier; information on the schedule can also be provided.

Bodrum Feribot
W bodrumferibot.com
Gestaş
W gdu.com.tr
IDO
W ido.com.tr
Van Gölü Feribot İşletme Müdürlüğü
T (0434) 827 80 40

Public Transport

All Turkish cities have extensive public transport networks. The largest cities incorporate trams, light-rail or metro lines, buses and dolmuşes.

Tickets

Nearly every Turkish city has swapped from cash payment on transport to prepaid transport cards, which allow holders discounted fares for that particular city's public transport routes. In most cities, a contactless debit or credit card can also be used. However in Istanbul, the bus network is the only part of the system where contactless card regularly works. Visitors planning to use Istanbul's public transport system should purchase an **Istanbulkart**, which can be bought and topped up at vending machines at airports, in metro, tram and train stations, and at kiosks or market shops near major transport stops. In the province of Muğla, the Muğla Card covers public transport within, as well as dolmuş transport between, several different towns.

Istanbulkart

W istanbulkart.istanbul

Taxis

All Turkish taxis have meters, which should be turned on at the start of the ride. Taxis typically wait at taxi stands rather than being hailed off the street. Taxis can be hired for half- and full-day trips to sights outside of town. For these types of trips, it's normal to negotiate a price for the trip upfront instead of using the meter.

Driving

Driving in Turkey is generally very good, with excellent road conditions (except in very rural areas) and clear road signage. The major issue is driving into larger cities such as Istanbul, İzmir and Ankara due to high traffic congestion and a lack of on-street parking. Drivers should be prepared for a more aggressive style of driving.

Car

Visitors must be over 21 to hire a car. Check the vehicle is registered for the High-Speed Toll System (HGS; Hızlı Geçiş Sistemi). When returning the car, you may be charged by the hire company for toll use, though some companies charge a daily base-rate instead. Most of the big car hire companies, such as **Europcar**, **Sixt** and **Avis**, have branches in larger towns as well as at airports.

Avis

W avis.com

Europcar

W europcar.com

Sixt

W sixt.com.tr

Rules of the Road

Always drive on the right. Road distances and speed regulations are only posted in kilometres. Winter tyres are mandatory in the winter months and must be stored in the boot at all times. Visitors from countries that use roman script can drive in Turkey using their national driver's licence; foreign drivers should always have their passport easily to hand. Mobile phone use while driving is illegal, but hands-free systems are allowed. The blood alcohol limit is 0.05 per cent; those found over the limit will incur a heavy fine, and foreign tourists will also have their driver's licence confiscated (they must then apply to have it returned after they've departed Turkey). If involved in an accident, do not move your vehicle until the **traffic police** arrive.

Traffic police

T 154

Toll Roads

Turkish *otoyols* (tolled motorways) and tolled bridges use the High-Speed Toll System (HGS; Hızlı Geçiş Sistemi). An HGS electronic chip is fitted to vehicles that tracks their passage and automatically adds toll fees to a registered account. Driving on a tolled road or bridge without HGS registration incurs steep fines. Driving into Turkey, drivers can enrol foreign vehicles for HGS at any Turkish post office (PTT). The **Touring and Automobile Association of Turkey** has a useful HGS guide on its website.

Touring and Automobile Association of Turkey

W turing.tr

Parking

There are no on-street parking meters in Turkey. Instead, a parking attendant collects the fee either when you park or when you leave. Multi-storey car parks are the norm in Istanbul; the city's **Ispark** website has a map of all multi-storey car parks, their fees, and live data on how many available spaces each car park has.

Ispark

W ispark.istanbul

Cycling

Turkey's motorists rarely cede space for cyclists, and a lack of bike-lane infrastructure makes it a less than ideal location for cyclists. Nevertheless, the astounding scenery on many routes attracts bike tourists to the country, and road cycling is gaining popularity. For a safer cycling experience, use secondary roads wherever possible.

Bicycle Hire

Eğirdir is one of the best places in Turkey for hiring a bike to explore. The **Eğirdir Outdoor Center** hires mountain bikes and offers information on routes. In Göreme, **Middle Earth Travel** is the main adventure-activity operator and runs biking tours as well as hiring bikes.

Eğirdir Outdoor Center

W egirdiroutdoorcenter.com

Middle Earth Travel

W middleearthtravel.com

Walking

In the cities, walking is one of the best ways to explore. The **Culture Routes in Turkey** website offers plenty of information on trekking trails in Turkey.

Culture Routes in Turkey

W cultureroutesinturkey.com

PRACTICAL INFORMATION

A little local know-how goes a long way in Turkey. Here you can find all the essential advice and information you will need during your stay.

AT A GLANCE

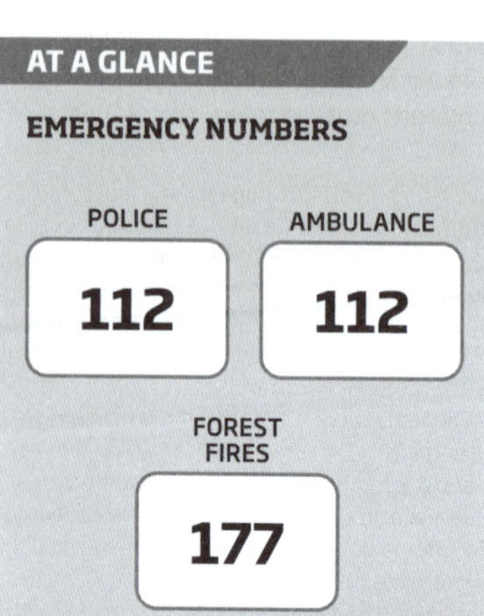

TIME ZONE

Eastern European Summer Time (EES) runs all year (no changes for daylight saving).

TAP WATER

Unless otherwise stated, tap water is safe to drink.

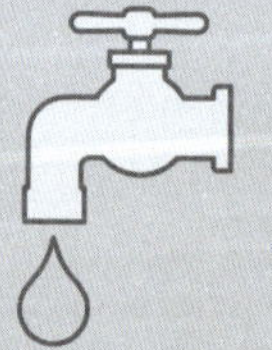

WEBSITES

Go Türkiye
Turkey's official tourism website (*goturkiye.com*).

Müze
Turkey's official tourist attractions website (*muze.gov.tr*).

Visit Istanbul
Istanbul's official tourism website (*visit.istanbul*).

İstanbul National Palaces
The website for Istanbul's palaces and pavilions (*millisaraylar.gov.tr*).

Personal security

Turkey is generally safe, but petty crime can occur. If anything is stolen, report the crime at the nearest police station and get a copy of the crime report in order to make a claim on your insurance. Contact your embassy immediately if your passport is stolen or in the event of a serious crime or accident.

Turkey overall has become markedly more conservative on issues of LGBTQ+ rights in recent years. Istanbul Pride has been cancelled by the authorities since 2015, same-sex marriage isn't recognized and there are no anti-discrimination laws protecting people on the basis of their gender or sexual preference (though it also has no legislation that prosecutes people based on their chosen gender or sexual preference). Despite this, as long as foreign LGBTQ+ couples refrain from public displays of affection, they are unlikely to run into problems or negative attention.

Health

The Turkish healthcare system is on par with many European nations, and there are both private and state facilities. Medical treatment for foreign visitors at private hospitals is expensive, so taking out travel medical insurance *(p365)* before visiting is highly recommended. English-speaking doctors or medical staff are rare in most medical facilities, but many private hospitals provide translators for foreign patients. Pharmacies are common and can supply over-the-counter remedies for minor ailments. They are called *Eczanes* and are marked with a red "E".

Smoking, Alcohol and Drugs

Smoking and vaping are banned in all interior public spaces. Outdoor cafés, restaurants and bar terraces are considered acceptable smoking areas, and a few establishments offer a dedicated no-smoking outdoor zone.

Turkey's drinking age is 18. Drinking in the street is not accepted. The drink-drive limit is

strictly enforced *(p369)*. Turkey has a zero-tolerance recreational drugs policy. Possession is a criminal offence and will incur either a harsh fine or a jail sentence.

ID

All foreign nationals in Turkey are required to carry ID on their person. Passports are necessary when checking into a hotel, and when booking organized tours, as well as seats on inter-city trains and buses, and domestic flights.

Local Customs

Turkey is a large country with many regional differences, so observe how locals dress and behave and adjust accordingly. Take Turkey's lese-majesty laws against insulting or defaming Atatürk or the Turkish Republic seriously. Being reported for making a derogatory comment can result in jail time or deportation. If invited into a Turkish home, it is customary to remove shoes at the door. Although many locals don't fast during the holy month of *Ramazan* (Ramadan), visitors to Turkey during this period should be discreet about drinking, eating and smoking on the street.

Visiting Places of Worship

Act respectfully when entering sacred sites. To visit mosques, all visitors should have upper arms and legs covered and remove shoes before entering. Women should also wear a headscarf. Non-worshippers should avoid prayer times.

Responsible Travel

Tourism has contributed to water-shortage issues in rural areas with large tourism industries. Take quick showers and don't choose accommodation that wastes water with pools and fixtures such as spa baths. The widespread housing crisis (many locals unable to afford sky-rocketing rents) has partly been caused by houses used for tourist accommodation. Visitors can help by staying in a hotel rather than an apartment.

Due to the climate crisis, forest fires are becoming increasingly frequent in summer. Be vigilant about forest fire safety and carefully dispose of any cigarette butts or flammable litter. Whenever possible, travel on Turkey's public transport networks instead of using private vehicles, and turn off air-conditioning (or in winter, radiators) in your room when you are out.

Mobile Phones and Wi-Fi

Free Wi-Fi is standard at hotels. There are also free Wi-Fi networks at many cafés and restaurants; you often have to register with your phone number. Turkish SIM cards and data packages are available to buy at airports, as well as newsagent kiosks and mobile phone shops. A passport is required at the point of purchase. Turkish SIM cards will automatically stop working in a foreign-bought phone after 120 days.

Post

The Turkish postal system, **Posta ve Telgraf Teşkilatı (PTT)**, is slow but reliable. Post offices are generally found in all town centres. Sending parcels by "registered post" is faster and doesn't cost much extra.

Posta ve Telgraf Teşkilatı (PPT)
W ptt.gov.tr

Taxes and Refunds

Turkey's VAT rate is 20 per cent. Visitors can get VAT refunds of 12 per cent on purchases of more than 1,000 TL at participating Tax Free Shopping stores, where a Tax Free receipt and regular receipt will be issued. When departing, present these at the airport's customs-office kiosk to be stamped before receiving your refund from the airport's tax-refund office.

Discount Cards

Travellers can purchase various museum cards from Turkey's official Müze website. If you are going to be spending a lot of time exploring the big heritage attractions, and visiting a few different regions, consider buying the **Museumpass Türkiye**, which includes entrance to 350 sites, is valid for 15 days and costs €165. This can offer a significant discount (depending on your itinerary), as entry fees for some of the most popular historic sites can cost €40.

Museumpass Türkiye
W muze.gen.tr

INDEX

Index

Page numbers in **bold** refer to main entries.

N

O

P

R

S

PHRASE BOOK

PRONUNCIATION

Turkish uses a Roman alphabet. It has 29 letters: 8 vowels and 21 consonants. Letters that differ from the English alphabet are: **c**, pronounced "j" as in "jolly"; **ç**, pronounced "ch" as in "church"; **ğ**, which lengthens the preceding vowel and is not pronounced; **ı**, pronounced "uh"; **ö**, pronounced "ur" (like the sound in "further"); **ş**, pronounced "sh" as in "ship"; **ü**, pronounced "ew" as in "few".

IN AN EMERGENCY

Help!	**İmdat!**	*eem-**dat**!*
Stop!	**Dur!**	*door!*
Call a doctor!	**Bir doktor çağırın!**	*beer dok-**tor chah**-ruhn!*
Call an ambulance!	**Bir ambulans çağırın!**	*beer am-boo-**lans chah**-ruhn!*
Call the police!	**Polis çağırın!**	*po-**lees chah**-ruhn!*
Fire!	**Yangın!**	*yan-**guhn**!*
Where is the nearest telephone?	**En yakın telefon nerede!**	*en ya-**kuhn** teh-leh-**fon** **neh**-reh-deh?*
Where is the nearest hospital?	**En yakın hastane nerede!**	*en ya-**kuhn** has-ta-**neh** **neh**-reh-deh?*

COMMUNICATION ESSENTIALS

Yes	**Evet**	*eh-**vet***
No	**Hayır**	*h-'**eye**'-uhr*
Thank you	**Teşekkür ederim**	*teh-shek-**kewr** **eh**-deh-reem*
Please	**Lütfen**	***lewt**-fen*
Excuse me	**Affedersiniz**	***af**-feh-der-see-neez*
Hello	**Merhaba**	***mer**-ha-ba*
Goodbye	**Hoşça kalın**	*hosh-**cha ka**-luhn*
Good morning	**Günaydın**	*gewn-'eye'-**duhn***
Good evening	**İyi akşamlar**	*ee-**yee** ak-sham-**lar***
Morning	**Sabah**	*sa-**bah***
Afternoon	**Öğleden sonra**	*ur-leh-**den son**-ra*
Evening	**Akşam**	*ak-**sham***
Yesterday	**Dün**	*dewn*
Today	**Bugün**	***boo**-gewn*
Tomorrow	**Yarın**	***ya**-ruhn*
Here	**Burada**	***boo**-ra-da*
There	**Şurada**	***shoo**-ra-da*
Over there	**Orada**	***o**-ra-da*
What?	**Ne?**	*neh?*
When?	**Ne zaman?**	***neh za**-man?*
Why?	**Neden**	*neh-**den**?*
Where?	**Nerede**	***neh**-reh-deh?*

USEFUL PHRASES

How are you?	**Nasılsınız?**	***na**-suhl-suh-nuhz?*
I'm fine	**İyiyim**	*ee-**yee**-yeem*
Pleased to meet you	**Memnun oldum**	*mem-**noon ol**-doom*
See you soon	**Görüşmek üzere**	*gur-rewsh-**mek** **ew**-zeh-reh*
That's fine	**Tamam**	*ta-**mam***
Where is/are ...?	**... nerede?**	*... **neh**-reh-deh?*
How far is it to...?	**... ne kadar uzakta?**	*... **neh ka**-dar oo-zak-ta?*
I want to go to ...	**... a/e gitmek istiyorum**	*... a/eh geet-**mek** ees-**tee**-yo-room*
Do you speak English?	**İngilizce biliyor musunuz?**	*een-gee-**leez**-jeh bee-**lee**-yor moo-soo-nooz?*
I don't understand	**Anlamıyorum**	*an-**la**-muh-yo-room*
Can you help me?	**Bana yardım edebilir misiniz?**	*ba-**na** yar-**duhm** eh-deh-bee-**leer** mee-see-neez?*

USEFUL WORDS

big	**büyük**	*bew-**yewk***
small	**küçük**	*kew-**chewk***
hot	**sıcak**	*suh-**jak***
cold	**soğuk**	*soh-**ook***
good/well	**iyi**	*ee-**yee***
bad	**kötü**	*kur-**tew***
enough	**yeter**	*yeh-**ter***
open	**açık**	*a-**chuhk***
closed	**kapalı**	*ka-pa-**luh***
left	**sol**	*sol*
right	**sağ**	*saa*
straight on	**doğru**	*doh-**roo***
near	**yakın**	*ya-**kuhn***
far	**uzak**	*oo-**zak***
up	**yukarı**	*yoo-ka-**ruh***
down	**aşağı**	*a-shah-**uh***
early	**erken**	*er-**ken***
late	**geç**	*gech*
entrance	**giriş**	*gee-**reesh***
exit	**çıkış**	*chuh-**kuhsh***
toilets	**tuvaletler**	*too-va-let-**ler***
push	**itiniz**	***ee**-tee-neez*
pull	**çekiniz**	***cheh**-kee-neez*
more	**daha fazla**	*da-**ha faz**-la*
less	**daha az**	*da-**ha az***
very	**çok**	*chok*

SHOPPING

How much is this?	**Bu kaç lira?**	*boo **kach** lee-ra?*
I would like ...	**... istiyorum**	*... ees-**tee**-yo-room*
Do you have ...?	**... var mı?**	*... **var** muh?*
Do you take credit cards?	**Kredi kartı kabul ediyor musumuz?**	***kreh**-dee **kar**-tuh ka-**bool** eh-**dee**-yor moo-soo-nooz?*
What time do you open/close?	**Saat kaçta açılıyor/kapanıyor?**	*Sa-**at** kach-**ta** a-chuh-**luh**-yor/ka-pa-**nuh**-yor?*
this one	**bunu**	*boo-**noo***
that one	**şunu**	*shoo-**noo***
expensive	**pahalı**	*pa-ha-**luh***
cheap	**ucuz**	*oo-**jooz***
size (clothes)	**beden**	*beh-**den***
size (shoes)	**numara**	*noo-ma-**ra***
white	**beyaz**	*bay-**yaz***
black	**siyah**	*see-**yah***
red	**kırmızı**	*kuhr-muh-**zuh***
yellow	**sarı**	*sa-**ruh***
green	**yeşil**	*yeh-**sheel***
blue	**mavi**	*ma-**vee***
brown	**kahverengi**	*kah-**veh**-ren-gee*
shop	**dükkan**	*dewk-**kan***
till	**kasa**	*ka-**sa***
bargaining	**pazarlık**	*pa-zar-**luhk***
That's my final offer	**Daha fazla veremen**	*da-**ha faz**-la veh-**reh**-mem*

TYPES OF SHOP

antiques shop	**antikacı**	*an-**tee**-ka-juh*
bakery	**fırın**	*fuh-**ruhn***
bank	**banka**	***ban**-ka*
bookshop	**kitapçı**	*kee-tap-**chuh***
butcher's	**kasap**	*ka-**sap***
cake shop	**pastane**	*pas-ta-**neh***
chemist's/pharmacy	**eczane**	*ej-za-**neh***
fishmonger's	**balıkçı**	*ba-luhk-**chuh***
greengrocer's	**manav**	*ma-**nav***
grocery	**bakkal**	*bak-**kal***
hairdresser's (ladies)	**kuaför**	*kwaf-**fur***
(mens)	**berber**	*ber-**ber***
leather shop	**derici**	*deh-ree-**jee***
market/bazaar	**çarşı/pazar**	*char-**shuh**/pa-**zar***
newsstand	**gazeteci**	*ga-**zeh**-teh-jee*
post office	**postane**	*pos-ta-**neh***
shoe shop	**ayakkabıcı**	*'eye'-**yak**-ka-buh-juh*
stationer's	**kırtasiyeci**	*kuhr-**ta**-see-yeh-jee*
supermarket	**süpermarket**	*sew-per-mar-**ket***
tailor	**terzi**	*ter-**zee***
travel agency	**seyahat acentesi**	*say-ya-**hat** a-jen-teh-**see***

SIGHTSEEING

castle	**hisar**	*hee-**sar***
church	**kilise**	*kee-**lee**-seh*
island	**ada**	*a-**da***
mosque	**cami**	***ja**-mee*
museum	**müze**	***mew**-zeh*
palace	**saray**	*sar-'**eye**'*
park	**park**	*park*
square	**meydan**	*may-**dan***
theological college	**medrese**	*med-**reh**-seh*
tomb	**türbe**	*tewr-**beh***
tourist information office	**turizm danışma bürosu**	*too-**reezm** da-nuhsh-**mah** **bew**-ro-soo*
tower	**kule**	*koo-**leh***
town hall	**belediye sarayı**	*beh-leh-dee-**yeh** sar-'**eye**'-uh*
Turkish bath	**hamam**	*ha-**mam***

TRANSPORT

airport	**havalimanı**	*ha-**va**-lee-ma-nuh*
bus/coach	**otobüs**	*o-to-**bewss***

bus stop	otobüs durağı	o-to-**bewss** doo-**ra**-uh
coach station	otogar	o-to-**gar**
dolmuş	dolmuş	dol-**moosh**
fare	ücret	ewj-**ret**
ferry	vapur	va-**poor**
sea bus	deniz otobüsü	deh-**neez** o-to-**bew**-sew
station	istasyon	ees-tas-**yon**
taxi	taksi	**tak**-see
ticket	bilet	bee-**let**
ticket office	bilet gişesi	bee-**let** gee-sheh **ee**
timetable	tarife	ta-ree-**feh**

STAYING IN A HOTEL

Do you have a vacant room?	Boş odanız var mı?	bosh o-da-**nuhz** **var** muh?
double room	iki kişilik bir oda	ee-**kee** kee-shee-**leek** beer o-**da**
room with a double bed	çift kişilik yataklı bir oda	**cheeft** kee-shee-**leek** ya-**tak**-luh beer o-**da**
twin room	çift yataklı bir oda	**cheeft** ya-**tak**-luh beer o-**da**
for one person	tek kişilik	**tek** kee-shee-**leek**
room with a bath	banyolu bir oda	**ban**-yo-loo beer o-**da**
shower	duş	doosh
porter	komi	ko-**mee**
key	anahtar	a-nah-**tar**
room service	oda servisi	o-**da** ser-vee-**see**
I have a reservation	Rezervasyonum var	reh-zer-vas-yo-**noom** var
Does the price include breakfast?	Fiyata kahvaltı dahil mi?	fee-ya-**ta** kah-val-tu**h** da-**heel** mee?

EATING OUT

A table for ... please	... kişilik bir masa lütfen	... kee-shee-**leek** beer **ma**-sa **lewt**-fen
I want to reserve a table	Bir masa ayırtmak istiyorum	beer **ma**-sa 'eye'-uhrt-**mak** ees-**tee**-yo-room
The bill please	Hesap lütfen	heh-**sap** **lewt**-fen
I am a vegetarian	Et yemiyorum	et **yeh**-mee-yo-room
restaurant	lokanta	lo-**kan**-ta
waiter	garson	gar-**son**
menu	yemek listesi	ye-**mek** **lees**-teh-see
fixed-price menu	fiks menü	feeks meh-**new**
wine list	şarap listesi	sha-**rap** **lees**-teh-see
breakfast	kahvaltı	kah-val-**tuh**
lunch	öğle yemeği	ur-**leh** yeh-meh-**ee**
dinner	akşam yemeği	ak-**sham** yeh-meh-**ee**
starter	meze	**meh**-zeh
main course	ana yemek	a-**na** yeh-**mek**
dish of the day	günün yemeği	gew-**newn** yeh-meh-**ee**
dessert	tatlı	tat-**luh**
rare	az pişmiş	**az** peesh-meesh
medium	orta pişmiş	or-**ta** peesh-meesh
well done	iyi pişmiş	ee-**yee** peesh-meesh
glass	bardak	bar-**dak**
bottle	şişe	shee-**sheh**
knife	bıçak	buh-**chak**
fork	çatal	cha-**tal**
spoon	kaşık	ka-**shuhk**

MENU DECODER

badem	ba-**dem**	almond
bal	bal	honey
balık	ba-**luhk**	fish
bira	**bee**-ra	beer
bonfile	**bon**-fee-leh	fillet steak
buz	booz	ice
çay	ch-'eye'	tea
çilek	chee-**lek**	strawberry
çorba	chor-**ba**	soup
dana eti	da-**na** eh-**tee**	veal
dondurma	don-door-**ma**	ice cream
ekmek	ek-**mek**	bread
elma	el-**ma**	apple
et	et	meat
fasulye	fa-**sool**-yeh	beans
fırında	fuh-ruhn-**da**	roast
fıstık	fuhs-**tuhk**	pistachio nuts
gazoz	ga-**zoz**	fizzy drink
hurma	hoor-**ma**	dates
içki	eech-**kee**	alcohol
incir	**een**-jeer	figs
ızgara	uhz-**ga**-ra	charcoal grilled
kahve	kah-**veh**	coffee
kara biber	ka-**ra** bee-**ber**	black pepper
karışık	ka-ruh-**shuhk**	mixed
karpuz	kar-**pooz**	water melon
kavun	ka-**voon**	melon
kayısı	k-'eye'-uh-**suh**	apricots
kaymak	k-'eye'-**mak**	cream
kıyma	kuhy-**ma**	minced meat
kızartma	kuh-zart-**ma**	fried
köfte	kurf-**teh**	meatballs
kuru	koo-**roo**	dried
kuzu eti	koo-**zoo** eh-**tee**	lamb
lokum	lo-**koom**	Turkish delight
maden suyu	ma-**den** soo-**yoo**	mineral water (fizzy)
meyve suyu	may-**veh** soo-**yoo**	fruit juice
midye	**meed**-yeh	mussels
muz	mooz	banana
patlıcan	pat-luh-**jan**	aubergine
peynir	pay-**neer**	cheese
pilav	pee-**lav**	rice
piliç	pee-**leech**	roast chicken
şarap	sha-**rap**	wine
sebze	seb-**zeh**	vegetables
şeftali	shef-ta-**lee**	peach
şeker	sheh-**ker**	sugar
su	soo	water
süt	sewt	milk
sütlü	sewt-**lew**	with milk
tavuk	ta-**vook**	chicken
tereyağı	teh-**reh**-yah-uh	butter
tuz	tooz	salt
üzüm	ew-**zewm**	grapes
vişne	**veesh**-neh	sour cherry
yoğurt	yoh-**urt**	yogurt
yumurta	yoo-moor-**ta**	egg
zeytin	zay-**teen**	olives
zeytinyağı	zay-**teen**-yah-uh	olive oil

NUMBERS

0	sıfır	**suh**-fuhr
1	bir	beer
2	iki	ee-**kee**
3	üç	ewch
4	dört	durt
5	beş	besh
6	altı	al-**tuh**
7	yedi	yeh-**dee**
8	sekiz	seh-**keez**
9	dokuz	doh-**kooz**
10	on	on
11	on bir	**on** beer
12	on iki	**on** ee-kee
13	on üç	**on** ewch
14	on dört	**on** durt
15	on beş	**on** besh
16	on altı	**on** al-tuh
17	on yedi	**on** yeh-dee
18	on sekiz	**on** seh-keez
19	on dokuz	**on** doh-kooz
20	yirmi	yeer-**mee**
21	yirmi bir	yeer-mee **beer**
30	otuz	o-**tooz**
40	kırk	kuhrk
50	elli	eh-**lee**
60	altmış	alt-**muhsh**
70	yetmiş	yet-**meesh**
80	seksen	sek-**sen**
90	doksan	dok-**san**
100	yüz	yewz
110	yüz on	yewz **on**
200	iki yüz	ee-**kee** yewz
1,000	bin	been
100,000	yüz bin	**yewz** been
1,000,000	bir milyon	**beer** meel-**yon**

TIME

one minute	bir dakika	**beer** da-**kee**-ka
one hour	bir saat	**beer** sa-at
half an hour	yarım saat	ya-**ruhm** **sa**-at
day	gün	gewn
week	hafta	haf-**ta**
month	ay	'eye'
year	yıl	yuhl
Sunday	pazar	pa-**zar**
Monday	pazartesi	pa-**zar**-teh-see
Tuesday	salı	sa-**luh**
Wednesday	çarşamba	char-sham-**ba**
Thursday	perşembe	per-shem-**beh**
Friday	cuma	joo-**ma**
Saturday	cumartesi	joo-**mar**-teh-see

ACKNOWLEDGMENTS

This edition updated by
Contributors Jennifer Hattam, Jess Lee, Lisa Morrow, Owen Morton
Senior Editor Keith Drew
Senior Art Editor Stuti Tiwari
Project Editor Tijana Todorinović
Art Editor Divyanshi Shreyaskar
Editor Vineet Singh
Proofreader Kathryn Glendenning
Indexer Helen Peters
Assistant Picture Research Administrator Manpreet Kaur
Rights and Permissions Specialist Vagisha Pushp
Deputy Picture Research Manager Virien Chopra
Jacket and Sales Coordinator Serena Sclocco
Jacket Designers Katie Cavanagh, Divyanshi Shreyaskar
Jacket Picture Researcher Kate Hockenhall
Senior Cartographer Mohammed Hassan
Cartography Manager Suresh Kumar
Pre-production Coordinator Tanveer Zaidi
Pre-production Designer Rohit Rojal
Pre-production Manager Balwant Singh
Pre-production Image Editors Vijay Kandwal, Pankaj Sharma
Production Controller Rebecca Short
Deputy Managing Editor Dharini Ganesh
Managing Editor Beverly Smart
Managing Art Editor Michael Duffy
Senior Managing Art Editor Priyanka Thakur
Editorial Director Hollie Teague
Art Director Maxine Pedliham
Publishing Director Georgina Dee

DK would like to thank the following for their contributions to the previous edition: Rosie Ayliffe, Rose Baring, Barnaby Rogerson, Canan Sılay, Suzanne Swan, Dominic Whiting

The publisher would like to thank the following for their kind permission to reproduce their photographs:

Key: a-above; b-below/bottom; c-center; f-far; l-left; r-right; t-top

Adobe Stock: EdNurg 201tl; efired 202–203, 243t; elenvd 139; enesdigital 155cr; Gabrielle 355crb, 355bl; Hasan 338b; Ali Kabas 362–363; muratart 18cb, 230–231, 260; Serg Zastavkin 347tl.

Alamy Stock Photo: Album 51tr, 70t, 71tr, 71c; Ayhan Altun 80, 117, 135, 142bl, 156–157b, 160–161t, 162–163b, 187cr; Amazing Aerial / Ali Kabas 11cr, 46-47t, 246-247; Jon Arnold 258cra; John Bracegirdle 55cra, 89cra; Michele Burgess 355br; Giovanni Camici 51tl; Cavan Images 6–7, 335tr, 335cra; CHROMORANGE 333tc; David Coleman | Have Camera Will Travel 91b; Roy Conchie 25tr, 217b; Helmut Corneli 40–41t; CPA Media Pte Ltd / Pictures From History 98bc; Chris Craggs 47cr; D and S Photography Archives 53tr; Ian Dagnall 77tl; directphoto.bz 113b; Marius Dobilas 13t; eFesenko 120; Douglas Peebles Photography 323cra; Jens Kalaene / dpa-Zentralbild / ZB 35crb; F1online digitale Bildagentur GmbH / Bianca Schauer 287tl; Neil Farrin 149tr; frantic 166t; funkyfood London - Paul Williams 149br; Ihsan Gercelman 134; GRANT ROONEY PREMIUM 10clb; Özen Güney Güvenç 348–349t; Serkant Hekimci 55br; Gavin Hellier 81cra; Hemis / Bertrand Gardel 138t; Serrano Anna / Hemis.fr 26–27t 181bl; Heritage Image Partnership Ltd 168tr; Historic Images 53cb; Tolga Ildun 266clb; Image Source Limited / Ken Welsh / Destinations 121; imageBROKER / Raimund Franken 19, 272; imageBROKER / G&M Therin-Weise 21cb, 342; imageBROKER / K. Kreder 256; imageBROKER / Juergen Pfeiffer 347ca; imageBROKER.com / Martin Siepmann 8cla, 8–9b, 37cla, 89tl, 155tl, 207cra, 252, 280t; Images & Stories 45cla, 237tl; Jon Arnold Images Ltd / Ivan Vdovin 233; Evren Kalinbacak 69crb; Mehmet Kalkan 314–315b; Izzet Keribar 13cr, 332b; Cem Kurtuluş 48bl; Lanmas 52cr, 54bl; Ian Littlewood 215; Pascal Mannaerts 45cr; Altan Gocher / NurPhoto 49bl; Mustafa Olgun 251cr; photomobilet 183tl; Juergen Ritterbach 336t, 338clb, 339; Uwe Seidner 37t; SOPA Images Limited 49tl; Mehmet Masum Suer / SOPA Images via ZUMA Press Wire 349clb; Dave Stamboulis 257; Sueddeutsche Zeitung Photo 55bl; The Picture Art Collection 50t, 52cb, 54tl, 54–55t; Ivan Vdovin 97, 158, 271, 341tl, 346–347b, 352tl; Westend61 GmbH / Matthew Dixon 61t, 84; Westend61 GmbH / Hans Lippert 12clb; Westend61 GmbH / Martin Siepmann 52–53t, 332–333t; ZUMA Press, Inc. / Tolga Ildun 148–149t; Tolga Ildun / ZUMA Press Wire 100t, 151crb, 289tr.

AWL Images: Jon Arnold 16, 22bl, 32t, 56–57, 63, 98–99t, 109t, 110–111t, 144; ClickAlps 174–175; Danita Delimont Stock 20, 296–297, 300, 317b; Cahir Davitt 94–95; Michele Falzone 210t; Neil Farrin 242; Francesco Riccardo Iacomino 207tl; Stefano Politi Markovina 213tr, 288–289b; Jan Miracky 27tr, 60, 64, 90t, 166–167b, 324cra; Jane Sweeney 31tr, Ivan Vdovin 37br, 89tl, 304–305, 330–331.

Bridgeman Images: Lebrecht History 51cb.

Depositphotos Inc: epicimages 268b;

franticOO 12-13b; halukcigsar 195; RuslanKal 30tl, 77cla.

Dreamstime.com: Husame Akcelik 39br, 356t; Acelya Aksunkur 184cb; Anton Aleksenko 93t, 153b; Murat An 206bl; Mihai Andritoiu 325cr; Leonid Andronov 356–357b; Nikolay Antonov 35cla; Stefano Armaroli 279tl; Serdar Basak 236b; Roksana Bashyrova 49tr; Scott Biales 8clb; Lukas Bischoff 17bl, 196; Bizoon 21tl, 318; Boggy 75br; Mehmet Cetin 359cra; Chandu09 74b; Sener Dagasan 31clb, 113crb, 306bl, 307tl; Utku Demirsoy 34–35t; Tiana Den 17t, 176; Birol Dincer 283; Dragoncello 90b; Tatiana Dyuvbanova 26tl; Oscar Espinosa 164tl, 182–183b, 193tl; Sergey Fedoskin 150–151b; Evgeniy Fesenko 143cra; Iakov Filimonov 227; FranticOO 40bl, 254–255; Gerasimovvv 245t; Ozgur Guvenc 163cr; Guvencan 276; H368k742 13br, 77tr; Ioannaalexa 78–79; Jackmalipan 11br; Evren Kalinbacak 43cl, 49cr, 69bl, 289cla, 340; Bilal Kocabas 295b, 298; Ahmet Kus 329tr; Irina Lepneva 164–165b; Brian Logan 225t; Aliaksandr Mazurkevich 280b; Mitzobs 98tc, 226b; Monticelllo 248; Denis Moskvinov 249, 251b; Oskanov 171; Ozdereisa 133tl, 360–361; Oleh Panasenko 2–3; Aleksandar Pavlovic 270; Alexey Pevnev 112; Photonsk 208b; Halit Sadik 22cr, 157cra; Saiko3p 217t; Sailingstone Travel 44–45t; Firdes Sayilan 43b, 313; Cagkan Sayin 234bl; Scaliger 161b; Serturvetan 201cra; Todor Stoyanov 50bl; Theendup 235br; Tigger76 204–205b; Tminaz 186, 192bl; Bekir Ugur 10ca; Aleh Varanishcha 11t, 266b; Galih Wisnu 42bl, 132; Hakan Can Yalcin 184bl, 358b; Yalcinsonat 253, 278–279b, 279cla; Zeytun Images 204t; Znm 162tl.

Getty Images: Ozan KOSE / AFP 49br; Emin Menguarslan / Anadolu Agency 48cr; Mehmet Emin Menguarslan / Anadolu Agency 49cl; Hasan Tascan / Anadolu 308–309; Gokhan Zobar / Anadolu Agency 48tl; Archiv Gerstenberg / ullstein bild 52tl; Bettmann 50crb, 55tr; Hakan Akgun / dia images 48cl; Sercan Ozkurnazli / dia images 48br; Cem Tekkesinoglu / dia images 42–43t; Godong / Universal Images Group 149c; Hulton Archive / Ann Ronan Pictures / Print Collector 53bl; Hulton Archive / Print Collector 54crb; Hulton Archive / Stringer 51cla; Moment / Ali CAN 10–11b; Moment / Ayhan Altun 137b, 190, 191b, 194, 207tr; Moment / Salvator Barki 137clb, 149bl; Moment / Malcolm P Chapman 211crb; Moment / Sebastian Condrea 209tr; Moment / Francesco Riccardo Iacomino 38bl; Moment / mikroman6 51bl; Moment / nejdetduzen 228–229b; Moment / Anton Petrus 218–219; Moment / Tanatat pongphibool, thailand 214; Moment Unreleased / Emad aljumah 310–311t; Moment Unreleased / Ayhan Altun 154–155b, 168–169b; Stone / Izzet Keribar 116, 156tl, 258t; Burak Kara / Stringer 114; The Image Bank / Marc Dozier 93cra.

Getty Images / iStock: Bahadr AY 234; cemagraphics 292–293t; daphnusia 24tl; dem10 36crb; Esin Deniz 220–221t, 226t, 264t; E+ / 1001Love 311tr; E+ / alxpin 125; E+ / Mehmet Hilmi Barcin 170; E+ / benstevens 94bc; E+ / byakkaya 323t; E+ / Circle Creative Studio 38–39t; E+ / minemero 8cl; E+ / mrtekmekci 41b; E+ / Guven Ozdemir 188; E+ / ugurhan 62, 126; E+ / wildart 211br; E+ / yasindmrblk 290; efired 133tr, 244t; EgyptianStudio 138b; franticOO 22crb, 28bl; Gökçen TUN 251cra; KenanOlgun 295t; Nataliia Milko 282; minemero 31br; murattopay 294; nejdetduzen 118, 299; NekomuraKatsuo 110b; Kenan Olgun 39cr; Selcuk Oner 336–337b; resulmuslu 358–359t; RockingStock 52bl; Kenan Talas 180–181t, 220b, 312; Thankful Photography 341tr; tunart 68-69t; Takayuki Ueda 29b, 326–327; zak00 48tr.

Istanbul Modern: 44–45b; Cemal Emden 130–131b, 131tl; Flufoto 131tr; Kayhan Kaygusu 131cra.

Osman Sezener Restaurant Group: Buket Yaşar 34–35b.

Rahmi M. Koç Museum: 165t, 281.

Shutterstock.com: acsen 36tl; ahmetozkanphotography 136; ali.can0707 47bl; Suleyman Alkan 314tl; Guillaume Angleraud 208clb; art of line 286bl; Fokke Baarssen 18tl, 238; Kayihan Bolukbasi 141b; Yasemin Yurtman Candemir 41cl; Mehmet Cetin 123tl; Esin Deniz 30–31b, 264b; Gokhan Dogan 71br; Duman Stock 103br; Nejdet Duzen 12t, 70–71b, 191clb; f9project 213tl; franticOO 24–25t, 222, 223; huseyinturk_photograph 229t; iremt 237br; Lepneva Irina 119; Kadagan 224–225b; karakartal 244–245b; Bilal Kocabas 293br; lapas77 22t, 28–29t; legacy1995 83tl; LizCoughlan 232; maitrecortex 250; Alex_Mastro 72–73t, 74–75t; Yavuz Meyveci 124cl; Morrowind 325cra; Resul Muslu 24–25ca; Photo Oz 267; Rasim Rasimoglu 285cra; saaton 96; Sanatkar 173; SeyyaaH 61bl, 104; Liu Yu Shan 26–27ca; SinanDogan34 53cra, 115; Kenan Talas 29cl, 184clb, 316–317t, 328–329t, 350–351; TravelPhotoBloggers 46bl, 325tr; yusuf.yilmaz 284–285t, 352–353b; zcebeci 268t, 269, ZMD-Design 159.

Cover images:
Front and Spine: **Getty Images / iStock:** Givaga.
Back: **AWL Images:** Stefano Politi Markovina cl; **Dreamstime.com:** Nikolay Antonov c; **Getty Images / iStock:** E+ / Mehmet Hilmi Barcin tr; Givaga b.
Front Flap: **Alamy Stock Photo:** Ayhan Altun bl; **AWL Images:** Jane Sweeney cb; **Depositphotos Inc:** halukcigsar cra; **Dreamstime.com:** Aleh Varanishcha tr; **Getty Images:** Moment / Ali CAN cla; **Shutterstock.com:** yusuf.yilmaz br.

First edition 2003

Published in Great Britain by Dorling Kindersley Limited, 20 Vauxhall Bridge Road, London SW1V 2SA

The authorised representative in the EEA is Dorling Kindersley Verlag GmbH. Arnulfstr. 124, 80636 Munich, Germany

Published in the United States by DK Publishing, 1745 Broadway, 20th Floor, New York, NY 10019, USA

26 27 28 29 10 9 8 7 6 5 4 3 2 1

A CIP catalog record for this book is available from the British Library.

A catalog record for this book is available from the Library of Congress.

ISSN: 1542 1554
ISBN: 978 0 2417 9820 1

Printed and bound in Malaysia.

www.dk.com

MIX
Paper | Supporting responsible forestry
FSC™ C018179

This book was made with Forest Stewardship Council™ certified paper – one small step in DK's commitment to a sustainable future.
Learn more at **www.dk.com/uk/information/sustainability**

A NOTE FROM DK

The rate at which the world is changing is constantly keeping the DK travel team on our toes. While we've worked hard to ensure that this edition of Turkey is accurate and up-to-date, we know that opening hours alter, standards shift, prices fluctuate, places close and new ones pop up in their stead. So, if you notice we've got something wrong or left something out, we want to hear about it.
Please get in touch at travelguides@dk.com